NAES COLLEGE LIBRARY
2838 WEST PETERSON
CHICAGO, IL 60659

IDEAS OF CULTURE
Sources and Uses

IDEAS OF CULTURE
Sources and Uses

EDITED BY
FREDERICK C. GAMST
University of Massachusetts, Boston

EDWARD NORBECK
Rice University, Houston

HOLT, RINEHART AND WINSTON
New York   Chicago   San Francisco   Atlanta
Dallas   Montreal   Toronto   London   Sydney

Library of Congress Cataloging in Publication Data

Main entry under title:

Ideas of culture.

    Includes index.
    1. Culture—Addresses, essays, lectures. 2. Ethnology—Addresses, essays, lectures. I. Gamst, Frederick C II. Norbeck, Edward, 1915–
GN357.I33   301.2   75–41356
ISBN 0-03-015866-4

Copyright © 1976 by Holt, Rinehart and Winston
All rights reserved
Printed in the United States of America
6 7 8 9 0 038 9 8 7 6 5 4 3 2 1

Preface

This book of selected writings and introductory editorial comments concerns the concept of culture, an idea that is central to cultural anthropology and has often been viewed as the outstanding contribution to knowledge made by anthropology. Shadowy antecedents of the anthropological concept of culture are ancient, and we have not attempted to include discussion of them. Acknowledging that the idea has deeper roots, we have traced the emergence and development of the concept of culture after it had taken fairly clear-cut form, that is, after culture had been seen by scholars as a distinctive category of phenomena in human experience and had become the subject of study of the new field of anthropology.

    The period of time embraced by the various writings in this book is thus about one century. During that time, definitions of culture and somewhat varying views of the nature of culture have grown to be numerous. We have not attempted to present all of the definitions and views in the history of anthropology but have selected those which appear to have been the most prominent and fruitful. Any definition is, of course, valid as a definition, and the customary procedure in making judgments of "validity" has been to appraise the consequences of use of a definition, whether or not it has been useful in contributing to knowledge and stimulating further investigation. Our selection of readings has been made principally on this basis of judgment. In future years and, in some opinion perhaps presently, certain of our selections may be judged as outmoded; they will, however, continue to record trends of anthropological thought. Most of the writings reproduced here are the work of anthropologists, but anthropology has often been enriched by other fields of study and we have accordingly included writings by influential authors in other fields of study.

The categories used to organize this book are not always mutually exclusive, and some readings and references might appropriately appear under more than one heading. Our division of the book into Part 1 and Part 2 is exempletive. Part 2 concerns dynamic aspects of culture, but many of the writings in Part 1 are also so concerned. Part 2 similarly concerns "the nature of culture," which we have used as the title of Part 1. Our division into these two parts nevertheless classifies: Part 1 focuses primarily upon varying views of what constitutes culture and Part 2 upon the internal and external relationships of culture.

Our introductory editorial comments on the sections of the book vary considerably in length. This variation is largely a reflection of our judgment of the adequacy of coverage of the subjects that is provided by the selected readings. Where, as in the section on personality, the quantity and topical variety of relevant writings is too great to permit the inclusion of a fully representative selection, we have attempted to amplify the coverage by our introductory statements.

Our aim in preparing this book has been to present the thoughts and views about culture in a coherent and reasonable way that will allow the reader to see both the general direction of growth of the concept of culture and the narrower paths of particular bents of thought that lead to, and derive from, specialized goals of anthropological study. Much in the past and present thinking about culture is held in common, even when the exponents of particular views have regarded themselves as opposing other views. The selected writings which follow accordingly try to show consensus and continuity as well as divergence of thought.

Listed at the end of each section as suggestions for further study are a number of published works. References cited in our editorial introductions to the sections of this book are marked with asterisks in these lists. Individual reading references and notes are at the end of the book, starting on p. 330.

F. C. G.
E. N.

Acknowledgements

The editors acknowledge with gratitude and fond remembrance the friendship and influence of Leslie A. White (1900–1975), who might appropriately be considered the dean of the scholars of the science of culture during the middle decades of the twentieth century. His death at the time we put the final editing touches to this work caused us to reflect all the more on the intellectual debt owed to him.

We thank our many students in various courses who by their questioning aided in the preparation of this book. These courses include Introductory Cultural and Social Anthropology, the Evolution of Culture, the Nature of Culture, Ethnological Theory, and Ethnological Research Methods. We give special thanks to Marilou Gamst, who helpfully reviewed the first draft and typed several later drafts, and to Barbara Podratz, who typed the final draft and assisted in various other ways in producing the manuscript.

We wish also to express our appreciation to the authors and publishers who gave permission to reprint the readings included in this book.

Contents

Preface   v

Acknowledgements   vii

PART 1   **THE NATURE OF CULTURE**

SECTION I   **Introduction: Cultural Anthropology and Concepts of Culture**   **3**
- 1   CULTURAL ANTHROPOLOGY: VIEWS OF MAN AND CULTURE   Edward Norbeck   7

SECTION II   **Culture as Symbols**   **18**
- 2   A CLUE TO THE NATURE OF MAN: THE SYMBOL   Ernst Cassirer   20
- 3   FROM ANIMAL REACTION TO HUMAN RESPONSES   Ernst Cassirer   21
- 4   SYMBOLING: A KIND OF BEHAVIOR   Leslie A. White   26

SECTION III   **Culture as a Superorganic Phenomenon**   **32**
- 5   THE SCIENCE OF CULTURE   Edward B. Tylor   36
- 6   AUTHOR'S PREFACE TO *THE RULES OF SOCIOLOGICAL METHOD*   Emile Durkheim   44
- 7   WHAT IS A SOCIAL FACT?   Emile Durkheim   45
- 8   THE SUPERORGANIC   A. L. Kroeber   48
- 9   THE CONCEPT OF CULTURE   Leslie A. White   55
- 10   ON THE CONCEPT OF CULTURE AND SOME CULTURAL FALLACIES   David Bidney   71
- 11   THE SUPERORGANIC: SCIENCE OR METAPHYSICS?   David Kaplan   81

SECTION IV   **The Social Order as Culture**   **94**
- 12   ON SOCIAL STRUCTURE   A. R. Radcliffe-Brown   99
- 13   STATUS AND ROLE   Ralph Linton   107
- 14   THE CONCEPT OF SOCIETY: THE COMPONENTS AND THEIR INTER-RELATIONS   Talcott Parsons   111
- 15   THE CONCEPTS OF CULTURE AND OF SOCIAL SYSTEM   A. L. Kroeber and Talcott Parsons   115

x   Contents

SECTION V   The Patterning of Culture   119
    16 PATTERNS   A. L. Kroeber   121
    17 PATTERNING AS EXEMPLIFIED IN NAVAHO CULTURE
        Clyde Kluckhohn   128

SECTION VI   Personality as Culture   148
    18 THE PSYCHOLOGICAL APPROACH IN ANTHROPOLOGY
        Edward M. Bruner   154
    19 PSYCHOLOGICAL ANTHROPOLOGY   John J. Honigmann   160
    20 BIOSOCIAL INFLUENCES ON CULTURE—A NEGLECTED CATEGORY
        Edward Norbeck   168

SECTION VII   Culture as a Cognitive System   174
    21 INTRODUCTION TO *COGNITIVE ANTHROPOLOGY*
        Stephen A. Tyler   177
    22 LANGUAGE AND THE MIND   Noam Chomsky   188
    23 AMERICAN KINSHIP TERMS ONCE MORE   Robbins Burling   198

PART 2   DYNAMIC ASPECTS OF CULTURE

SECTION VIII   Culture and Biology   213
    24 SOCIETY   Elman R. Service   216
    25 MAN'S CAPACITY FOR CULTURE   John Buettner-Janusch   220
    26 HOW CULTURE AFFECTS GENETICS   Frederick S. Hulse   231
    27 BIOLOGICAL ADAPTATION TO CULTURE   Frederick S. Hulse   234

SECTION IX   Culture and Geographic Environment   247
    28 CULTURAL AND NATURAL AREAS OF NATIVE NORTH AMERICA
        A. L. Kroeber   250
    29 THE ECOLOGICAL APPROACH IN ANTHROPOLOGY
        June Helm   257
    30 THE CONCEPT AND METHOD OF CULTURAL ECOLOGY
        Julian H. Steward   265
    31 CULTURAL ECOLOGY AND ETHNOGRAPHY   Charles O. Frake   270

SECTION X   Cultural Evolution   278
    32 PRIMITIVE SOCIETY AND ANCIENT LAW   Henry S. Maine   282
    33 ENERGY AND THE EVOLUTION OF CULTURE   Leslie A. White   283
    34 EVOLUTION: SPECIFIC AND GENERAL   Marshall D. Sahlins   298

SECTION XI   Function in Culture   311
    35 ON THE CONCEPT OF FUNCTION IN SOCIAL SCIENCE
        A. R. Radcliffe-Brown   313
    36 THE GROUP AND THE INDIVIDUAL IN FUNCTIONAL ANALYSIS
        Bronislaw Malinowski   319
    37 THE ROLE OF RELIGION: INTRODUCTION   Edward Norbeck   322
    38 HISTORY, EVOLUTIONISM, AND FUNCTIONALISM: THREE TYPES OF
        INTERPRETATION OF CULTURE   Leslie A. White   327

        READING REFERENCES AND NOTES   330

        NAME INDEX   347

        SUBJECT INDEX   349

The Nature of Culture

PART 1

section I

Introduction: Cultural Anthropology and Concepts of Culture

The term "culture" is used today as a scientific concept by all of the social sciences. It also often appears, with meanings derived from the anthropological usages of the term, in modern writings in philosophy and other fields of the humanities. Increasingly, the term appears in the vocabulary of ordinary life outside the realms of professional scholarship. In university classes today it is rarely necessary to explain that, in the social sciences, the word culture does not mean beaux arts. Despite its wide and varied usage among all of the social sciences, however, the concept of culture is primarily the child of anthropology. Since the beginning of anthropology as a systematically-pursued branch of study, culture has been the central idea of ethnology and archeology, and it has been a matter of important, if not always principal, concern to physical anthropologists studying the biological evolution and physical nature of man. Unquestionably anthropology has done the most to formulate the concept and use it to gain an understanding of man's nature and ways of life.

The following reading in Section I introduces the concept of culture by providing an introduction to cultural anthropology, its interests, goals, and procedures. The attention of the reader is then called to continuities as well as differences of thought about man and culture that are evident in the history of cultural anthropology. This introductory essay and others that follow make clear that "the study of man" in cultural anthropology has been principally the study of his culture. Man has been considered by anthropologists as a biological organism in dealing with special problems that relate to both culture and biological traits; this includes attempts to understand cultural differences between males and females, or between any two individuals who have differing physical characteristics that influence cultural participation. It is, of course, also sometimes obvious that various elements of culture which are cultural universals, various elements of culture found in all human societies, are cultural responses to innate, biological characteristics of *Homo sapiens*. For example, man must eat to survive; therefore the cultures of all societies include technologic and economic procedures to supply food. The period of immaturity and consequent helplessness of human beings is extraordinarily long, the longest of any living form; the human cultural response to these needs of dependency takes the form of family groupings consisting of adults of both sexes and the immature. But explanations of differences in technologic-economic systems and forms of the family and, in fact, most questions which cultural anthropology has asked, cannot reasonably be related to biological traits. The most remarkable feature of man as a living entity, an animal among thousands of other animals, is that only humans create and transmit culture, thereby maintaining life and perpetuating the species. Thus, through the study of culture, especially of the relationships among the elements or distinguishable components of culture, anthropologists have tried to ascertain the nature of man.

Readings in Part 1 following the introductory essay present varying views of culture and discuss what may be called aspects of culture, such as the cultural nature of the human personality. As these writings show, the concept of culture arose from a broader and less sharply defined idea. Early students of man's ways of life used interchangeably the concepts of culture and human society in referring to a general sociocultural realm which they called "social" or "societal." This practice continues today among social scientists in various fields who do not think that a distinction between the social and the cultural is necessary although they are able to make such a distinction. Cultural anthropologists, whose basic interest is not limited to the social but covers the entire range of what is man-made in ideas, attitudes, social relations, and objects, distinguish the social from the cultural, customarily by regarding the social realm as a major component or element of the larger realm of culture.

Culture is regarded in at least a threefold hierarchy. *Generically*, culture refers to the learned way of life of all mankind, past and present; *specifically*, it means the way of life of a people or a particular society, such as the Navajos, Zulus, Russians, or Koreans; and *subspecifically*, it may mean any of a large range of somewhat different ways of life of groups of people within a society, such as, in the United States, the cultures or subcultures of the lower class, upper class, Appalachians, urban people, rural people, college students, ecclesiastics, physicians, males, females, the aged or the young, or individual people. Certain aspects of culture may be labeled *interspecific;* that is, they are subspecific but common to two or more cultures. No specific culture is truly autonomous or independent of all other specific cultures. Even so-called "isolated" primitive societies share interspecific traits of culture with their neighbors. Various features or aspects of culture are *universal*, existing in every society, a subject which several readings in this book discuss.

During the past century, several hundred definitions of culture have been formulated by anthropologists. This abundance does not, however, reflect a chaotic battle of many opinions. Most definitions are similar and the entire number may be reduced to a few categories, as is shown in the often cited analysis by A. L. Kroeber and Clyde Kluckhohn (1952). Perhaps the most outstanding difference is in two categories of definitions that may be called *realistic* and *idealistic,* which reflect diverging views of the nature of knowledge and reality. Realism is a body of philosophical thought holding that things may be regarded as existing independently and distinctly from knowledge of them and the mind which encounters them. Idealism is the view that all things are part of the human knowledge of them and of the mind which knows them. Idealistic concepts of culture are usually couched in terms of patterns and configurations of behavioral norms or rules abstracted from the observation of behavior. Idealistically, then, culture is an organization of "laws" or norms of behavior that exist in the minds of the bearers of a culture, who transmit these norms to succeeding generations. As such, culture is an abstraction of human behavior; and for various formulators of idealistic concepts of culture, an additional step has been to view culture as unreal because it is abstract.

In realistic formulations, culture is an abstraction only in the sense that the terms mathematics, cow, and magazine are abstractions or modal categories, single configurations that abstract the characteristics of many individual configurations. Culture, in realistic conceptions, is a natural phenomenon among other natural phenomena, a distinguishable category of things with characteristics and behavior unique to its class that is observable and amenable to scientific study in the same manner as other categories of phenomena. Thus, culture is as "concrete" as mathematics, cows, and magazines, and, for the purpose of study, its reality is not doubted. As the essay in Section III by David Kaplan suggests, the difference in views of culture as being "unreal" or "real" applies mostly when anthropologists formally discuss their views of culture. In the actual conduct of research and the presentation of interpretations of culture, idealists as well as realists have generally proceeded as if culture were indeed "real."

Early definitions often saw culture as being distinctive because it was learned rather than genetically transmitted or instinctive behavior. But this trait alone was soon seen as inadequate to set culture apart as unique since the behavior of many forms of animal life includes learned acts. In formulating definitions of culture, the mode of its transmission was also considered. A common definition of culture during the period from about 1920 to 1950 was "learned behavior, socially transmitted, and the concrete products of such behavior." Many definitions of culture from early times were *functional*, identifying culture as man's way of maintaining life. An element commonly added to the definition after the 1940s concerns the way that culture comes into existence. Writing about the concept of culture in 1948, A. L. Kroeber (1948a:253) stated, "perhaps *how it comes to be* is more distinctive of culture than what it *is*." How culture comes to be is certainly important to understanding it. Distinctively human behavior (as distinguished from man-animal behavior that is unlearned, such as blinking the eyes) is regarded as synonymous with culture, and the creation of culture is seen to depend upon the unique ability of man to create symbols (see Section II).

By the middle of the twentieth century, anthropological definitions of culture often included all of these various traits; culture was conceived as a learned, socially transmitted, symbolically based mechanism for survival, which, like other phenomena of our universe, had order or pattern. The principal trend for the past three or four decades has been to view the order or pattern as composing a system; that is, culture is a unit composed of interrelated parts which affect and are affected by each other.

Whether culture is regarded as idealistically "abstract" or realistically "concrete," its definition today generally continues to include all of these distinguishing traits: culture is viewed as man's way of maintaining life and perpetuating his species, a system of learned and socially transmitted ideas, sentiments, social arrangements, and objects that depend for their formulation and continuation upon man's ability to create symbols. In accordance with this definition, culture is unique to man and may be described as a distinctive class of phenomena forming the subject matter of a superorganic science just as minerals, plants, and other categories of phenomena form the subject matter of the inorganic and organic sciences.

Not every modern anthropologist has regarded the concept of culture as useful (Laughlin and d'Aquili 1974:195–206) and some have called it anthropocentric. For example, John H. Moore says, "Anthropology's culture concept is intimately related to theories of instinct in biology. The ideological function of both concepts is to preserve traditional Christian-Cartesian views of human uniqueness" (1974:537). However, the idea of culture continues to be the main concept of cultural anthropology and, as in the past, for most purposes the system of culture is studied as if it had an existence of its own apart from man the animal, its creator. As in the past, culture is also generally conceived as being limited in its range of variation by common elements of a human psychological and biological unity that are genetically transmitted and are everywhere essentially alike among all races and societies of mankind.

1 CULTURAL ANTHROPOLOGY: VIEWS OF MAN AND CULTURE
EDWARD NORBECK

Anthropology is one of the most youthful of the sciences and perhaps the most ambitious in scope. Scholars identified as anthropologists study subjects as diverse as the behavior of bands of baboons in Africa; the distribution of blood types among American Indians; stone tools of early man of the ice age; the beginnings of plant and animal husbandry in the Near East many thousands of years later in time; probable reasons why many peoples of the world marry one kind of cousin but do not marry another kind; the relationships between languages spoken throughout the world; the customs of Australian aborigines and other primitive peoples, and the effects of industrialization upon the social structure of the African tribes and of the populations of the United States, Japan, and other culturally elaborate civilizations.

All of these subjects are well within the conventional compass of anthropology. All focus upon man, as a living organism, or upon his culture, the things he has created. These subjects also reflect, if unevenly, the principal divisions of anthropology: physical anthropology, archaeology, and cultural anthropology. The physical anthropologist concerns himself with the physical aspects of man; his innate capacities and probable evolutionary origins; the evolution of his capacity for creating and transmitting culture; physical differences among races and populations of mankind; problems of bodily growth; the effect of culture upon man's physical traits, and other questions regarding the bodily characteristics of man. The archaeologist and the cultural anthropologist share as their central concern a common subject, culture, and in large measure have common goals. The archaeologist studies culture in a general sense and also specific cultures, focusing his attention on cultural events of the past. In drawing inferences from materials yielded by his archaeological excavations, it is often to his advantage to have a thorough knowledge of cultural anthropology. The cultural anthropologist studies primarily living or historically known culture and cultures, and it is advantageous for him to be acquainted with the findings and interpretations of archaeologists, for his concern is the nature of culture without necessary limitation on the time of its existence. It is also important for him to know the findings and opinions of physical anthropologists with respect to the innate capabilities and limitations of human beings.

The cultural anthropologist is interested in culture in a generic sense and also in specific cultures, their contents, similarities and differences; the manner of growth and change of individual cultures and of culture in a generalized sense; the interrelationships of different aspects of culture; the relationships between culture and physical environment; and the relationship between culture and human personality. He seeks to observe and compare, and on the basis of his comparative study to formulate principles of regularity.

Reprinted by permission of the publisher from Edward Norbeck, "Cultural Anthropology: Views of Man and Culture," *Thought,* vol. 39, no. 153 (New York: Fordham University Press, 1964), Copyright © 1964 by Fordham University Press, pp. 253–256, 261–263, 264–265, 270.

Depending upon his specific interests, the cultural anthropologist may be known among his colleagues by various titles such as linguist, folklorist, and comparative musicologist, or be identified by the names of the cultures he studies. He may be identified by the problems that interest him or by his theoretical leanings. The cultural ecologist, for example, tries to understand the relationship between the physical environment and culture, and the cultural evolutionist seeks to deduce sequences of cultural forms and to understand processes that bring them into existence. If the identifying title is ethnologist, a term often used interchangeably with cultural anthropologist, the scholar's research concerns cultures of living peoples, whether primitive or civilized. If the term is ethnographer, it means to indicate that the scholar's work is primarily descriptive rather than analytic or interpretive. If the title is social anthropologist, as most British and many American anthropologists call themselves, interests center on social structure and social relationships rather than the whole of culture, and theoretical orientations resemble those of sociologists.

According to popular opinion, cultural anthropologists study primitive societies, and the elaborate societies of the modern world are the province of sociologists. Anthropologists have indeed given much attention to the simpler societies of the world, a course of action that has been followed for several reasons. Most important among these is that study of foreign cultures, whether simple or complex, provides information necessary for comparison. Primitive societies also seem to offer in simple, comprehensible miniature the elements fundamental to human society, and, in the absence of recorded history, to offer a glimpse of the conditions of our past. During the early part of the present century, anthropologists hastened to study primitive cultures while they could. Following the expansion of Europeans into Asia, Africa, the Americas, and the islands of the Pacific Ocean, primitive peoples of these areas began discarding indigenous ways of life in favor of those of the civilized world, and sometimes whole societies as well as their aboriginal cultures became extinct. If the potentially valuable information on aboriginal ways of life in some areas of the world were ever to be recorded, it needed to be done quickly. With these circumstances in mind, programs of salvage anthropology were fostered by university departments of anthropology. Modern cultural anthropologists continue to pursue their traditional interest in primitive societies, but they have not lost sight of their fundamental concern, the culture of all mankind, and their efforts in recent years have been weighted increasingly toward the study of the great industrialized nations.

If we seek the ultimate origins of anthropology, it might be appropriate to say that the earliest anthropologist was the human being who first attempted to examine himself and his fellow men objectively and analytically. Following this line of thought, we can assume that the earliest men were also the earliest anthropologists. As a discipline of study wittingly and systematically pursued, however, anthropology began only about a century ago. At that time, science in general began a spurt of development which has since moved at an accelerated rate of speed. Anthropology was first an activity of men of means or of those gaining their livelihood in established professional fields of the time. By the turn of the century, it had entered the curricula of only a handful of colleges and universities. Although its growth in the following three decades was relatively great, the number of professional anthropologists in the United States in 1930 was still small enough so that most of the men and women knew each other personally. By far the greatest growth has come since World War II. . . . By the 1970s most of the approximately 2,200 colleges and universities of the United States included anthropology among their curricula, and the number of professional anthropologists had increased severalfold.

One of the inevitable concomitants of expansion has been specialization. Anthropologists of the nineteenth and early twentieth centuries might fruitfully pursue research as universal anthropologists, working in all of its major subfields. This time has passed. The death of Alfred L. Kroeber in 1960 after six decades of highly outstanding research and publication undoubtedly marked its end. Information in the field of cultural anthropology is now so extensive that the modern cultural anthropologist is challenged to maintain a thorough knowledge of research within the boundaries of his own broad specialty and can no longer also be an archaeologist and physical anthropologist. All indications point to increasingly accelerated expansion of teaching and research in cultural anthropology, ever finer specialization and, doubtless, the addition of new terms to label the new specializations. . . .

Cultural evolutionism, thoroughly alive again and finding increasing acceptance in professional ranks, also concerns interrelations or functional relationships, injecting into the study the idea of temporal progression in attempts to deduce a sequence of forms and the manner of interplay, the actions and reactions, that bring them about.

At a casual glance the diversity of modern cultural anthropology seems great. There are, nevertheless, common meeting grounds more specific than the general subject of study, and an examination of the most fundamental and commonly prevailing of these provides a revealing view of the total field. One of these is the idea that culture comprises a distinctive class of phenomena and that either culture in an abstract sense or individual species of culture compose units. To expand on this subject, it is useful to look first at anthropological views of man.

Anthropologists regard man as a biological organism, a member of the animal kingdom that emerged on our planet by the same general route as other living forms. Man is, however, unique in his capacity to create culture and transmit it to fellow members of his species and succeeding generations. Man's existence is dependent upon culture; without it he could not compete successfully with other living things. Culture has allowed him to live in a wide range of physical environments and to assume a position of dominance over other forms of life. The anthropological definition of man, and thus the dividing line between man and his evolutionary ancestors of the primate order, has in fact long been expressed in terms of culture. Man is the toolmaker, the creator and transmitter of culture.

Characteristically, anthropologists regard all varieties of modern man as sufficiently alike so that for the purpose of most studies in cultural anthropology, variations in the human organism may be omitted from consideration. This is the view expressed by the pioneer Tylor in 1871 and, implicitly or explicitly, it remains the prevailing view today. This assumption is not a democratic article of faith and it does not necessarily indicate a belief that all peoples and races are precisely equal in innate intellectual capacities. The question of physical differences among human beings is primarily the concern of physical anthropology. It is useful here, however, to summarize briefly some of the views of scientists who have concerned themselves directly with this topic. Race is a biological concept, and there is little agreement on the proper classification of human beings into races and subraces. The question of racial difference in intelligence is a vexing one, beset by problems of classification and hampered by a lack of tests valid for making judgments. At present, no conclusive scientific evidence exists to allow judgments of inferiority or superiority. To the unknown extent that "intelligence" might be biologically based, it seems reasonable to think that innate differences in intellectual ability exist among the people of a single society and among different populations and races, quite as differences in other physical traits exist. But attempts to appraise all the physical differences of anatomy and physiology that have been noted among populations and races have allowed no conclusions of general biological superiority and inferiority. It has long been observed that the individual of any race may acquire any culture, given the social opportunity to do so from infancy. It is also clear that recourse to putative biological differences in "intelligence" to explain differences in the cultural attainments of the societies of the world leads only to confusion. The anthropological view is that if one is to gain an understanding of societal differences in cultural development he must, against the background of the physical environment and natural resources, look to the culture itself, to differences in modes of subsistence, technological knowledge and efficiency, related ways of aligning the members of society into social groups, and resultant and accompanying attitudes and values.

Another idea of the relationship between man and culture is often involved when cultural anthropologists exclude from consideration the biological aspects of man. Again, it is an old view, first clearly expressed by Tylor, and commonly shared by modern cultural evolutionists as well as many if not all cultural anthropologists of other theoretical persuasions. Tylor looked for causality in man's behavior and saw that causality in culture. Writing in a similar vein, Morgan referred to inventions and discoveries as standing in serial relations along the lines of human progress and observed that social and civil institutions exhibited a similar register of progress. When collated and compared, he stated, these institutions, inventions and discoveries ". . . tend to show the unity of origin of mankind, the similarity of human wants in the same stage of advancement and the uniformity of the operations of the human mind in similar conditions of society."

The idea under discussion here has been elaborated in the twentieth century and has come to be called the superorganic concept of culture, a name bestowed by Alfred L. Kroeber. According to this concept, culture is looked upon as if it had an existence of its own apart from the biological organism, man. Man is the active agent in creating and transmitting culture but he does not determine its nature or content in any arbitrary, independent, or willful way. Culture comes to him from outside his bodily organism, giving him the peculiar set of attitudes and ideals that distinguish his culture or subculture from others, suggesting to him and compelling him to carry on the way of life taught to him, to add new traits of culture derived from old traits, to invent others, and to change or abandon certain traits. Man's personality is the reflection of his culture, the attitudes, values, ideals that have come to him, shaped by his society's manner of gaining a livelihood, its social alignments, and his total social life. In this view, culture engenders culture, and the human organism is the agency through which it operates, an agent that is of course indispensable for the creation, modification, and perpetuation of culture but dispensable and distracting if one desires to understand processes of cultural change and development.

Writing on the subject of the role of the individual with reference to culture, contemporary cultural anthropologists have elaborated upon these ideas, citing in support of their arguments such things as the high incidence of simultaneous but independent inventions and discoveries; the high incidence of geniuses in particular societies at certain times followed by periods when no geniuses appear in the records, and the acceleration of cultural growth in a pattern that resembles an exponential curve as elements of culture increase and are combined to form new traits subject to further synthesis. . . .

Whatever their theoretic views of the nature of man's behavior, it is clear that the primary, direct concern of cultural anthropologists has been culture and only indirectly man as a biological organism. Only secondarily and for restricted kinds of problems has attention been given to man's innate qualities and to biologically inherited differences among individuals and groups. Reference to the human organism is useful and sometimes necessary in attempts to understand cultural universals, a name given to traits of culture, such as family organization and the institution of marriage, that have been found to exist in all historically known societies. It is useful to try to determine whether cultural universals represent traits invented in one society that spread by contact from society to society throughout the world or whether the universals are responses to drives or needs on an innate level that are essential for the survival of the species *Homo sapiens*. It is obvious, for example, that man's ways of exploiting the resources of nature to get food are as they are in part because man's biological equipment sets limitations on the kinds of things he can successfully ingest. It is clear also that human infants are born helpless and mature slowly, and that to permit the human species to survive they must be given protection and nurture for many years by adults. Consideration of these facts sheds some light on reasons for the existence of the family. Only consideration of influencing cultural circumstances, including modes of subsistence in a given physical environment, however, can offer explanations to account for differing forms of the family and other kin groups among societies of the world. If one is investigating individual variations in cultural behavior or personality, it is also necessary to examine differences on a biological level, but we may note that anthropology thus far has tended strongly to study the culture of groups and to deal with modes. . . .

Anthropologists interested in distinguishing sharply the realm of things called culture have held that there is a qualitative difference between the kinds of learning of which man and other animals are capable. According to this view, man has both innate, man-animal behavior and distinctively human or cultural behavior. As with any other species of the animal kingdom, some of the behavior of man, including scratching, blinking the eyes, and, very probably, smiling, laughing, and bipedal locomotion or walking, may be regarded as biologically inherited traits. Other behavior derives from experience or learning. Only man, however, is capable of the kind of learned behavior that involves symbolizing; that is, only man can arbitrarily attach meanings to things. . . .

The definition of culture on the basis of symbolism has become common, but, as with many other ideas, it is not possible to state whether or not it is the general conception. It offers the advantage of setting sharper boundaries on culture than does a definition as learned behavior, and it makes man unique, the lone living creature with culture.

Let us now examine anthropological concepts of culture and working procedures against the background of the basic views and methods of other sciences, comparing them to note similarities and differences. Like all sciences, cultural anthropology sets up a distinctive field of investigation. Together with the other sciences, it looks for regularities and seeks to formulate principles. To be sure, men have often failed to understand their own acts and those of fellow human beings and they have sometimes declared human behavior inexplicable. The occasional anthropologist has declared culture to be an unordered aggregation, but he has generally met the stern censure of his colleagues. A example is provided by the experience of the late, distinguished anthropologist Robert H. Lowie (1883–1957), who once referred to culture as a "planless hodgepodge, that thing of shreds and patches." Although Lowie's many writings made it very clear that this remark was a slip of the pen in an unguarded moment and that it strongly misrepresented his own views, he was subjected for many years to severe criticism from his colleagues.

Rather than being unreasonable, the idea that the "behavior" of culture exhibits regularities appears to be the only reasonable view available to us. A moment's reflection on the classes of phenomena in our universe shows everywhere among them the existence of patterns and regularities. Although individual objects and living things are unique, all classes of things and events—including starfish, raindrops, winds, ocean currents, falling bodies, cows, and forms of mental illness—that have been subjected to examination have been seen to display regularities. If, as cultural anthropologists hold, culture comprises a valid scientific category, it would be most surprising to find that it lacked regularities peculiar to its class.

We may say that modern cultural anthropologists are characteristically committed to the views that culture represents a distinctive and scientifically meaningful part of the universe, that culture may be observed objectively, and that from this observation the scholar may formulate generalizations concerning the nature of culture. This view, like so many other assumptions and premises current in modern cultural anthropology, was expressed nearly a century ago when anthropology first took form as a discipline of study. In Tylor's words, "The tendency of modern enquiry is more and more towards the conclusion that if law is anywhere, it is everywhere." In the physical and natural sciences, essentially identical views are platitudes that rarely find or need statement.

The methods of cultural anthropology are similarly unexceptional. The anthropologist is faced with the task of setting order into his realm by classifying culture into subcategories comparable with the classifications of biology, chemistry, and astronomy. It is safe to say that no science regards itself as having thus far solved with full success its problems of classification. Cultural anthropology, as one of the youngest sciences, still faces many tasks of this kind. Various classifications of culture that divide it into components or elements—for example, the broad categories of religion, economics, technology, and social structure—have become conventional. Using these and many subcategories, anthropologists have sought to understand the interaction of individual elements and their relationship to the whole. The foregoing sentence constitutes a restatement of the anthropological view that culture comprises a system. Cultural anthropology is, of course, unexceptional among the sciences in this respect also. Since it shares the concept of system with many other branches of study, it seems reasonable to expect that many of its assumptions concerning the system called culture should find parallels elsewhere. These are precisely the circumstances.

The similarities of concepts and fundamental assumptions obtaining among the various sciences concerned with systems are striking, although this seems as yet hardly to have come to the attention of most scientists. Although differences of view exist that stem in part from the characteristics of the distinctive phenomena that compose the various conceptualized systems, many similarities may be noted between the ideas of cultural anthropologists and those held in biology, chemistry, physics, astronomy, psychology, sociology, cybernetics, linguistics, genetics, mathematics, and all other branches of study that concern systems. As implied by the definition of system as a unit composed of interacting parts, theories in these various sciences concern interrelationships of components of the system, ideas concerning the ways in which they modify and affect each other and enmesh to form a whole. Common also is the concept of equilibrium, the idea that the elements are in a state of balanced interaction or functional integration that obtains indefinitely unless change in one or more elements is brought about from within or without the system. Change in any important element is assumed to result in either adjustive alteration of other elements, resulting in a new state of equilibrium, or else inefficient operation and breakdown of the system. These are familiar and explicitly stated ideas of functionalist study in cultural anthropology, and they are also familiar although often less explicit in cultural evolutionism and studies in culture and personality. . . .

Whether or not the joint efforts of these scientists representing the whole spectrum of science will be successful in reaching the goal of formulating and deriving principles valid for systems in general, their efforts have revealed that the fundamental viewpoints of cultural anthropology are essentially those of any science. Let me make it clear that these observations concern the *scientific* views and goals of cultural anthropology. It is doubtless true that a minority of anthropologists are not concerned with scientific objectives. These are scholars of humanitarian leaning, who look upon anthropology as history or as an art rather than as a science. It is noteworthy, however, that the general trend in the scientific world is toward viewing anthropology, and the social sciences in general, as sciences rather than arts. . . .

We may summarize these remarks by saying that the scientific aims of cultural anthropology are to formulate principles concerning the nature of culture, and, since man and culture are intimately associated, thereby also to contribute to our understanding of ourselves. A question that naturally follows concerns the degree of success attained in meeting these goals. Few attempts to state precise scientific laws have met general acceptance, and attainment of the goals doubtless lies far ahead. The work of the past century has, however, greatly increased our objective knowledge of man and culture. It has also done much to overcome the particular obstacles that face cultural anthropology: lack of objectivity and imperfection of methods of observation. The anthropologist himself is in and of culture, so deeply immersed in personal life in the subject of his study that a wholly objective view has been difficult to gain. Knowledge gained during the past century of both differences and striking similarities in ways of life of the many societies of the world has done much to free us from the rigidity of thought imposed by acquaintance with only one mode of life. The prospects for the future seem increasingly hopeful.

SECTION INTRODUCTION REFERENCES* AND SUGGESTIONS FOR FURTHER STUDY

Allport, Floyd H., 1924a, "The Group Fallacy in Relation to Social Science." *Journal of Abnormal and Social Psychology* 19:60–73.
———, 1924b, "The Group Fallacy in Relation to Culture." *Journal of Abnormal and Social Psychology* 19:185–191.
Beals, Ralph L., and Harry Hoijer, 1971, "The Nature of Culture." In *An Introduction to Anthropology*, 4th ed. New York: Macmillan, pp. 101–122.
Becker, Ernest, 1971, *The Lost Science of Man*. New York: Braziller.
Bierstedt, Robert, 1938, "The Meanings of Culture." *Philosophy of Science* 5:204–216.
Bohannan, Paul, 1973, "Rethinking Culture: A Project for Current Anthropologists." *Current Anthropology* 14:367–372.
Burling, Robbins, 1970, *Man's Many Voices: Language in its Cultural Context*. New York: Holt, Rinehart and Winston.
Clarke, J. J., 1970, "On the Unity and Diversity of Cultures." *American Anthropologist* 72:545–554.

Coulbourne, R., 1952, "Causes in Culture." *American Anthropologist* 54:112–116.

Cowell, Frank R., 1959, *Culture in Private and Public Life*. New York: Praeger.

Dole, G., and R. Carneiro, eds., 1960, *Essays in the Science of Culture*. New York: Crowell.

Erasmus, Charles, and W. Smith, 1967, "Cultural Anthropology in the United States Since 1900: A Quantitative Analysis." *Southwestern Journal of Anthropology* 23:111–140.

Fairchild, Henry P., ed., 1967, *Dictionary of Sociology*. Totowa, N.J.: Littlefield, Adams & Co.

Febvre, Lucien, M. Mauss, E. Tonnelat, A. Nicefore, and L. Weber, 1930, *Civilizations: Le mot et l'idee, exposes par*. Paris: La Renaissance du Livre.

Firth, Raymond, ed., 1957, *Man and Culture: An Evaluation of the Work of Bronislaw Malinowski*. London: Routledge.

Fried, Morton H., 1972, *The Study of Anthropology*. New York: Crowell.

Goldschmidt, Walter, 1971, "On Man and Culture: A Response to J. J. Clarke." *American Anthropologist* 73:798–810.

Goldstein, Leon J., 1957, "On Defining Culture." *American Anthropologist* 59:1075–1081.

Goodenough, Ward H., 1971, *Culture, Language, and Society*. Addison-Wesley Modular Publications.

Gould, Julius, and William L. Kolb, eds., 1964, *A Dictionary of the Social Sciences*. New York: Free Press.

Hallowell, A. Irving, 1960, "The Beginnings of Anthropology in America." In F. deLaguna, ed., *Selected Papers from the American Anthropologist, 1888–1920*. New York: Harper & Row, pp. 1–104.

Harris, Marvin, 1968, *The Rise of Anthropological Theory: A History of Theories of Culture*. New York: Crowell.

Holloway, Ralph L., Jr., 1969, "Culture: A *Human* Domain." *Current Anthropology* 10:395–412.

Hultkrantz, Ake, 1960, "General Ethnological Concepts." In *International Dictionary of Regional European Ethnology and Folklore, Vol. I*. Copenhagen: Rosenkilde and Bagger.

Hymes, Dell, ed., 1974, *Reinventing Anthropology*. New York: Vintage Books.

Jaeger, Gertrude, and Philip Selznick, 1964, "A Normative Theory of Culture." *American Sociological Review* 29:653–669.

Kaplan, David, 1974, "The Anthropology of Authenticity: Everyman His Own Anthropologist." *American Anthropologist* 76:824–839.

Kaplan, David, and Robert A. Manners, 1972, *Culture Theory*. Englewood Cliffs, N.J.: Prentice-Hall.

Kluckhohn, Clyde, 1953, "Universal Categories of Culture." In A. L. Kroeber, ed., *Anthropology Today*. Chicago: University of Chicago Press, pp. 507–523.

Kluckhohn, Clyde, and William H. Kelley, 1945, "The Concept of Culture." In R. Linton, ed., *The Science of Man in the World Crisis*. New York: Columbia University Press, pp. 78–106.

*Kroeber, Alfred L., 1948, *Anthropology*. New York: Harcourt.

*Kroeber, A. L., and Kluckhohn, Clyde, 1952, "Culture: A Critical Review of Concepts and Definitions." In *Papers of the Peabody Museum of American Archaeology and Ethnology* 47(1).

Langness, L. L., 1974, *The Study of Culture*. San Francisco: Chandler & Sharp.

*Laughlin, Charles D., Jr., and Eugene G. d'Aquili, 1974, *Biogenetic Structuralism*. New York: Columbia University Press.

Leacock, Eleanor Burke, 1971, "Introduction." In *The Culture of Poverty: A Critique.* New York: Simon & Schuster, pp. 9–37.

Lehrman, Daniel S., 1970, "Semantic and Conceptual Issues in the Nature-Nurture Problem." In L. R. Aronson, et al., eds., *Development and Evolution of Behavior.* San Francisco: Freeman, pp. 17–52.

Levin, Harry, 1965, "Semantics of Culture." *Daedalus* 94:1–13.

Lowie, Robert H., 1936, "Cultural Anthropology: A Science." *American Journal of Sociology* 42:301–320.

Malinowski, Bronislaw, 1931, "Culture." *Encyclopaedia of the Social Sciences* 4:621–646.

———, 1939, "Review of: *Six Essays on Culture,* by Albert Blumenthal." *American Sociological Review* 4:588–592.

Merton, Robert K., 1936, "Civilization and Culture." *Sociology and Social Research* 21:103–113.

Mitchell, G. Duncan, ed., 1968, *A Dictionary of Sociology.* Chicago: Aldine.

*Moore, John H., 1974, "The Culture Concept as Ideology." *American Ethnologist* 1:537–549.

Moore, Omar K., 1952, "Nominal Definitions of 'Culture'." *Philosophy of Science* 19:245–256.

Muhsin, Mahdi, 1957, *Ibn Khaldun's Philosophy of History: A Study in the Philosophic Foundation of the Science of Culture.* London: Allen and Unwin.

Murdock, George P., 1932, "The Science of Culture." *American Anthropologist* 34:200–215.

———, 1945, "The Common Denominator of Cultures." in R. Linton, ed., *The Science of Man in the World Crisis.* New York: Columbia University Press, pp. 123–142.

———, 1957, "Anthropology as a Comparative Science." *Behavioral Scientist* 2:249–254.

———, 1963, *Outline of World Cultures.* New Haven: Human Relations Area Files.

———, 1965, *Culture and Society.* Pittsburgh: University of Pittsburgh Press.

———, 1971, "Anthropology's Mythology." In *Proceedings of the Royal Anthropological Institute of Great Britain and Ireland for 1971,* pp. 17–24.

Naroll, Raoul, and Ronald Cohen, eds., 1970, *A Handbook of Method in Cultural Anthropology.* Garden City, N.Y.: The Natural History Press.

Ogburn, W. F., 1922, *Social Change.* New York: Heubsch.

Opler, Morris E., 1948, "Some Recently Developed Concepts Relating to Culture." *Southwestern Journal of Anthropology* 4:107–122.

Seligman, Edwin R. A., ed., 1930–1935, *Encyclopedia of the Social Sciences.* New York: Macmillan.

Sills, David L., ed., 1968, *International Encyclopedia of the Social Sciences.* New York: Macmillan.

Social Science Quarterly, 1972, Special Issue on "The Idea of Culture in the Social Sciences" 53:221–392.

Sorokin, Pitirim A., 1966, "Part Three: Theories of Cultural Systems." In *Sociological Theories of Today.* New York: Harper & Row, pp. 133–383.

Spencer, Robert F., 1954, "The Humanities in Cultural Anthropology." In R. F. Spencer, ed., *Method and Perspective in Anthropology.* Minneapolis: University of Minnesota Press, pp. 126–144.

Spradley, James P., 1972, "Foundations of Cultural Knowledge." in J. P. Spradley, ed., *Culture and Cognition.* San Francisco: Chandler, pp. 3–38.

Stocking, George W., Jr., 1968, *Race, Culture, and Evolution: Essays in Honor of Anthropology*. New York: Free Press.

Wallis, Wilson D., 1930, *Culture and Progress*. New York: Whittlesey House, McGraw-Hill.

Willey, Malcolm M., and Melville J. Herskovits, 1927, "Psychology and Culture." *Psychological Bulletin* 24:253–283.

Winick, Charles, 1958, *Dictionary of Anthropology*. Totowa, N.J.: Littlefield, Adams.

White, Leslie A., 1963, "The Culturological Revolution." *Colorado Quarterly* 11:367–382.

White, Leslie A., with Beth Dillingham, 1973, *The Concept of Culture*. Minneapolis: Burgess.

Wolf, Eric R., 1974, *Anthropology*. New York: Norton.

Verene, Donald, ed., 1970, *Man and Culture: A Philosophical Anthology*. New York: Dell.

Voget, Fred W., 1960, "Man and Culture: An Essay in Changing Anthropological Interpretation." *American Anthropologist* 62:943–946.

Znaniecki, Florian, 1952, *Cultural Sciences: Their Origin and Development*. Urbana, Ill.: University of Illinois Press.

section II

Culture as Symbols

Attempts to define culture in a way that might set it clearly apart from other phenomena of our universe at first sometimes referred to language as the element of human culture that served as the primary means for its transmission. Growing awareness that people communicated with each other in a large variety of learned ways different from those of other animals but alike in one fundamental respect, culminated in the concept of symbolism. In his early writing on "the science of culture," Edward Tylor discussed the idea "that the power of using words as signs to express thoughts with which their sound does not directly connect them, in fact as arbitrary symbols, is the highest grade of the special human faculty in language, the presence of which binds together all races of mankind in substantial mental unity" (1875:118). The central and common element, and also the defining trait of symbols, is their arbitrary meaning; that is, symbols are objects and events which in themselves have no inherent meaning but to which humans have attached meaning. Man's primary form of symbolizing is language, in which he arbitrarily assigns significance to sounds of speech. Man also symbolizes through music, dance, and other forms of art, writing, mathematics, smoke signals, facial expressions, gestures, bodily postures, bodily ornaments, clothing, and in still other ways. It is clear that man can attribute meaning to any event or object and that these attributions may have great emotional significance for him.

Perception of the symbolic nature of culture undoubtedly has roots reaching back into antiquity. It was not until the twentieth century, however, that this line of thought became common in the social sciences and philosophy, and not until midcentury that symbolism became a feature of the definition of culture. The symbolic nature of religion was clearly evident, for example, to the sociologist Emile Durkheim (*The Elementary Forms of the Religious Life,* 1915). In 1942 the sociologist Read Bain stated that "culture is all behavior mediated by . . . symbols" (1942:87). The anthropologically-minded, idealistic philosopher Ernst Cassirer (1944:25) wrote of man as existing in a universe that was not merely physical but mitigated by symbols, and he defined man as an *animal symbolicum.* Describing the two decades before 1940, the philosopher Suzanne Langer similarly refers to symbolism as the subject of a trend of changing thought, a "Philosophy in a New Key" (1951). She sees the direction of change as a concern with human "intellectual activities determined by 'symbolic modes'" and with "the function of *symbolic transformation* as a natural activity, a high form of nervous response, characteristic of man among the animals" (1951:xi–xii).

The first detailed and widely read statement in anthropology about the symbolic nature of culture and the first use of symbolizing as a primary defining characteristic of culture, however, as provided in an essay by Leslie A. White which long ago became one of the classic writings in the field. Since the time of its original publication in 1940, this essay has been reproduced in publications in anthropology and other fields of study perhaps twenty times, suggesting that the world of professional social scientists had already striven to formulate the ideas expressed in the essay and had at last found, and welcomed, a suitable spokesman. A later version of White's ideas about symbols is reproduced here. White makes a clear distinction between symbols and signs, and is thereby able to limit symbols and symbolizing to human beings. In his well-supported view, the distinction between human and nonhuman animals is one of kind rather than degree because of man's unique ability to symbolize.

The ability to symbolize is today generally assumed by anthropologists to be as old as man. Although the neurophysiological basis of this capability is not understood, an evolutionary development of the trait in the hominid line is assumed; that is, development occurred in the central nervous systems of the members of the Order of Primates—early monkey-like forms, monkeys, apes, near-men such as extinct *Australopithecinae,* and early forms of the genus *Homo.* Symbols and culture have thus come to be regarded as essentially synonymous. In the words of White, "The symbol is the universe of humanity."

2 A CLUE TO THE NATURE OF MAN: THE SYMBOL
ERNST CASSIRER

In the human world we find a new characteristic which appears to be the distinctive mark of human life. The functional circle of man is not only quantitively enlarged; it has also undergone a qualitative change. Man has, as it were, discovered a new method of adapting himself to his environment. Between the receptor system and the effector system, which are to be found in all animal species, we find in man a third link which we may describe as the *symbolic system*. This new acquisition transforms the whole of human life. As compared with the other animals man lives not merely in a broader reality; he lives, so to speak, in a new *dimension* of reality. There is an unmistakable difference between organic reactions and human responses. In the first case a direct and immediate answer is given to an outward stimulus; in the second case the answer is delayed. It is interrupted and retarded by a slow and complicated process of thought. At first sight such a delay may appear to be a very questionable gain. Many philosophers have warned man against this pretended progress. "L'homme qui médite," says Rousseau, "est un animal dépravé": it is not an improvement but a deterioration of human nature to exceed the boundaries of organic life.

Yet there is no remedy against this reversal of the natural order. Man cannot escape from his own achievement. He cannot but adopt the conditions of his own life. No longer in a merely physical universe, man lives in a symbolic universe. Language, myth, art, and religion are parts of this universe. They are the varied threads which weave the symbolic net, the tangled web of human experience. All human progress in thought and experience refines upon and strengthens this net. No longer can man confront reality immediately; he cannot see it, as it were, face to face. Physical reality seems to recede in proportion as man's symbolic activity advances. Instead of dealing with the things themselves man is in a sense constantly conversing with himself. He has so enveloped himself in linguistic forms, in artistic images, in mythical symbols or religious rites that he cannot see or know anything except by the interposition of this artificial medium. His situation is the same in the theoretical as in the practical sphere. Even here man does not live in a world of hard facts, or according to his immediate needs and desires. He lives rather in the midst of imaginary emotions, in hopes and fears, in illusions and disillusions, in his fantasies and dreams. "What disturbs and alarms man," said Epictetus, "are not the things, but his opinions and fancies about the things."

From the point of view at which we have just arrived we may correct and enlarge the classical definition of man. In spite of all the efforts of modern irrationalism this definition of man as an *animal rationale* has not lost its force. Rationality is indeed an inherent feature of all human activities. Mythology itself is not simply a crude mass of superstitions or gross delusions. It is not merely chaotic,

---

Reprinted by permission of Yale University Press from Ernst Cassirer, *An Essay on Man*, pp. 23–26. Copyright © 1944 by Yale University Press.

for it possesses a systematic or conceptual form. But, on the other hand, it would be impossible to characterize the structure of myth as rational. Language has often been identified with reason, or with the very source of reason. But it is easy to see that this definition fails to cover the whole field. It is a *pars pro toto;* it offers us a part for the whole. For side by side with conceptual language there is an emotional language; side by side with logical or scientific language there is a language of poetic imagination. Primarily language does not express thoughts or ideas, but feelings and affections. And even a religion "within the limits of pure reason" as conceived and worked out by Kant is no more than a mere abstraction. It conveys only the ideal shape, only the shadow, of what a genuine and concrete religious life is. The great thinkers who have defined man as an *animal rationale* were not empiricists, nor did they ever intend to give an empirical account of human nature. By this definition they were expressing rather a fundamental moral imperative. Reason is a very inadequate term with which to comprehend the forms of man's cultural life in all their richness and variety. But all these forms are symbolic forms. Hence, instead of defining man as an *animal rationale,* we should define him as an *animal symbolicum.* By so doing we can designate his specific difference, and we can understand the new way open to man—the way to civilization.

3 FROM ANIMAL REACTIONS TO HUMAN RESPONSES
ERNST CASSIRER

By our definition of man as an *animal symbolicum* we have arrived at our first point of departure for further investigations. But it now becomes imperative that we develop this definition somewhat in order to give it greater precision. That symbolic thought and symbolic behavior are among the most characteristic features of human life, and that the whole progress of human culture is based on these conditions, is undeniable. But are we entitled to consider them as the special endowment of man to the exclusion of all other organic beings? Is not symbolism a principle which we may trace back to a much deeper source, and which has a much broader range of applicability? If we answer this question in the negative we must, as it seems, confess our ignorance concerning many fundamental questions which have perennially occupied the center of attention in the philosophy of human culture. The question of the *origin* of language, of art, of religion becomes unanswerable, and we are left with human culture as a given fact which remains in a sense isolated and, therefore, unintelligible.

It is understandable that scientists have always refused to accept such a solution. They have made great efforts to connect the fact of symbolism with other well-known and more elementary facts. The problem has been felt to be of paramount importance, but unfortunately it has very rarely been approached with an

Reprinted by permission of Yale University Press from Ernst Cassirer, *An Essay on Man,* pp. 27–41. Copyright © 1944 by Yale University Press.

entirely open mind. From the first it has been obscured and confused by other questions which belong to a quite different realm of discourse. Instead of giving us an unbiased description and analysis of the phenomena themselves the discussion of this problem has been converted into a metaphysical dispute. It has become the bones of contention between the different metaphysical systems: between idealism and materialism, spiritualism and naturalism. For all these systems the question of symbolism has become a crucial problem, on which the future shape of science and metaphysics has seemed to hinge.

With this aspect of the problem we are not concerned here, having set for ourselves a much more modest and concrete task. We shall attempt to describe the symbolic attitude of man in a more accurate manner in order to be able to contradistinguish it from other modes of symbolic behavior found throughout the animal kingdom. That animals do not always react to stimuli in a direct way, that they are capable of an indirect reaction, is evidently beyond question. The well-known experiments of Pavlov provide us with a rich body of empirical evidence concerning the so-called representative stimuli. . . .

Everyone who examines the different psychological theses and theories with an unbiased and critical mind must come at last to the conclusion that the problem cannot be cleared up by simply referring to forms of animal communication and to certain animal accomplishments which are gained by drill and training. All such accomplishments admit of the most contradictory interpretations. Hence it is necessary, first of all, to find a correct logical starting point, one which can lead us to a natural and sound interpretation of the empirical facts. This starting point is the *definition of speech* . . . . But instead of giving a ready-made definition of speech, it would be better perhaps to proceed along tentative lines. Speech is not a simple and uniform phenomenon. It consists of different elements which, both biologically and systematically, are not on the same level. We must try to find the order and interrelationships of the constituent elements; we must, as it were, distinguish the various geological strata of speech. The first and most fundamental stratum is evidently the language of the emotions. A great portion of all human utterance still belongs to this stratum. But there is a form of speech that shows us quite a different type. Here the word is by no means a mere interjection; it is not an involuntary expression of feeling, but a part of a sentence which has a definite syntactical and logical structure. It is true that even in highly developed, in theoretical language the connection with the first element is not entirely broken off. Scarcely a sentence can be found—except perhaps the pure formal sentences of mathematics—without a certain affective or emotional tinge. Analogies and parallels to emotional language may be found in abundance in the animal world. As regards chimpanzees Wolfgang Koehler states that they achieve a considerable degree of expression by means of gesture. Rage, terror, despair, grief, pleading, desire, playfulness, and pleasure are readily expressed in this manner. Nevertheless one element, which is characteristic of and indispensable to all human language, is missing: we find no signs which have an objective reference or meaning. . . .

Here we touch upon the crucial point in our whole problem. The difference between *propositional language* and *emotional language* is the real landmark between the human and the animal world. All the theories and observations concerning animal language are wide of the mark if they fail to recognize this fundamental difference. In all the literature of the subject there does not seem to be a single conclusive proof of the fact that any animal ever made the decisive step from subjective to objective, from affective to the propositional language. . . . The logical analysis of human speech always leads us to an element of prime importance which has no parallel in the animal world. The general theory of evolution in no sense stands in the way of the acknowledgment of this fact. Even in the field of the phenomena of organic nature we have learned that evolution does not exclude a sort of original creation. The fact of sudden mutation and of emergent evolution has to be admitted. Modern biology no longer speaks of evolution in terms of earlier Darwinism; nor does it explain the causes of evolution in the same way. We may readily admit that the anthropoid apes, in the development of certain symbolic processes, have made a significant forward step. But again we must insist that they did not reach the threshold of the human world. They entered, as it were, a blind alley.

For the sake of a clear statement of the problem we must carefully distinguish between *signs* and *symbols*. That we find rather complex systems of signs and signals in animal behavior seems to be an ascertained fact. We may even say that some animals, especially domesticated animals, are extremely susceptible to signs. A dog will react to the slightest changes in the behavior of his master; he will even distinguish the expressions of a human face or the modulations of a human voice. But it is a far cry from these phenomena to an understanding of symbolic and human speech. The famous experiments of Pavlov prove only that animals can easily be trained to react not merely to direct stimuli but to all sorts of mediate or representative stimuli. A bell, for example, may become a "sign for dinner," and an animal may be trained not to touch its food when this sign is absent. But from this we learn only that the experimenter, in this case, has succeeded in changing the food-situation of the animal. He has complicated this situation by voluntarily introducing into it a new element. All the phenomena which are commonly described as conditioned reflexes are not merely very far from but even opposed to the essential character of human symbolic thought. Symbols—in the proper sense of this term—cannot be reduced to mere signals. Signals and symbols belong to two different universes of discourse: a signal is a part of the physical world of being; a symbol is a part of the human world of meaning. . . .

Nature itself has here, so to speak, made an experiment capable of throwing unexpected light upon the point in question. We have the classical cases of Laura Bridgman and Helen Keller, two blind deaf-mute children, who by means of special methods learned to speak. . . .

The principle of symbolism, with its universality, validity, and general applicability, is the magic word, the Open Sesame! giving access to the specifically human world, to the world of human culture. Once man is in possession of this magic key further progress is assured. Such progress is evidently not obstructed or made impossible by any lack in the sense material. . . . The free development of symbolic thought and symbolic expression is not obstructed by the use of tactile signs in the place of vocal ones. If the child has succeeded in grasping the meaning of human language, it does not matter in which particular material this meaning is accessible to it. As the case of Helen Keller proves, man can construct his symbolic world out of the poorest and scantiest materials. The thing of vital importance is not the individual bricks and stones but their general *function* as architectural form. In the realm of speech it is their general symbolic function which vivifies the material signs and "makes them speak." Without this vivifying principle the human world would indeed remain deaf and mute. With this principle, even the world of a deaf, dumb, and blind child can become incomparably broader and richer than the world of the most highly developed animal.

Universal applicability, owing to the fact that everything has a name, is one of the greatest prerogatives of human symbolism. But it is not the only one. There is still another characteristic of symbols which accompanies and complements this one, and forms its necessary correlate. A symbol is not only universal but extremely variable. I can express the same meaning in various languages; and even within the limits of a single language a certain thought or idea may be expressed in quite different terms. A sign or signal is related to the thing to which it refers in a fixed and unique way. Any one concrete and individual sign refers to a certain individual thing. In Pavlov's experiments the dogs could easily be trained to reach for food only upon being given special signs: they would not eat until they heard a particular sound which could be chosen at the discretion of the experimenter. But this bears no analogy, as it has often been interpreted, to human symbolism; on the contrary, it is in opposition to symbolism. A genuine human symbol is characterized not by its uniformity but by its versatility. It is not rigid or inflexible but mobile. It is true that the full *awareness* of this mobility seems to be a rather late achievement in man's intellectual and cultural development. In primitive mentality this awareness is very seldom attained. Here the symbol is still regarded as a property of the thing like other physical properties. In mythical thought the name of a god is an integral part of the nature of the god. If I do not call the god by his right name, then the spell or prayer becomes ineffective. The same holds good for symbolic actions. A religious rite, a sacrifice, must always be performed in the same invariable way and in the same order if it is to have its effect. Children are often greatly confused when they first learn that not every name of an object is a "proper name," that the same thing may have quite different names in different languages. They tend to think that a thing "is" what it is called. But this is only a first step. Every normal child will learn very soon that it can use various symbols to express the same wish or thought. For this variability and mobility there is apparently no parallel in the animal world. . . .

Another important aspect of our general problem now emerges—the problem of the *dependence of relational thought upon symbolic thought*. Without a complex system of symbols relational thought cannot arise at all, much less reach its full development. It would not be correct to say that the mere *awareness* of relations presupposes an intellectual act, an act of logical or abstract thought. Such an awareness is necessary even in elementary acts of perception. . . . The mere awareness of relations cannot, therefore, be regarded as a specific feature of human consciousness. We do find, however, in man a special type of relational thought which has no parallel in the animal world. In man an ability to isolate relations—to consider them in their abstract meaning—has developed. In order to grasp this meaning man is no longer dependent upon concrete sense data, upon visual, auditory, tactile, kinesthetic data. He considers these relations "in themselves" . . . as Plato said. Geometry is the classic example of this turning point in man's intellectual life. Even in elementary geometry we are not bound to the apprehension of concrete individual figures. We are not concerned with physical things or perceptual objects, for we are studying universal spatial relations for whose expression we have an adequate symbolism. Without the preliminary step of human language such an achievement would not be possible. In all the tests which have been made of the processes of abstraction or generalization in animals, this point has become evident. Koehler succeeded in showing the ability of chimpanzees to respond to the *relation* between two or more objects instead of to a particular object. Confronted by two food-containing boxes, the chimpanzee by reason of previous general training would constantly choose the larger—even though the particular object selected might in a previous experiment have been rejected as the smaller of the pair. Similar capacity to respond to the nearer object, the brighter, the bluer, rather than to a particular box was demonstrated. Koehler's results were confirmed and extended by later experiments. It could be shown that the higher animals are capable of what has been called the "isolation of perceptual factors." They have the potentiality for singling out a particular perceptual quality of the experimental situation and reacting accordingly. In this sense animals are able to abstract color from size and shape or shape from size and color. In some experiments made by Mrs. Kohts a chimpanzee was able to select from a collection of objects varying extremely in visual qualities those which had some one quality in common; it could, for instance, pick out all objects of a given color and place them in a receiving box. These examples seem to prove that the higher animals are capable of that process which Hume in his theory of knowledge terms making a *"distinction of reason."* But all the experimenters engaged in these investigations have also emphasized the rarity, the rudimentariness, and the imperfection of these processes. Even after they have learned to single out a particular quality and to reach toward this, animals are liable to all sorts of curious mistakes. If there are certain traces of a *distinctio rationis* in the animal world, they are, as it were, nipped in the bud. They cannot develop because they do not possess that invaluable and indeed indispensable aid of human speech, of a system of symbols. . . .

Speech is not an object, a physical thing for which we may seek a natural or a supernatural cause. It is a process, a general function of the human mind. . . . Without symbolism the life of man would be like that of the prisoners in the cave of Plato's famous simile. Man's life would be confined within the limits of his biological needs and his practical interests; it could find no access to the "ideal world" which is opened to him from different sides by religion, art, philosophy, science.

4 SYMBOLING: A KIND OF BEHAVIOR
LESLIE A. WHITE

There is a fundamental difference between the mind of man and the minds, or *mindings,* of all other species; this difference is one of kind, not merely one of degree. Only man has the ability to originate and bestow meanings upon things and events and to comprehend such meanings bestowed by others.

Holy water is a good example of this kind of behavior. Holy water has a meaning that ordinary water does not have. This meaning has, of course, a value, an importance, to millions of people. Upon what does this meaning, or value, depend? Certainly not upon the physical structure or chemical composition of the fluid. It depends upon the unique ability of the human organism to originate and bestow meanings upon acts and upon objects external to itself.

Fetishes provide another example. We have a museum specimen identified as a "calcite concretion." But, in the context from which the ethnologist obtained it, it was not "just a calcite concretion"; it was the "home," or the embodiment, of a spirit. And this spirit is the creation and projection of the human mind.

Acts, singly or in rituals and ceremonies, as well as objects, may acquire meanings from the human mind. "Biting your thumb" at someone (*Romeo and Juliet,* Act I, Sc. 1), or tugging the lobe of your left ear, may be made to mean anything one wants it to mean.

Articulate speech, however, provides us with the most significant manifestation of symboling. What does *doko* mean? It is a combination of sounds, of wave phenomena in the atmosphere, or a series of marks upon a piece of paper. But human beings can give it meaning, any meaning they choose. Like the x in algebra, *doko* can be made to mean a dozen eggs, ten minutes, "close your eyes," or "that class of adult males of *Homo sapiens* who are between 30 and 40 years of age, have one gold incisor tooth, and play the clarinet." As Humpty Dumpty observed, in his discourse on semantics with Alice, "When *I* use a word it means just what I choose it to mean—neither more nor less."

A *symbol* may be defined as a thing or event, an act or an object, upon which meaning has been bestowed by human beings: holy water, a fetish, a ritual, a word. A symbol is, therefore, a composite of (1) a meaning, and (2) a physical structure. A symbol must have a physical form otherwise it and its meaning can not enter our

Reprinted from Leslie A. White, "Symboling: A Kind of Behavior," *The Journal of Psychology,* 1962, 59, 311–317. Copyright by The Journal Press.

experience—unless we are willing to accept the claims of telepathy or clairvoyance. But there is no necessary relationship between the meaning of a symbol and its physical basis; the relationship between the two is purely arbitrary.

The meanings of symbols cannot be grasped and appreciated (comprehended) with the senses. One cannot distinguish holy water from natural water, or discover the meaning of biting one's thumb at someone, or ascertain the meaning of *doko,* by sensory means. Symboling is that kind of behavior in which imperceptible meanings are originated and bestowed, on the one hand, and comprehended on the other. Symboling is trafficking in non-sensory meanings. And, be it repeated, no animal other than man can have, or be brought to, any comprehension of holy water or fetishes—or sin or Sunday.

But there is another class of things or events whose meanings may be related in purely arbitrary fashion to their physical forms: a green triangle may mean food to a laboratory rat, or it may mean an electric shock, or something else. But this is a *sign*, not a *symbol*.

A *sign* is a thing or event that indicates something else. There are two kinds of signs: (1) those whose meanings are inherent in themselves and their contexts (steam issuing from the radiator of an automobile, geese flying south, jaundiced eyeballs), and (2) those whose meanings are not inherent in their physical structures and situations (the green triangle that means food, the yellow quarantine flag). One learns the meanings of signs by experience (observation, the conditioned reflex). The meanings of signs which are extrinsic to their physical forms become identified with their physical forms by means of the conditioned reflex. And, having become identified with their respective physical forms, these meanings can be comprehended and differentiated with the senses: the rat comprehends the meaning of the green triangle and distinguishes it from the red circle with its eyes. How, then, are some signs to be distinguished from all symbols if the relationship between meaning and physical form is purely arbitrary?

The nature of the English language tends to confuse the issue here. There is no such thing as a *sign* or a *symbol* in the same sense that there is a *cat* and a *dog*. A cat, a dog, is an animal having certain parts and properties. But there is no thing which, in and of itself, is either a sign or a symbol. A thing or an event is a sign or a symbol only when it is in a certain context, just as a vase is a commodity, an object of art, or a scientific specimen depending upon context; or as a person is a slave only in a certain context. The fundamental distinction then is not between *a* sign and *a* symbol, but between contexts, between kinds of behavior, between "symboling" and "signing" (again the shortcomings of the English language). A thing or event, act or object, is a symbol when it is significant in the context of symboling, i.e., originating and bestowing non-sensory meanings, and in comprehending such meanings. A thing or event is a sign when its meaning is either inherent in it and its context, or has become identified through experience with its physical form and, as a consequence of this, the meaning can be grasped and appreciated with the senses. The meanings of symbols can be comprehended but not perceived; in sign behavior perception and comprehension are congruent and inseparable.

It is clear from the above that a thing or event may be significant and have meaning in either symboling or signing contexts. *Doko* originates as a symbol. But after its meaning has become identified through experience with its physical form, it becomes a sign, and its meaning is grasped with the senses: "Did you say 'pig' or 'fig'?" the Cheshire Cat asked Alice; it was a matter of hearing.

There is, then, a kind of behavior that is peculiar to an animal species, *Homo sapiens*. It consists of originating and bestowing meanings upon things and events and in comprehending these meanings. This kind of behavior should have a name. We propose the term *symboling*. A human being *symbols*, just as it performs any other function of which it is capable. It breathes with its respiratory organs, sees with its eyes, smells with its nose, and it symbols with its unique neurological equipment. The fact that we know very little about the anatomy of this function does not affect by one whit the validity of the assertion just made. We may not know much about the anatomy (the structural basis and operations) of sleep, but we know that people do sleep.

Why is the word *symbol* preferable to *symbolize* to designate this kind of behavior? The answer is, because *symbolize* already has established meanings which do not include, or encompass, the meaning that we wish here to express. To symbolize is "to represent, express, or identify by a symbol, or symbols; as, a nimbus enclosing a cross symbolizes Christ" (*Webster's New International Dictionary*). To symbolize is to do something *to* something *with* something: we symbolize Christ with a nimbus enclosing a cross. But we can symbol directly and immediately (not mediately): We can symbol an object just as we can see it or feel it. We can symbol water, i.e., give it a meaning, make it holy. We can symbol a calcite concretion, i.e., give it a meaning, make it a fetish. We can symbol the sun, an owl, bathing, wine, in short, anything that we can experience. We see the world chromatically and stereoscopically because we have a certain kind of optical equipment. We symbol the world because we have a certain kind of neurological equipment. And because we symbol, we human beings can never experience the external, physical world precisely as non-human beings experience it. We do not see the same sun that they do—or rather, they do not see the same sun that we do, for it is we who have added something to the purely optical experience. To us the sun is never "just a bright, shining, heat-giving object in the sky." It is the Sun Father, the Giver of Life, or a vast mass of physical particles in a process of thermonuclear transformation. No dog or ape can experience *any* of *these* suns.

It might be well, at this point, to call attention to the fact that not all of the behavior of *Homo sapiens* is *human*. Human is distinguished from non-human, and it is symboling that makes this distinction. Man is a human being because he can symbol, but much of his behavior is not-symboling and is therefore not human: coughing, scratching, walking, and so on. It goes without saying, however, that any element of the behavior of man can be placed in a context of symboling, i.e., can be symboled. A belch, for example, may be, and in some cultures is, given the meaning "I have enjoyed my host's meal"; a cough can be made to mean "pull the trigger."

We would do well here to make another distinction, namely, between *human behavior* and *culture*. Many anthropologists have defined culture as learned behavior, or socially transmitted behavior. But some have seen in this definition a threat to anthropology, for if culture is behavior and behavior is the proper subject matter of psychology, what is left to the cultural anthropologist? Kroeber and Kluckhohn solved this dilemma by awarding behavior to psychology, reserving abstractions of behavior for the cultural anthropologist. This had unfortunate consequences, for these abstractions became first imperceptible and eventually unreal; the cultural anthropologist was left with no real subject matter.

But the solution of Kroeber and Kluckhohn was as unnecessary as it was unfortunate. The products of symboling are: acts (tipping one's hat), objects (holy water, arrow heads), concepts (sin, hot), and attitudes (loathing of milk). These products of symboling are just what they are: products of symboling. As a class of phenomena they have no name in the lexicon of science. This is indeed a remarkable fact, for what class of phenomena is more important than that which distinguishes man as a unique species? I have ventured to give these phenomena a name: *symbolates* (if an isolate is a product of isolating, may not a product of symboling be a symbolate?).

Anything may be considered in any context for purposes of scientific interpretation: astronomic, physiologic, sociologic, culturologic, etc. More specifically, symbolates may be considered in either a somatic or an extrasomatic context. That is, they may be treated in terms of their relationship to the human organism, or they may be dealt with in terms of their relationships to one another. Thus, smoking a cigarette may be interpreted in terms of habit formation, satisfactions, conforming to custom, and so on. Or, we may consider it in terms of its relationship to other symbolates, such as ideas and attitudes of right and wrong, the social roles of age and sex, the distinction between the custom of cigarette-smoking (which women may be permitted to indulge in) and cigar-smoking (which may be denied to women), the relationship between cigarette-smoking and advertising, merchandising of tobacco, beliefs (assertions) with regard to the carcinogenic effect of smoking, and so on.

Symbolates (instances, or products, of symboling) in a somatic context may be called *human behavior,* the scientific study of which is psychology. In an extrasomatic context, symbolates become culture, the scientific study of which is culturology. Students of words (word phenomena) have long made this distinction between somatic and extrasomatic contexts, which they have called *la parole* and *la langue,* respectively. In the somatic context, word phenomena constitute *speech*—a kind of human behavior—the scientific study of which is psychology (conception, imagination, habituation, etc.). In the extrasomatic context words constitute a *language,* and are considered, not in terms of their relationship to the human organism, but in terms of their relationship to one another. Here we have the science of linguistics, concerned with such things as syntax, lexicon, grammar and phonetics.

Summary

There is a kind of behavior of which man, and man alone, is capable. It consists in originating and bestowing meanings, freely and arbitrarily, upon things (objects) and events (acts), and of comprehending such meanings. These meanings cannot be grasped and appreciated with the senses. Things and events upon which meanings have thus been bestowed may be called *symbolates*. *Symbols* (symboling) are to be distinguished from *signs* (signing). Human behavior (consisting of, or dependent upon, symboling) is to be distinguished from the non-human behavior of man. Symbolates viewed in a somatic context are to be regarded as human behavior, the scientific study of which is psychology. Symbolates viewed in an extrasomatic context are to be regarded as a culture, the scientific study of which is culturology. Symboling is a distinct kind of behavior, and it should be called symboling, not symbolizing.

SECTION INTRODUCTION REFERENCES*
AND SUGGESTIONS FOR FURTHER STUDY

*Bain, Reed, 1942, "A Definition of Culture." *Sociology and Social Research* 27:87-94.

Bidney, David, 1949, "The Philosophical Anthropology of Ernst Cassirer and its Significance in Relation to the History of Anthropological Thought." In P. A. Schilpp, ed., *The Philosophy of Ernst Cassirer.* Evanston, Ill.: Library of Living Philosophers, pp. 465-544.

Bruyn, Severyn T., 1962, "The Methodology of Participant Observation." *Human Organization* 21:224-235.

Cassirer, Ernst, 1953, *The Philosophy of Symbolic Forms* (3 vols.). (Trans. by R. Manheim.) New Haven, Conn.: Yale University Press.

*———, 1944, *An Essay on Man: An Introduction to a Philosophy of Human Culture.* New Haven, Conn.: Yale University Press.

Chapple, Eliot D., and C. S. Coon, 1942, "The Conditioned Nature of Symbols," "Ritual Symbols—The Supernatural World." "Symbols and Human Relations." In *Principles of Anthropology.* New York: Henry Holt, pp. 465-483, 551-565, 566-696.

*Durkheim, Emile, 1915, *The Elementary Forms of Religious Life* (Trans. by J. W. Swain.) London: Allen & Unwin.

Eaton, Ralph M., 1925, *Symbolism and Truth.* Cambridge, Mass.: Harvard University Press.

Furness, William H., 1916, "Observations on the Mentality of Chimpanzees and Orangutans." American Philosophical Society, *Proceedings* 55:281-290.

Gesell, Arnold, 1941, "The Biography of a Wolf-Child." *Harper's Magazine* 182:183-193.

Keller, Helen, 1902, *The Story of My Life.* New York: Doubleday.

Landar, Herbert, 1966, *Language and Culture.* New York: Oxford University Press.

*Langer, Susanne K., 1951, *Philosophy in a New Key: A Study in the Symbolism of Reason, Rite, and Art.* Cambridge, Mass.: Harvard University Press (First published in 1942).

Mistler-Lachman, Janet L., and Roy Lachman, 1974, "Language in Man, Monkeys, and Machines." *Science* 185:871-872.

Morris, Charles W., 1938, "Foundations of the Theory of Signs." *International Encyclopedia of Unified Science* 1(2):3–59.
_____, 1946, *Signs, Language and Behavior*. New York: Prentice-Hall.
_____, 1964, *Signification and Significance: A Study of the Relations of Signs and Values*. Cambridge, Mass.: MIT Press.
Nagel, Ernest, 1956, "Symbolism and Science." In *Logic without Metaphysics*. New York: Free Press, pp. 103–141.
Nida, Eugene A., 1964, *Toward a Science of Translating*. Leiden, Netherlands: Brill.
Ogden, C. K., and I. A. Richards, 1947, *The Meaning of Meaning: A Study of the Influence of Language upon Thought and of the Science of Symbolism*, 8th ed. New York: Harcourt.
Premack, David, 1971, "Language in a Chimpanzee?" *Science* 172:808–822.
Premack, A. J., and David Premack, 1972, "Teaching Language to an Ape." *Scientific American* 227:92–99.
Reichenbach, Hans, 1947, "Introduction." In *Elements of Symbolic Logic*. New York: Free Press, pp. 1–22.
Sapir, Edward, 1934, "Symbolism." *Encyclopaedia of the Social Sciences* 14:492–495.
*Tylor, Edward B., 1875, "Anthropology." *Encyclopaedia Britannica*, 9th ed. 2:107–123.
Urban, Wilbur M., 1939, *Language and Reality: The Philosophy of Language and the Principles of Symbolism*. London: Allen & Unwin.
*White, Leslie A., 1940, "The Symbol: The Origin and Basis of Human Behavior." *Philosophy of Science* 7:451–463.
_____, 1942, "On The Use of Tools by Primates." *Journal of Comparative Psychology* 34:369–374.
_____, 1946, "The Origin and Nature of Speech." In W. S. Knickerbocker, ed., *Twentieth-Century English*. New York: Philosophical Library, pp. 93–103.
_____, 1960, "Four Stages in the Evolution of Minding." In S. Tax, ed., *Evolution After Darwin*, Vol. 2. Chicago: University of Chicago Press, pp. 239–253.
*_____, 1974, "Reply to S. M. Willhelm." *Current Anthropology* 15:466–467.
Whitehead, Alfred North, 1927, *Symbolism: Its Meaning and Effect*. New York: Macmillan.
*Willhelm, Sidney M., 1974, "On Leslie A. White's Concept of the Symbol: A Reinterpretation." *Current Anthropology* 15:463–467.

For further references see Section VII, on cognition; for example, see Victor Turner.

section III

Culture as a Superorganic Phenomenon

The view of culture as a superorganic or extraorganic phenomenon—a system of things that may, and for certain purposes of study should, be studied apart from man, its creator—dates back to scholars of the eighteenth century and is foreshadowed in still earlier writings that try to formulate "ideal histories." The idea is evident in the nineteenth and early twentieth centuries in fields outside anthropology, for example, in the writings of Karl Marx and the sociologists Herbert Spencer and Emile Durkheim, although it is sometimes obscured or disguised by lack of a suitable vocabulary. In the excerpt from Emile Durkheim included here, a fairly clear statement of the superorganic view of culture becomes evident if the term "culture" is substituted for Durkheim's expressions, "collective representations" and "collective consciousness."

The word culture, derived from the Latin *cultura*, to cultivate land, has a long history of use in French and English. In these two related languages it has meant tilling land, raising plants, and also the worship of spiritual beings. By extension of its meaning of tillage, in French it also came to mean cultivation of the fine arts and of the mind (*Dictionaire de l'Academie Francoise* 1762, 2:398).

The source of some meanings of culture currently used in the social sciences was apparent in France during the latter part of the Enlightenment, particularly in the views of Voltaire (see Scherer 1875:81). Although his use of the word culture was restricted to mean cultivation of the mind (see GLLF 1972:1094), Voltaire was the first to use the procedure of study that later came to be called culture history. Gustav Klemm, an early German student of culture, noted:

Voltaire was the first to shove aside [the preoccupation of scholars with] dynasties, lists of kings, and battles and to seek out what is essential in the study of the history of man, culture—as manifest in customs, in beliefs, and in governmental forms. (Klemm 1843, 1:18)

After partial formulation by Voltaire and other French writers, principally Montesquieu, a formative idea of culture in a new sense was introduced to German scholars by historian Johann J. Winckelmann. The idea was then developed in the late eighteenth century by Johann Christoph Adelung, a lexicographer and grammarian. He appears to have been the first to use the term culture as a precursor of its modern meaning of human acts and artifacts (see Scherer 1875:81; Vogel 1898; Basler 1953:65). To Adelung, a member of the scholarly elite of Germany, *Cultur* was in part cultivation of the mind. Indeed, his discussion of the word in the second edition of his dictionary of High German is as restricted as Voltaire's (Adelung 1793:1354–1355; GLLF 1972:1094). However, his earlier discussion of the term (Adelung 1782) is broader than the meaning of cultivation of the mind: "Refinement, enlightenment, development of the faculties, all say something [with reference to *Cultur*], but not everything" (1782:ix). In this statement, and elsewhere in his work, we find the beginnings of the enumerative definition of culture developed at a later date by Edward Tylor as part of his conception of this subject (see the first page of reading 5). Beyond his discussion, Adelung's use of *Cultur* also included ideas that later became known as cultural relativism, holism, and the view that cultures should be studied comparatively, all of which are embodied in or relate to later concepts of culture as a superorganic system.

Adelung rejected the theory then prevailing that human society had retrogressed from a previous golden age of higher development and held that from their beginnings human beings have been on a continued course of cultural development, which he describes as being "incessant" and "geometric" in its progression. Following a somewhat ecological framework of thought, Adelung stated that culture is produced by ecological pressures upon a population in a restricted territory (1782:viii–xiii).

Adelung's ideas and procedures were developed further by Gustav Klemm, who stated "the science of culture has the duty to bring to contemplation the entire human activity and its monuments in all places and times" (Klemm 1854, 2:38). Building directly upon statements of Adelung, Klemm notes, "Culture is the result of the interaction between man and nature and from this time, the reciprocal social intercourse of men" (1854, 2:37). A basic interest of Klemm, noted in *Allgemeine Cultur-Geschichte der Menschheit,* was in stages of "the gradual evolution of mankind . . . with regard to custom, knowledge, skills, domestic and public life in peace and war, religion, science, and art" (1843, 1:21). This statement closely resembles Tylor's classic definition.

Developing further the ideas of Adelung and earlier scholars in Germany and elsewhere, Klemm used the term *Cultur* to label a concept of culture which he had only incompletely formulated. Nevertheless, his views appear to be the intellectual antecedent of later formulations of the concept and are so acknowledged by Edward Tylor. Developing the ideas of Klemm and other scholars, Tylor presented the first fully clear statement of the superorganic concept of culture as Chapter 1 of his *Primitive Culture* (1871), which is reproduced here. Tylor's writing expresses awareness of the revolutionary nature of his views and discusses the opposition it evoked. As the writings of an eminent scholar and outstanding pioneer in anthropology who has often been called the "father of anthropology," Tylor's ideas were presumably known to other scholars of the time and acceptable to at least some of them. We know that the turn of the century saw a general turning away from ideas of cultural evolution, which were closely associated with Tylor's views on the nature of culture, and anthropological history then shows no evidence of interest in this view of culture for some years. Like other scholars of the nineteenth century, Tylor lacked a vocabulary tailored to his subject. He thus uses the term "adhesions" where modern scholars might use "correlations" or "functional relationships," and employs "civilization" as a synonym for "culture" (with no intent of limiting culture to the civilized nations of the world). Tylor's writing is nevertheless a clear and rounded expression essentially identical with modern views.

In 1917 this view of culture appears again in still clearer and more detailed expression in an essay, excerpted here, by the distinguished anthropologist A. L. Kroeber, whose formulation was apparently made without direct awareness of Tylor's much earlier writing. From this essay the label "superorganic concept of culture" arose. Again this view met strong opposition and criticism, strong enough to move Kroeber to amend his statements somewhat in a later essay (Kroeber 1948). Kroeber's views of the superorganic concept of culture were first published in 1915 and were paralleled in a book by Robert Lowie, who said, "the principles of psychology are as incapable of accounting for the phenomena of culture as is gravitation to account for architectural styles" (1917:25–26). Malcolm Willey, a "cultural sociologist," was influential in countering attacks from outside anthropology upon the concept of "superindividual (superorganic)" culture (1929).

Subsequently, the view of culture as a superorganic entity has been most clearly and cogently expressed in numerous writings of Leslie A. White, beginning in the 1940s. For White, this conception has been central to the study of culture as a scientific pursuit, a field which he has variously called culturology and the science of culture. As in the past, expression of the superorganic encountered opposition, and some years passed before any substantial number of professional colleagues found it acceptable. A formulation of this view by White and an example of the opposition by the idealistic philosopher-anthropologist David Bidney are included here.

Reasons for the general reaction of opposition seem clear. Describing culture as a superorganic phenomenon may be considered revolutionary because it opposes cherished traditional views of the nature of man and the universe. In evoking percussive, emotionally charged antagonism, the theory of biological evolution has probably been the most revolutionary departure from traditional thinking in the history of science. (The theory of biological evolution is, of course, not a formulation of anthropology, which only later contributed to its elaboration and refinement.) Explosive, antagonistic reaction to the superorganic concept of culture has so far been limited to the world of scholarship, and the view has not as yet reached even the educated citizenry beyond those who have had contact with anthropology. Its revolutionary aspects seem nevertheless greater than those of the theory of biological evolution.

The theory of biological evolution, like the earlier Copernican theory of a heliocentric solar system, challenged traditional religious views of genesis and, especially, of man as a special creation. The superorganic concept of culture does much more, if its implications are fully comprehended. It seemingly opposes the very essence of Christian theology, seeing man as a vehicle for culture and God as the creation of man rather than the reverse; it opposes the idea of free will; and it views man as moved by culture rather than as a free prime mover.

Among professional anthropologists, the past three decades have seen increasing acceptance of this concept and its implications, but explicit rejection continues on the part of those who hold what we have called idealistic views of culture. It is not difficult to demonstrate, however, that the explicit rejectors are often implicit acceptors in the sense that their procedures of study accord with the view of culture as a superorganic entity. Within the folds of anthropology and also as a separate field of study, linguistic science has consistently proceeded from this viewpoint, treating one element of culture, language, as a superorganic phenomenon, and on this basis has developed a rigorously scientific discipline. If looked at dispassionately, the superorganic concept is wholly congruent with views and associated procedures of research of the sciences in general. It may be seen as an application of Tylor's idea that if scientific law is anywhere it is everywhere. The revolutionary and repulsive force of this view seems to stem from the fact that it does not concern chemical substances or other things somehow remote from man but pertains most intimately to them, seemingly denying the existence of cherished human attributes. It seems probable that the reception this idea might meet today outside scholarly circles would differ little from the circumstances described by Tylor in 1871:

> To many educated minds there is something presumptuous and repulsive in the view that the history of mankind is part and parcel of the history of nature, that our thoughts, will, and actions accord with laws as definite as those which govern the motion of waves, the combination of acids and bases, and the growth of plants and animals.

Yet, if fruitfulness is accepted as a judgment of validity, this concept must be judged as valid. In the entire range of studies of modern cultural anthropology, implicit use of the concept has been the rule.

5 THE SCIENCE OF CULTURE
EDWARD B. TYLOR

Culture or Civilization, taken in its wide ethnographic sense, is that complex whole which includes knowledge, belief, art, morals, law, custom, and any other capabilities and habits acquired by man as a member of society. The condition of culture among the various societies of mankind, in so far as it is capable of being investigated on general principles, is a subject apt for the study of laws of human thought and action. On the one hand, the uniformity which so largely pervades civilization may be ascribed, in great measure, to the uniform action of uniform causes: while on the other hand its various grades may be regarded as stages of development or evolution, each the outcome of previous history, and about to do its proper part in shaping the history of the future. To the investigation of these two great principles in several departments of ethnography, with especial consideration of the civilization of the lower tribes as related to the civilization of the higher nations, the present volumes are devoted.

Our modern investigators in the sciences of inorganic nature are foremost to recognize, both within and without their special fields of work, the unity of nature, the fixity of its laws, the definite sequence of cause and effect through which every fact depends on what has gone before it, and acts upon what is to come after it. They grasp firmly the Pythagorean doctrine of pervading order in the universal Kosmos. They affirm, with Aristotle, that nature is not full of incoherent episodes, like a bad tragedy. They agree with Leibnitz in what he calls 'my axiom, that nature never acts by leaps (la nature n'agit jamais par saut),' as well as in his 'great principle, commonly little employed, that nothing happens without sufficient reason.' Nor again, in studying the structure and habits of plants and animals, or in investigating the lower functions even of man, are these leading ideas unacknowledged. But when we come to talk of the higher processes of human feeling and action, of

Reprinted from Edward B. Tylor, *Primitive Culture*, 2nd edition, 1873. Published by John Murray (Publishers) Ltd.

thought and language, knowledge and art, a change appears in the prevalent tone of opinion. The world at large is scarcely prepared to accept the general study of human life as a branch of natural science, and to carry out, in a large sense, the poet's injunction to 'Account for moral as for natural things.' To many educated minds there seems something presumptuous and repulsive in the view that the history of mankind is part and parcel of the history of nature, that our thoughts, wills, and actions accord with laws as definite as those which govern the motion of waves, the combination of acids and bases, and the growth of plants and animals.

The main reasons of this state of the popular judgment are not far to seek. There are many who would willingly accept a science of history if placed before them with substantial definiteness of principle and evidence, but who not unreasonably reject the systems offered to them, as falling too far short of a scientific standard. Through resistance such as this, real knowledge always sooner or later makes its way, while the habit of opposition to novelty does such excellent service against the invasions of speculative dogmatism, that we may sometimes even wish it were stronger than it is. But other obstacles to the investigation of laws of human nature arise from considerations of metaphysics and theology. The popular notion of free human will involves not only freedom to act in accordance with motive, but also a power of breaking loose from continuity and acting without cause,—a combination which may be roughly illustrated by the simile of a balance sometimes acting in the usual way, but also possessed of the faculty of turning by itself without or against its weights. This view of an anomalous action of the will, which it need hardly be said is incompatible with scientific argument, subsists as an opinion patent or latent in men's minds, and strongly affecting their theoretic views of history, though it is not, as a rule, brought prominently forward in systematic reasoning. Indeed the definition of human will, as strictly according with motive, is the only possible scientific basis in such enquiries. . . .

Now it appears that this view of human will and conduct as subject to definite law, is indeed recognized and acted upon by the very people who oppose it when stated in the abstract as a general principle, and who then complain that it annihilates man's free will, destroys his sense of personal responsibility, and degrades him to a soulless machine. He who will say these things will nevertheless pass much of his own life in studying the motives which lead to human action, seeking to attain his wishes through them, framing in his mind theories of personal character, reckoning what are likely to be the effects of new combinations, and giving to his reasoning the crowning character of true scientific enquiry, by taking it for granted that in so far as his calculation turns out wrong, either his evidence must have been false or incomplete, or his judgment upon it unsound. . . .

The philosophy of history at large, explaining the past and predicting the future phenomena of man's life in the world by reference to general laws, is in fact a subject with which, in the present state of knowledge, even genius aided by wide research seems but hardly able to cope. Yet there are departments of it which, though difficult enough, seem comparatively accessible. If the field of enquiry be narrowed from History as a whole to that branch of it which is here called Culture, the history, not of tribes or nations, but of the condition of knowledge, religion, art, custom, and the like among them, the task of investigation proves to lie within far more moderate compass. We suffer still from the same kind of difficulties which beset the wider argument, but they are much diminished. The evidence is no longer so wildly heterogeneous, but may be more simply classified and compared, while the power of getting rid of extraneous matter, and treating each issue on its own proper set of facts, makes close reasoning on the whole more available than in general history. This may appear from a brief preliminary examination of the problem, how the phenomena of Culture may be classified and arranged, stage by stage, in a probable order of evolution. . . .

For the present purpose it appears both possible and desirable to eliminate considerations of hereditary varieties or races of man, and to treat mankind as homogeneous in nature, though placed in different grades of civilization. The details of the enquiry will, I think, prove that stages of culture may be compared without taking into account how far tribes who use the same implement, follow the same custom, or believe the same myth, may differ in their bodily configuration and the colour of their skin and hair.

A first step in the study of civilization is to dissect it into details, and to classify these in their proper groups. Thus, in examining weapons, they are to be classed under spear, club, sling, bow and arrow, and so forth; among textile arts are to be ranged matting, netting, and several grades of making and weaving threads; myths are divided under such headings as myths of sunrise and sunset, eclipse-myths, earthquake-myths, local myths which account for the names of places by some fanciful tale, eponymic myths which account for the parentage of a tribe by turning its name into the name of an imaginary ancestor; under rites and ceremonies occur such practices as the various kinds of sacrifice to the ghosts of the dead and to other spiritual beings, the turning to the east in worship, the purification of ceremonial or moral uncleanness by means of water or fire. Such are a few miscellaneous examples from a list of hundreds, and the ethnographer's business is to classify such details with a view to making out their distribution in geography and history, and the relations which exist among them. What this task is like, may be almost perfectly illustrated by comparing these details of culture with the species of plants and animals as studied by the naturalist. To the ethnographer the bow and arrow is a species, the habit of flattening children's skulls is a species, the practice of reckoning numbers by tens is a species. The geographical distribution of these things, and their transmission from region to region, have to be studied as the naturalist studies the geography of his botanical and zoological species. . . . And just as distant regions so often produce vegetables and animals which are analogous, though by no means identical, so it is with the details of the civilization of their inhabitants. How good a working analogy there really is between the diffusion of plants and animals and the diffusion of civilization, comes well into view when we notice how far the same causes have produced both at once. In district after district, the same causes which have introduced the cultivated plants and domesticated animals of civilization, have brought in with them a corresponding art and knowledge. . . . Experience leads the student after a while to expect and find that the phenomena of culture, as resulting from widely-acting similar causes, should recur again and again in the world. He even mistrusts isolated statements to which he knows of no parallel elsewhere, and waits for their genuineness to be shown by corresponding accounts from the other side of the earth, or the other end of history. . . .

To turn from the distribution of culture in different countries, to its diffusion within these countries. The quality of mankind which tends most to make the systematic study of civilization possible, is that remarkable tacit consensus or agreement which so far induces whole populations to unite in the use of the same language, to follow the same religion and customary law, to settle down to the same general level of art and knowledge. It is this state of things which makes it so far possible to ignore exceptional facts and to describe nations by a sort of general average. It is this state of things which makes it so far possible to represent immense masses of details by a few typical facts, while, these once settled, new cases recorded by new observers simply fall into their places to prove the soundness of the classification. There is found to be such regularity in the composition of societies of men, that we can drop individual differences out of sight, and thus can generalize on the arts and opinions of whole nations, just as, when looking down upon an army from a hill, we forget the individual soldier, whom, in fact, we can scarce distinguish in the mass, while we see each regiment as an organized body, spreading or concentrating, moving in advance or in retreat. . . .

That a whole nation should have a special dress, special tools and weapons, special laws of marriage and property, special moral and religious doctrines, is a remarkable fact, which we notice so little because we have lived all our lives in the midst of it. It is with such general qualities of organized bodies of men that ethnography has especially to deal. Yet, while generalizing on the culture of a tribe or nation, and setting aside the peculiarities of the individuals composing it as unimportant to the main result, we must be careful not to forget what makes up this main result. There are people so intent on the separate life of individuals that they cannot grasp a notion of the action of a community as a whole—such an observer, incapable of a wide view of society, is aptly described in the saying that he 'cannot see the forest for the trees.' But, on the other hand, the philosopher may be so intent upon his general laws of society as to neglect the individual actors of whom that society is made up, and of him it may be said that he cannot see the trees for the forest. We know how arts, customs, and ideas are shaped among ourselves by the combined actions of many individuals, of which actions both motive and effect often come quite distinctly within our view. The history of an invention, an opinion, a ceremony, is a history of suggestion and modification, encouragement and opposition, personal gain and party prejudice, and the individuals concerned act each according to his own motives, as determined by his character and circumstances. Thus sometimes we watch individuals acting for their own ends with little thought of their effect on society at large, and sometimes we have to study movements of national life as a whole, where the individuals co-operating in them are utterly beyond our observation. But seeing that collective social action is the mere resultant of many individual actions, it is clear that these two methods of enquiry, if rightly followed, must be absolutely consistent.

In studying both the recurrence of special habits or ideas in several districts, and their prevalence within each district, there come before us ever-reiterated proofs of regular causation producing the phenomena of human life, and of laws of maintenance and diffusion according to which these phenomena settle into permanent standard conditions of society, at definite stages of culture. . . .

It being shown that the details of Culture are capable of being classified in a great number of ethnographic groups of arts, beliefs, customs, and the rest, the consideration comes next how far the facts arranged in these groups are produced by evolution from one another. It need hardly be pointed out that the groups in question, though held together each by a common character, are by no means accurately defined. To take up again the natural history illustration, it may be said that they are species which tend to run widely into varieties. And when it comes to the question what relations some of these groups bear to others, it is plain that the student of the habits of mankind has a great advantage over the student of the species of plants and animals. Among naturalists it is an open question whether a theory of development from species to species is a record of transitions which actually took place, or a mere ideal scheme serviceable in the classification of species whose origin was really independent. But among ethnographers there is no such question as to the possibility of species of implements or habits or beliefs being developed one out of another, for development in Culture is recognized by our most familiar knowledge. . . . And thus, in the other branches of our history, there will come again and again into view series of facts which may be consistently arranged as having followed one another in a particular order of development, but which will hardly bear being turned round and made to follow in reversed order. Such for instance are the facts I have here brought forward in a chapter on the Art of Counting, which tend to prove that as to this point of culture at least, savage tribes reached their position by learning and not by unlearning, by elevation from a lower rather than by degradation from a higher state.

Among evidence aiding us to trace the course which the civilization of the world has actually followed, is that great class of facts to denote which I have found it convenient to introduce the term 'survivals.' These are processes, customs, opinions, and so forth, which have been carried on by force of habit into a new state of society different from that in which they had their original home, and they thus remain as proofs and examples of an older condition of culture out of which a newer has been evolved. Thus, I know an old Somersetshire woman whose hand-loom dates from the time before the introduction of the 'flying shuttle,' which newfangled appliance she has never even learnt to use, and I have seen her throw her shuttle from hand to hand in true classic fashion; this old woman is not a century behind her times, but she is a case of survival. . . . The serious business of ancient society may be seen to sink into the sport of later generations, and its serious belief to linger on in nursery folk-lore, while superseded habits of old-world life may be modified into new-world forms still powerful for good and evil. Sometimes old thoughts and practices will burst out afresh, to the amazement of a world that thought them long since dead or dying; here survival passes into revival, as has lately happened in so remarkable a way in the history of modern spiritualism, a subject full of instruction from the ethnographer's point of view. The study of the principles of survival has, indeed, no small practical importance, for most of what we call superstition is included within survival, and in this way lies open to the attack of its deadliest enemy, a reasonable explanation. Insignificant, moreover, as multitudes of the facts of survival are in themselves, their study is so effective for tracing the course of the historical development through which alone it is possible to understand their meaning, that it becomes a vital point of ethnographic research to gain the clearest possible insight into their nature. . . .

Progress, degradation, survival, revival, modification, are all modes of the connexion that binds together the complex network of civilization. It needs but a glance into the trivial details of our own daily life to set us thinking how far we are really its originators, and how far but the transmitters and modifiers of the results of long past ages. Looking round the rooms we live in, we may try here how far he who only knows his own time can be capable of rightly comprehending even that. . . . In fact, the books of costume, showing how one garment grew or shrank by gradual stages and passed into another, illustrate with much force and clearness the nature of the change and growth, revival and decay, which go on from year to year in more important matters of life. . . . The study of language has, perhaps, done more than any other in removing from our view of human thought and action the ideas of chance and arbitrary invention, and in substituting for them a theory of development by the co-operation of individual men, through processes ever reasonable and intelligible where the facts are fully known. Rudimentary as the science of culture still is, the symptoms are becoming very strong that even what seem its most spontaneous and motiveless phenomena will, nevertheless, be shown to come within the range of distinct cause and effect as certainly as the facts of mechanics. What would be popularly thought more indefinite and uncontrolled than the products of the imagination in myths and fables? Yet any systematic investigation of mythology, on the basis of a wide collection of evidence, will show plainly enough in such efforts of fancy at once a development from stage to stage, and a production of uniformity of result from uniformity of cause. Here, as elsewhere, causeless spontaneity is seen to recede farther and farther into shelter within the dark precincts of ignorance; like chance, that still holds it place among the vulgar as a real cause of events otherwise unaccountable, while to educated men it has long consciously meant nothing but this ignorance itself. It is only when men fail to see the line of connection in events, that they are prone to fall upon the notions of arbitrary impulses, causeless freaks, chance and nonsense and indefinite unaccountability. . . . In carrying on the great task of rational ethnography, the investigation of the causes which have produced the phenomena of culture, and of the laws to which they are subordinate, it is desirable to work out as systematically as possible a scheme of evolution of this culture along its many lines. In the following chapter, on the Development of Culture, an attempt is made to sketch a theoretical course of civilization among mankind, such as appears on the whole most accordant with the evidence. By comparing the various stages of civilization among races known to history, with the aid of archaeological inference from the remains of prehistoric tribes, it seems possible to judge in a rough way of an early general condition of man, which from our point of view is to be regarded as a primitive condition, whatever yet earlier state may in reality have lain behind it. This hypothetical primitive condition corresponds in a considerable degree to that of modern savage tribes, who, in spite of their difference and distance, have in common certain elements of civilization, which seem remains of an early state of the human race at large. If this hypothesis be true, then, notwithstanding the continual interference of degeneration, the main tendency of culture from primaeval up to modern times has been from savagery towards civilization. On the problem of this relation of savage to civilized life, almost every one of the thousands of facts discussed in the succeeding chapters has its direct bearing. Survival in Culture, placing all along the course of advancing civilization way-marks full of meaning to those who can decipher their signs, even now sets up in our midst primaeval monuments of barbaric thought and life. . . .

Nowhere, perhaps, are broad views of historical development more needed than in the study of religion. Notwithstanding all that has been written to make the world acquainted with the lower theologies, the popular ideas of their place in history and their relation to the faiths of higher nations are still of the mediaeval type. It is wonderful to contrast some missionary journals with Max Müller's Essays, and to set the unappreciating hatred and ridicule that is lavished by narrow hostile zeal on Brahmanism, Buddhism, Zoroastrism, besides the catholic sympathy with which deep and wide knowledge can survey those ancient and noble phases of man's religious consciousness; nor, because the religions of savage tribes may be rude and primitive compared with the great Asiatic systems, do they lie too low for interest and even for respect. The question really lies between understanding and misunderstanding them. Few who will give their minds to master the general principles of savage religion will ever again think it ridiculous, or the knowledge of it superfluous to the rest of mankind. Far from its beliefs and practices being a rubbish-heap of miscellaneous folly, they are consistent and logical in so high a degree as to begin, as soon as even roughly classified, to display the principles of their formation and development; and these principles prove to be essentially rational, though working in a mental condition of intense and inveterate ignorance. . . . In these investigations, however, made rather from an ethnographic than a theological point of view, there has seemed little need of entering into direct controversial argument, which indeed I have taken pains to avoid as far as possible. The connection which runs through religion, from its rudest forms up to the status of an enlightened Christianity, may be conveniently treated of with little recourse to dogmatic theology. The rites of sacrifice and purification may be studied in their stages of development without entering into questions of their authority and value, nor does an examination of the successive phases of the world's belief in a future life demand a discussion of the arguments adduced for or against the doctrine itself.

The ethnographic results may then be left as materials for professed theologians, and it will not perhaps be long before evidence so fraught with meaning shall take its legitimate place. To fall back once again on the analogy of natural history, the time may soon come when it will be thought as unreasonable for a scientific student of theology not to have a competent acquaintance with the principles of the religions of the lower races, as for a physiologist to look with the contempt of past centuries on evidence derived from the lower forms of life, deeming the structure of mere invertebrate creatures matter unworthy of his philosophic study.

Not merely as a matter of curious research, but as an important practical guide to the understanding of the present and the shaping of the future, the investigation into the origin and early development of civilization must be pushed on zealously. Every possible avenue of knowledge must be explored, every door tried to see if it is open. No kind of evidence need be left untouched on the score of remoteness or complexity, of minuteness or triviality. The tendency of modern enquiry is more and more towards the conclusion that if law is anywhere, it is everywhere. To despair of what a conscientious collection and study of facts may lead to, and to declare any problem insoluble because difficult and far off, is distinctly to be on the wrong side in science; and he who will choose a hopeless task may set himself to discover the limits of discovery. One remembers Comte starting in his account of astronomy with a remark on the necessary limitation of our knowledge of the stars: we conceive, he tells us, the possibility of determining their form, distance, size, and movement, whilst we should never by any method be able to study their chemical composition, their mineralogical structure, etc. Had the philosopher lived to see the application of spectrum analysis to this very problem, his proclamation of the dispiriting doctrine of necessary ignorance would perhaps have been recanted in favour of a more hopeful view. And it seems to be with the philosophy of remote human life somewhat as with the study of the nature of the celestial bodies. The processes to be made out in the early stages of our mental evolution lie distant from us in time as the stars lie distant from us in space, but the laws of the universe are not limited with the direct observation of our senses. There is vast material to be used in our enquiry; many workers are now busied in bringing this material into shape, though little may have yet been done in proportion to what remains to do; and already it seems not too much to say that the vague outlines of a philosophy of primaeval history are beginning to come within our view.

6 AUTHOR'S PREFACE TO THE SECOND EDITION OF *THE RULES OF SOCIOLOGICAL METHOD*
EMILE DURKHEIM

In no case can sociology simply borrow from psychology any one of its principles in order to apply it, as such, to social facts. Collective thought, in its form as in its matter, must be studied in its entirety, in and for itself, with an understanding of its peculiar nature. How much it resembles the thought of individuals must be left for future investigation. It is a problem which is rather within the jurisdiction of general philosophy and abstract logic than in the science of social facts. . . .

Quite obviously the social fact may be characterized in several different ways, and there is no reason why any one certain distinctive characteristic should be attached to it oftener than any other. It is only important to choose that characteristic which appears the best for one's purpose; and it is even quite possible to use, concurrently, several criteria, according to the circumstances. This is what we ourselves have occasionally found necessary in sociology; for there are cases where the character of constraint is not easily recognizable. Since we are here concerned with an initial definition, it is necessary only that the criteria we use be immediately discernible and relevant to the intended research. These considerations have not been manifest in the definitions that have at times been opposed to ours. Critics have said, for example, that the social fact is "all that takes place in and through society," or again, "what interests and affects the group in some way." But only when the science is already advanced can one determine whether or not society is the cause of a fact, or whether this fact has social effects. Such definitions could not therefore serve to determine the subject matter of the investigation at its beginning. In order that these definitions may be utilized, the study of social facts must already have made considerable progress, and consequently one must have discovered earlier some other means of finding and identifying them. . . .

We must not be surprised, moreover, if other phenomena of nature display the very characteristic by which we have defined social phenomena. This parallelism arises chiefly from the fact that both are real things. For everything that is real has a definite nature that asserts control, that must be taken into account and is never completely overcome, even when we succeed in neutralizing it. And, fundamentally, this is the very essence of the idea of social constraint; for it merely implies that collective ways of acting or thinking have a reality outside the individuals who, at every moment of time, conform to it. These ways of thinking and acting exist in their own right. The individual finds them completely formed, and he cannot evade or change them. He is therefore obliged to reckon with them. It is difficult (we do not say impossible) for him to modify them in direct proportion to the extent that they share in the material and moral supremacy of society over its members. Of course, the individual plays a role in their genesis. But in order that there may be a

Reprinted with permission of Macmillan Publishing Co., Inc, from the *The Rules of Sociological Method*, 8th edition, by Emile Durkheim. Copyright 1938 by George E. G. Catlin, renewed 1966 by Sarah A. Solovay, John H. Mueller, and George E. G. Catlin.

social fact, several individuals, at the very least, must have contributed their action; and in this joint activity is the origin of a new fact. Since this joint activity takes place outside each one of us (for a plurality of consciousnesses enters into it), its necessary effect is to fix, to institute outside us, certain ways of acting and certain judgments which do not depend on each particular will taken separately. . . .

7 WHAT IS A SOCIAL FACT?

EMILE DURKHEIM

Each individual drinks, sleeps, eats, reasons; and it is to society's interest that these functions be exercised in an orderly manner. If, then, all these facts are counted as "social" facts, sociology would have no subject matter exclusively its own, and its domain would be confused with that of biology and psychology.

But in reality there is in every society a certain group of phenomena which may be differentiated from those studied by the other natural sciences. When I fulfil my obligations as brother, husband, or citizen, when I execute my contracts, I perform duties which are defined, externally to myself and my acts, in law and in custom. Even if they conform to my own sentiments and I feel their reality subjectively, such reality is still objective, for I did not create them; I merely inherited them through my education. How many times it happens, moreover, that we are ignorant of the details of the obligations incumbent upon us, and that in order to acquaint ourselves with them we must consult the law and its authorized interpreters! Similarly, the church-member finds the beliefs and practices of his religious life ready-made at birth; their existence prior to his own implies their existence outside of himself. The system of signs I use to express my thought, the system of currency I employ to pay my debts, the instruments of credit I utilize in my commercial relations, the practices followed in my profession, etc., function independently of my own use of them. And these statements can be repeated for each member of society. Here, then, are ways of acting, thinking, and feeling that present the noteworthy property of existing outside the individual consciousness.

These types of conduct or thought are not only external to the individual but are, moreover, endowed with coercive power, by virtue of which they impose themselves upon him, independent of his individual will. Of course, when I fully consent and conform to them, this constraint is felt only slightly, if at all, and is therefore unnecessary. But it is, nonetheless, an intrinsic characteristic of these facts, the proof thereof being that it asserts itself as soon as I attempt to resist it. If I attempt to violate the law, it reacts against me so as to prevent my act before its accomplishment, or to nullify my violation by restoring the damage, if it is ac-

Reprinted with permission of Macmillan Publishing Co., Inc. from *The Rules of Sociological Method,* 8th edition, by Emile Durkheim. Copyright 1938 by George E. G. Catlin, renewed 1966 by Sarah A. Solovay, John H. Mueller, and George E. G. Catlin.

complished and reparable, or to make me expiate it if it cannot be compensated for otherwise.

In the case of purely moral maxims, the public conscience exercises a check on every act which offends it by means of the surveillance it exercises over the conduct of citizens, and the appropriate penalties at its disposal. In many cases the constraint is less violent, but nevertheless it always exists. If I do not submit to the conventions of society, if in my dress I do not conform to the customs observed in my country and in my class, the ridicule I provoke, the social isolation in which I am kept, produce, although in an attenuated form, the same effects as a punishment in the strict sense of the word. The constraint is nonetheless efficacious for being indirect. I am not obliged to speak French with my fellow-countrymen nor to use the legal currency, but I cannot possibly do otherwise. If I tried to escape this necessity, my attempt would fail miserably. As an industrialist, I am free to apply the technical methods of former centuries; but by doing so, I should invite certain ruin. Even when I free myself from these rules and violate them successfully, I am always compelled to struggle with them. When finally overcome, they make their constraining power sufficiently felt by the resistance they offer. The enterprises of all innovators, including successful ones, come up against resistance of this kind.

Here, then, is a category of facts with very distinctive characteristics: it consists of ways of acting, thinking, and feeling, external to the individual, and endowed with a power of coercion, by reason of which they control him. These ways of thinking could not be confused with biological phenomena, since they consist of representations and of actions; nor with psychological phenomena, which exist only in the individual consciousness and through it. They constitute, thus, a new variety of phenomena; and it is to them exclusively that the term ''social'' ought to be applied. And this term fits them quite well, for it is clear that, since their source is not in the individual, their substratum can be no other than society, either the political society as a whole or some one of the partial groups it includes, such as religious denominations, political, literary, and occupational associations, etc. On the other hand, this term ''social'' applies to them exclusively, for it has a distinct meaning only if it designates exclusively the phenomena which are not included in any of the categories of facts that have already been established and classified. These ways of thinking and acting therefore constitute the proper domain of sociology. It is true that, when we define them with this word ''constraint,'' we risk shocking the zealous partisans of absolute individualism. For those who profess the complete autonomy of the individual, man's dignity is diminished whenever he is made to feel that he is not completely self-determinant. It is generally accepted today, however, that most of our ideas and our tendencies are not developed by ourselves but come to us from without. How can they become a part of us except by imposing themselves upon us? This is the whole meaning of our definition. And it is generally accepted, moreover, that social constraint is not necessarily incompatible with the individual personality.[1]

---

[1] We do not intend to imply, however, that all constraint is normal. We shall return to this point later.

Since the examples that we have just cited (legal and moral regulations, religious faiths, financial systems, etc.) all consist of established beliefs and practices, one might be led to believe that social facts exist only where there is some social organization. But there are other facts without such crystallized form which have the same objectivity and the same ascendency over the individual. These are called "social currents." Thus the great movements of enthusiasm, indignation, and pity in a crowd do not originate in any one of the particular individual consciousnesses. They come to each one of us from without and can carry us away in spite of ourselves. Of course, it may happen that, in abandoning myself to them unreservedly, I do not feel the pressure they exert upon me. But it is revealed as soon as I try to resist them. Let an individual attempt to oppose one of these collective manifestations, and the emotions that he denies will turn against him. Now, if this power of external coercion asserts itself so clearly in cases of resistance, it must exist also in the first-mentioned cases, although we are unconscious of it. We are then victims of the illusion of having ourselves created that which actually forced itself from without. If the complacency with which we permit ourselves to be carried along conceals the pressure undergone, nevertheless it does not abolish it. . . .

To confirm this definition of the social fact by a characteristic illustration from common experience, one need only observe the manner in which children are brought up. Considering the facts as they are and as they have always been, it becomes immediately evident that all education is a continuous effort to impose on the child ways of seeing, feeling, and acting which he could not have arrived at spontaneously. From the very first hours of his life, we compel him to eat, drink, and sleep at regular hours; we constrain him to cleanliness, calmness, and obedience; later we exert pressure upon him in order that he may learn proper consideration for others, respect for customs and conventions, the need for work, etc. If, in time, this constraint ceases to be felt, it is because it gradually gives rise to habits and to internal tendencies that render constraint unnecessary. . . . This unremitting pressure to which the child is subjected is the very pressure of the social milieu which tends to fashion him in its own image, and of which parents and teachers are merely the representatives and intermediaries. . . .

Currents of opinion, with an intensity varying according to the time and place, impel certain groups either to more marriages, for example, or to more suicides, or to a higher or lower birthrate, etc. These currents are plainly social facts. At first sight they seem inseparable from the forms they take in individual cases. But statistics furnish us with the means of isolating them. They are, in fact, represented with considerable exactness by the rates of births, marriages, and suicides, that is, by the number obtained by dividing the average annual total of marriages, births, suicides, by the number of persons whose ages lie within the range in which marriages, births, and suicides occur. Since each of these figures contains all the individual cases indiscriminately, the individual circumstances which may have had a share in the production of the phenomenon are neutralized and, consequently, do not contribute to its determination. The average, then, expresses a certain state of the group mind (*l'âme collective*). . . .

8 THE SUPERORGANIC
A. L. KROEBER

It has long been the custom to say that the difference [between man and animals] is that between body and mind; that animals have their physiques adapted to their circumstances, but that man's superior intelligence enables him to rise superior to such lowly needs. But this is not the significant point of the difference. It is true that without the much greater mental faculties of man, he could not achieve the attainments the lack of which keeps the brute chained to the limitations of his anatomy. But the greater human intelligence in itself does not cause the differences that exist. This psychic superiority is only the indispensable condition of what is peculiarly human: civilization. Directly, it is the civilization in which every Eskimo, every Alaskan miner or arctic discoverer is reared, and not any greater inborn faculty, that leads him to build houses, ignite fire, and wear clothing. The distinction between animal and man which counts is not that of the physical and mental, which is one of relative degree, but that of the organic and social, which is one of kind. The beast has mentality, and we have bodies; but in civilization man has something that no animal has. . . .

There have been many attempts to make precise the distinction between instinct and civilization, between the organic and the social, between animal and man. Man as the clothing animal, the fire-using animal, the tool-using or tool-making animal, the speaking animal, are all summations that contain some approximation. But for the conception of the discrimination that is at once most complete and most compact, we must go back, as for the first precise expression of so many of the ideas with which we operate, to the uniquely marvelous mind that impelled Aristotle. "Man is a political animal." The word political has changed in import. We use instead the Latin term social. This, both philosopher and philologist tell us, is what the great Greek would have said were he speaking in English today. Man is a social animal, then; a social organism. He has organic constitution; but he has also civilization. To ignore one element is as short-sighted as to overlook the other; to convert one into the other, if each has its reality, is negation. With this basic formulation more than two thousand years old, and known to all the generations, there is something puny, as well as obstinately destructive, in the endeavor to abrogate the distinction, or to hinder its completest fruition. The attempt today to treat the social as organic, to understand civilization as heredity, is as essentially narrow minded as the alleged mediaeval inclination to withdraw man from the realm of nature and from the ken of the scientist because he was believed to possess an immaterial soul. . . .

The problem being in the present state of our knowledge unprovable, is really also not arguable. What is possible, however, is to realize that a complete and consistent explanation can be given, for all so-called racial differences, on a basis of

Reproduced by permission of the American Anthropological Association from the *American Anthropologist*, vol. 19, no. 2, 1917.

purely civilizational and non-organic causes; and to attain also to the recognition that the mere fact of the world in general assuming that such differences between one people and another are inborn and ineradicable except by breeding, is no evidence whatever in favor of the assumption being true. . . .

Most ethnologists, at any rate, are convinced that the overwhelming mass of historical and miscalled racial facts that are now attributed to obscure organic causes, or at most are in dispute, will ultimately be viewed by everyone as social and as intelligible only in their social relations. That there may be a residuum in which hereditary influences have been operative, it would be dogmatic to deny; but even this residuum of organic agencies will perhaps be found to be operative in quite other manners than those which are customarily adduced at present.

The opinion may further be uncompromisingly maintained, that for the historian—him who wishes to understand any sort of social phenomena—it is an unavoidable necessity, today, to disregard the organic as such and to deal only with the social. For the larger number who are not professional students of civilization, insistence upon these articles would be an unreasonable demand, under our present inability to substantiate them by proof. On the other hand, the social as something distinct from the organic is an old enough concept, and is a plain enough phenomenon about us in daily life, to warrant the claim that it cannot be outright dispensed with. It is perhaps too much to expect any one wedded, deliberately or unknowingly, to organic explanations, to discard these wholly before such incomplete evidence as is available to the contrary of these explanations. But it does seem justifiable to stand unhesitatingly on the proposition that civilization and heredity are two things that operate in entirely separate ways; that therefore any outright substitution of one for the other in the explanation of human group phenomena is crass; and that the refusal to recognize at least the logical possibility of an explanation of human achievement totally different from the prevailing tendency toward a biological one, is an act of illiberality. When once such recognition, of the rationality of this attitude of mind which is diametrically opposed to the current one, shall have become general, far more progress will have been made on the road towards a useful agreement as to the truth, than by any present attempts to win converts by argument. . . .

The whole theory of heredity by acquirement rests upon the confusion of these two so diverse processes, that of heredity and that of civilization. It has been nourished, perhaps, by unsatisfied needs of biological science, but it has never obtained the slightest unchallengeable verification from biology, and has in fact long been assailed, by a sound and vigorous instinct, as well as in consequence of the failure of observation and experiment, from within that science. It is a doctrine that is the constant blazon of the dilettante who knows something of both history and life, but has no care to understand the workings of either. . . .

The reason why mental heredity has nothing to do with civilization, is that civilization is not mental action but a body or stream of products of mental exercise. Mental activity, as biologists have dealt with it, being organic, any demonstration concerning it consequently proves nothing whatever as to social events. Mentality relates to the individual. The social or cultural, on the other hand, is in its very essence non-individual. Civilization, as such, begins only where the individual ends; and whoever does not in some measure perceive this fact, though as a brute and rootless one, can find no meaning in civilization, and history for him must be only a wearying jumble, or an opportunity for the exercise of art.

All biology necessarily has this entire reference to the individual. A social mind is as meaningless a nonentity as a social body. There can be only one kind of organicness: the organic on another plane would no longer be organic. The Darwinian doctrine relates, it is true, to the race; but the race, except as an abstraction, is only a collection of individuals; and the bases of this doctrine, heredity, variation, and competition, deal with the relation of individual to individual, from individual, and against individual. The whole key of the success of the Mendelian methods of studying heredity lies in isolating traits and isolating individuals.

But a thousand individuals do not make a society. They are the potential basis of a society; but they do not themselves cause it; and they are also the basis of a thousand other potential societies.

The findings of biology as to heredity, mental and physical alike, may then, in fact must be, accepted without reservation. But that therefore civilization can be understood by psychological analysis, or explained by observations or experiments in heredity, or, to revert to a concrete example, that the destiny of nations can be predicted from an analysis of the organic constitution of their members, assumes that society is merely a collection of individuals; that civilization is only an aggregate of psychic activities and not also an entity beyond them; in short, that the social can be wholly resolved into the mental as it is thought this resolves into the physical.

It is accordingly in this point of the tempting leap from the individually mental to the culturally social which presupposes but does not contain mentality, that the source of the distracting transferences of the organic into the social is to be sought. A more exact examination of the relation of the two is therefore desirable. . . .

[A]ll so-called inventors of appliances or discoverers of thoughts of note were unusually able men, endowed from before birth with superior faculties, which the psychologist can hope to analyze and define, the physiologist to correlate with functions of organs, and the genetic biologist to investigate in their hereditary origins until he attains not only system and law but verifiable power of prediction. And, on the other hand, the content of the invention or discovery springs in no way from the make-up of the great man, or that of his ancestors, but is a product purely of the civilization into which he with millions of others is born as a meaningless and regularly recurring event. Whether he in his person becomes inventor, explorer, imitator, or user, is an affair of forces that the science of mechanical causality is concerned with. Whether his invention is that of the cannon or the bow, his achievement a musical scale or a system of harmony, his formulation that of the soul or that of the categorical imperative, is not explainable by the medium of mechanistic science—at least, not by any methods at the command of biological science—but finds its meaning only in such operations with the material of civilization as history is occupied with. . . .

The whole history of inventions is one endless chain of parallel instances. An examination of patent office records, in any other than a commercial or anecdotic spirit, would alone reveal the inexorable order that prevails in the advance of civilization. The right to the monopoly of the manufacture of the telephone was long in litigation; the ultimate decision rested on an interval of hours between the recording of concurrent descriptions by Alexander Bell and Elisha Gray. Though it is part of our vulgar thinking to dismiss such conflicts as evidences only of unscrupulous cupidity and legal inadequacy or as melodramatic coincidences, it behooves the historian to see beyond such childlike plays of the intellect.

The discovery of oxygen is credited to both Priestley and Scheele; its liquefaction to Cailletet as well as to Pictet, whose results were attained in the same month of 1877 and announced in one session. Kant as well as La Place can lay claim to the promulgation of the nebular hypothesis. Neptune was predicted by Adams and by Leverrier; the computation of the one, and the publication of that of the other, had precedence by a few months.

For the invention of the steamboat, glory is claimed by their countrymen or partisans for Fulton, Jouffroy, Rumsey, Stevens, Symmington, and others; of the telegraph, for Steinheil and Morse; in photography Talbot was the rival of Daguerre and Niepce. The doubly flanged rail devised by Stevens was reinvented by Vignolet. Aluminum was first practically reduced by the processes of Hall, Héroult, and Cowles. Leibnitz in 1684 as well as Newton in 1687 formulated calculus. Anaesthetics, both ether and nitrous oxide, were discovered in 1845 and 1846, by no less than four men of one nationality. So independent were their achievements, so similar even in details and so closely contemporaneous, that polemics, lawsuits, and political agitation ensued for years, and there was not one of the four but whose career was embittered, if not ruined, by the animosities arising from the indistinguishability of the priority. Even the south pole, never before trodden by the foot of human beings, was at last reached twice in one summer.

A volume could be written, with but few years' toil, filled with endlessly repeating but ever new accumulation of such instances. When we cease to look upon invention or discovery as some mysterious inherent faculty of individual minds which are randomly dropped in space and time by fate; when we center our attention on the plainer relation of one such advancing step to the others; when, in short, interest shifts from individually biographic elements, which can be only dramatically artistic, didactically moralizing, or psychologically interpretable, and attaches whole heartedly to the social, evidence on this point will be infinite in quantity, and the presence of a majestic order pervading civilization will be irresistibly evident.

Knowing the civilization of an age and a land, we can then substantially affirm that its distinctive discoveries, in this or that field of activity, were not directly contingent upon the personality of the actual inventors that graced the period, but would have been made without them; and that, conversely, had the great illuminating minds of other centuries and climates been born in the civilization referred to, instead of their own, its first achievements would have fallen to their lot. Ericsson or Galvani eight thousand years ago would have polished or bored the first stone; and in turn the hand and mind whose operation set in inception the neolithic age of human culture, would, if held in its infancy in unchanging catalepsy from that time until today, now be devising wireless telephones and nitrogen extractors. . . .

If, therefore, any one's interpretation of mentality is disturbed by some of the particular equivalences that have been suggested, he can easily find others that seem more just, without dissenting from the underlying principle that the march of history, or as it is current custom to name it, the progress of civilization, is independent of the birth of particular personalities; since these, apparently averaging alike, both as regards genius and normality, at all times and places, furnish the same substratum for the social.

Here, then, we have an interpretation which allows to the individual, and through him to heredity, all that the science of the organic can legitimately claim on the strength of its actual accomplishments; and which also yields the fullest scope to the social in its own distinctive field. The accomplishment of the individual measured against other individuals depends, if not wholly then mainly, on his organic constitution as compounded by his heredity. The accomplishments of a group, relative to other groups, are uninfluenced by heredity because sufficiently large groups average alike in organic make-up.

This identity of average is incontestable for some instances of the same nations in closely successive ages—as Athens in 550 and 450, or Germany in 1800 and 1900—during which brief periods their hereditary composition could not possibly have altered to even a small fraction of the degree in which cultural achievement varied; it is certainly probably even for people of the same blood separated by long intervals of time and wide divergences of civilization; and it is, while neither proved nor disproved, likely to be substantially true, as suggested before, for the most distant races.

The difference between the accomplishments of one group of men and those of another group is therefore of another order from the difference between the faculties of one person and another. It is through this distinction that one of the essential qualities of the nature of the social is to be found.

The physiological and the mental are bonded as aspects of the same thing, one resolvable into the other; the social is, directly considered, irresolvable into the mental. That it exists only after mentality of a certain kind is in action, has led to confusion of the two, and even to their identification. The error of this identification is a fault that tends to pervade modern thinking about civilization, and which must be overcome by self-discipline before our understanding of this order of phenomena that fill and color our lives can become either clear or serviceable.

If the relation of the individual to culture here outlined is a true one, a conflicting view sometimes held and already alluded to, is unentertainable. This view is the opinion that all personalities are, while not identical, potentially equal in capacity, their varying degrees of accomplishment being due solely to different measures of accord with the social environment with which they are in touch. This view has perhaps been rarely formulated as a generic principle; but it seems to underlie, though usually vaguely and by implication only, many tendencies toward social and educational reform, and is therefore likely to find formal enunciation at some time. . . .

But, that a social enviroment may somewhat affect the fortunes and career of the individual as measured against other individuals, does not prove that the individual is wholly the product of circumstances outside of himself, any more than it means that the opposite is true and that a civilization is only the sum total of the products of a group of organically shaped minds. The concrete effect of each individual upon civilization is determined by civilization itself. Civilization appears even in some cases and in some measure to influence the effect of the individual's native activities upon himself. But to proceed from these realizations to the inference that all the degree and quality of accomplishment by the individual is the result of his moulding by the society that encompasses him, is pure assumption, extreme at that, and directly at variance with all observation, both as immediate apperception and as it survives critical analysis.

Therefore it is possible to hold to the historical or civilizational interpretation of social phenomena without proceeding to occupy the position that the human beings that are the given channels through which civilization courses, are only and wholly the products of its stream. Because culture rests on specific human faculty, it does not follow that this faculty, the thing in man that is supra-animal, is of social determination. The line between the social and the organic may not be randomly or hastily drawn. The threshold between the endowment that renders the flow and continuance of civilization possible and that which prohibits even its inception, is the demarcation—doubtful enough once, in all probability, but gaping for a longer period than our knowledge covers—between man and animal. The separation between the social itself, however, the entity that we call civilization, and the non-social, the pre-social or organic, is the diversity of quality or order or nature which exists between animal and man conjointly on the one hand, and the products of the interactions of human beings on the other. In the previous pages the mental has already been subtracted from the social and added to the physically organic which is subject to the influence of heredity. In the same way it is necessary to eliminate the factor of individual capacity from the consideration of civilization. But this elimination means its transfer to the group of organically conceivable phenomena, not its denial. In fact nothing is further from the path of a just prosecution of the understanding of history than such a negation of differences of degree of the faculties of individual men.

In short, social science, if we may take that word as equivalent to history, does not deny individuality any more than it denies the individual. It does refuse to deal with either individuality or individuals. And it bases this refusal solely on its denial of the validity of either factor for the achievement of its proper aims. . . .

We may sketch the relation which exists between the evolutions of the organic and of the social (Figure 8–1). A line, progressing with the flow of time, rises slowly, but ever gatheringly. At a certain point, another line begins to diverge from it, insensibly at first, but ascending ever farther above it on its own course; until, at the moment where the curtain of the present cuts off our view, each is advancing, but far from the other, and uninfluenced by it.

In this illustration, the continuous line denotes the level inorganic; the broken line, the evolution of the organic; the line of dots, the development of civilization. Height above the base is degree of advancement, whether that be complexity, heterogeneity, degree of coördination, or anything else. A is the beginning of time on this earth as revealed to our understandings. B marks the point of the true missing link, of the first human precursor, the first animal that carried and accumulated tradition. C would denote the state reached by what we are accustomed to call primitive man, that Neandertal *homo* who was our forefather in culture if not in blood; and D, the present moment.

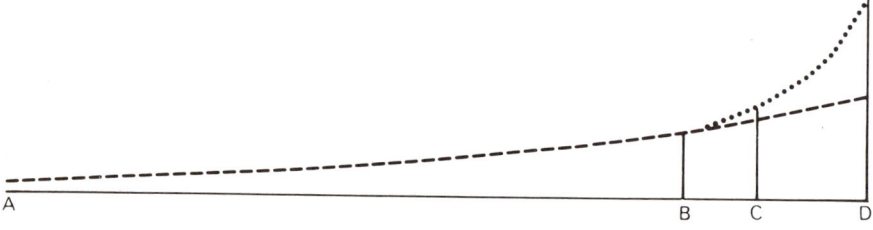

FIGURE 8-1.

It is inevitable that if there is any foundation for the contentions that have been set forth, an arguing from one of these lines to the other must be futile. To assert, because the upper line has risen rapidly just before it is cut off, that the one below it must also have ascended proportionally more in this period than in any before, is obviously uncompelling. That our institutions, our knowledge, the exercising of our minds, have advanced dizzyingly in twenty thousand years is no reason that our bodies and brains, our mental equipment and its physiological basis, have advanced in any corresponding measure, as is sometimes argued by scientists and generally taken for granted by men at large. If anything, it might rather be an evidence that the lower, organic line has fallen off in its rate of ascent. The bodies and minds in this line have continued to carry civilization; but this civilization has met the struggle of the world in such a way that much of the stress has been directed from these bodies and minds. We do not argue that the progress of organic evolution is *prima facie* indication that inorganic matter is more complex, more advanced in its combinations, or in any sense "higher," than it was fifty million years ago; much less that organic evolution has taken place through an inorganic evolution as cause. And no more can we infer from social development to a progress of the hereditary forms of life.

In fact, not only is the correlation of the lines of organic and social development as unjustifiable theoretically as it would be to argue from the compressibility or weight of water to that of steam; but all the evidence known directs us to the conviction that in recent periods civilization has raced at a speed so far outstripping the pace of hereditary evolution, that the latter has, if not actually standing still, afforded all the seeming, relatively, of making no progress. There are a hundred elements of civilization where there was one in the time when the Neandertal skull enclosed a living brain; and not only the content of civilization but the complexity of its organization has increased a hundredfold. But the body and the associated mind of that early man have not, by any scale that can be applied, attained a point a hundred times, nor even twice, as fine, as efficient, as delicate, or as strong, as they were then; it is doubtful if they have improved by a fifth. There are, it is true, those who make the contrary assertion. Yet it seems the fair-minded must avow that such assertions rest not on any objective interpretation of the facts, but on a wish to find a correlation, a desire to make the thread of evolution a single, unbranching one, to see the social only as organic.

Here, then, we have to come to our conclusion; and here we rest. The mind and the body are but facets of the same organic material or activity; the social substance—or unsubstantial fabric, if one prefers the phrase,—the existence that we call civilization, transcends them utterly for all its being forever rooted in life. The processes of civilizational activity are almost unknown to us. The self-sufficient factors that govern their workings are unresolved. The forces and principles of mechanistic science can indeed analyze our civilization; but in so doing they destroy its essence, and leave us without understanding of the very thing which we seek. The historian as yet can do little but picture. He traces and he connects what seems far removed; he balances; he integrates; but he does not really explain, nor does he transmute phenomena into something else. His method is not science; but neither can the scientist deal with historical material and leave it civilization, nor anything resembling civilization, nor convert it wholly into concepts of life and leave nothing else to be done. What we all are able to do is to realize this gap, to be impressed by its abyss with reverence and humility, and to go our paths on its respective sides without self-deluding attempts to bridge the eternal chasm, or empty boasts that its span is achieved.

9 THE CONCEPT OF CULTURE
LESLIE A. WHITE

Virtually all cultural anthropologists take it for granted, no doubt, that *culture* is the basic and central concept of their science. There is, however, a disturbing lack of agreement as to what they mean by this term. To some, culture is learned behavior. To others, it is not behavior at all, but an abstraction from behavior—whatever that is. Stone axes and pottery bowls are culture to some anthropologists, but no material object can be culture to others. Culture exists only in the mind, according to some; it consists of observable things and events in the external world to others. Some anthropologists think of culture as consisting of ideas, but they are divided upon the

Reproduced by permission of the American Anthropological Association from the *American Anthropologist*, vol. 61, no. 2, 1959.

question of their locus: some say they are in the minds of the peoples studied, others hold that they are in the minds of ethnologists. We go on to "culture is a psychic defense mechanism," "culture consists of n different social signals correlated with m different responses," "culture is a Rorschach of a society," and so on, to confusion and bewilderment. One wonders what physics would be like if it had as many and as varied conceptions of energy!

There was a time, however, when there was a high degree of uniformity of comprehension and use of the term culture. During the closing decades of the nineteenth century and the early years of the twentieth, the great majority of cultural anthropologists, we believe, held to the conception expressed by E. B. Tylor, in 1871, in the opening lines of *Primitive Culture:* "Culture . . . is that complex whole which includes knowledge, belief, art, morals, law, custom, and any other capabilities and habits acquired by man as a member of society." Tylor does not make it explicit in this statement that culture is the peculiar possession of man; but it is therein implied, and in other places he makes this point clear and explicit (Tylor 1881:54, 123,[1] where he deals with the "great mental gap between us and the animals"). Culture, to Tylor, was the name of all things and events peculiar to the human species. Specifically, he enumerates beliefs, customs, objects—"hatchet, adze, chisel," and so on—and techniques—"wood-chopping, fishing . . ., shooting and spearing game, fire-making," and so on (Tylor 1913:5–6).

The Tylorian conception of culture prevailed in anthropology generally for decades. In 1920, Robert H. Lowie began *Primitive Society* by quoting "Tylor's famous definition." In recent years, however, conceptions and definitions of culture have multiplied and varied to a great degree. One of the most highly favored of these is that *culture is an abstraction.* . . .

Those who define culture as an abstraction do not tell us what they mean by this term. They appear to take it for granted (1) that they themselves know what they mean by "abstraction," and (2) that others, also, will understand. We believe that neither of these suppositions is well founded; we shall return to a consideration of this concept later in this essay. But whatever an abstraction in general may be to these anthropologists, when culture becomes an "abstraction" it becomes imperceptible, imponderable, and not wholly real. According to Linton, "culture itself is intangible and cannot be directly apprehended even by the individuals who participate in it" (1936:288–89). Herskovits also calls culture "intangible" (1945:150). Anthropologists in the imaginary symposium reported by Kluckhohn and Kelly (1945:79, 81) argue that "one can see" such things as individuals and their actions and interactions, but "has anyone ever seen 'culture'?" Beals and Hoijer (1953:210) say that "the anthropologist cannot observe culture directly; . . ."

If culture as an abstraction is intangible, imperceptible, does it exist, is it real? Ralph Linton (1936:363) raises this question in all seriousness: "If it [culture] can be said to exist at all. . . ." Radcliffe-Brown (1940:2) declares that the word culture "denotes, not any concrete reality, but an abstraction, and as it is commonly

---

[1]For individual reading references and notes, see pp. 330 ff.

used a vague abstraction." And Spiro (1951:24) says that according to the predominant "position of contemporary anthropology . . . culture has no ontological reality. . . ."

Thus when culture becomes an abstraction it not only becomes invisible and imponderable; it virtually ceases to exist. It would be difficult to construct a less adequate conception of culture. Why, then, have prominent and influential anthropologists turned to the "abstraction" conception of culture?

A clue to the reason—if, indeed, it is not an implicit statement of the reason itself—is given by Kroeber and Kluckhohn (1952:155):

> Since behavior is the first-hand and outright material of the science of psychology, and culture is not—being of concern only secondarily, as an influence on this material—it is natural that psychologists and psychologizing sociologists should see behavior as primary in their field, and then extend this view farther to apply to the field of culture also.

The reasoning is simple and direct: if culture is behavior, then (1) culture becomes the subject matter of psychology, since behavior is the proper subject matter of psychology; culture would then become the property of psychologists and "psychologizing sociologists"; and (2) nonbiological anthropology would be left without a subject matter. The danger was real and imminent; the situation, critical. What was to be done?

The solution proposed by Kroeber and Kluckhohn was neat and simple: let the psychologists have behavior, anthropologists will keep for themselves abstractions from behavior. These abstractions become and constitute *culture*.

But in this rendering unto Caesar, anthropologists have given the psychologists the better part of the bargain, for they have surrendered unto them real things and events, locatable and observable, directly or indirectly, in the real external world, in terrestrial time and space, and have kept for themselves only intangible, imponderable abstractions that "have no ontological reality." But at least, and at last, they have a subject matter—however insubstantial and unobservable—of their own!

Whether or not this has been the principal reason for defining culture as "not behavior, but abstractions from behavior," is perhaps a question; we feel, however, that Kroeber and Kluckhohn have made themselves fairly clear. But whatever the reason, or reasons—for there may have been several—may have been for the distinction, the question whether culture is to be regarded as behavior or as abstractions from it is, we believe, the central issue in recent attempts to hammer out an adequate, usable, fruitful, and enduring conception of culture.

The present writer is no more inclined to surrender culture to the psychologists than are Kroeber and Kluckhohn; indeed, few anthropologists have taken greater pains to distinguish psychological problems from culturological problems than he has. But he does not wish to exchange the hard substance of culture for its wraith, either. No science can have a subject matter that consists of intangible, invisible, imponderable, ontologically unreal "abstractions"; a science must have real stars, real mammals, foxes, crystals, cells, phonemes, gamma rays, and culture traits to work with. We believe that we can offer an analysis of the situation that will distinguish between psychology, the scientific study of behavior on the one hand,

and culturology, the scientific study of culture, on the other, and at the same time give a real, substantial subject matter to each.

Science makes a dichotomy between the mind of the observer and the external world—things and events having their locus outside the mind of this observer. The scientist makes contact with the external world with and through his senses, forming percepts. These percepts are translated into concepts which are manipulated in a process called thinking in such a way as to form premises, propositions, generalizations, conclusions, and so on. The validity of these premises, propositions, and conclusions is established by testing them in terms of experience of the external world. This is the way science proceeds and does its work.

The first step in scientific procedure is to observe, or more generally to experience, the external world in a sensory manner. The next step—after percepts have been translated into concepts—is the classification of things and events perceived or experienced. Things and events of the external world are thus divided into classes of various kinds: acids, metals, stones, liquids, mammals, stars, atoms, corpuscles, and so on. Now it turns out that there is a class of phenomena, one of enormous importance in the study of man, for which science has as yet no name: this is the class of things and events consisting of or dependent upon symboling. It is one of the most remarkable facts in the recent history of science that this important class has no name, but the fact remains that it does not. And the reason why it does not is because these things and events have always been considered and designated, not merely and simply as the things and events that they are, in and of themselves, but always as things and events in a particular context.

A thing is what it is; "a rose is a rose is a rose." Acts are not first of all ethical acts or economic acts or erotic acts. An act is an act. An act becomes an ethical datum or an economic datum or an erotic datum when—and only when—it is considered in an ethical, economic, or erotic context. Is a Chinese porcelain vase a scientific specimen, an object of art, an article of commerce, or an exhibit in a lawsuit? The answer is obvious. Actually, of course, to call it a "Chinese porcelain vase" is already to put it into a particular context; it would be better first of all to say "a glazed form of fired clay is a glazed form of fired clay." As a Chinese porcelain vase, it becomes an object of art, a scientific specimen, or an article of merchandise when, and only when, it is considered in an esthetic, scientific, or commercial context.

Let us return now to the class of things and events that consist of or are dependent upon symboling: a spoken word, a stone axe, a fetich, avoiding one's mother-in-law, loathing milk, saying a prayer, sprinkling holy water, a pottery bowl, casting a vote, remembering the sabbath to keep it holy—"and any other capabilities and habits [and things] acquired by man as a member of [human] society" (Tylor 1913:1). They are what they are: things and acts dependent upon symboling.

We may consider these things-and-events-dependent-upon-symboling in a number of contexts: astronomical, physical, chemical, anatomical, physiological, psychological, and culturological, and, consequently, they become astronomic, physical, chemical, anatomical, physiological, psychological and culturological phenomena in turn. All things and events dependent upon symboling are dependent also upon solar energy which sustains all life on this planet; this is the astronomic context. These things and events may be considered and interpreted in terms of the anatomical, neurological, and physiological processes of the human beings who exhibit them. They may be considered and interpreted also in terms of their relationship to human organisms, i.e., in a somatic context. And they may be considered in an extrasomatic context, i.e., in terms of their relationship to other like things and events rather than in relationship to human organisms.

When things and events dependent upon symboling are considered and interpreted in terms of their relationship to human organisms, i.e., in a somatic context, they may properly be called *human behavior,* and the science, *psychology.* When things and events dependent upon symboling are considered and interpreted in an extrasomatic context, i.e., in terms of their relationships to one another rather than to human organisms, we may call them *culture,* and the science, *culturology.* . . .

A thing or event dependent upon symboling—a symbolate—is just what it is, but it may become significant in any one of a number of contexts. As we have already seen, it may be significant in an astronomic context: the performance of a ritual requires the expenditure of energy which has come from the sun. But within the sciences of man we may distinguish two significant contexts: the somatic and the extrasomatic. Symbolates may be considered and interpreted in terms of their relationship to the human organism, or they may be considered in terms of their relationships to one another, quite apart from their relationship to the human organism. Let us illustrate with some examples.

I smoke a cigarette, cast a vote, decorate a pottery bowl, avoid my mother-in-law, say a prayer, or chip an arrowhead. Each one of these acts is dependent upon the process of symboling; each therefore is a symbolate. As a scientist, I may consider these acts (events) in terms of their relationships to me, to my organism; or, I may treat them in terms of their relationships to one another, to other symbolates, quite apart from their relationship to my organism.

In the first type of interpretation I consider the symbolate in terms of its relationship to my bodily structure: the structure and functions of my hand, for example; or to my stereoscopic, chromatic vision; or to my needs, desires, hopes, fears, imagination, habit formation, overt reactions, satisfactions, and so forth. How do I feel when I avoid my mother-in-law or cast a ballot? What is my attitude toward the act? What is my conception of it? Is the act accompanied by heightened emotional tone, or do I perform it in a mechanical, perfunctory manner? And so on. We may call these acts *human behavior;* our concern is *psychological.*

What we have said of acts (events) will apply to objects (things) also. What is my conception of a pottery bowl, a ground axe, a crucifix, roast pork, whisky, holy water, cement? What is my attitude and how do I react toward each of these things? In short, what is the nature of the relationship between each of these things and my own organism? We do not customarily call these things human behavior, but they are the embodiments of human behavior; the difference between a nodule of flint and a stone axe is the factor of human labor. An axe, bowl, crucifix—or a haircut—is congealed human labor. We have then a class of objects dependent upon symboling that have a significance in terms of their relationship to the human organism. The scientific consideration and interpretation of this relationship is *psychology*.

But we may treat symbolates in terms of their relationships to one another, quite apart from their relationship to the human organism. Thus, in the case of the avoidance of a mother-in-law, we would consider it in terms of its relationship to other symbolates, or symbolate clusters, such as customs of marriage—monogamy, polygyny, polyandry—place of residence of a couple after marriage, division of labor between the sexes, mode of subsistence, domestic architecture, degree of cultural development, etc. Or, if we are concerned with voting we would consider it in terms of forms of political organization (tribal, state), kind of government (democratic, monarchical, fascist); age, sex, or property qualifications; political parties and so on. In this context our symbolates become *culture*—culture traits or trait clusters, i.e., institutions, customs, codes, etc., and the scientific concern is *culturology*.

It would be the same with objects as with acts. If we were concerned with a hoe we would regard it in terms of its relationships to other symbolates in an extrasomatic context: to other instruments employed in subsistence, the digging stick and plow in particular; or to customs of division of labor between the sexes; the stage of cultural development, etc. We would be concerned with the relationship between a digital computer and the degree of development of mathematics, the stage of technological development, division of labor, the social organization within which it is used (corporation, military organization, astronomical laboratory), and so on.

Thus we see that we have two quite different kinds of sciencing with regard to things and events—objects and acts—dependent upon symboling. If we treat them in terms of their relationship to the human organism, i.e., in an organismic, or somatic context, these things and events become *human behavior* and we are doing *psychology*. If, however, we treat them in terms of their relationship to one another, quite apart from their relationship to human organisms, i.e., in an extrasomatic, or extraorganismic, context, the things and events become *culture*—cultural elements or culture traits—and we are doing *culturology*. Human psychology and culturology have the same phenomena as their subject matter: things and events dependent upon symboling (symbolates). The difference between the two sciences derives from the difference between the contexts in which their common subject matter is treated. . . .

Culture, then, is a class of things and events, dependent upon symboling, considered in an extrasomatic context. This definition rescues cultural anthropology from intangible, imperceptible, and ontologically unreal abstractions and provides it with a real, substantial, observable subject matter. And it distinguishes sharply between behavior—behaving organisms—and culture; between the science of psychology and the science of culture.

It might be objected that every science should have a certain class of things per se as its subject matter, not things-in-a-certain-context. Atoms are atoms and mammals are mammals, it might be argued, and as such are the subject matter of physics and mammalogy, respectively, regardless of context. Why therefore should cultural anthropology have its subject matter defined in terms of things in context rather than in terms of things in themselves? At first glance this argument might appear to be a cogent one, but actually it has but little force. What the scientist wants to do is to make intelligible the phenomena that confront him. And very frequently the significant thing about phenomena is the context in which they are found. Even in the so-called natural sciences we have a science of organisms-in-a-certain-context: parasitology, a science of organisms playing a certain role in the realm of living things. And within the realm of man-and-culture we have dozens of examples of things and events whose significance depends upon context rather than upon the inherent qualities of the phenomena themselves. An adult male of a certain animal species is called a man. But a man is a man, not a slave; a man becomes a slave only when he enters a certain context. So it is with commodities: corn and cotton are articles of use-value, but they were not commodities—articles produced for sale at a profit—in aboriginal Hopi culture; corn and cotton become commodities only when they enter a certain socioeconomic context. A cow is a cow, but she may become a medium of exchange, money (*pecus,* pecuniary) in one context, food in another, mechanical power (Cartwright used a cow as motive power for his first power loom) in another, and a sacred object of worship (India) in still another. We do not have a science of cows, but we do have scientific studies of mediums of exchange, of mechanical power, and of sacred objects in each of which cows may be significant. And so we have a science of symboled things and events in an extrasomatic context.

The locus of culture. If we define culture as consisting of real things and events observable, directly or indirectly, in the external world, where do these things and events exist and have their being? What is the locus of culture? The answer is: the things and events that comprise culture have their existence, in space and time, (1) within human organisms, i.e., concepts, beliefs, emotions, attitudes; (2) within processes of social interaction among human beings; and (3) within material objects (axes, factories, railroads, pottery bowls) lying outside human organisms but within the patterns of social interaction among them. The locus of culture is thus intraorganismal, interorganismal, and extraorganismal.

But, someone might object, you have said that culture consists of extrasomatic phenomena and now you tell me that culture exists, in part, within human organisms. Is this not a contradiction? The answer is, No, it is not a contradiction; it is a misunderstanding. We did not say that culture consists of extrasomatic things and events, i.e., phenomena whose locus is outside human organisms. What we said is that culture consists of things and events considered within an extrasomatic context. This is quite a different thing.

Every cultural element has two aspects: subjective and objective. It might appear that stone axes are ''objective,'' and ideas and attitudes are ''subjective.'' But this is a superficial and inadequate view. An axe has a subjective component; it would be meaningless without a concept and an attitude. On the other hand, a concept or an attitude would be meaningless without overt expression, in behavior or speech (which is a form of behavior). Every cultural element, every culture trait, therefore, has a subjective and an objective aspect. But conceptions, attitudes, and sentiments—phenomena that have their locus within the human organism—may be considered for purposes of scientific interpretation in an extrasomatic context, i.e., in terms of their relation to other symboled things and events rather than in terms of their relationship to the human organism. Thus, we may consider the subjective aspect of the mother-in-law taboo, i.e., the conceptions and attitudes involved, in terms of their relationship, not to the human organism, but to other symbolates such as forms of marriage and the family, place of residence after marriage, and so on. On the other hand, we may consider the axe in terms of its relationship to the human organism—its meaning; the person's conception of it; his attitude toward it—rather than to other symboled things and events such as arrows, hoes, and customs regulating the division of labor in society.

We shall now pass in review a number of conceptions of culture, or conceptions with regard to culture, widely current in ethnological literature, and comment critically upon each one from the standpoint of the conception of culture set forth in this paper.

"Culture consists of ideas." Some anthropologists like to define culture in terms of ideas only. The reason for this, apparently, is the notion that ideas are both basic and primary, that they are prime movers and as such originate behavior which in turn may produce objects such as pottery bowls. "Culture consists of ideas," says Taylor (1948:98–110, passim), it "is a mental phenomenon . . . not . . . material objects or observable behavior. . . . For example, there is present in an Indian's mind the idea of a dance. This is the trait of culture. This idea influences his body so that he behaves in a certain way," i.e., he dances.

This conception of sociocultural reality is a naive one. It is based upon a primitive, prescientific, and now obsolete metaphysics and psychology. It was Thought-Woman among the Keresan Pueblo Indians who brought about events by thinking and willing them to happen. Ptah created Egyptian culture by objectifying his thoughts. And God said "Let there be light," and there was light. But we no longer explain the origin and development of culture by simply saying that it has resulted from man's ideas. To be sure, an idea was involved in the invention of firearms, but we have explained nothing when we say that firearms are the fruit of thought, because the ideas themselves have not been accounted for. Why did the idea occur when and where it did rather than at some other time and place? And, actually, ideas—matter of fact, realistic ideas—enter the mind from the outside world. It was working with soils that gave man, or woman, the idea of pottery; the calendar is a by-product of intensive agriculture. Culture does indeed consist in part of ideas; but attitudes, overt acts, and objects are culture, also.

"Culture consists of abstractions." We return now to the presently popular definition: "culture is an abstraction, or consists of abstractions." As we observed earlier, those who define culture in these terms do not tell us what they mean by

"abstraction," and there is reason to believe that they are not very clear as to what they do mean by it. They make it emphatically clear, however, that an abstraction is not an observable thing or event. The fact that doubts have been raised as to the "reality" of an abstraction indicates that those who use this term are not sure what "it means," i.e., what they mean by it. We do have some clues, however.

Culture is "basically a form or pattern or way," say Kroeber and Kluckhohn (1952:155, 159), "even a culture trait is an abstraction. A trait is an 'ideal type' because no two pots are identical nor are two marriage ceremonies ever held in precisely the same way." The culture trait "pot" therefore appears to be the ideal form of which each particular pot is an exemplification—a sort of Platonic idea, or ideal. Each and every pot, they reason, is real; but the "ideal" is never realized in any particular pot. It is like the "typical American man": 5'8½" high, weighs 164.378 pounds, is married, has 2.3 children, and so on. This is, we suppose, what they mean by an abstraction. If so, we know it well: it is a conception in the mind of the observer, the scientist.

There is a slightly different way of looking at an "abstraction." No two marriage ceremonies are ever held in precisely the same way. Well, let us tabulate a large sample of marriage ceremonies. We find that 100 percent contain element a (mutual acceptance of spouses). Ninety-nine percent contain element b. Elements c, d, and e appear in only 96, 94, and 89 percent, respectively, of the cases. We construct a distribution curve and determine an average or norm about which all particular instances are distributed. This is the typical marriage ceremony. But, like the typical American who has 2.3 children, this ideal is never fully and perfectly realized in any actual instance. It is an "abstraction," that is, a conception, worked out by the scientific observer and which exists in his own mind.

The failure to recognize the fact that abstractions are conceptions has led to confusion both as to their locus and their reality. Recognition of the fact that the so-called abstractions of science (such as a "rigid body" in physical theory; rigid bodies do not exist in actuality) are conceptions in the mind of the scientist clears up both these points: cultural "abstractions" are conceptions ("ideas") in the mind of the anthropologist. And as for their "ontological reality," conceptions are none the less real for being in the minds of men—nothing is more real, for example, than an hallucination.

This point was well made by Bidney (1954:488–89) in his review of *Culture, a Critical Review etc.*:

> The real crux of the problem centers about what is meant by abstraction and what is its ontological import. Some anthropologists maintain that they are dealing only with logical abstractions and that culture has no reality other than that of an abstraction, but they can hardly expect other social scientists to agree with them, conceding that the objects of their sciences have no ontological, objective reality. *Thus Kroeber and Kluckhohn have confused the concept culture, which is a logical construct, with the actual existential culture* . . . [emphasis ours].

It is interesting to note in this connection that one anthropological theorist, Cornelius Osgood (1951:208; 1940), has defined culture explicitly as consisting of ideas in the minds of anthropologists: "Culture consists of all ideas of the manufactures, behavior, and ideas of the aggregate of human beings which have been directly observed or communicated to one's mind and of which one is conscious." Spiro (1951:24), also, holds that "culture is a logical construct, abstracted from human behavior, and as such, it exists only in the mind of *the investigator*" (Spiro's emphasis).

"There is no such thing as 'material' culture." Those who define culture in terms of ideas, or as an abstraction, or as behavior, find themselves obliged logically to declare that material objects are not, and cannot be, culture. "Strictly speaking," says Hoebel (1956:176), "material culture is really not culture at all." Taylor (1948:102, 98) goes farther: ". . . the concept of 'material culture' is fallacious" because "culture is a mental phenomenon." Beals and Hoijer (1953:210): ". . . culture is an abstraction from behavior and not to be confused with acts of behavior or with material artifacts, such as tools. . . ." This denial of material culture is rather awkward in view of the long established tradition among ethnographers, archeologists, and museum curators of calling tools, masks, fetiches, and so on, "material culture."

Our definition extricates us from this dilemma. As we have already seen, it would not be absurd to speak of sandals or pottery bowls as behavior; their significant attribute is not mere deer hide or clay, but human labor; they are congelations of human labor. But in our definition, symboling is the common factor in ideas, attitudes, acts, and objects. There are three kinds of symbolates: (1) ideas and attitudes, (2) overt acts, and (3) material objects. All may be considered in an extrasomatic context; all are to be reckoned as culture. This conception brings us back to long established usage in cultural anthropology: "Culture is that which is described in an ethnographic monograph."

"Reification of culture." There is a kind of conception of culture held by some anthropologists that is much deplored by others who call it "reification." As one who has been especially singled out as a "reifier" of culture, I may say that the term is singularly inappropriate. To reify is to make a thing of that which is not a thing, such as hope, honesty, or freedom. But it is not I who have made culture things. I have merely found real things and events in the external world which are distinguishable as a class by being dependent upon symboling, and which may be treated in an extrasomatic context, and I have called these things and events culture. This is precisely what E. B. Tylor did. It is what Lowie, Wissler, and most early American anthropologists have done. To Durkheim (1938:xliii) "the proposition which states that social facts [i.e., culture traits] are to be treated as things" lay "at the very basis of our method." It is not we who have reified culture; the elements comprising culture, according to our definition, were things to start with.

To be sure, if culture is defined as consisting of intangible, imponderable, ontologically unreal "abstractions," then to transform these wraiths into real, substantial bodies would indeed be to reify them. But we do not subscribe to such a definition.

"Culture: a process sui generis." "Culture is a thing *sui generis* . . ." said Lowie many years ago (1917:66, 17). This view has been held also by Kroeber, Durkheim, and others. It has been misunderstood and opposed by many. But what Lowie meant by this statement is made clear in the rest of the passage cited above (1917:66): "Culture is a thing *sui generis* which can be explained only in terms of itself . . . the ethnologist . . . will account for a given cultural fact by merging it in a group of cultural facts or by demonstrating some other cultural fact out of which it has been developed." For example, the custom of reckoning descent patrilineally may be explained in terms of customs of division of labor between the sexes, customs of residence—patrilocal, matrilocal, or neolocal—of a married couple; mode of subsistence; rules of inheritance, and so on. Or, to express it in terms of our definition of culture: "a symbolate in an extrasomatic context (i.e., a culture trait) is to be explained in terms of its relationship to other symbolates in the same context."

This conception of culture, like "reification" with which it is closely related, has been much misunderstood and opposed. In general, it has been regarded as "mystical." How can culture grow and develop by itself? ("Culture . . . seems to grow of itself"; Redfield 1941:134.) "It seems hardly necessary," says Boas (1928:235), "to consider culture a mystic entity that exists outside the society of its individual carriers, and that moves by its own force." Bidney (1946:535) brands this view of culture as a "mystical metaphysics of fate." And it has been opposed by Benedict (1934:231), Hooton (1939:370), Spiro (1951:23), and others.

But no one has ever said that culture is an entity that exists and moves by, and of, itself, quite apart from people. Nor has anyone ever said, as far as we know, that the origin, nature, and functions of culture can be understood without taking the human species into consideration. Obviously, if one is to understand culture in these aspects he must consider the biological nature of man. What has been asserted is that, given culture, its variations in time and place, and its processes of change are to be explained in terms of culture itself. This is precisely what Lowie meant when he said that "culture is a thing [process would have been a better term] *sui generis*," as the above quotation from him (1917:66) makes clear. A consideration of the human organism, individually or collectively, is irrelevant to an explanation of processes of culture change. "This is not mysticism," says Lowie (1917:66), "but sound scientific method." And, as everyone knows, scholars have been working in accordance with this principle of interpretation for decades. One does not need to take human organisms into account in a scientific explanation of the evolution of currency, writing, or of Gothic art. The steam engine and textile machinery were introduced into Japan during the closing decades of the nineteenth century and certain changes in social structure followed; we add nothing to our explanation of these events by remarking that human beings were involved. Of course they were. And they were not irrelevant to the events which took place, but they are irrelevant to an explanation of these events.

"It is people, not culture, that does things." "Culture does not 'work,' 'move,' 'change,' but is worked, is moved, is changed. It is people who do things,"

says Lynd (1939:39). He supports this argument with the bold assertion that "culture does not enamel its fingernails . . . but people do . . ." (ibid). He might have clinched it by demonstrating that culture has no fingernails.

The view that "it is people, not cultures, that do things" is widely held among anthropologists. Boas (1928:236) tells us that "the forces that bring about the changes are active in the individuals composing the social group, not in the abstract culture." Hallowell (1945:175) remarks that "in a literal sense cultures never have met nor will ever meet. What is meant is that peoples meet and that, as a result of the processes of social interaction, acculturation—modifications in the mode of life of one or both peoples—may take place. Individuals are the dynamic centers of this process of interaction." And Radcliffe-Brown (1940:10–11) pours fine scorn on the notion that cultures, rather than peoples, interact:

> A few years ago, as a result perhaps of re-defining social anthropology as the study, not of society, but of culture, we were asked to abandon this kind of investigation in favor of what is now called the study of "culture contact." In place of the study of the formation of new composite societies, we are supposed to regard what is happening in Africa as a process in which an entity called African culture comes into contact with an entity called European or Western culture, and a third new entity is produced . . . which is to be described as Westernized African culture. To me this seems a fantastic reification of abstractions. European culture is an abstraction and so is the culture of an African tribe. I find it fantastic to imagine these two abstractions coming into contact and by an act of generation producing a third abstraction.

We call this view, that people rather than culture do things, the fallacy of pseudo-realism. Of course culture does not and could not exist independently of people. But, as we have pointed out earlier, cultural processes can be explained without taking human organisms into account; a consideration of human organisms is irrelevant to the solution of certain problems of culture. Whether the practice of mummification in pre-Columbian Peru was indigenous or the result of Egyptian influence is an example of a kind of problem that does not require a consideration of human organisms. To be sure the practice of mummification, its invention in Peru, or its diffusion from Egypt to the Andean highlands, could not have taken place without the action of real, flesh-and-blood human beings. Neither could Einstein have worked out the theory of relativity without breathing, but we do not need to take his respiration into account when we trace the history, or explain the development, of this theory.

Those who argue that it is people, not culture, that do this or that mistake a description of what they see for an explanation of these events. Seated in the Senate gallery they see men making laws; in the shipyards men are building freighters; in the laboratory human beings are isolating enzymes; in the fields they are planting corn, and so on. And, for them, a description of these events, as they observe them, is a simple explanation of them: it is people who pass laws, build freighters, plant corn, and isolate enzymes. This is a simple and naive form of anthropocentrism. . . .

Culture "cannot be realistically disconnected from those organizations of ideas and feelings which constitute the individual," i.e., culture cannot be realistically disconnected from individuals, says Sapir (1932:233). He is quite right, of course, in actuality culture is inseparable from human beings. But if culture cannot be realistically (in actuality) disconnected from individuals it most certainly can be disconnected in logical (scientific) analysis, and no one has done a better job of "disconnecting" than Edward Sapir: there is not a single Indian—or even a nerve, muscle, or sense organ—in his monograph, *Southern Paiute, a Shoshonean Language* (1930). Nor are there any people roaming about in his *Time Perspective in Aboriginal American Culture* (1916). "Science must abstract some elements and neglect others," says Morris Cohen (1931:226) "because *not all things that exist together are relevant to each other*" (emphasis ours). Comprehension and appreciation of this fact would be an enormous asset to ethnological theory. "Citizenship cannot be realistically disconnected from eye color," i.e., every citizen has eyes and every eye has a color. But, in the United States at least, color of eyes is not relevant to citizenship: "things that exist together are not always relevant to each other."

And so it is perfectly true, as Hallowell, Radcliffe-Brown, and others say, that "it is *peoples* who meet and interact." But this should not keep us from confining our attention, in the solution of certain problems, to symbolates in an extrasomatic context: to tools, utensils, customs, beliefs, and attitudes, in short, to culture. The meeting and mixing of European culture with African culture and the production thereby of a mixture, Euro-African culture, may seem "a fantastic reification of abstractions" to Radcliffe-Brown and others. But anthropologists have been concerned with problems of this sort for decades and will continue to deal with them. The intermingling of customs, technologies, and ideologies is just as valid a scientific problem as the intermingling of human organisms or genes.

We have not asserted, nor do we imply, that anthropologists in general have failed to treat culture as a process sui generis, i.e., without taking human organisms into account; many, if not most, cultural anthropologists have in fact done this. But some of them, when they turn to theory, deny the validity of this kind of interpretation. Radcliffe-Brown himself provides us with examples of purely culturological problems and culturological solutions thereof—in "The Social Organization of Australian Tribes" (1930–31), "The Mother's Brother in South Africa" (1924), etc. But when he dons the philosopher's cap he denies that this procedure is scientifically valid.

However, some anthropologists have recognized, on the theoretical level, that culture can be scientifically studied without taking human organisms into account, that a consideration of human organisms is irrelevant to the solution of problems dealing with extrasomatic traditions. We have cited a number—Tylor, Durkheim Kroeber, Lowie, et al.—who have done this. But we may add one or two new references here. "The best hope . . . for parsimonious description and 'explanation' of cultural phenomena," say Kroeber and Kluckhohn (1952:167) "seems to rest in the study of cultural forms and processes as such, largely . . . abstracted from individuals and personalities." And Steward (1955:46) remarks that "certain aspects of a modern culture can best be studied quite apart from individual behavior. The structure and function of a system of money, banking, and credit, for example, represents supra-individual aspects of culture." Also, he says: "form of government, legal system, economic institutions, religious organizations, educational systems," and so on, "have aspects which are national . . . in scope and which must be understood apart from the behavior of the individuals connected with them" (ibid:47).

There is nothing new about this; anthropologists and other social scientists have been doing this for decades. But it seems to be difficult for some of them to accept this as a matter of theory and principle as well as of actual practice.

"It takes two or more to make a culture." There is a conception, not uncommon in ethnological theory, that whether a phenomenon is an element of culture or not depends upon whether it is expressed by one, two, or "several" individuals. Thus Linton (1945:35) says that "any item of behavior . . . which is peculiar to a single individual in a society is not to be considered as a part of the society's culture. . . . Thus a new technique for weaving baskets would not be classed as a part of culture as long as it was known only to one person." Wissler, Osgood, Malinowski, Durkheim, et al., have subscribed to this view.

Two objections may be raised against this conception of culture: (1) if plurality of expression of learned behavior be the significant distinction between culture and not-culture, then the chimpanzees described by Wolfgang Köhler in *The Mentality of Apes* (New York, 1925) had culture, for innovations made by a single individual were often quickly adopted by the whole group. Other subhuman species also would have culture according to this criterion. (2) The second objection is: if expression by one person is not enough to qualify an act as a cultural element, how many persons will be required? Linton (1936:274) says that "as soon as this new thing has been transmitted to and is shared by even one other individual in the society, it must be reckoned as a part of culture." Osgood (1951:208) requires "two or more." Durkheim (1938:lvi) needs "several individuals, at the very least." Wissler (1929:358) says that an item does not rise to the level of a culture trait until a standardized procedure is established in the group. And Malinowski (1941:73) states that a "cultural fact starts when an individual interest becomes transformed into public, common, and transferable systems of organized endeavor."

Obviously such a conception does not meet the requirements of science. What agreement could one find on the point at which an "individual interest becomes transformed into public, common, and transferable systems of organized endeavor"? Or, suppose an ornithologist said that if there were but one specimen of a kind of bird it could not be a carrier pigeon or a whopping crane, but that if there were an indefinite number then they could be pigeons or cranes. Or, suppose a physicist said that if there were but one atom of a certain element that it could not be copper, but if there were "a lot of such atoms" then it might properly be called copper. One wants a definition that says that item x belongs to class y or it does not, regardless of how many items of x there may be (and a class, in logic, may have only one member, or even none).

Our definition meets the requirements of a scientific definition: an item—a conception or belief, an act, or an object—is to be reckoned an element of culture (1) if it is dependent upon symboling, and (2) when it is considered in an extrasomatic context. To be sure, all cultural elements exist in a social context; but so do such nonhuman (not dependent upon symboling) traits as grooming, suckling, and mating exist in a social matrix. But it is not sociality, duality, or plurality that distinguishes a human, or cultural, phenomenon from a nonhuman or noncultural phenomenon. The distinguishing characteristic is symboling. Secondly, whether a thing or an event can be considered in an extrasomatic context does not depend upon whether there is only one such thing or event, or two, or "several." A thing or event may be properly considered an element of culture even if it is the only member of its class, just as an atom of copper would still be an atom of copper even if it were the only one of its kind in the cosmos.

And, of course, we might have pointed out in the first place that the notion that an act or an idea in human society might be wholly the work of a single individual is an illusion, another one of the sorry pitfalls of anthropocentrism. Every member of human society is of course always subjected to sociocultural stimulation from the members of his group. Whatever a man does as a human being, and much of what he does as a mere animal, is a function of his group as well as of his organism. Any human act, even in its first expression in the person of a single individual, is a group product to begin with.

Culture as "characteristic" traits. "Culture may be defined," says Boas (1938:159), "as the totality of the mental and physical reactions and activities that *characterize* the behavior of the individuals composing a social group . . ." (emphasis ours). Herskovits (1948:28) tells us that "when culture is closely analyzed, we find but a series of patterned reactions that characterize the behavior of the individuals who constitute a given group." (Just what "close analysis" has to do with this conception is not clear.) Sapir (1917:442): "The mass of typical reactions called culture. . . ." This view has, of course, been held by others.

Two objections may be raised against this conception of culture: (1) how does one determine which traits characterize a group and which traits do not—how does one draw the line between the two classes, culture and not-culture? And, (2) if we call the traits that characterize a group *culture,* what are we to call those traits that do not characterize it?

It seems probable that anthropologists who hold this view are really thinking of *a* culture, or cultures, plural, rather than of culture in general, culture as a particular kind of phenomena. Thus, "French culture" might be distinguished from "English culture" by those traits which characterize each. But if, on the one hand, the French and the English may be distinguished from each other by differences of traits, they will on the other hand be found to be very similar to each other in their possession of like traits. And the traits that resemble each other are just as much a part of the "way of life" of each people as the traits that differ. Why should only one class be called culture?

These difficulties and uncertainties are done away with by our conception of culture: culture consists of all of the ways of life of each people which are dependent upon symboling and which are considered in an extrasomatic context. If one wished to distinguish the English from the French on the basis of their respective culture traits he could easily specify "those traits which characterize" the people in question. But he would not assert that nontypical traits were not culture.

In this connection we may note a very interesting distinction drawn by Sapir (1917:442) between the behavior of individuals and "culture."

It is always the individual that really thinks and acts and dreams and revolts. Those of his thoughts, acts, dreams, and rebellions that somehow contribute in sensible degree to the modification or retention of the mass of typical reactions called culture we term social data; *the rest, though they do not, psychologically considered, in the least differ from these, we term individual and pass by as of no historical or social moment* [i.e., they are not culture]. It is highly important to note that the differentiation of these two types of reaction is essentially arbitrary, resting, as it does, entirely on a principle of selection. The selection depends on the adoption of a scale of values. Needless to say, the threshold of the social (or historical) [i.e., cultural] *versus* the individual shifts according to the philosophy of the evaluator or interpreter. I find it utterly inconceivable to draw a sharp and eternally valid dividing line between them [emphases ours].

Sapir finds himself confronted by a plurality, or aggregation, of individuals. (He would have preferred this wording rather than "society," we believe, for he speaks of "a theoretical [fictitious?] community of human beings," adding that "the term 'society' itself is a cultural construct"; Sapir, 1932:236.) These individuals do things: dream, think, act, and revolt. And "it is always the individual," not society or culture, who does these things. What Sapir finds then is: individuals and their behavior; nothing more.

Some of the behavior of individuals is culture, says Sapir. But other elements of their behavior are not-culture, although, as he says, psychologically considered they do not differ in the slightest from those elements which he calls culture. The line thus drawn between "culture" and "not-culture" is purely arbitrary, and depends upon the subjective evaluation of the one who is drawing the line.

A conception of culture could hardly be less satisfactory than this one. It says, in effect: "culture is the name that we give to some of the behavior of some individuals, the selection being arbitrary and made in accordance with subjective criteria."

In the essay from which we have been quoting, "Do We Need a Superorganic?" (1917), Sapir is opposing the culturological point of view presented by Kroeber in "The Superorganic." He (Sapir) virtually makes culture disappear; it is dissolved into the totality of the reactions of individuals. Culture becomes, as he has elsewhere called it, a "statistical fiction" (Sapir 1932:237). If there is no significant reality that one can call culture, then there can be no science of culture. Sapir's argument was skillful and persuasive. But it was also unsound, or at least misleading.

Sapir's argument was persuasive because he bolstered it with authentic, demonstrable fact. It was unsound or misleading because he makes it appear that the only significant distinction between the behavior of individuals and culture is the one that he had made.

It is perfectly true that the elements which comprise the human behavior of individuals and the elements which comprise culture are identical classes of things and events. All are symbolates—dependent upon man's unique ability to symbol. It is true, also, that "psychologically considered," they are all alike. But Sapir overlooks, and by his argument effectively obscures, the fact that there are two fundamentally different kinds of contexts in which these "thinkings, actings, dreamings, and revolts" can be considered for purposes of scientific interpretation and explanation: the somatic and the extrasomatic. Considered in a somatic context, i.e., in terms of their relationship to the human organism, these acts dependent upon symboling constitute *human behavior*. Considered in an extrasomatic context, i.e., in terms of their relationships to one another, these acts constitute *culture*. Instead, therefore, of arbitrarily putting some in the category of culture and the rest in the category human behavior, we put all acts, thoughts, and things dependent upon symboling in either one context or the other, somatic or extrasomatic, depending upon the nature of our problem.

10 ON THE CONCEPT OF CULTURE AND SOME CULTURAL FALLACIES
DAVID BIDNEY

One of the most encouraging features of contemporary social science is the increasing recognition of the importance of conceptual analysis. The social scientists, it is held, must endeavor to emancipate themselves from the "armchair taboo" and from the blind worship of the "totem" of barren experimentalism. The isolation of theory from practical research, it is claimed, leads to empty, unverified speculation on the one hand, and to incoherent aggregates of data on the other. The essential requirement is that the concepts employed in any science be consistent with one another and connote some specific class of empirically verifiable facts.

One concept which is being increasingly employed in contemporary social thought is that of culture. Anthropologists and sociologists are in general agreement that human culture is acquired or created by man as a member of society and that it is communicated largely by language. There is disagreement, however, as to the definition and role of culture. Anthropologists such as Tylor, Boas, Wissler, Ben-

Reproduced by permission of the American Anthropological Association from the *American Anthropologist,* vol. 46, no. 1, 1944.

edict and Mead, maintain that culture consists of acquired capabilities, habits or customs and that culture is a quality or attribute of human social behavior and has no independent existence of its own. From a philosophical point of view, this position may be designated as realistic since culture is regarded as an attribute of actual or real individuals and societies which exist independent of the observer. Other anthropologists, notably Marett, Redfield and Osgood, tend to define culture in terms of "communicable intelligence," "conventional understandings" or "communicated ideas." Their implicit presupposition seems to be that the distinguishing feature of culture is the fact that it is communicated knowledge. Philosophically, this position may be described as epistemological idealism, since those who hold it maintain that culture is to be defined primarily in terms of ideas.

Culture is also conceived objectively and impersonally as "the social heritage," as the sum of the historical achievements or products of human social life which have been transmitted in the form of a tradition from one generation to another. Man is said to be born into a cumulative, artificial environment to which he is trained to adapt himself in addition to the natural environment which he shares with other animals. The social heritage is, however, conceived differently by realists and idealists. The former hold that culture consists of the body of material artifacts and non-material customs and ideals. This position is maintained by Boas, Sapir and Dixon. On the other hand, idealists such as Kroeber, implicitly following the Platonic tradition, maintain that the social heritage is a "superorganic" stream of ideas and that any particular culture is an abstraction from the historical complex of ideational traditions. This position may be termed objective idealism since its advocates regard culture as a heritage of ideas which have a transcendent reality of their own independent of the individuals or societies which happen to bear them. Objective or Platonic cultural idealism is the antithesis of the humanistic position according to which man is the creator of his social heritage. That is to say, for the objective impersonal idealist culture is a transcendental, metaphysical entity which has made man what he is and to which he conforms as to his historical destiny, whereas, for the personal or humanistic idealist, culture consists of norms or ideals of behavior which man himself has created and which have no existence apart from the human mind. On either basis, material culture is a contradiction in terms, since the real cultural entities are the conceptual norms or patterns and not the particular artifacts which exemplify them.

It is important to bear in mind in this connection that although social scientists agree that culture is "superorganic" they interpret the notion in diverse ways. Thus for Herbert Spencer, who originated the term, the superorganic refers to the cumulative aggregate of human achievements which constitute the artificial hereditary environment of man. Among contemporary writers, Winston aptly expresses Spencer's meaning when he writes that "the superorganicness of culture lies in the fact that traits are in one important sense independent of man. To an important degree culture is a heritage achieved, retained (in large part) and passed down from one generation to another." A second meaning of the term, and one which most social scientists would find acceptable, is that the superorganic refers to the fact that cultural evolution is not limited by man's organic structure as is the case with animal instincts. Human culture is superorganic in the psychological sense that man's capacity for invention and communication enables him to create and acquire new forms of cultural life without any corresponding change in his organic structure. This conception of the superorganic not only fails to exclude, but even necessitates, an intimate relation between culture and the psychological nature of man. That is to say, while the facts of psychology and biology are not considered sufficient in themselves to explain the diversity of human cultures, they are nevertheless indispensable for explaining the universal functions of cultural institutions. The functionalists and pragmatists in general, following the lead of Malinowski and John Dewey, have tended to stress the psychobiological significance of cultural phenomena.

There is, however, a third usage of the term which many would not find acceptable. According to the theory of emergent evolution as developed by Kroeber and Warden, there are three basic levels of reality; namely, the inorganic, the organic and the superorganic. The organic level is thought to have emerged from the inorganic and the superorganic from the organic level. The significant point of the doctrine of emergent cultural evolution is that each level of reality is considered to be autonomous and understood only in terms of itself. As Warden put it, "An emergent system has new properties and new modes of organization that seem to bear no definite relation to the old order from which it arose." According to Kroeber, the realm of culture—which is for him identical with the social and superorganic—is to be explained without reference to man's biological or psychological nature; culture is "superpsychic." Similarly, according to Warden, culture is an emergent from the biosocial level which in turn has emerged from the subsocial level. In brief, according to the view of the superorganic based on the theory of emergent evolution, there is an ontological difference between superorganic and organic phenomena such that neither level can be explained in terms of the other. Cultural reality appears to be an impersonal force which acts upon individuals but which is not to be understood in terms of their psychobiological needs. It is this transcendental view of the superorganic which has evoked the criticism of Sapir and Allport and led the former to question whether we need a superorganic. Warden's position, it seems to me, is equivocal since on the one hand he would agree with the functionalists that "the primary culture pattern cannot be divorced from its natural biosocial functions," and on the other hand, he would also accept Kroeber's thesis that culture is superpsychic. The two theses, I believe, are logically incompatible. Murdock, it appears, adopts a similar eclectic position.

One major source of confusion in contemporary theory of culture is, I should say, the fact that many social scientists have attempted to combine the dynamic, personal conception of culture together with the static, impersonal conception involved in the notion of the social heritage. The issue is whether culture is to be understood as essentially a state or mode of living in which each individual participates actively, or whether it is a reified objective achievement or entity which man acquires from his ancestors more or less passively. Current social theory seems to be divided on the issue, some writers defining culture in terms of physical and mental activities and reactions, while others enumerate the various kinds of material and non-material culture products which comprise the entity called culture. The confusion is increased by the fact that some anthropologists and sociologists first present a dynamic definition of culture and then proceed to specify the contents of culture in terms of cultural achievements. Thus Sapir informs us that a culture is "what a society does and thinks" and then, in another paper writes that culture "embodies any socially inherited element in the life of man, material and spiritual." Similarly Dixon writes that "the culture of any people comprises the sum of all their activities, customs and beliefs" and later states that it comprises "the totality of a people's products and activities."

As my purpose in writing this paper is not only to present an analysis of contemporary conceptions of culture but also to indicate how these conflicting views may be reconciled or best eliminated, I shall in the following state briefly what I consider to be the essential facts of experience with which any theory of culture must reckon.

Looked at genetically, the notion of culture is, as Marett has reminded us, closely related to that of cultivation or tillage and involves a process of growth. To cultivate an object is to develop the potentialities of its nature in a specific manner with a view to a definite result. Thus agriculture is the process of cultivation of the potentialities of the earth and seeds by means of implements with a view to producing or growing plants. In like manner, human culture is the process of the development of the potentialities of human nature with a view to fitting man for life in society. Man conditions his natural potentialities in diverse ways in order to adapt himself to his natural, geographical environment as well as to other human beings with whom he finds it necessary to live and cooperate.

By a logical transition of thought the term culture is used to refer to the product of the process of cultivation or culturation. In this sense the biologist speaks of a germ-colony which he has been instrumental in growing as "a culture." In like manner the product of human self-cultivation is called culture. Human culture is, so to speak, an acquired or secondary nature supervening upon the primary, innate, potential human nature. Empirically, this cultured nature is manifested through acquired forms of technique, behavior, feeling and thought and it is to these that we refer when we speak of the culture of a given people.

Paraphrasing Aristotle's normative dictum that "man is by nature a social animal," we can say that *man is by nature a cultural animal*, meaning thereby that man attains to the full development of his potentialities and exercises his distinctively human functions only insofar as he lives a cultural life. As contrasted with other animals who develop naturally to maturity and for the most part follow fixed, instinctive or innate patterns of behavior, man is largely a self-made or self-formed animal. That is to say, most patterns of human behavior are acquired or learned in the life time of the individual and are not biologically inherited. The diverse cultural forms of society are due to the way in which various groups have developed the potentialities of human nature in relation to diverse geographical environments. The universal aspects of culture, such as the manufacture of implements and the regulation of morals, are expressions of universal human needs. Cultural forms of behavior differ from natural, instinctive forms in that the cultural expressions are not uniform even though they have implicit, universal functions.

A given form of culture once originated and practiced by members of a given society is imitated by members of the new generation either directly and without any special training or indirectly through verbal instruction and conditioning. Modern anthropologists are inclined to stress the role of language as all-important in the communication of cultural traditions. But the fact that the acquisition of behavior may be facilitated through linguistic instruction does not imply that culture consists exclusively or primarily of ideas. Culture may be acquired through communication of ideas but it is more than knowledge. To argue otherwise is to be committed to Berkeleyan subjective idealism with regard to culture.

Furthermore, a particular cultural trait may be either individual or social; that is, characteristic of a society as a whole or peculiar to one or more individuals within that society. As Boas and Allport have held, cultural behavior may be socially acquired by man as a member of society without being social or common to all members of his group. All culture is "socialized" or socially modified but it is not necessarily social in the sense of being an ideal pattern conformed to by all members of a society. Certainly, if the seventeenth century philosophers erred in conceiving a cultureless individual living in "a state of nature," modern thinkers seem to be going to the opposite extreme in socializing culture.

As Plato has pointed out in the famous myth of the *Protagoras*, man compensates for his deficiencies as compared with other animals by his inventive ability, particularly by the invention of fire, which is the basis for so many other techniques. The inventive ability of man is not, however, limited to techniques for the making of artifacts. More important is man's social inventiveness, his success in creating language which is the means of social communication as well as social institutions which facilitate cooperation and mutual helpfulness. Psychologically, Plato held, all social cooperation is based on an innate sense of shame and justice. Put in modern terms this means, as Aldrich has noted, that cooperation has been a more important factor in human evolution than competition. Man's social institutions or folkways are truly conservative in the sense that they have made for human conservation.

It is obvious that if human culture consists primarily of acquired forms of behavior, sentiment and thought, no inventions or culture-objects *per se* are essentially culture; they are products of human culture which must be included in any description of a given culture but they are not constituent elements thereof. Artifacts, social institutions or socifacts, and "mentifacts" or the accumulated folklore and "clerk-lore," are, so to speak, "cultural capital" or the surplus which results from and facilitates cultural living but they are not in themselves, and apart from their relation to members of a society, constituent elements of culture. It is therefore proper from this standpoint to distinguish culture from cultural achievements. The same thesis may also be argued from the functionalist's premises. As Malinowski and his followers have contended, the nature or essence of an artifact is relative to its function in, or significance for, a given society and one must not therefore speak of an object as being the same when its cultural function has been changed, even though its perceptible form remains identical. This explains why the functionalists are generally more concerned with giving an integral description of the interdependence of cultural institutions than with tracing the history of a custom or the diffusion of material trait-complexes. An adequate functionalistic division of culture would, it seems to me, be one in which the dichotomy of technical and non-technical culture would supersede the tripartite division into material, social and intellectual culture.

Furthermore, the identification of culture with the social heritage is, according to our theory, not only a "vicious misnomer" but also a serious error, since it implies that the essential feature of culture is the fact of communication and transmission, whereas we maintain that the essential feature is the combination of invention and acquisition through habituation. It is not at all essential for a cultural achievement to be communicated even though it usually is. This point may be illustrated by comparing the anthropologist who acquires ideas about a native culture with the natives themselves. The visiting anthropologist obtains information about a native culture but the culture itself would not be attributed to him because he is not "acculturated," that is, because he does not practice and profess the ideals of the native culture in his daily life. Similarly, artifacts gathered by archaeologists and placed in museums are not *our* culture-objects because thay are not made or actively utilized by us, even though we have acquired or "inherited" them. Besides, it is a commonplace of daily experience that man is not content to live by the practices or customs of his ancestors but driven by a sense of wonder and boredom and by a desire for improving the conditions of his life, he is led to introduce new ways of life and technical inventions. In brief, human culture is historical because it involves change as well as continuity, creation and discovery of novelties together with the assimilation of traditions. To define culture as a social heritage from the past is to ignore the equally significant element of historical change.

In a preceding paragraph I stated that man is by nature a cultural animal and explained that this meant that man is largely a self-formed or self-made animal. Man is not, so to speak, a ready-made product of nature. On the contrary, nature provides only the raw material of biological potentiality which man himself molds in conformity with his ideals and experiences. This implies that there is a close connection between human culture and human rationality. Man, it appears, is a cultural animal because he is also a rational animal. Man lives in accordance with his ideals of what he thinks he ought to be and acts as he thinks he is. But then, sooner or later, he discovers that some of the social ideals communicated to him by his society are not to his liking or do not lead to satisfactory results. Institutions and practices originally intended as means for the amelioration of human existence become sanctified as ends-in-themselves and lose their connection with human well-being. But instead of changing ideals to conform to change of practice, societies frequently continue to profess allegiance to the old ideals. Or else, they may change their theories without a corresponding change of practice. In either case there results a disparity between professed social theory and the actual practice of individuals and societies.

It should be noted in this connection that the terms theory and practice have a double meaning. On the one hand, practice refers to the actual behavior and beliefs of members of a society as contrasted with their professed ideals. So conceived practice is not identical with empirical or observable behavior, since beliefs which actually serve to regulate conduct are communicated but not observed. On the other hand, the terms theory and practice may also be used in a more limited sense to refer to thought and action respectively. In this latter sense theory or thought is communicable but not observed, whereas practice or action is observed but not communicated. In either case, however, the dichotomy of theory and practice is not an epistemic distinction among ideas and refers to cultural phenomena of different orders. Theory and practice are the irreducible, constituent categories of culture and not merely different kinds of ideas. The basic epistemological question which may arise is one of the degree of correspondence or agreement between the theoretical and practical elements *within* a given culture. The integration of a culture is evaluated by the degree of conformity between the theory and practice of the society to which it is attributed.

From this standpoint we can appreciate the significance of the conflict between the realistic and idealistic positions outlined at the beginning of this paper. The realists, we have seen, defined culture in terms of acquired habits, customs, folkways and mores and tended to ignore the ideal, unpracticed aspects of culture. On this basis, social ideals are logically nothing but a sort of statistical average of individual practices. The realists tend to confuse the actual aspects of culture with ideal culture by assuming that the covert or professed ideals are carried out in practice when this often is not the case. This I should call *the positivistic fallacy*. On the other hand, normative idealists define culture in terms of social ideals and values and exclude the actual practices of society as not properly belonging to culture. That is to say, they identify a culture with a given system of behavioral ideals and neglect all practices whether they be "divergent" or "conforming." This may be called *the normative fallacy*. In brief, it is as fallacious to assume that an account of what occurs or is practiced is a sufficient description of a culture as it is to assume that the ideals professed by members of a society are in themselves the complete culture. As field anthropologists and sociologists know from experience, every culture has its ideal and practical aspects and it is an indispensable function of the social scientist to show their interrelation and the measure of their integration in the society which he is investigating. One must not assume a priori that practice conforms to professed theory or vice versa since that is an empirical question which will be answered differently for various societies. The degree of cultural "lag" between the ideals and practices of a given society is, as Ogburn and Lynd have urged, an important indication of the extent of its cultural integration.

Recently Dollard and Linton, following some psychiatrical suggestions of Sapir, have attempted to harmonize the notion of normative culture with the facts of individual psychology and sociology by postulating reciprocal interaction between culture, society and the individual. Linton maintains that society and culture are phenomena of different orders. "A society," he writes, "is an organized aggregation of persons, a culture an organized aggregation of ideas and attitudes. . . . The society as a whole interacts with the culture as a whole, the two being existing continua." Linton admits that cultural norms are arrived at by a process of abstraction but leaves open the metaphysical question "as to whether cultures are anything more than constructs developed by the investigator." In any event, he argues, whether cultures in the sense of aggregates of norms of behavior exist or not, "things happen as though they existed." Similarly Dollard distinguishes between culture, society and individual impulse. "Culture," he explains, "is the name given to these abstracted (from men), intercorrelated customs of a social group. . . . Some writers extend the term 'culture' to designate the living group of persons as well as the abstracted habits of the group; this is inexpedient since it leads to confusion. For the actual group, conceived as an association of persons, society should always be used. . . . Society seems to be the broader term since it includes the manifestations of culture and impulse." Dollard stresses the point that man is not "a cultural robot" wholly determined by the cultural patterns and society. The process of "socialization" is never complete; there is always the residual, ineradicable element of individual psychobiological impulse which resists automatic socialization and is the source of the perennial conflict between the individual and his society.

The difficulty remains, however, of explaining how it is possible for abstract entities such as behavioral ideals and attitudes to act in any efficient sense of the term. It seems to me but common sense to insist with Lynd and Murphy that the only concrete entities capable of initiating change are the cultural man and the cultural society. Human nature as well as culture taken by itself is an abstraction or mental construct. Man as we know him actually is a union of the material of human nature with the forms of culture. To attribute power of activity to cultural ideals is to commit *the metaphysical fallacy* for which Aristotle originally criticized Plato, namely, the fallacy of attributing efficiency to mental forms which are not actual, concrete substances. Only by viewing culture in both its theoretical and practical aspects do we eliminate the necessity of juxtaposing human impulse, society and culture and thereby avoid the metaphysical fallacy of hypostatizing cultural ideals into dynamic agents capable of interacting with individuals and societal forces.

The dispute among sociologists and social psychologists concerning the role of culture in social science may therefore be settled by a recognition of the diverse meanings of the term cause as used in this connection. Cultural inventions, whether they be artifacts, mentifacts, or socifacts, are the material and formal causes or conditions of cultural development but they are not the efficient causes or active agents. Culture is not an efficient cause and does not make or develop itself; hence it is not capable of interacting with any other entity as Linton and Dollard seem to presuppose. On the other hand, cultural achievements do influence individual and social life by providing the material and formal stimuli or conditions for the acquisition of a specific form of behavior and thought, and to this extent the study of abstract cultural objects and ideas is of value for the social sciences. The problem of the ontological or metaphysical status of culture, it appears, is not one that the practical social scientist can ignore by relegating it to the limbo of philosophical speculation, since his basic assumptions (especially when held uncritically) have a direct bearing on his methods and results.

The major contribution of anthropology to contemporary social science has undoubtedly been the insight it has provided into the diversity of human cultures and the role of cultural conditioning in transforming the potentialities of human nature. We have come to realize that tendencies previously regarded as the necessary expression of human nature or of the biological character of a particular race are due to special historical factors. Thus modern anthropologists and sociologists no longer take seriously the doctrines of Comte, Spencer and the evolutionary school of anthropology insofar as they have attempted to deduce the universal, evolutionary stages of human cultural development from the postulate of the uniform nature of man. As Boas and other American anthropologists have established, the historical diffusion of customs and artifacts plus the empirical evidence concerning the diversity of cultural sequences has rendered the evolutionary theory of natural laws of cultural development untenable. This attempt to deduce a priori natural laws of cultural development may be called *the naturalistic fallacy*. This fallacy, it appears, dies hard since it fosters racial and national pride. This may be illustrated by the Nazi conception of Aryan culture as well as by Spengler's theory of monadic types of culture arising from Apollonian, Magian and Faustian types of soul. Even so careful a thinker as Freud seems to have fallen victim to this fallacy when he regarded the Oedipus Complex as essential to human nature in an attempt to explain the origin of totem and taboo, in spite of the evidence from matrilineal societies which contradicts his hypothesis. Unlike the German romanticists, however, Freud was led to this position by his uncritical acceptance of the evolutionary theory of the inheritance of acquired characteristics and of an unconscious racial memory.

On the other hand, the tendency to hypostatize culture and to conceive it as a transcendental, superorganic or superpsychic force which alone determines human, historical destiny has led to the opposite extreme of cultural determinism. This *culturalistic fallacy*, as it may be called, is based on the assumption that culture is a force that may make and develop itself and that individuals are but its passive vehicles or instruments. The following passage from Kroeber's *Anthropology* illustrates this position clearly:

> Lawgivers, statesmen, religious leaders, discoverers, inventors, therefore only seem to shape civilization. The deep-seated, blind and intricate forces that shape culture also mold the so-called creative leaders of society as essentially as they mold the mass of humanity. Progress, so far as it can objectively be considered as such, is something that makes itself. We do not make it. Our customary conviction to the contrary is probably the result of an unconscious desire not to realize our individual impotence as regards the culture we live in.

Social influence of a sort we do have as individuals, but it is a personal influence on the fortunes and careers of other members of society and is concerned largely with aims of personal security, relative dominance or affection among ourselves. This obviously is a different thing from the exertion of influence on the form or content of civilization as such.

This position obviously involves cultural determinism and is the antithesis of the humanistic, individualistic position that man creates his culture and is capable of regulating the course of his historical development.

It is noteworthy that the position of cultural determinism may be maintained either by cultural idealists or materialists. According to objective idealism, cultural ideas are the determining forces of history; technology and social institutions are but the symbols of expressions of these spiritual forces. In addition to Kroeber, this position has been maintained with variations by Hegel, Spengler and Sorokin. Among contemporary writers, Sorokin has developed this thesis at greatest length. The latter maintains that phenomenological or sociocultural meanings are the primary, determining elements of culture and that there are three basic types of cultural mentality which serve to integrate all the data of culture whether primitive or civilized, namely, the sensate, ideational and idealistic types of mentality and their various combinations. The history of culture, he believes, shows a cyclical tendency. Unlike Spengler, therefore, Sorokin believes optimistically that the present sensate or materialistic culture far from marking "the decline of the west," is due to be followed by an ideational or idealistic form of culture in which non-empirical, normative values will be paramount once more. On the other hand, according to the materialistic philosophy of history, technological and economic practices are the primary factors which determine the course of history and the ideologies of societies at various stages of development. This doctrine of "dialectical materialism" is, as its leading proponent Marx has observed, simply Hegelian idealism turned upside down. In either case, individual initiative as the factor in historical development is discounted.

By means of the thesis of this paper, namely, the recognition that culture has its theoretical and practical elements and that culture is essentially the product of human creativeness, we shall avoid the extremes of the positivistic and normative fallacies on the one hand, and the metaphysical, naturalistic and culturalistic fallacies on the other. Culture, we maintain, is a historical creation of man and depends for its continuity upon free, conscious transmission and invention. Since culture is in part the cultivation of man in relation to the physical environment, it is necessarily subject to the laws and limitations of human nature as well as of nature as a whole. Similarly, cultural ideals and practices when assimilated and conformed to, do influence or condition the course of human development. But neither natural forces nor cultural achievements taken separately or by themselves can serve to explain the emergence and evolution of cultural life.

11 THE SUPERORGANIC: SCIENCE OR METAPHYSICS?
DAVID KAPLAN

The following discussion is an attempt to reexamine the superorganic conception of culture in the light of the logic of scientific methodology. Put more specifically, the central problem of this paper is whether from the viewpoint of the logic of scientific explanation it makes any sense to speak of explaining "culture in terms of culture"; or whether, as we have so often been told, cultural phenomena must, in the final analysis, be explained in psychological terms. The crux of this issue, as I see it, hinges not upon a determination of the ontological structure of the world, but rather upon a formulation of those conditions under which one science is reducible to some other one, i.e., the logical and empirical requirements which must be satisfied if the laws and other theoretical statements of one discipline can be said to be explained by the theoretical statements of a second discipline. There are, of course, a number of different theoretical perspectives which have as their focus the relationship between cultural and psychological phenomena, and not all of them are reductive in their implications. One might, for instance, be interested in exploring the psychological concomitants of cultural events in an attempt to supplement culturological explanations with some statements about the character of such psychological processes; or one might wish to investigate the congruence or lack of congruence between certain types of personality systems and certain kinds of cultural systems. But since these theoretical concerns, as I understand them, would not entail a denial of the logical possibility of explaining cultural phenomena in terms of themselves, I will not be concerned with them here.

Perhaps it ought to be emphasized at the outset that this paper lays no claim to settling this issue once and for all. Its purpose is essentially a more modest one, namely, to shift the dialogue from the spongy ground of metaphysics to the arena of scientific methodology—where the whole question properly belongs.

Probably the best place to begin is with a few brief remarks about the concept of culture itself. I think it is fair to say that most anthropologists, at least in the United States, look upon culture as their master concept. Yet if one were to judge from the recent exhaustive review of the concept by Kroeber and Kluckhohn (1952),* it would appear that anthropologists are sharply at odds about the nature of their subject-matter, as well as where to set the logical limits of its boundaries. On the face of it, this is a curious state of affairs for a discipline to find itself in—somewhat like a group of mammalogists at loggerheads over what a mammal is. I think, however, that if we put aside what anthropologists assert to be the essential nature of culture when they don their philosophic caps, and instead look at how they actually work with the concept in the context of their empirical research, we will find a greater degree of agreement than the bewildering array of definitions contained in the Kroeber-Kluckhohn compendium might suggest. After all, despite their diverse

Reproduced by permission of the American Anthropological Association from the *American Anthropologist*, vol. 67, no. 4, 1965.

*See pp. 331–332 for references.

metascientific conceptions of culture, most of the time anthropologists do manage to communicate with each other about the kinds of things they are doing. When we undertake a piece of research, whether it be in the field or the library, we do not first spend time in deciding what and where culture is—as though culture were some object to be located out there in the external world: we allow our theoretical interests to dictate the kinds of phenomena and conceptual "entities" with which we will be concerned. As a matter of fact, a cursory glance through a sample of ethnographic monographs will reveal that anthropologists concern themselves with roughly the same kinds of conceptual "entities": modes of subsistence, kinship systems, political institutions, magical and religious rituals, and so on.

I would suggest that the basis for this common universe of discourse—beneath all the ostensible definitional diversity—is that anthropologists engaged in empirical research, however they may philosophically define the concept, tend to view culture as a class of phenomena, conceptualized for the purpose of serving their methodological and scientific needs. . . .

Most of the critiques which have been levelled at the superorganic conception of culture can be grouped within two broad categories. The first—and probably the one that anthropologists have found most convincing—would reject the possibility of explaining cultural phenomena wholly in terms of themselves on the grounds that such phenomena have no independent ontological existence, but in "reality" are always found intimately associated with psychological phenomena. In other words, because culture cannot exist without its human carriers, and because in "reality" man and culture are inseparably linked, this position would maintain that to separate culture conceptually from man does violence to the nature of this "reality."

The second type of critique is of a different sort and stems from a moralistic stance. This position would reject the attempt to explain cultural phenomena in terms of themselves on the grounds that this view entails a kind of determinism which reduces man to a mere cipher caught up by impersonal cultural forces over which he has no control. Each of these arguments will now be taken up in turn.

We are indebted to David Bidney for one of the most explicit and thoroughgoing expositions of what can be called the ontological critique of the superorganic position. . . .

The crux of Bidney's argument seems to be as follows: that each of the sciences strive to isolate for special consideration its own particular segment of reality; but the interdependence of the levels of reality makes for certain difficulties in this endeavor. Some scientific disciplines, such as physics, chemistry and biology find it methodologically easy to accomplish because they deal with "disparate objects which may be segregated for special treatment." In the case of the cultural sciences, however, it is clearly impossible. Since there is no separate segment of reality (ontological level) which corresponds to cultural phenomena, we cannot speak of explaining these phenomena in terms of themselves, but must always include as an integral part of our explanations, statements about psychological phenomena as well.

Now one can readily agree that in "reality" all cultural phenomena are intimately linked with psychological phenomena; but is it not also the case that psychological phenomena are at the same time intimately associated with physiological phenomena and these in turn with physicochemical and subatomic phenomena. Yet it is not claimed (at least not by Bidney) that to explain cultural or psychological phenomena we must show how they are related to the biochemical and sub-cellular physical processes going on within human organisms—although some writers might contend that this is the ultimate goal of science.

Bidney, it should be pointed out in all fairness, explicitly asserts that his psychocultural approach does not seek to reduce cultural phenomena to the psychological level—as a matter of fact, he labels any such attempt the "naturalistic fallacy" (1953:51). I must confess, however, to being somewhat uncertain as to the meaning which Bidney attaches to the terms "reduction" and "psychocultural." In support of his psychocultural approach, for example, he contends (1953:65): "An adequate theory of culture must explain the origin of culture and its intrinsic relations to the psychobiological nature of man. To insist upon the self-sufficiency and autonomy of culture, as if culture were a closed system requiring only historical explanations in terms of other cultural phenomena, is not to explain culture, but to leave its origin a mystery or an accident of time."

Bidney is so acutely attuned to the detection of logical fallacies, it is surprising that he should be guilty in the above passage of the genetic fallacy. The psychobiological nature of man, to be sure, *is* relevant to explaining the origins of culture (who ever denied this). But to account for the initial origins of culture is quite a different matter from providing an explanation of its present-day diversity of content and form.

Basic to Bidney's view of culture is his notion of "human nature." He maintains that "culture is a direct necessary expression of human nature" and furthermore that this "human nature, like culture evolves or unfolds in time" (1953:76). He then goes on to add (1953:76): ". . . while the innate biological potentialities of man remain more or less constant the actual, effective psychophysical powers and capabilities are subject to development in time. . . . The point I wish to make does not raise the problem of racial differences, but only the possibility of the cultural perfectibility of human nature as an acquired, historical achievement which varies with different cultures."

But how are we to determine empirically what these "psychophysical powers and capabilities" are, which seem to unfold independently of man's innate biological potentialities, and which give rise to cultural variations in time and space? Bidney does not tell us, except to say that they vary with the state of human culture. Ultimately what we are left with is a mode of explanation that goes something like this: Cheyenne culture differs from Arunta culture because they are expressions of different human natures. And how do we know that Cheyenne and Arunta human natures are different? Obviously, because their cultures are different. The sterility of this kind of verbal explanation is, I think, apparent and scarcely needs further comment.

As for Bidney's disavowal of reductionism, his remarks about the connection between chemical and physical phenomena and the development of psychosomatic medicine casting light on the interdependence between cultural, psychological and biological phenomena, indicate not only a readiness to deal with several (and perhaps even all) levels simultaneously, but also a conviction that phenomena at the "higher," levels *can* be explained by those at the "lower" levels. If we are to deal with a number of different levels at once, however, what is required are empirical laws which permit us to connect logically the phenomena (or more accurately the concepts and statements which describe and explain these phenomena) of the several levels. The success of a field such as biochemistry, for example, stems from the fact that as a result of empirical developments in biology and chemistry, such laws and hypotheses have been formulated, making it possible logically to derive statements about certain biological phenomena from statements about certain chemical phenomena. We will return to this issue shortly, when considering reductionism more fully.

What appears to be involved in Bidney's position, and, indeed, in the whole ontological critique of the superorganic, is an erroneous view of the rationale for the division of labor between the various scientific disciplines, as well as the basis for making logical distinctions between them. Bidney sees the world in terms of a series of emergent levels of reality. Moreover, he writes about these levels of reality as though the "nature" of things and the interrelationships between those natures were somehow given to us to be read off by direct inspection. But the world does not present itself to us neatly packaged into cultural events, psychological events, biological events or physicochemical events; nor does it present itself to us in terms of "levels of reality" or "natural phenomena." It comes to us as a stream of concrete events which are "just what they are." Out of the countless properties associated with any given event, the ones that are selected out for special concern will depend upon one's theoretical interests and scientific purposes. Since language is by its very nature abstractive—and all knowledge about the world if it is not to remain private must be stated in propositional form—we can never exhaust the total "concreteness" of an event. Nor is it the purpose of any theoretical science to faithfully reproduce "reality," either in whole or in part. We are, in effect, constantly engaged in a process of theoretical selecting-out, and it is for this reason that the notion of "pure" description is a chimera. To put it in a slightly different way, while there may be one "reality," there are many different kinds of questions which one can address to that reality and in consequence many different ways of conceptualizing it. And since this reality is never grasped directly, but only through our conceptualizations of it, the nature of reality turns out to be as varied as there are different theoretical formulations of it. We cannot somehow get behind our concepts to a non-conceptualized "real" world. The point of all this is that the *logical* independence of a science is not based upon having its own separate "chunk of reality" with which to deal—for this is not true of any science. Rather, it is based upon the fact that it has a set of distinct questions or problems which are its special concern, and that in seeking answers to these problems it has developed a body of distinct terms and concepts (which determine its subject-matter), as well as laws and theories (which organize and explain its subject-matter).

Now, I would submit that cultural anthropology has a set of *cultural* questions which it has traditionally sought to answer (e.g., the relationship between types of residence, types of descent and types of kinship terminology; the relationship between changing modes of subsistence and complexity of social organization; the relationship between centralized political systems and such features as trade or the construction and maintenance of large-scale public works or ecological differentiation—to name but a few that come readily to mind). I am aware that in addition to the kinds of questions mentioned above, anthropologists have, especially within recent decades, been interested in asking questions about all sorts of things, e.g., national character, socialization, basic personality structure, values, themes, etc. I am not much concerned here, however, with the special interests of particular anthropologists, as I am in logical distinctions between different theoretical structures and the modes of questioning from which they issue. If an anthropologist wishes to ask psychological questions, then he is obliged to operate within the conceptual and theoretical framework of psychology. But this does not mean that anthropology as a discipline is *about* psychology, it merely signifies that some anthropologists are interested in psychological questions. It is the failure to fully appreciate the fact that different kinds of questioning logically necessitate the use of different concepts and theoretical schemes which has sometimes made culture-personality research so vulnerable to criticism. For example, in an excellent survey of recent work in this field, Bert Kaplan (1957:113 ff.) has made the point that all-too-frequently anthropologists have inferred personality configurations wholly or in large part from cultural data, rather than dealing with personality in more autonomous, i.e., psychological, terms. Since they then want to relate personality back to culture, their methodological procedure becomes circular and a great deal of their theoretical statements tautological.

Some of the questions traditionally posed by cultural anthropologists have also been asked by some of the other cultural sciences such as sociology; some are unique to anthropology. The science of psychology, on the other hand, has focused on problems relating to the intraorganismic psychic processes of individuals, usually in relation to a specific environmental setting. Anthropologists, in contrast, have not been so much concerned with the inner processes of individuals *qua* individuals, as they have in *traditional ways* or *patterns* of behaving. Moreover, in seeking answers to its questions about these traditional patterns of behaving, anthropology has developed a body of concepts (e.g., segmentary lineage, virilocal residence, cross-cousin marriage, ramage, redistribution, irrigation state, etc.)—as well as theoretical statements relating these concepts to each other—which appear nowhere in the conceptual framework of psychology. This, at least in part, is the logical rationale for the methodological assertion that cultural phenomena can be explained in terms of themselves.

To many anthropologists, who view culture as merely an "abstraction" or a "logical construct," the notion that cultural phenomena can be said to explain or cause anything (no less themselves) would seem to be patent nonsense. Thus, Wallace (1961:42) quotes with an approving nod the well-known remark by Radcliffe-Brown that, "To say of culture patterns that they act upon an individual . . . is as absurd as to hold a quadratic equation capable of committing a murder." Woodger (cited by Jessor 1958:173) has graphically characterized the type of philosophy expressed in the above quote as "finger and thumb" metaphysics—the view that a "thing is real or exists only if it can in principle be picked up between the finger and thumb." But its metaphysics to one side, Radcliffe-Brown's comment is also highly misleading because it tends to confuse the purely formal or logical structure of a science with the empirical implications or relevance of that structure. From a strictly formal point of view, all conceptual entities in science are in some sense "abstractions" or "logical constructs"—since science is a form of sociolinguistic behavior, what else could they conceivably be? But those who espouse a logical-construct view of culture are claiming much more than this: they mean to assert that while culture patterns are constructed (or abstracted) out of a welter of observations, they are not in themselves directly observable—the implication being that this makes them somehow less real and causally significant than, say, persons or sticks and stones.

First, we ought to be reminded that scientific concepts, while they may be suggested by empirical data, are not abstracted from such data by a simple process of induction. They are, rather, the products of an informed and creative imagination, or as it has so often been put "free inventions of the human intellect." What is more, few conceptual entities in science are directly observable, or can be said to be physically real in the sense in which sticks and stones are real. (It is not inappropriate to note here that *names*, in addition to sticks and stones, *can* hurt me). This does not mean, however, that such entities have no empirical referents, although their logical relationship to observational data is rarely a simple and direct one; nor does it mean that such entities may not form part of the logical structure of causal explanations. . . . From the standpoint of the development of a science, the explanatory power of conceptual entities is of far greater importance than are questions about their ontological status. . . .

Within recent decades the whole problem of the ontological status of theoretical entities has come in for a great deal of discussion in the physical sciences because of certain conceptual difficulties arising out of developments in subatomic physics. But anthropologists do not deal in sub-microscopic phenomena; they are concerned with what, by contrast, are macroscopic events. And as far as the conceptual entities formulated by anthropologists to explain these events are concerned, there are two crucial questions that ought to be asked of them: Do they have empirical referents which can be specified with any degree of precision? And do they have explanatory power, i.e., where would we be in organizing and interpreting our data without them? In this sense at least, culture patterns such as, for example, "castes," "markets," "lineages" are just as real and may be as casually significant in scientific explanations as "atoms," "genes," and "gravitational fields"—or for that matter, "drives," "habit strengths" and "cognitive maps."

Thus far in the discussion we have been skirting the problem of reduction in the sciences, and it is time that we faced it more directly. The term "reduction" turns up frequently in social science literature, usually appended to the phrase "the fallacy of," as though reductionism were some sort of illicit logical practice. Actually, the reduction of one science, either wholly or in part, to some other one may, under certain conditions, represent a significant advance of scientific knowledge.

One science is said to be reducible to another science (or one part of a science to another part) when all the terms and concepts of the one science are logically "connected" to those of the other (either by terms of the one being explicitly defined in terms of the scientific vocabulary of the other, or more commonly through suitable empirical hypotheses) in such a way so as to make it possible for all the theoretical statements of the one science to be derived logically from the theoretical statements of the other. Thus, to reduce one science to another does not somehow decrease the diversity of the natural world or make a certain range of phenomena illusory, as some writers believe; it merely implies that the theoretical structure of one science can, either entirely or in part, be subsumed under or explained by, the theoretical structure of a second.

To cite one of the classic cases of a successful reduction in science, physicists are agreed that the laws of thermodynamics which contain such concepts as heat, temperature, and entropy are reducible to the laws of mechanics which contain no references to these concepts at all. Making this reduction possible are certain empirical hypotheses which logically connect the concept of the two sciences, e.g., temperature is posited as being proportional to the mean kinetic energy of gas molecules. As a result, physicists are enabled to introduce as premises in their explanations hypotheses (kinetic theory of matter) which omit all references to such concepts as heat, temperature, etc., and which substitute in their place only concepts referring to the things that are part of the subject-matter of mechanics, such as the motion of molecules. In consequence, all the statements in thermodynamics can be logically derived—and without these statements losing in the process any of the theoretical content that they have in thermodynamics—from statements in mechanics.

The same formal requirements would hold in the case of reducing the science of culture to psychology. Concepts such as "lineage," "caste," "polygyny," "levirate" would have to be logically connected to such terms as "drive," "sublimation," "ego processes," "aggression" and "condition reflex," so as to provide a basis for specifying in *psychological* terms the conditions which give rise to the occurrence of different cultural phenomena. Clearly, we are a long way from any such reduction. Take the concept of "lineage," for example. A lineage, to be sure, is a particular grouping of individuals interacting in certain ways. But a lineage also has an organizational structure which persists through time irrespective of the particular individuals who may be members of the lineage at any given moment; and it is precisely these organizational features of the lineage in which anthropologists have been most interested. In other words, the kinds of questions we want to ask of lineage organization are not the same questions we wish to ask about the psychological make-up of the individuals who may be members of the lineage at any given moment in time. Nor is it possible, and this is really the crux of the argument, to derive logically, statements about the organizational features of the lineage from statements about the psychological characteristics of its members. Any attempt to explain lineage organization in terms of the behaving of its individual members would require that we conceive of these individuals not in psychological terms, but in terms of the statuses they occupy and the roles they perform. And since the concepts of status and roles would be meaningless except if interpreted as part of the organizational structure of the lineage, we would, in effect, be assuming a knowledge of the very phenomena we were trying to explain. The point here is that the lineage concept, while its scientific usefulness may be validated by observing individuals interacting in certain social situations, is not simply an abstraction from these observations. Rather, it is "invented" precisely for the purpose of making sense out of that observed behavior. . . .

The main drift of the argument up to this point has been to show that given the present stage of development of both sciences, the science of culture is not fully and without loss of theoretical meaning reducible to the science of psychology. But what of the future? Has not the general trend in science been toward greater reductionism? And is it not likely therefore that eventually the science of culture will be reduced to psychology (or indeed that psychology will be reduced to physiology and so on)? This is clearly an empirical question which relates to the future state of the sciences being considered, and therefore is not answerable on logical grounds alone. Culturology may at some future date be reduced to psychology, it may not—we can only wait and see. In either case, the outcome will depend upon the direction taken by the empirical development of both disciplines. In this connection, it is important to emphasize that the reducibility or irreducibility of a science is not an inherent characteristic of it; the possibility and scientific significance of reduction is always relative to the given state of development of the sciences concerned. If future theoretical developments should make it possible for the science of culture, or portions of it, to be reduced to psychology—and from the vantage point of this moment in time such developments seem very remote indeed—then psychology will have become a very different science from what it now is.

Turning from the future to the present state of the sciences of culture and psychology, it is difficult to imagine what would be gained scientifically if one were reduced to the other at the current time, assuming that such a reduction was now logically feasible. One can scarcely speak in any meaningful way of reducing culturology to psychology until there is a science of culture to be reduced, and a science of psychology for it to be reduced to. As Nagel (1961:363) has noted, if reduction is to represent a genuine advance of scientific knowledge, and not merely an arid formal exercise, the sciences concerned must be at appropriately mature levels of development. It need hardly be pointed out that the sciences being considered here are a long way from achieving such levels of theoretical sophistication. And if we can further judge from the history of science, scientific knowledge has never been significantly advanced by the simple addition of the terms and theories of one science to another. What I am suggesting here is this: that given the present undeveloped state of both the sciences of culture and psychology, the cause of the advancement of the two disciplines in particular, and scientific knowledge in general, can best be served by each continuing to further develop and refine their own conceptual and theoretical structures.

From everything that has been said it should be apparent that it is not sufficient merely to assert, as Spiro (1961a:470–471) has done, that ". . . personality variables are as important for the maintenance of social systems as for their change. Without the use of personality concepts, attempts fully to explain the operation of these [cultural] systems, either in terms of efficient causes or in terms of functional consequences, are seldom convincing." One must demonstrate how personality variables are to be logically connected to cultural variables through empirical hypotheses so as to yield explanations of how cultural systems undergo change as well as how they operate. This Spiro has not done. As a matter of fact, in the essay from which the above quote was excerpted, it is evident that Spiro is not concerned with explaining why different cultures are the way they are and how they have come to be that way, but with the very different question of how individuals are motivated to assume the social roles necessary to keep the cultural system going. In other words, his entire analysis assumes an on-going cultural system, and then provides an explanation of how it perpetuates itself; it does not explain the cultural system itself (why this set of roles rather than some others?).

This matter of keeping the questions being posed sorted out, as this paper has tried to show, is an important one. Anthropology has often been characterized by a great deal of futile and unproductive controversy because some writers have accused others of not adequately answering questions that they did not ask in the first place. White (1949:190ff.) and Kroeber (1944), for example, have sought to explain cultural innovations by the antecedent cultural matrix out of which they arise (I am not so much concerned with the substantive content of the explanations offered by these writers, as with their methodological approach). The question White and Kroeber are concerned with is why it is that certain innovations are made in certain cultures and not others, and why in certain historic periods and not others. In short, theirs is essentially a question about *rates* or *patterns* of innovation. They are not asking why in a particular culture at a particular time, individual A makes an innovation rather than individual B. This is patently a biographical question which cannot be answered by their methodological approach. Thus, Copeland's (1963:114) recent remarks that White's thesis fails to explain why Ghandi, Churchill, Hitler and Mussolini and not some other persons did what they did, misconstrues White's intention.

Nor will the Kroeber-White approach tell us anything about the psychological processes involved in making an innovation. Barnett (1953) in his book on innovation views the innovative process as being essentially a mental one, involving the recombination of two or more "mental configurations." A major limitation of this perspective, as Wallace (1961:124) sees it, is that it fails to ". . . state the conditions under which a particular innovation will occur; i.e., to predict which of several possible recombinations will be made, by whom, and when." Wallace has his own view of the innovative process, based upon what he calls the "principle of maximal organization," which asserts (1961:125); ". . . that an organism acts in such a way as to maximize under existing conditions, and to the extent of its capacity, the amount of organization in the dynamic system represented in its mazeway; that is to say, it works to increase both the complexity and the orderliness of its experience."

Wallace adds that if a particular innovative recombination is to occur, the necessary "proto-typical and stimulus configurations" must be present. He then sums up his position by saying (1961:127) that ". . . in itself innovation is an 'instinctive' propensity of the human organism activated under the merest provocation of desire for richer or more orderly experience."

Now, one can conceptualize innovation in any way that one's theoretical interests demand, but if I understand them correctly, I do not see how either Barnett's or Wallace's conceptualization of the innovative process will help us very much in answering questions about varying *rates* of innovation in time and space.

The ontological objection to the superorganic view of culture has been discussed at considerable length because it is clearly the most frequently expressed criticism of that position. The second type of critique can be dealt with more summarily.

As mentioned earlier, one gets the impression from reading many of the strictures directed at the superorganic view of culture that often the objection is not a logical or scientifiic one but rather a moralistic one; that is, the objection is to the alleged deterministic implications of the position. Opler (1963:902), for instance, has recently fired a verbal fusillade at those deterministic "culturologists" who would strip anthropology of its "warmth and purpose, its concern with humanity." Why the attempt to explain cultural phenomena in terms of other cultural phenomena should indicate a lack of concern with humanity, or turn men into mechanical robots, is not readily apparent. One would think that, on the contrary, only to the extent man is able to develop a body of reliable knowledge about how cultural systems work, will his efforts to exert some measure of control over his cultural environment meet with any degree of success. I suspect one of the major reasons some writers find the superorganic position so repugnant is they tend to see it as entailing the view that, regardless of what man does, cultural forces will grind away inexorably to their fated end. But this is to wholly misinterpret the character of causal explanation in science and to confuse it with some brand of metaphysical fatalism. Causal explanations do not somehow shape and constrain events in the phenomenal world, they merely enable us to understand and predict them. The laws of gravitation do not cause apples to fall from trees, nor can we object to meteorology for making it rain so often.

This is not the place to undertake a full-scale review of the logic of scientific explanation and its relationship to the issue of determinism versus indeterminism, but a few brief remarks are warranted.

Whether or not a universal determinism can be attributed to the world in the sense that for every event there is a unique set of conditions without whose presence the event would not have occurred, and that given these conditions the event in question will always occur, is a doctrine which cannot be proved or disproved on either *a priori* grounds or by citing empirical evidence. It is an *assumption* that we make about the world which says, in effect, that all events have determinate causes and that we ought to look for them. Some such assumption would seem to be a precondition of our very ability to understand and effectively cope with the world in which we live, for the opposite assumption calls up a kind of Kafkaesque world in which events occur with maddening whimsicality, without apparent rhyme or reason. As a heuristic principle, determinism is basic to doing science, since the goal of the scientific enterprise is explanation, and the ideal of scientific explanation is to be able to state the necessary and sufficient conditions for the occurrence of an event. It is of course true that many events cannot now be explained in strictly causal terms (some may never be so explained), and that much of our knowledge about the world is of a statistical or probabilistic nature. But to say this is to say something about the present state of our theoretical knowledge of the world, and not to describe its ontological structure. For to argue from the epistemic fact that our theories do not at the present time permit us to causally explain the occurrence of a specific event to the conclusion that "this event has no cause," is to advance a metaphysical proposition which can never be verified. And it may, of course, with future theoretical developments, be falsified.

The superorganic position, therefore, is neither more nor less deterministic than any other scientific procedure. It merely asserts that from a methodological standpoint, cultural events can be explained in terms of other cultural events, and that the motives, drives and psychological dispositions of individuals are not relevant to answering certain cultural questions. If an investigator comes back with the counterassertion that such psychological phenomena are relevant, then he must demonstrate logically and empirically in what way they are. But the introduction of individuals and their psychological characteristics as explanatory factors would not make his explanations any the less deterministic than they would be if these phenomena were excluded. The science of psychology, in short, is no less deterministic than the science of culture.

Conclusions

The development of a naturalistic and autonomous science of culture for which Tylor argued so cogently rests squarely upon the possibility of explaining cultural phenomena in terms of themselves. For if this cannot be done, then there can be no autonomous science of culture, and the study of cultural phenomena becomes a branch of whichever scientific discipline can provide explanations for them. This paper has attempted to demonstrate that there are no *logical* or *scientific* reasons why culture cannot be explained in terms of culture, and that in answering certain kinds of questions it makes perfectly good methodological sense to do so. This position, as I have tried to show, does not commit us to any metaphysical view of the constitution of the world—although it is true that often proponents of superorganicism have phrased their arguments in terms (e.g., "levels of reality" or "reality *sui generis*") which might lead one to believe that this is the case. It does not, in other words, compel one (as Bidney contends) to conceive of culture as some sort of metaphysically closed system. Obviously, cultural phenomena do in "reality" interact with all kinds of noncultural phenomena. But our attempts to explain cultural phenomena are something else again, and it is here that we strive to achieve logical closure. The ultimate ideal of any science is the formulation of a comprehensive and systematic theoretical structure, i.e., a set of highly interconnected, hierarchically ordered and "logically closed" theoretical propositions. Few sciences have ever even approached this kind of theoretical maturity, and there are good reasons for thinking that a science of culture may never do so. But certainly we ought not to abandon the quest, since much can be learned from just trying.

The main burden of this paper has been a logical one. It has been maintained that there is indeed a set of strictly cultural questions and problems which have never been the concern of the science of psychology, and that these have formed the traditional core of the anthropological enterprise. Moreover, in seeking answers to these problems, anthropology has formulated concepts, theoretical entities, laws (or if one prefers, generalizations) and theories which do not form any part of the theoretical apparatus of psychology and cannot be reduced to it. This is the logical basis for treating culture as an autonomous sphere of phenomena, explainable in terms of itself. It is wholly beside the point to maintain that anthropologists cannot proceed in this way or that they ought not proceed in this way, for the brute fact of the matter is that in their empirical research this is precisely the way they do most often proceed. In this regard, it is a curious fact that when cultural phenomena are explained in terms of themselves in the context of anthropological empirical work, few eyebrows are raised. It is only when anthropologists get philosophical and start to talk about what they are doing that all the trouble begins.

SECTION INTRODUCTION REFERENCES* AND SUGGESTIONS FOR FURTHER STUDY

*Adelung, Johann Christoph, 1782, *Versuch einer Geschichte der Cultur des menschlichen Geschlechts*. Leipzig: Hertel.
*_____, 1793–1801, *Grammatisch-kritisches Wörterbuch der Hochdeutschen Mundart. . .*, zweyte Ausgabe. Leipzig: Breitkopf.
*Basler, Otto, 1953, "Adelung, Sprachforscher und Historiker, 2) Johann Christoph." *Neue Deutsche Biographie*, Vol. 1. Berlin: Duncker & Humblot.
Bidney, David, ed., 1963, *The Concept of Freedom in Anthropology*. The Hague: Mouton.
Copeland, John W., 1963, "Culture and Man: Leslie A. White's Thesis Re-examined." *Southwestern Journal of Anthropology* 19:109–120.
Durkheim, Emile, 1915, *The Elementary Forms of Religious Life* (Trans. by J. W. Swain). London: Allen & Unwin.
Dictionnaire de l'Académie Françoise, 4th ed., 1762, Vol.1, A-K. Paris: Brunet.
*GLLF (*Grand Larousse de la langue francaise*), 1972, Vol. 2. Paris: Librairie Larousse.
Hartog, Philip, 1938, " 'Kultur' As a Symbol in Peace and in War." *The Sociological Review* 30:317–345. (Written in 1917.)

*Klemm, Gustav Friedrich, 1843, *Allgemeine Cultur – Geschichte der Menschheit* (10 Vols.). Leipzig: Teubner.

*_____, 1854–1855, *Allgemeine Culturwissenschaft: Die materiellen Grundlagen menschlicher Cultur* (2 Vols.). Leipzig: Romberg's Verlag.

*Kroeber, Alfred L., 1915, "Eighteen Professions." *American Anthropologist* 17:283–288.

_____, 1928, "The Anthropological Attitude." *American Mercury* 13:490-496.

_____, 1936, "So-called Social Science." *Journal of Social Philosophy* 1:317-340.

_____, 1943, "Review of Arnold J. Toynbee, A Study of History." *American Anthropologist* 45:294-299.

*_____, 1948, "White's View of Culture." *American Anthropologist* 50:405–415.

*Lowie, Robert H., 1966, *Culture and Ethnology*. New York: Basic Books. (First published in 1917.)

Ogburn, W. F., and D. Thomas, 1922, "Are Inventions Inevitable? A Note on Social Evolution." *Political Science Quarterly* 37:83–84.

Opler, Morris E., 1964, "The Human Being in Culture Theory." *American Anthropologist* 66:507–528.

Radcliffe-Brown, 1949, "White's View of a Science of Culture." *American Anthropologist* 51:503–512

Sapir, Edward, 1917, "Do We Need a Superorganic?" *American Anthropologist* 19:441–447.

*Scherer, Wilhelm S., 1875, "Adelung: Johann Christoph." *Allgemeine Deutsche Biographie* 1:80–84. Leipzig: Duncker & Humblot.

Sumner, William Graham, 1906, *Folkways. A Study of the Sociological Importance of Usages, Manners, Customs, Mores, and Morals*. Boston: Ginn.

*Tylor, Edward B., 1958, *Primitive Culture*. New York: Harper Torchbooks. (First published in 1871.)

*Vogel, Julius, 1898, "Winckelmann: Johann Joachim." *Allgemeine Deutsche Biographie* 43:343–362. Leipzig: Duncker & Humblot.

White, Leslie A., 1949, "Ethnological Theory." In R. W. Sellars et al., eds., *Philosophy for the Future*. New York: Macmillan, pp. 357–384.

*Willey, Malcolm M., 1929, "The Validity of the Culture Concept." *American Journal of Sociology* 35:204–219.

section IV

The Social Order as Culture

In sociology and social and cultural anthropology the term *society* has various meanings which reflect the differing interests of the scholars concerned and are reflected in their procedures of study. Some conceptions, especially the sociological, scarcely mention culture or define it obscurely as some sort of appendage to human society. Other views clearly distinguish culture from society, sometimes seeing culture as an element, attribute, or aspect of society, and other times regarding society as an element of a systemic unit called culture. The view taken here, common in cultural anthropology, conceives society or the social order as a major element of culture, distinguishable from other elements but intimately related to them. From this viewpoint, society is composed of people in orderly arrangements of relationships; that is, society, the social order, and social groups have structural or formal arrangements and also sets of associated institutionalized relationships or modes of interaction, both of which—the structures, and the interactions of people that are the dynamic aspect of the structures—are cultural.

The study of culture then importantly includes the study of the social order. Like ants, whales, monkeys and many other nonhuman species of animal life, man is by biological nature a social animal. Unlike nonhuman societies, however, the societies of man, the particular forms of social structure and the accompanying relationships of people that distinguish one society from another, are cultural. Thus, in attempting to understand similarities and differences in the social order among societies of the world, the primary subjects of investigation are differences and similarities in other components of culture, as they are conditioned by the physical environment and by innate needs of human beings as biological organisms. All subsystems, or aspects of culture, such as economics, technology, and religion are simultaneously social phenomena, and the study of culture is in one way or another also a study of human social relationships.

Society is customarily seen as a unit composed of a number of distinguishable constituents: structural, ideological, attitudinal, and behavioral. Using differing terminology, most views in cultural anthropology concerning the composition of society separate it into two major divisions, one of which is structural or formal and the other dynamic or functional. A third division or aspect of society, the ideological, ideational, or attitudinal, is sometimes distinguished although this is sometimes merged with the functional aspect. A simple analogy, now old-fashioned in anthropology but nevertheless useful, compares society with a living organism. The relationship of the structure and the functions of society are like those between the anatomy and physiology of the organism. Society is seen as a network of social structures, such as forms of the family, lineages, clans, common-interest associations of many kinds, and occupational groups, that form a composite structural whole, and also an accompanying set of institutions, that is, institutionalized ideas, values and acts that involve social interaction. The family is a structure, for example, and marriage is one of its accompanying institutions.

Many of the writings in the following section reflect this view, although the terminology may differ somewhat. For example, the early functionalist A. R. Radcliffe-Brown used the word *structure* in a way that accords with our definition and saw structures as being accompanied by "social usage," a term that appears to coincide in meaning with what we have called institutions. The term *social institution* is far more variable in meaning than "social structure," however, and it is sometimes loosely used to include both structures and institutions, as we have defined them. Some scholars see society as having two basic levels of integration, (1) social structures with their particular institutions, and (2) social statuses, or social positions, with their institutionalized social roles. Each structure is a network of statuses, each of which in turn has an appropriate role.

Social structures and institutions are usually regarded as functionally supporting or maintaining the unity of the entire society. Many are seen as responses to fundamental human needs, such as securing food. Although structures overlap, for purposes of study and interpretation, many may usefully be distinguished—the family, concerned with rearing children and meeting the sexual needs of adults; religious structures, such as sects, congregations, and religious societies, accompanied by institutionalized ideas and procedures of supernaturalism that relate to human welfare in numerous ways and often sanction social norms; the economic realm of structures and accompanying institutions concerned with the production, distribution, and consumption or use of goods and services; and political organization, regulating and controlling the behavior of individuals as members of society. All structures and institutions have "charters," explanatory and validating rationales which often appear or claim to be the reasons for the existence of the structures and institutions they support. These may take the form of myths and of ideals and moral values supported by religious and other sanctions, or they may be codified in oral or written law.

The relationship of the concepts of status and role is closely analogous with that between structure and institution previously described. In loose usage, the terms *status* and *role* are sometimes used interchangeably, but scholarly custom has long distinguished status as the formal or structural aspect and role as the dynamic or behavioral aspect. A social status is then a position held by a member of society in a network of social interaction. Any person ordinarily enters several or many networks so that he has many distinguishable social statuses, as, for example, the combination of statuses of being male, middle-aged, husband, father, merchant, Presbyterian, Democrat, and sponsor of Little League baseball. Status may also be considered hierarchically as superior or inferior, by social class, and as an individual compared with other individuals. Statuses are added as social contexts of an individual increase or enlarge. In an international context one's national identity as German, English, Japanese, American or whatever becomes a status. Statuses are either *ascribed*, determined by sex, age, race, birth order, hereditary social position, and similar circumstances over which the individual has no control, or they are *achieved*, acquired through individual effort or action.

Role is the dynamic aspect of status. In simplest analogy, role is to status as swimming is to fish. Roles represent social consensus concerning privileges and obligations associated with statuses, and they may be realistically described as ideals or expectations of behavior necessary for social interaction and cohesion rather than rigid patterns of behavior from which no deviation is allowed. Although some societies allow great variation or idiosyncracy in the performance of certain roles, all roles impose restraints upon behavior since all are defined in relation to other persons and other roles of a society. The roles are learned and are elements of culture, which may be looked upon as the script enabling and perhaps forcing the actors to learn their roles.

As discussed in the foregoing paragraphs, the readings in this section include a variety of views on the nature of culture and society. Within anthropology, the greatest differences have been between the views of cultural anthropology and social anthropology. It is useful to note that social anthropology has strong and acknowledged roots in sociology and, accordingly, reflects the ideas and interests of that field of study. The pioneers of British social anthropology A. R. Radcliffe-Brown and Bronislaw Malinowski acknowledged intellectual indebtedness to the French sociologist Emile Durkheim, and elsewhere in the work of British social anthropologists the influence of sociologists, such as the German scholar Georg Simmel, is readily evident. Following the sociological tradition, the primary interest of social anthropology has been society rather than culture. Radcliffe-Brown sometimes identified himself as a sociologist and he made no explicit use of the concept of culture. His ideas of structure and function, however, refer to what we have called culture. He notes, as we do, that social structure is intertwined with "social usages in which that structure appears and on which it depends for its continued existence" (1935:397). In his definition, social usages include morals, law, etiquette, religion, government, and education (1940:6). He refers also to patterns: "social structure has . . . to be described by the patterns of behavior to which individuals and groups conform"; and "these patterns are partially formulated in rules" (1940:8). These ideas of Radcliffe-Brown might well introduce the section that follows on cultural patterns.

Particularly in the United States, cultural anthropology has long included and valued the interpretations and working methods of social anthropology. The intensive attention of social anthropology to the social sphere, particularly through its view of social life as a system of social interaction, has yielded results that have improved our understanding of religion, economics, politics, and other distinguishable major spheres of culture. Far more than cultural anthropology, social anthropology has given attention to and increased awareness of the social identities of actors (statuses) and their social acts (roles) and to the social groups (structures) and institutions. We may also note that the concept of system in social anthropology has never been adapted to evolutionary interpretation (discussed later on in Section X), and that, unlike cultural anthropology, comparative studies are poorly developed in social anthropology. No large-scale comparative studies have ever been made in social anthropology and most studies concentrate on the structural and functional aspects of a single society, without consideration of change in the society through time. But let us note especially that the fundamental view of social anthropology is remarkably like that of cultural anthropology, as described in Section I. Both deal with systems, units composed of parts that are in functional relationship. For social anthropology, the system is society, placed by cultural anthropology within the system of culture. Little adaptation is necessary for cultural anthropologists to make use of the interpretations of social anthropologists.

The compatibility of social anthropology with cultural anthropology has, in fact, long been taken for granted by cultural anthropologists, who combine in their professional inventories much of social anthropological thought. Characteristically, North American anthropologists who identify themselves as social anthropologists include in their inventory the concept of culture. The validity of both social and cultural perspectives is probably rarely questioned today. Our readings include an article, now almost two decades old, centering on this theme which, in the persons of the distinguished scholars A. L. Kroeber and Talcott Parsons, represents the fields of anthropology and sociology. Kroeber and Parsons end their article with the statement that the question of the value of the two views is no longer an issue but what is important is how studies reflecting the two views operate and relate to each other. A similar view of the complementary positions of functionalist and evolutionist interpretations expressed by the cultural evolutionist Leslie A. White appears in Section XI as the concluding selection of this book.

The range of interest of cultural anthropology may be broader than that of social anthropology, but both lines of study have followed trends of special emphasis which have sometimes coincided, as is reflected by the readings in this section. Most anthropological studies of the social order of recent decades have concerned tribal societies organized principally on the basis of kinship. Accordingly, the greatest emphasis has been given to the study of kin groups, especially forms of the family, and to associated institutions, especially marriage.

Associations—sometimes called common-interest associations and sodalities—have as yet been given little attention despite their common existence in tribal societies of middle levels of cultural development and their acknowledged importance in societies such as our own. Three of the relatively few broad writings on this subject are included in our bibliography (Bohannan 1963; Banton 1968; Anderson 1971). Social differentiation into class and caste has long been an important subject of anthropological interest, and summary articles on this subject (Berreman 1968; Lipset 1968) are also included in our selected references to further reading.

Throughout the readings, it is not difficult to share the cultural anthropological view that culture is the ordering principle in social structure and social relations.

12 ON SOCIAL STRUCTURE
A. R. RADCLIFFE-BROWN

I conceive of social anthropology as the theoretical natural science of human society, that is, the investigation of social phenomena by methods essentially similar to those used in the physical and biological sciences. I am quite willing to call the subject "comparative sociology," if any one so wishes. It is the subject itself, and not the name, that is important. As you know, there are some ethnologists or anthropologists who hold that it is not possible, or at least not profitable, to apply to social phenomena the theoretical methods of natural science. For these persons social anthropology, as I have defined it, is something that does not, and never will, exist. For them, of course, my remarks will have no meaning, or at least not the meaning I intend them to have.

While I have defined social anthropology as the study of human society, there are some who define it as the study of culture. It might perhaps be thought that this difference of definition is of minor importance. Actually it leads to two different kinds of study, between which it is hardly possible to obtain agreement in the formulation of problems.

For a preliminary definition of social phenomena it seems sufficiently clear that what we have to deal with are relations of association between individual organisms. In a hive of bees there are the relations of association of the queen, the workers and the drones. There is the association of animals in a herd, of a mother-cat and her kittens. These are social phenomena; I do not suppose that any one will call them cultural phenomena. In anthropology, of course, we are only concerned with human beings, and in social anthropology, as I define it, what we have to investigate are the forms of association to be found amongst human beings.

Let us consider what are the concrete, observable facts with which the social anthropologist is concerned. If we set out to study, for example, the aboriginal inhabitants of a part of Australia, we find a certain number of individual human beings in a certain natural environment. We can observe the acts of behaviour of these individuals, including, of course, their acts of speech, and the material products of past actions. We do not observe a "culture," since that word denotes, not any concrete reality, but an abstraction, and as it is commonly used a vague abstraction. But direct observation does reveal to us that these human beings are connected by a complex network of social relations. I use the term "social structure" to denote this network of actually existing relations. It is this that I regard it as my business to study if I am working, not as an ethnologist or psychologist, but as a social anthropologist. I do not mean that the study of social structure is the whole of social anthropology, but I do regard it as being in a very important sense the most fundamental part of the science.

Reprinted by permission of the Royal Anthropological Institute of Great Britain and Ireland from A. R. Radcliffe-Brown, "On Social Structure," abridged version, *Journal of the Royal Anthropological Institute,* vol. 70, 1940.

My view of natural science is that it is the systematic investigation of the structure of the universe as it is revealed to us through our senses. There are certain important separate branches of science, each of which deals with a certain class or kind of structures, the aim being to discover the characteristics of all structures of that kind. So atomic physics deals with the structure of atoms, chemistry with the structure of molecules, crystallography and colloidal chemistry with the structure of crystals and colloids, and anatomy and physiology with the structures of organisms. There is, therefore, I suggest, place for a branch of natural science which will have for its task the discovery of the general characteristics of those social structures of which the component units are human beings.

Social phenomena constitute a distinct class of natural phenomena. They are all, in one way or another, connected with the existence of social structures, either being implied in or resulting from them. Social structures are just as real as are individual organisms. A complex organism is a collection of living cells and interstitial fluids arranged in a certain structure; and a living cell is similarly a structural arrangement of complex molecules. The physiological and psychological phenomena that we observe in the lives of organisms are not simply the result of the nature of the constituent molecules or atoms of which the organism is built up, but are the result of the structure in which they are united. So also the social phenomena which we observe in any human society are not the immediate result of the nature of individual human beings, but are the result of the social structure by which they are united.

It should be noted that to say we are studying social structures is not exactly the same thing as saying that we study social relations, which is how some sociologists define their subject. A particular social relation between two persons (unless they be Adam and Eve in the Garden of Eden) exists only as part of a wide network of social relations, involving many other persons, and it is this network which I regard as the object of our investigations.

I am aware, of course, that the term "social structure" is used in a number of different senses, some of them very vague. This is unfortunately true of many other terms commonly used by anthropologists. The choice of terms and their definitions is a matter of scientific convenience, but one of the characteristics of a science as soon as it has passed the first formative period is the existence of technical terms which are used in the same precise meaning by all the students of that science. By this test, I regret to say, social anthropology reveals itself as not yet a formed science. One has therefore to select for oneself, for certain terms, definitions which seem to be the most convenient for the purposes of scientific analysis.

There are some anthropologists who use the term social structure to refer only to persistent social groups, such as nations, tribes and clans, which retain their continuity, their identity as individual groups, in spite of changes in their membership.

In the first place, I regard as a part of the social structure all social relations of person to person. For example, the kinship structure of any society consists of a number of such dyadic relations, as between a father and son, or a mother's brother and his sister's son. In an Australian tribe the whole social structure is based on a network of such relations of person to person, established through genealogical connections.

Secondly, I include under social structure the differentiation of individuals and of classes by their social role. The differential social positions of men and women, of chiefs and commoners, of employers and employees, are just as much determinants of social relations as belonging to different clans or different nations.

In the study of social structure, the concrete reality with which we are concerned is the set of actually existing relations, at a given moment of time, which link together certain human beings. It is on this that we can make direct observations. But it is not this that we attempt to describe in its particularity. Science (as distinguished from history or biography) is not concerned with the particular, the unique, but only with the general, with kinds, with events which recur. The actual relations of Tom, Dick and Harry or the behaviour of Jack and Jill may go down in our field note-books and may provide illustrations for a general description. But what we need for scientific purposes is an account of the form of the structure. For example, if in an Australian tribe I observe in a number of instances the behaviour towards one another of persons who stand in the relation of mother's brother and sister's son, it is in order that I may be able to record as precisely as possible the general or normal form of this relationship, abstracted from the variations of particular instances, though taking account of those variations.

This important distinction, between structure as an actually existing concrete reality, to be directly observed, and structural form, as what the field-worker describes, may be made clearer perhaps by a consideration of the continuity of social structure through time, a continuity which is not static like that of a building, but a dynamic continuity, like that of the organic structure of a living body. Throughout the life of an organism its structure is being constantly renewed; and similarly the social life constantly renews the social structure. Thus the actual relations of persons and groups of persons change from year to year, or even from day to day. New members come into a community by birth or immigration; others go out of it by death or emigration. There are marriages and divorces. Friends may become enemies, or enemies may make peace and become friends. But while the actual structure changes in this way, the general structural form may remain relatively constant over a longer or shorter period of time. Thus if I visit a relatively stable community and revisit it after an interval of ten years, I shall find that many of its members have died and others have been born; the members who still survive are now ten years older and their relations to one another may have changed in many ways. Yet I may find that the kinds of relations that I can observe are very little different from those observed ten years before. The structural form has changed little.

But, on the other hand, the structural form may change, sometimes gradually, sometimes with relative suddenness, as in revolutions and military conquests. But even in the most revolutionary changes some continuity of structure is maintained. . . .

Closely connected with this conception of social structure is the conception of "social personality" as the position occupied by a human being in a social structure, the complex formed by all his social relations with others. Every human being living in society is two things: he is an individual and also a person. As an individual, he is a biological organism, a collection of a vast number of molecules organised in a complex structure, within which, as long as it persists, there occur physiological and psychological actions and reactions, processes and changes. Human beings as individuals are objects of study for physiologists and psychologists. The human being as a person is a complex of social relationships. He is a citizen of England, a husband and a father, a brick-layer, a member of a particular Methodist congregation, a voter in a certain constituency, a member of his trade union, an adherent of the Labour Party, and so on. Note that each of these descriptions refers to a social relationship, or to a place in a social structure. Note also that a social personality is something that changes during the course of the life of the person. As a person, the human being is the object of study for the social anthropologist. We cannot study persons except in terms of social structure, nor can we study social structure except in terms of the persons who are the units of which it is composed. . . .

I have now sufficiently defined, I hope, the subject matter of what I regard as an extremely important branch of social anthropology. The method to be adopted follows immediately from this definition. It must combine with the intensive study of single societies (i.e., of the structural systems observable in particular communities) the systematic comparison of many societies (or structural systems of different types). The use of comparison is indispensable. The study of a single society may provide materials for comparative study, or it may afford occasion for hypotheses, which then need to be tested by reference to other societies; it cannot give demonstrated results.

Our first task, of course, is to learn as much as we can about the varieties, or diversities, of structural systems. This requires field research. Many writers of ethnographical descriptions do not attempt to give us any systematic account of the social structure. But a few social anthropologists, here and in America, do recognise the importance of such data and their work is providing us with a steadily growing body of material for our study. Moreover, their researches are no longer confined to what are called "primitive" societies, but extend to communities in such regions as Sicily, Ireland, Japan, Canada and the United States.

If we are to have a real comparative morphology of societies, however, we must aim at building up some sort of classification of types of structural systems. That is a complex and difficult task, to which I have myself devoted attention for thirty years. It is the kind of task that needs the co-operation of a number of students and I think I can number on my fingers those who are actively interested in it at the present time. Nevertheless, I believe some progress is being made. Such work, however, does not produce spectacular results and a book on the subject would certainly not be an anthropological best-seller. . . .

Besides this morphological study, consisting in the definition, comparison and classification of diverse structural systems, there is a physiological study. The problem here is: how do structural systems persist? What are the mechanisms which maintain a network of social relations in existence, and how do they work? In using the terms morphology and physiology, I may seem to be returning to the analogy between society and organism which was so popular with mediaeval philosophers, was taken over and often misused by nineteenth century sociologists, and is completely rejected by many modern writers. But analogies, properly used, are important aids to scientific thinking and there is a real and significant analogy between organic structure and social structure.

In what I am thus calling social physiology, we are concerned not only with social structure, but with every kind of social phenomenon. Morals, law, etiquette, religion, government, and education are all parts of the complex mechanism by which a social structure exists and persists. If we take up the structural point of view, we study these things, not in abstraction or isolation, but in their direct and indirect relations to social structure, i.e., with reference to the way in which they depend upon, or affect, the social relations between persons and groups of persons. I cannot do more here than offer a few brief illustrations of what this means. . . .

If we take the social life of a local community over a period, let us say a year, we can observe a certain sum total of activities carried out by the persons who compose it. We can also observe a certain apportionment of these activities, one person doing certain things, another doing others. This apportionment of activities, equivalent to what is sometimes called the social division of labour, is an important feature of the social structure. Now activities are carried out because they provide some sort of "gratification," as I propose to call it, and the characteristic feature of social life is that activities of certain persons provide gratifications for other persons. In a simple instance, when an Australian blackfellow goes hunting, he provides meat, not only for himself, but for his wife and children and also for other relatives to whom it is his duty to give meat when he has it. Thus in any society there is not only an apportionment of activities, but also an apportionment of the gratifications resulting therefrom, and some sort of social machinery, relatively simple or, sometimes, highly complex, by which the system works.

It is this machinery, or certain aspects of it, that constitutes the special subject-matter studied by the economists. They concern themselves with what kinds and quantities of goods are produced, how they are distributed (i.e., their flow from person to person, or region to region), and the way in which they are disposed of. Thus what are called economic institutions are extensively studied in more or less complete abstraction from the rest of the social system. This method does undoubtedly provide useful results, particularly in the study of complex modern societies. Its weaknesses become apparent as soon as we attempt to apply it to the exchange of goods in what are called primitive societies.

The economic machinery of a society appears in quite a new light if it is studied in relation to the social structure. The exchange of goods and services is dependent upon, is the result of, and at the same time is a means of maintaining a certain structure, a network of relations between persons and collections of persons. For the economists and politicians of Canada the potlatch of the Indians of the north-west of

America was simply wasteful foolishness and it was therefore forbidden. For the anthropologist it was the machinery for maintaining a social structure of lineages, clans and moieties, with which was combined an arrangement of rank defined by privileges.

Any full understanding of the economic institutions of human societies requires that they should be studied from two angles. From one of these the economic system is viewed as the mechanism by which goods of various kinds and in various quantities are produced, transported and transferred, and utilised. From the other the economic system is a set of relations between persons and groups which maintains, and is maintained by, this exchange or circulation of goods and services. From the latter point of view, the study of the economic life of societies takes its place as part of the general study of social structure.

Social relations are only observed, and can only be described, by reference to the reciprocal behaviour of the persons related. The form of a social structure has therefore to be described by the patterns of behaviour to which individuals and groups conform in their dealings with one another. These patterns are partially formulated in rules which, in our own society, we distinguish as rules of etiquette, of morals and of law. Rules, of course, only exist in their recognition by the members of the society; either in their verbal recognition, when they are stated as rules, or in their observance in behaviour. These two modes of recognition, as every field-worker knows, are not the same thing and both have to be taken into account.

If I say that in any society the rules of etiquette, morals and law are part of the mechanism by which a certain set of social relations is maintained in existence, this statement will, I suppose, be greeted as a truism. But it is one of those truisms which many writers on human society verbally accept and yet ignore in theoretical discussions, or in their descriptive analyses. The point is not that rules exist in every society, but that what we need to know for a scientific understanding is just how these things work in general and in particular instances. . . .

I have talked about social relations, but I have not so far offered you a precise definition. A social relation exists between two or more individual organisms when there is some adjustment of their respective interests, by convergence of interest, or by limitation of conflicts that might arise from divergence of interests. I use the term "interest" here in the widest possible sense, to refer to all behaviour that we regard as purposive. To speak of an interest implies a subject and an object and a relation between them. Whenever we say that a subject has a certain interest in an object we can state the same thing by saying that the object has a certain value for the subject. Interest and value are correlative terms, which refer to the two sides of an asymmetrical relation.

Thus the study of social structure leads immediately to the study of interests or values as the determinants of social relations. A social relation does not result from similarity of interests, but rests either on the mutual interest of persons in one another, or on one or more common interests, or on a combination of both of these. The simplest form of social solidarity is where two persons are both interested in bringing about a certain result and co-operate to that end. When two or more persons have a *common interest* in an object, that object can be said to have a *social value* for the persons thus associated. If, then, practically all the members of a society have an interest in the observance of the laws, we can say that the law has a social value. The study of social values in this sense is therefore a part of the study of social structure.

It was from this point of view that in an early work I approached the study of what can conveniently be called ritual values, i.e., the values expressed in rites and myths. It is perhaps again a truism to say that religion is the cement which holds society together. But for a scientific understanding we need to know just how it does this, and that is a subject for lengthy investigations in many different forms of society. . . .

From the point of view that I have attempted briefly to describe, social institutions, in the sense of standardised modes of behaviour, constitute the machinery by which a social structure, a network of social relations, maintains its existence and its continuity. I hesitate to use the term "function," which in recent years has been so much used and misused in a multitude of meanings, many of them very vague. Instead of being used, as scientific terms ought to be, to assist in making distinctions, it is now used to confuse things that ought to be distinguished. For it is often employed in place of the more ordinary words "use," "purpose" and "meaning." It seems to be more convenient and sensible, as well as more scholarly, to speak of the use or uses of an axe or digging stick, the meaning of a word or symbol, the purpose of an act of legislation, rather than to use the word function for these various things. "Function" has been a very useful technical term in physiology and by analogy with its use in that science it would be a very convenient means of expressing an important concept in social science. As I have been accustomed to use the word, following Durkheim and others, I would define the social function of a socially standardised mode of activity, or mode of thought, as its relation to the social structure to the existence and continuity of which it makes some contribution. Analogously, in a living organism, the physiological function of the beating of the heart, or the secretion of gastric juices, is its relation to the organic structure to the existence or continuity of which it makes its contribution. It is in this sense that I am interested in such things as the social function of the punishment of crime, or the social function of the totemic rites of Australian tribes, or of the funeral rites of the Andaman Islanders. But this is not what either Professor Malinowski or Professor Lowie mean by functional anthropology.

Besides these two divisions of the study of social structure, which I have called social morphology and social physiology, there is a third, the investigation of the processes by which social structures change, of how new forms of structures come into existence. Of this important branch of study I have time for only one illustration, from the field of colonial sociology.

Let us suppose that we wish to study and understand what is happening in a British or French colony or dependency in Africa, at the present time. Formerly the region was inhabited by Africans having their own social structure. Now a new and more complex social structure has been brought into existence. The population now includes a certain number of Europeans—government officials, traders, missionaries and, in some instances, settlers. The new political structure is one in which the Europeans have a large measure of control, and they generally play an important part in the new economic structure. The outstanding characteristic of this kind of social structure is that Europeans and Africans constitute different classes, with different languages, different customs and modes of life, and different sets of values and ideas. It is an extreme example of a society compounded of heterogeneous elements. As such it has a certain instability, due to the lack of adjustment of divergent interests.

In order to understand the social changes that are taking place in a society of this kind, it seems to me essential to study the whole set of relations amongst the persons involved. This kind of study was undertaken by some of us in South Africa twenty years ago and is still being continued, profitably, I think. A few years ago, as a result perhaps of re-defining social anthropology as the study, not of society, but of culture, we were asked to abandon this kind of investigation in favour of what is now called the study of "culture contact." In place of the study of the formation of new composite societies, we are supposed to regard what is happening in Africa as a process in which an entity called African culture comes into contact with an entity called European or Western culture, and a third new entity is produced, or is to be produced, which is to be described as Westernized African culture. To me this seems a fantastic reification of abstractions. European culture is an abstraction and so is the culture of an African tribe. I find it fantastic to imagine these two abstractions coming into contact and by an act of generation producing a third abstraction. There is contact, but it is between human beings, European and African, and it takes place within a definite structural arrangement. . . .

It is convenient, I think, to use the term "progress" for the process by which human beings attain to greater control over the physical environment through the increase of knowledge and improvement of technique by inventions and discoveries. The way in which we are now able to destroy considerable portions of cities from the air is one of the latest striking results of progress. Progress is not the same thing as social evolution, but it is, I believe, very closely connected with it.

Evolution, as I understand the term, refers specifically to a process of emergence of new forms of structure. Organic evolution has two important features: (1) in the course of it a small number of kinds of organisms have given rise to a very much larger number of kinds; (2) more complex forms of organic structure have come into existence by development out of simpler forms. While I am unable to attach any definite meaning to such phrases as the evolution of culture or the evolution of language, I think that social evolution is a reality which the social anthropologist should recognise and study. Like organic evolution, it can be defined by two features. There has been a process by which, from a small number of forms of social structure, many different forms have arisen in the course of history; that is, there has been a process of differentiation. Secondly, throughout this process more complex forms of social structures have developed out of, or replaced, simpler forms.

Just how structural systems are to be classified with reference to their greater or less complexity is a problem requiring investigation. But there is evidence of a fairly close correlation between complexity and another feature of structural systems, namely, the extent of the field of social relations. In a structural system with a narrow total social field, an average or typical person is brought into direct and indirect social relations with only a small number of other persons. In systems of this type we may find that the linguistic community—the body of persons who speak one language—numbers from 250 to 500, while the political community is even smaller, and economic relations by the exchange of goods and services extend only over a very narrow range. Apart from the differentiation by sex and age, there is very little differentiation of social role between persons or classes. We can contrast with this the systems of social structure that we observe to-day in England or the United States. Thus the process of human history to which I think the term social evolution may be appropriately applied might be defined as the process by which wide-range systems of social structure have grown out of, or replaced, narrow-range systems. Whether this view is acceptable or not, I suggest that the concept of social evolution is one which requires to be defined in terms of social structure. . . .

13 STATUS AND RÔLE
RALPH LINTON

In the preceding chapter we discussed the nature of society and pointed out that the functioning of societies depends upon the presence of patterns for reciprocal behavior between individuals or groups of individuals. The polar positions in such patterns of reciprocal behavior are technically known as *statuses*. The term *status*, like the term *culture*, has come to be used with a double significance. *A status*, in the abstract, is a position in a particular pattern. It is thus quite correct to speak of each individual as having many statuses, since each individual participates in the expression of a number of patterns. However, unless the term is qualified in some way, *the status* of any individual means the sum total of all the statuses which he occupies. It represents his position with relation to the total society. Thus the status of Mr. Jones as a member of his community derives from a combination of all the statuses which he holds as a citizen, as an attorney, as a Mason, as a Methodist, as Mrs. Jones's husband, and so on.

A status, as distinct from the individual who may occupy it, is simply a collection of rights and duties. Since these rights and duties can find expression only through the medium of individuals, it is extremely hard for us to maintain a distinction in our thinking between statuses and the people who hold them and exercise the rights and duties which constitute them. The relation between any individual and

From Ralph Linton, *The Study of Man,* © 1936, Renewed 1964. Reprinted by permission of Prentice-Hall, Inc., Englewood Cliffs, New Jersey.

any status he holds is somewhat like that between the driver of an automobile and the driver's place in the machine. The driver's seat with its steering wheel, accelerator, and other controls is a constant with ever-present potentialities for action and control, while the driver may be any member of the family and may exercise these potentialities very well or very badly.

A *rôle* represents the dynamic aspect of a status. The individual is socially assigned to a status and occupies it with relation to other statuses. When he puts the rights and duties which constitute the status into effect, he is performing a rôle. Rôle and status are quite inseparable, and the distinction between them is of only academic interest. There are no rôles without statuses or statuses without rôles. Just as in the case of *status,* the term *rôle* is used with a double significance. Every individual has a series of rôles deriving from the various patterns in which he participates and at the same time *a rôle,* general, which represents the sum total of these rôles and determines what he does for his society and what he can expect from it.

Although all statuses and rôles derive from social patterns and are integral parts of patterns, they have an independent function with relation to the individuals who occupy particular statuses and exercise their rôles. To such individuals the combined status and rôle represent the minimum of attitudes and behavior which he must assume if he is to participate in the overt expression of the pattern. Status and rôle serve to reduce the ideal patterns for social life to individual terms. They become models for organizing the attitudes and behavior of the individual so that these will be congruous with those of the other individuals participating in the expression of the pattern. Thus if we are studying football teams in the abstract, the position of quarter-back is meaningless except in relation to the other positions. From the point of view of the quarter-back himself it is a distinct and important entity. It determines where he shall take his place in the line-up and what he shall do in various plays. His assignment to this position at once limits and defines his activities and establishes a minimum of things which he must learn. Similarly, in a social pattern such as that for the employer-employee relationship the statuses of employer and employee define what each has to know and do to put the pattern into operation. The employer does not need to know the techniques involved in the employee's labor, and the employee does not need to know the techniques for marketing or accounting.

It is obvious that, as long as there is no interference from external sources, the more perfectly the members of any society are adjusted to their statuses and rôles the more smoothly the society will function. In its attempts to bring about such adjustments every society finds itself caught on the horns of a dilemma. The individual's formation of habits and attitudes begins at birth, and, other things being equal, the earlier his training for a status can begin the more successful it is likely to be. At the same time, no two individuals are alike, and a status which will be congenial to one may be quite uncongenial to another. Also, there are in all social systems certain rôles which require more than training for their successful performance. Perfect technique does not make a great violinist, nor a thorough book knowledge of tactics an efficient general. The utilization of the special gifts of individuals may be highly important to society, as in the case of the general, yet these gifts usually show themselves rather late, and to wait upon their manifestation for the assignment of statuses would be to forfeit the advantages to be derived from commencing training early.

Fortunately, human beings are so mutable that almost any normal individual can be trained to the adequate performance of almost any rôle. Most of the business of living can be conducted on a basis of habit, with little need for intelligence and none for special gifts. Societies have met the dilemma by developing two types of statuses, the *ascribed* and the *achieved*. *Ascribed* statuses are those which are assigned to individuals without reference to their innate differences or abilities. They can be predicted and trained for from the moment of birth. The *achieved* statuses are, as a minimum, those requiring special qualities, although they are not necessarily limited to these. They are not assigned to individuals from birth but are left open to be filled through competition and individual effort. The majority of the statuses in all social systems are of the ascribed type and those which take care of the ordinary day-to-day business of living are practically always of this type.

In all societies certain things are selected as reference points for the ascription of status. The things chosen for this purpose are always of such a nature that they are ascertainable at birth, making it possible to begin the training of the individual for his potential statuses and rôles at once. The simplest and most universally used of these reference points is sex. Age is used with nearly equal frequency, since all individuals pass through the same cycle of growth, maturity, and decline, and the statuses whose occupation will be determined by age can be forecast and trained for with accuracy. Family relationships, the simplest and most obvious being that of the child to its mother, are also used in all societies as reference points for the establishment of a whole series of statuses. Lastly, there is the matter of birth into a particular socially established group, such as a class or caste. The use of this type of reference is common but not universal. In all societies the actual ascription of statuses to the individual is controlled by a series of these reference points which together serve to delimit the field of his future participation in the life of the group.

The division and ascription of statuses with relation to sex seems to be basic in all social systems. All societies prescribe different attitudes and activities to men and to women. Most of them try to rationalize these prescriptions in terms of the physiological differences between the sexes or their different rôles in reproduction. However, a comparative study of the statuses ascribed to women and men in different cultures seems to show that while such factors may have served as a starting point for the development of a division the actual ascriptions are almost entirely determined by culture. Even the psychological characteristics ascribed to men and women in different societies vary so much that they can have little physiological basis. Our own idea of women as ministering angels contrasts sharply with the ingenuity of women as torturers among the Iroquois and the sadistic delight they took in the process. Even the last two generations have seen a sharp change in the psychological patterns for women in our own society. The delicate, fainting lady of the middle eighteen-hundreds is as extinct as the dodo.

When it comes to the ascription of occupations, which is after all an integral part of status, we find the differences in various societies even more marked. Arapesh women regularly carry heavier loads than men "because their heads are so much harder and stronger." In some societies women do most of the manual labor; in others, as in the Marquesas, even cooking, housekeeping, and baby-tending are proper male occupations, and women spend most of their time primping. Even the general rule that women's handicap through pregnancy and nursing indicates the more active occupations as male and the less active ones as female has many exceptions. Thus among the Tasmanians seal-hunting was women's work. They swam out to the seal rocks, stalked the animals, and clubbed them. Tasmanian women also hunted opossums, which required the climbing of large trees. . . .

The use of age as a reference point for establishing status is as universal as the use of sex. All societies recognize three age groupings as a minimum: child, adult, and old. Certain societies have emphasized age as a basis for assigning status and have greatly amplified the divisions. Thus in certain African tribes the whole male population is divided into units composed of those born in the same years or within two- or three-year intervals. However, such extreme attention to age is unusual, and we need not discuss it here. . . .

In the case of age, as in that of sex, the biological factors involved appear to be secondary to the cultural ones in determining the content of status. There are certain activities which cannot be ascribed to children because children either lack the necessary strength or have not had time to acquire the necessary technical skills. However, the attitudes between parent and child and the importance given to the child in the family structure vary enormously from one culture to another. The status of the child among our Puritan ancestors, where he was seen and not heard and ate at the second table, represents one extreme. At the other might be placed the status of the eldest son of a Polynesian chief. All the *mana* (supernatural power) of the royal line converged upon such a child. He was socially superior to his own father and mother, and any attempt to discipline him would have been little short of sacrilege. I once visited the hereditary chief of a Marquesan tribe and found the whole family camping uncomfortably in their own front yard, although they had a good house built on European lines. Their eldest son, aged nine, had had a dispute with his father a few days before and had tabooed the house by naming it after his head. The family had thus been compelled to move out and could not use it again until he relented and lifted the taboo. As he could use the house himself and eat anywhere in the village, he was getting along quite well and seemed to enjoy the situation thoroughly.

The statuses ascribed to the old in various societies vary even more than those ascribed to children. In some cases they are relieved of all heavy labor and can settle back comfortably to live off their children. In others they perform most of the hard and monotonous tasks which do not require great physical strength, such as the gathering of firewood. In many societies the old women, in particular, take over most of the care of the younger children, leaving the younger women free to enjoy themselves. In some places the old are treated with consideration and respect; in others they are considered a useless incumbrance and removed as soon as they are incapable of heavy labor. In most societies their advice is sought even when little attention is paid to their wishes. This custom has a sound practical basis, for the individual who contrives to live to old age in an uncivilized group has usually been a person of ability and his memory constitutes a sort of reference library to which one can turn for help under all sorts of circumstances. . . .

14 THE CONCEPT OF SOCIETY: THE COMPONENTS AND THEIR INTERRELATIONS
TALCOTT PARSONS

The . . . classification of four highly general sub-systems of human action—the organism, personality, social system, and cultural system—is an application of a general paradigm which can be used throughout the field of action, and which I shall use below to analyze social systems. This paradigm analyzes *any* action *system* in terms of the following four functional categories: (1) that concerned with the maintenance of the highest "governing" or controlling patterns of the system; (2) the internal integration of the system; (3) its orientation to the attainment of goals in relation to its environment; (4) its more generalized adaptation to the broad conditions of the environment—e.g., the non-action, physical environment. Within action systems, cultural systems are specialized around the function of pattern-maintenance, social systems around the integration of acting units (human individuals or, more precisely, personalities engaged in roles), personality systems around goal-attainment, and the behavioral organism around adaptation (see Table 14–1).

The Concept of the Social System

Since the social system is made up of the interaction of human individuals, each member is *both actor* (having goals, ideas, attitudes, etc.) *and object* of orientation for *both* other actors and himself. The interaction system, then, is an *analytical aspect abstractable* from the total action processes of its participants. At the same time, these "individuals" are also organisms, personalities, and participants in cultural systems.

From Talcott Parsons, *Societies: Evolutionary and Comparative Perspectives,* © 1966. Reprinted by permission of Prentice-Hall, Inc., Englewood Cliffs, New Jersey.

Because of such interpenetration, each of the other three action systems (Culture, Personality, Behavioral Organism) constitutes a part of the environment—or, we may say *an* environment—of a social system. Beyond these systems are the environments of action itself, standing above and below the general hierarchy of factors that control action in the world of life. These relationships are depicted in Table 14–1.

Below action in the hierarchy stands the physical-organic environment, including the sub-human species of organisms and the "nonbehavioral" components of human organisms. This is a particularly important boundary of action because, as humans, we know the physical world *only* through the organism. Our minds have no direct experience of an external physical object unless we perceive it through physical processes and the brain "processes" information about it. In their psychologically known sense, however, physical objects are aspects of action.

In principle, similar considerations apply to the environment above action—the "ultimate reality" with which we are ultimately concerned in grappling with what Weber called the "problems of meaning"—e.g., evil and suffering, the temporal limitations of human life, and the like. "Ideas" in this area, as cultural objects, are in some sense symbolic "representations" (e.g., conceptions of gods, totems, the supernatural) of the ultimate realities, but are not themselves such realities.

A fundamental principle about the organization of living systems is that their structures are differentiated in regard to the various exigencies imposed upon them by their environments. Thus the biological functions of respiration, nutrition-elimination, locomotion, and information-processing are bases of differentiated organ-systems, each of which is specialized about the exigencies of certain relations between the organism and its environment. We will use this principle to organize our analysis of social systems.

We will consider social systems in their relations to their most important environments. I will contend that the functional differentiations among the three sub-systems of action other than the social—the cultural system, the personality system, and the behavioral organism—and the articulation of two of them with the two environments of the entire action system, constitute very major references for analyzing the differences among social systems. That is, my analysis will be developed on the basis of the fundamental system-and-environment relations of Table 14–1.

In the functional terms of our paradigm, the social system is the *integrative* sub-system of action in general. The other three sub-systems of action constitute principal environments in relation to it. In the analysis of societies or other social systems, then, the above principle can be applied. We will see that three of the primary sub-systems of the society are functionally specialized around their inter-relations with the three principal environments of a social system, each relating most directly to one of these environments. Each of these three societal sub-systems may also be considered a distinct environment of the sub-system which is the society's integrative core. We will employ this *dual* application of the functional paradigm throughout the exposition of our general theoretical scheme, and in the analysis of particular societies in the body of the book.

Table 14-1 SUB-SYSTEMS OF ACTION

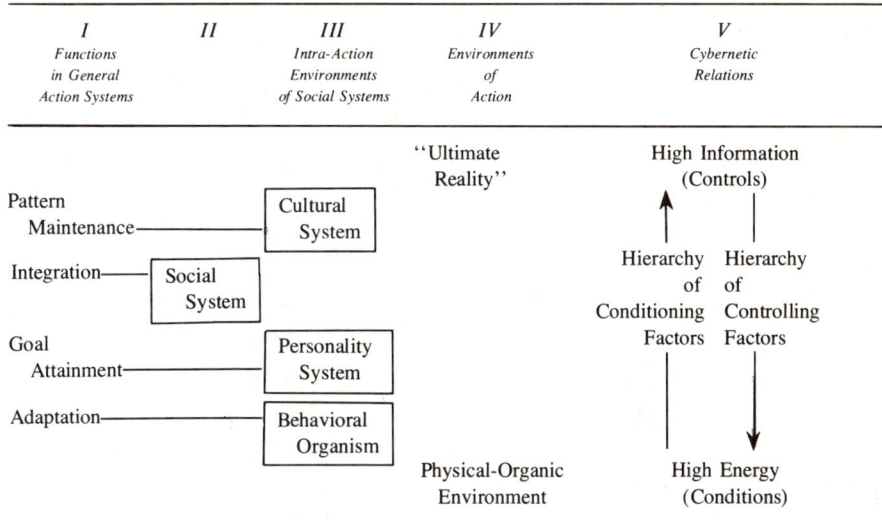

Table 14-1 presents the main relations between the social system and its total system of environments in terms of the functional scheme we have used. Column I lists the functional categories, interpreted here at the general action level. Column II singles out the social system from the others according to its integrative functions within the action system. Column III lists the other three primary sub-systems of action as immediate (i.e., as intra-action) environments of the social system. Column IV presents the two environments within which action systems function—at least so far as they are distinguished here—namely, the physical-organic environment, relations with which are mediated in the first instance through the behavioral organism, and the environment we have called "ultimate reality," relations with which are mediated through the constitutive symbol systems (i.e., religious components) of the cultural system. Finally, Column V indicates the two directions in which factors exert their effect on these systems. The upward-pointed arrow indicates the hierarchy of conditions, which at any given cumulative level in the upward series is, in the common formula, "necessary but not sufficient." The downward-pointed arrow designates the hierarchy of controlling factors, in the cybernetic sense. As we move downward, control of more and more necessary conditions makes the implementation of patterns, plans, or programs possible. Systems higher in the order are relatively high in information while those lower down are relatively high in energy.

The Concept of Society

In defining a society, we may use a criterion which goes back at least to Aristotle. A society is a type of social system, in any universe of social systems, which attains the highest level of self-sufficiency as a system in relation to its environments.

This definition refers to an abstracted system, of which the other, similarly abstracted sub-systems of action are the primary environments. This view contrasts sharply with our common-sense notion of society as being composed of concrete human individuals. Organisms and the personalities of members of the society would then be internal to the society, not part of its environment. We cannot argue the merits of these two views of societies here. But the reader must be clear about the usage in this book.

With this understanding, the criterion of self-sufficiency can be divided into five sub-criteria, each relating to one of the five environments of social systems—Ultimate Reality, Cultural Systems, Personality Systems, Behavioral Organisms, the Physical-Organic Environment. The self-sufficiency of a society is a function of the balanced *combination* of its controls over its relations with these five environments and of its own state of internal integration.

We have referred to a hierarchy of control which organizes the interrelations of the analytically distinguished systems. This includes the *cybernetic* aspect of control by which systems high in information but low in energy regulate other systems higher in energy but lower in information (Table 14–1, column V). Thus, a programmed sequence of mechanical operations (e.g., in a washing machine) can be controlled by a timing switch using very little energy compared with the energy actually operating the machine's moving parts or heating its water. Another example is the gene and its control over protein synthesis and other aspects of cell metabolism.

The cultural system structures commitments vis-à-vis ultimate reality into meaningful orientations toward the rest of the environment and the system of action, the physical world, organisms, personalities, and social systems. In the cybernetic sense, it is highest within the action system, the social system ranking next, and personality and organism falling respectively below that. The physical environment is ultimate in the *conditional,* as distinguished from the organizational, sense. Insofar as physical factors are not controllable by the cybernetically higher-order systems, we must adapt to them or human life will disappear. Human dependence on oxygen, food, tolerable temperatures, and so on, are very familiar examples.

Because of our wide evolutionary perspective, our major concern among the non-social sub-systems of action will be with the cultural system. Because they develop over long periods and under widely varying circumstances, forms of social organization emerge which have increasingly broad adaptive capacities. In their broad characteristics, they tend to become decreasingly subject to major change from narrow, particularized, conditional causes operating through specific physical circumstances or individual organic or personality differences. In the more advanced societies, the range of individual personalities may even broaden whereas the structure and processes of the society become less dependent on individual idiosyncracies. Thus we must focus on the cybernetically higher-order structures—the cultural system among the environments of the society—in order to examine the major sources of large-scale change.

15 THE CONCEPTS OF CULTURE AND OF SOCIAL SYSTEM
A. L. KROEBER AND TALCOTT PARSONS

There seems to have been a good deal of confusion among anthropologists and sociologists about the concepts of *culture* and *society* (or, *social system*). A lack of consensus—between and within disciplines—has made for semantic confusion as to what data are subsumed under these terms; but, more important, the lack has impeded theoretical advance as to their interrelation.

There are still some anthropologists and sociologists who do not even consider the distinction necessary on the ground that all phenomena of human behavior are sociocultural, with both societal and cultural aspects at the same time. But even where they recognize the distinction, which can be said now to be a commonplace, they tend to assume determinative primacy for the set of phenomena in which they are more interested. Sociologists tend to see all cultural systems as a sort of outgrowth or spontaneous development, derivative from social systems. Anthropologists are more given to being holistic and therefore often begin with total systems of culture and then proceed to subsume social structure as merely a part of culture. ("Social anthropology" perhaps represents a secession within anthropology that inclines to prefer the sociological assumption.)

Our objective in the present joint statement is to point out, so far as methodological primacy is concerned, that, either of these assumptions is a preferential *a priori* and cannot be validated in today's state of knowledge. Separating cultural from societal aspects is not a classifying of concrete and empirically discrete sets of phenomena. They are distinct systems in that they abstract or select two analytically distinct sets of components from the same concrete phenomena. Statements made about relationships within a cultural pattern are thus of a different order from those within a system of societal relationships. Neither can be directly reduced to terms of the other; that is to say, the order of relationships within one is independent from that in the other. Careful attention to this independence greatly increases the power of analytical precision. In sum, we feel that the analytical discrimination should be consistently maintained without prejudice to the question of which is more "important," "correct" or "fundamental," if indeed such questions turn out to be meaningful at all.

It is possible to trace historically two successive analytical distinctions that have increased this analytical precision. It might be suggested that the first differentiation was a division of subject-matter broadly along the lines of the heredity-environment distinction. In English-speaking countries, at least, the most important reference point is the biologically oriented thinking of the generation following the publication of Darwin's *Origin of Species*. Here the social scientists were concerned with defining a sphere of investigation that could not be treated as simply biological

Reprinted with permission of the authors and the American Sociological Association from A. L. Kroeber and Talcott Parsons, "The Concepts of Culture and of Social System," *American Sociological Review*, vol. 23, 1958.

in the then current meaning of that concept. Tylor's concept of culture and Spencer's of the social as superorganic were important attempts to formulate such a sphere. Thus the organism was assigned to the biological sciences and culture-society (as yet more or less undifferentiated) assigned to the sociocultural sciences.

In the formative period of both disciplines, then, culture and society were used with relatively little difference of meaning in most works of major influence. In the anthropological tradition, Tylor and Boas used culture to designate that aspect of total human social behavior (including its symbolic and meaningful products) that was independent of the genetic constitutions and biological characteristics of organisms. The ideas of continuity, creation, accumulation, and transmission of culture independent of biological heredity were the key ones. On the sociological side, Comte and Spencer, and Weber and Durkheim spoke of society as meaning essentially the same thing that Tylor meant by culture.

For a considerable period this condensed concept of culture-and-society was maintained, with differentiation between anthropology and sociology being carried out not conceptually but operationally. Anthropologists tended to confine their studies to nonliterate societies and sociologists concerned themselves with literate ones (especially their own.) It did not seem necessary to go much further. Now we believe that knowledge and interests have become sufficiently differentiated so that further distinctions need to be made and stabilized in the routine usage of the relevant professional groups. Such a need has been foreshadowed in the practice of many anthropologists in speaking of social organization as one major segment or branch of culture, and of some sociologists in discriminating such categories as values, ideologies, science, and art from social structure.

In this way a second analytical distinction has taken (or is taking) shape. We suggest that it is useful to define the concept *culture* for most usages more narrowly than has been generally the case in the American anthropological tradition, restricting its reference to transmitted and created content and patterns of values, ideas, and other symbolic-meaningful systems as factors in the shaping of human behavior and the artifacts produced through behavior. On the other hand, we suggest that the term *society*—or more generally, *social system*—be used to designate the specifically relational system of interaction among individuals and collectivities. To speak of a "member of a culture" should be understood as an ellipsis meaning a "member of the society of culture X." One indication of the independence of the two is the existence of highly organized insect societies with at best a minimal rudimentary component of culture in our present narrower sense.

Parenthetically we may note that a similar analytical distinction has begun to emerge with reference to the older concept of the organism, on the other side of the division outlined above by which the social sciences came to be differentiated from the biological. Where the term organism was once used to designate both biological and psychological aspects, it has recently come to be increasingly important to discriminate a specifically psychological component from the merely biological. Thus the term personality is being widely used as an appropriate or favored term expressive of the distinction.

To speak, then, of the analytical independence between culture and social system is, of course, not to say that the two systems are not related, or that various approaches to the analysis of the relationship may not be used. It is often profitable to hold constant either cultural or societal aspects of the same concrete phenomena while addressing attention to the other. Provided that the analytical distinction between them is maintained, it is therefore idle to quarrel over the rightness of either approach. Important work has been prosecuted under both of them. It will undoubtedly be most profitable to develop both lines of thinking and to judge them by how much each increases understanding. Secondly, however, building on the more precise knowledge thus gained, we may in time expect to learn in which area each type of conceptualization is the more applicable and productive. By some such procedure, we should improve our position for increasing understanding of the relations between the two, so that we will not have to hold either constant when it is more fruitful not to do so.

We therefore propose a truce to quarreling over whether culture is best understood from the perspective of society or society from that of culture. As in the famous case of heredity "versus" environment, it is no longer a question of how important each is, but of how each *works* and how they are interwoven with each other. The traditional perspectives of anthropology and sociology should merge into a temporary condominium leading to a differentiated but ultimately collaborative attack on problems in intermediate areas with which both are concerned.

SECTION INTRODUCTION REFERENCES* AND SUGGESTIONS FOR FURTHER STUDY

*Anderson, Robert T., 1971, "Voluntary Associations in History." *American Anthropologist* 73:209–222.

*Banton, M., 1968, "Voluntary Associations: Anthropological Aspects." *International Encyclopedia of the Social Sciences* 16:357–362.

Beattie, J. H. M., 1955, "Contemporary Trends in British Social Anthropology." *Sociologus* 5:1–14.

*Berreman, G. D., 1968, "Caste: The Concept of Caste." *International Encyclopedia of the Social Sciences* 2:333–338.

*Bohannan, Paul, 1963, "Contracts and Associations." In *Social Anthropology*. New York: Holt, Rinehart and Winston, pp. 144–163.

Fox, Robin, 1967, *Kinship and Marriage: An Anthropological Perspective*. Baltimore: Penguin.

Leach, E. R., 1954, "Introduction." In *Political Systems of Highland Burma*. London: Bellard, pp. 1–17.

———, 1961, "Rethinking Anthropology." In *London School of Economics Monographs on Social Anthropology, No. 22*. London: University of London Press, pp. 1–27.

Lévi-Strauss, Claude, 1953, "Social Structure." In A. L. Kroeber, ed., *Anthropology Today*. Chicago: University of Chicago Press, pp. 524–553.

*Lipset, S. M., 1968, "Stratification, Social: Social Class." *International Encyclopedia of the Social Sciences* 15:296–316.

Lowie, Robert H., 1948, *Social Organization.* New York: Holt, Rinehart and Winston.
Merton, Robert K., 1957, *Social Theory and Social Structure.* New York: Free Press.
Nadel, Siegfried F., 1957, "Preliminaries." In *The Theory of Social Structure.* London: Cohen & West Ltd., pp. 1–19.
Park, George, 1974, *The Idea of Social Structure.* Garden City, N.Y.: Anchor.
Parsons, Talcott, 1951, *The Social System.* New York: Free Press.
*Radcliffe-Brown, A. R., 1935, "On the Concept of Function in Social Structure." *American Anthropologist* 37:394–402.
*————, 1940, "On Social Structure." *Journal of the Royal Anthropological Institute* 70:1–12.
————, 1941, "The Study of Kinship Systems." *Journal of the Royal Anthropological Institute* 71:1–18.
Simmel, Georg, 1950, *Sociology.* (Trans. by Kurt H. Wolff.) New York: Free Press.
Stern, B. J., 1930, "Concerning the Distinction between the Social and the Cultural." *Social Forces* 8:265–271.
Thompson, Richard A., 1973, "A Theory of Instrumental Social Networks." *Journal of Anthropological Research* 29:244–265.

section V

The Patterning of Culture

To most readers of this book the expression "patterns of culture" probably brings to mind the well-known book bearing this title by Ruth Benedict, which abstracts in the more or less psychologically descriptive terms Apollonian and Dionysian two pervasive modes of thought, ideal, and action of a number of preliterate societies (Benedict 1928, 1934). These patterns, according to Benedict, characterize all aspects of life of the people concerned. Her technique of organizing and coherently presenting information on ways of life is effective, as the continuing popularity of her book attests. However, the work is often criticized as being a selective presentation of ethnographic data tailored to fit a preconceived scheme of organization. Her mode of organization is one example of a general anthropological and human trend to perceive patterns or regularities of one kind or another.

Many of the readings in preceding and following sections of this book and our comments about them explicitly and implicitly concern ideas about the patterning of culture. Human adjustment to the universe characteristically sees patterns in acts, events, objects, and other phenomena, thereby making them comprehensible and suggesting courses of action to take with regard to them. This human proclivity may thus be seen as adjustive behavior. Most of the words of any language—the nouns, pronouns, adjectives, adverbs, and verbs—may be seen as patterns or abstractions that present modal meanings from groups of semantic isolates. Man has, of course, never failed to see regularities or patterns in any class of phenomena to which he has given attention and verbal labels. Single events or objects are unique, but human interpretation has found patterns in classes of things as diverse as forms of mental illness, typhoons, the atomic structure of matter, and, as an evolutionary pattern, the plants and animals of the world.

As the writings in this book clearly show, anthropological conceptions of patterns cover a wide range that derives its diversity in large part from differing goals of scholarship. The writings which follow on the subject of personality and, still more markedly, the selections concerning cognition exemplify the concern with patterns; and the concepts of patterns vary in accord with the goals or subjects of study. The pioneer anthropologist Edward Tylor saw culture as a distinctive category of phenomena (a pattern) and also saw it as a system (also a pattern), a view which is generally found among anthropologists today. Many other views of culture which have already been discussed present concepts of cultural subsystems, such as religious, economic, and social systems, and readings in other sections of this book present information on the range of these kinds of interpretations. As we have also seen, these views of culture as a system or a number of levels of subsystems hold in common certain basic ideas—of relationships among elements, congruence of elements, and incongruence of elements—that prevail in any science making use of the concept of system. Although seldom so labeled, these views of culture may also be called patterns in the sense that they consist of cohering regularities of one kind or another, such as the repetitive and recurring arrangement of traits.

Our special concern in this section is with the regularities that have frequently been called "patterns" by their formulators. The scope of such patterns extends from relatively simple categories of culture to complexes of categories of various kinds. These are formulations that may be described as having primary goals of organizing or classifying. As such, they are probably seldom regarded by professional anthropologists as having great theoretical import in interpretations of the dynamics of culture, how its parts enmesh and how it changes and evolves. They are nevertheless fundamental and necessary tools of interpretive scholarship in anthropology, quite as the taxonomy of plants and animals of the world as formulated by Linnaeus was a preliminary interpretation necessary for Darwin's later formulation of his theory of biological evolution. Simply as an organizing scheme, for example, the concept of culture area is necessary to put order into the presentation of data; the instructor in anthropology attempting to give a course on Indians of North America would find it difficult or impossible to proceed without use of this formulation of pattern. The selection from A. L. Kroeber which follows concerns principally classificatory patterns of culture which have had lasting utility in anthropology. The selection by Clyde Kluckhohn similarly concerns classifications of cultural elements but goes farther in concerning the patterning of values and discussing "uniform modes of relationships between things" on the overt and covert levels.

16 PATTERNS
A. L. KROEBER

Patterns are those arrangements or systems of internal relationship which give to any culture its coherence or plan, and keep it from being a mere accumulation of random bits. They are therefore of primary importance. However, the concepts embraced under the term "pattern" are still a bit fluid; the ideas involved have not yet crystallized into sharp meanings. It will therefore be necessary to consider in order several kinds of patterns. We may call these provisionally the universal, the systemic, the societal or whole-culture, and the style type of patterns.

The Universal Pattern

The *universal pattern* was proposed by Wissler, with the alternative designation of "the culture scheme." It is a general outline that will more or less fit all cultures. It is therefore fundamentally different from the other kinds of pattern, since these all apply either to particular cultures or only to parts of cultures. The universal pattern consists of a series of nine heads under which all the facts of any culture may be comprehended. The nine heads are: Speech, Material Traits, Art, Knowledge ("mythological" as well as "scientific"), Religion, Society, Property, Government, and War. These subdivide further, as desirable. Thus under Society, Wissler suggests marriage, kinship, inheritance, control, and games; under Material Traits, food, shelter, transport, dress, utensils, weapons, and industries; Government is divided into political forms and legal procedures.

It is apparent at once that this universal pattern with its heads and subheads is like a table of contents in a book. It guides us around within the volume rather than giving us the essence or quality of it. Except for minor variations, the universal pattern is in fact identical with the table of contents of most books descriptive of a culture, such as a standard ethnographic report on a tribe. The main heads are conventional captions for those classes of facts which common sense and common experience lead us to expect to be represented in every culture. We know of no people without speech, food habits, artifacts, property, religion, society, and so on. We can say therefore that these captions represent a sort of common denominators found in all cultures, and that the universal pattern consists merely of the series of these common denominators expectably represented in any culture—represented perhaps very variably but represented somehow.

It is evident that the greater the range of cultures considered, and the more diverse these are, the more will the universal elements or common denominators shrink or become vague. The proportion of universal or common traits in the total range becomes less and less as this total grows more diverse, while at the same time the concepts corresponding to the captions have to be increasingly stretched to

---

Abridged from *Anthropology*, 2nd edition, by A. L. Kroeber, copyright 1923, 1948 by Harcourt Brace Jovanovich, Inc. and reprinted with their permission.

accommodate the facts or traits. Thereby the most characteristic features of each culture get blurred out. The Yurok, and again the Ifugao, have a highly intricate legal system, but a minimum of political institutions—in fact it might be argued whether they properly have any. This is certainly an interesting situation in that it differs so radically from our own culture, where not only both law and government are highly developed but law is made to depend on government or to derive from it. This characterizing distinction, which is obviously significant for the understanding of Yurok or Ifugao culture, and almost certainly significant also for understanding our own culture better—this and similar distinctions are lost in the degree that one does one's describing in terms of the common denominators of the universal pattern.

This universal pattern thus boils down to a rough plan of convenience for a preliminary ordering of facts awaiting description or interpretation. No one seems to have developed the idea since it was set forth in 1923, or to have made serious use of it toward deeper understanding. We will therefore pass on to other kinds of patterns.

Systemic Patterns

A second kind of pattern consists of a system or complex of cultural material that has proved its utility as a system and therefore tends to cohere and persist as a unit; it is modifiable superficially, but modifiable only with difficulty as to its underlying plan. Any one such systemic pattern is limited primarily to one aspect of culture, such as subsistence, religion, or economics; but it is not limited areally, or to one particular culture; it can be diffused cross-culturally, from one people to another. Examples are plow agriculture, monotheism, the alphabet, and, on a smaller scale, the *kula* ring of economic exchange among the Massim Melanesians. What distinguishes these systemic patterns of culture—or well-patterned systems, as they might also be called—is a specific interrelation of their component parts, a nexus that holds them together strongly, and tends to preserve the basic plan. This is in distinction to the great "loose" mass of material in every culture that is not bound together by any strong tie but adheres and again dissociates relatively freely. As a result of the persistence of these systemic patterns, their significance becomes most evident on a historical view.

As we mentally roam over the world or down the centuries, what is impressive about these systemic patterns is the point-for-point correspondence of their parts, plus the fact that all variants of the pattern can be traced back to a single original form. . . .

The exclusive-monotheistic pattern is Hebrew-Christian-Mohammedan. The three religions are outgrowths of one another and originated in a small area of southwestern Asia. The pattern comprises a single deity, of illimitable power, and exclusive of all others; so far as there are other spiritual beings, such as angels or saints, they are derivative from him; the deity is proclaimed by a particular human vessel inspired by the deity; and worship according to this revelation excludes and forbids any other worship. Cults and philosophies outside these three organized monotheisms have repeatedly attained to monotheism, or to a pantheism or a henotheism that would be hard to distinguish logically from monotheism. And many religions, even of backward peoples, recognize a supreme deity. But all these others regularly lack some of the features of the exclusive-monotheistic pattern, and their resemblances are thus only partial covergences of an analogical type. This merely analogical similarity of these "high-god" and miscellanously monotheistic religions goes hand in hand with their diversity of origin: they are not connected with the exclusive monotheisms, nor for the most part with one another. By contrast, the three exclusive monotheisms are homologous—structurally or part-for-part similar—and they are connected in origin: Jesus was a Jew, and Mohammed took his ideas from Jews and Christians.

The systemic type of pattern accordingly not only partakes of the quality of a system, but is a specific growth. It originates in one culture, is capable of spread and transplantation to others, and tends strongly to persist once it is established. It recalls the basic patterns of structure common to groups of related animals developed from a common origin, with the original pattern persisting through all superficial modifications as they occur under evolution. For instance, the basic vertebrate pattern includes a skull with lower jaw, vertebrate column, and, above the level of the fishes, two pairs of limbs each ending in five digits. Within the range of this pattern, there is endless variation. A snake has no legs, whales and some reptiles and amphibians possess only one pair. Birds have converted the front pair into wings; seals, into flippers; and moles, into "shovels." The digits carry claws in carnivores, hoofs in running mammals, nails in ourselves. They number five in man as in the salamander, never more than four in birds and in pigs, three in the emu, two in the ostrich and the cow, one only in the horse—not counting nonfunctioning vestiges. Not one of the thousand of species of amphibians, reptiles, birds, or mammals ever possesses more than two pairs of limbs or more than five digits; any six-fingered vertebrate is an individual malformation. . . .

In fact, the peculiar interest of these systemic patterns is that, within the endless kaleidoscope of human culture, they allow us to recognize things that are actually related in origin as against things that appear similar but are not connected in origin. The patterns differentiate homologies from analogies, the biologist would say. Thus, the several examples of exclusive monotheism are both homologous and historically interconnected through derivation of one from the other. But the Chinese Heaven, the Indian Brahma, the Egyptian Aten, "god" in the abstract of the Greek philosophers, the supreme deities of many primitive religions, represent analogies or convergences. They are distinct, separate developments which led to results that seem similar. And so, Egyptian hieroglyphs, Mesopotamian cuneiform, Indus Valley, Mayan, and other ancient ideographic or mixed systems of writing, and the surviving Chinese system are like alphabets in that they function as more or less effective methods of visible-speech communication. But they are like them only in that functioning. All alphabets are genetically one—derived from a single source;

the other methods of writing have separate sources, operate on different principles, are built on different plans. They resemble alphabets as a whale does a fish—both communicate or swim—but without genuine similarity of structure or meaningful relationship. But alphabet resembles alphabet as whale and porpoise and dolphin resemble one another.

It is in the working-out of these real relationships, structural and genetic relationships as against mere functional similarities, that the recognition of culture patterns of the systemic type finds one of its chief uses.

Total-Culture Patterns

Next, there are patterns that relate to whole cultures. There is an Italian, a French, a British pattern or form of European civilization. There is an Iroquoian, Algonkin, and Siouan aspect or facies of North American Indian Woodland culture. This Woodland culture in turn has its own larger total pattern, which, together with the Southeastern, Southwestern, North Pacific Coast, Mexican, and other patterns make up the still larger native North American pattern. It is evident that we are here dealing with culture wholes, not, as in the last section, with specific complexes or systems that form only part of any one culture but can be grafted onto others.

East is East and West is West, Kipling said in vivid allusiveness to the different physiognomies or qualities of Occidental and Asiatic civilizations. When he added that never the twain shall meet, he was technically overstating things, in that civilizations do borrow and learn from each other, do assimilate or "acculturate"—which fact he was perfectly aware of when he went on: "But there is neither East nor West, Border, nor Breed, nor Birth, when two strong men stand face to face." But the "never-meeting" is also a poetical way of saying that civilizations are vast things like great ocean currents flowing past each other, and perhaps of implying that the sets or trends of civilizations as wholes vary profoundly, quite apart from the sum total of the items which make up their content. Civilizations differ in "configuration," in modern scientific jargon; "spirit" would have been an earlier word, "genius" before that. . . .

A spirited depiction of the total pattern of any culture possesses much the same appeal and interest as a portrait by a good painter. Some cultures, like some faces, are more interesting than others, but all can be given an interest and meaning by the hand of the skilled master. This gift of "seizing" character, with its suffusion by insight, admittedly partakes as much of the faculties of the artist as of those of the scientist. Excellent delineations of culture patterns have in fact been presented by nonanthropologists, by historians and travelers. . . .

A requisite for the recognition of the whole-culture type of pattern, besides of course insight and articulateness, is willingness to see a culture in terms of itself, of its own structure, values, and style. There must be an interest in the culture for its own sake. Without this, the depiction tends to degenerate into a recital of oddments, or of those features in which the culture's standards differ from our own—to its own worsening, of course. The disengagement from the biases and values of the describer's own culture should be complete, at least for the time being. Such preconceptions should never block his sympathies for the culture he is describing, where its qualities call for sympathy. Of course the account must not be a laudation, but an appraisal of what the culture's own standards and valuations are, and how far they are adhered to.

This process is akin to recognition of style in art; to "appreciation" in the stricter sense of that word, before it acquired its popular meaning of mere liking. There too we do not judge Michelangelo by the standard of Rodin, or Mozart by that of Shostakovich; nor, for that matter, Shostakovich by the values of Mozart, though unconsciously that is what conservatives may tend to do. What is in question in such endeavors is the recognition of the art of a certain region and period as expressed by its best exponents, the evaluation of how far it achieved its aims, and the definition of what these aims and values were. Attempts to recognize and define whole-culture patterns are of the same kind, but are larger in that they try to grasp the totality of styles—the nexus of social, ethical, intellectual, and economic as well as aesthetic styles or manners which together constitute the master pattern of a culure. . . .

Style Patterns

The basic reason for the concentrations of productivity seems to be that for things to be done well they must be done definitely, and definite results can be achieved only through some specific method, technique, manner, or plan of operations. Such a particular method or manner is called a *style* in all the arts, as we have seen. And "style" is perhaps the best available word that will cover also the corresponding methods or plans in other activities. We can speak of styles of governing, of waging war, of prosecuting industry or commerce, of promoting science, even of speculative reasoning. For instance, all modern Occidental business is carried on in a style that includes banking and credit. But ancient and Byzantine and Islamic businessmen necessarily followed a quite different style or pattern because they did not seriously employ credit, and actual money had usually to be collected or moved for any and all transactions. A style, then, may be said to be a way of achieving definiteness and effectiveness in human relations by choosing or evolving one line of procedure out of several possibles ones, and sticking to it. That means, psychologically, that habits become channeled, facility and skill are acquired, and that this skill can then be extended to larger situations or to somewhat altered ones. This process may mount for a while, the original skill itself being developed farther or giving rise to subsidiary ones. Or it may mount through enlargement of the field to which it is being applied, and therewith the product achieved perhaps increases in quantity as well as improving in quality. But the process cannot go on mounting indefinitely, because it began with a limitation of choice, a selection among possibilities. Therefore every style is necessarily pre-limited: it is an essential commitment to one manner, to the exclusion of others.

Accordingly it cannot encompass everything. The range of its channeled skills will extend so far; beyond, they fail. Then we say that the style has exhausted itself, its characteristic pattern has broken down. Or the style may be able to maintain itself for a while, but without any longer increasing the range of its control or improving its achievements. When this termination has been reached, accordingly, there is either decline or a freezing. The style either loses its skill of touch and its products deteriorate; or it becomes frankly repetitive, which is usually equivalent to a slowed-up deterioration, interest and feeling having been lost when further change is eliminated. A pickup in quality will normally be possible only with a new start toward a new style. And the evolution of a new style is likely to be easier to outsiders or novices than to the group which has been reared in an old style. That is why nations replace one another in their achievements; or if one does repeat, it is usually after a considerable interval.

This course of development will be familiar to anyone who has ever followed through the history of any art style, whether in literature, sculpture, painting, architecture, or music. It is a commonplace that all aesthetic styles rise and fall and perish. All art has constantly to get itself reborn with a new set of impulses, and then run a new course. Why that is so is what has just been set forth. But, as has also been just said, the arts are by no means something wholly set apart from the rest of civilization. The same principles of style or method, and therefore of pulsation, tend to hold for most or all cultural activities except the basic day-by-day and year-by-year repetitive ones like plowing and reaping, making a living, cooking and eating, marrying and dying. And even in these day-by-day activities, style patterns do intrude: we certainly have changing styles of cookery—usually dignified as cuisines; of marrying—early or late, for love or convenience, and so on; of funerals and corpse disposals. However, let us consider a cultural activity that is obviously neither of the repetitive kind nor aesthetic, one that passes as cumulatively progressive: science. . . .

In much the same way, the style of ancient Greek science as a whole and the style of European science are distinguishable. The Greeks observed, but without instruments and without standard measures; and they did not experiment. These aids to the prosecution of science were developed only after A.D. 1500, as part of the western-European method of science. Galileo's trials with bodies falling from the leaning tower of Pisa were made about 1590. The telescope, invented in Holland in 1608, was used for astronomical discovery by Galileo within two or three years. The microscope was almost simultaneous. Since understanding of the subtler forms of energy and of the qualitative properties of matter seems to depend on systematic experimentation, the basic discoveries in electromagnetism and chemistry were made still later, about 1750 to 1800, after the modern European pattern or style of science was becoming mature.

We can assume, then, that the higher values of human civilization tend to be produced in bursts or spurts of growth. This is because their achievement is dependent on the development of specific methods or styles somewhat similar in kind to styles in art; and, like art styles, it is limited or exhaustible. Further progress, beyond the potentialities of a given style and pattern, normally requires a pause, followed by a fresh start with a new style or pattern—a new approach to the problem, we might say. This principle seems to apply almost equally to aesthetic activities, to intellectual ones, to politico-military or national fortunes, and even to major economic achievements. At any rate, such related items as machine versus manual manufacture, mass production, and credit suggest that industrial progress can also be due to the fact that a "style pattern" has been devised.

Basic Pattern and Style Variability

Dress obviously is heavily involved in the matters under discussion. The first association of many women to "pattern" is likely to be the paper model from which dresses are cut and shaped. Vulgarly, the word "style" refers to dress first of all; and it is certainly plain that dress in general is heavily conditioned by style. But beyond all this, dress excellently exemplifies even basic pattern and its influence.

For instance, Occidental civilization, Ancient Mediterranean, and East Asiatic are each characterized by a distinctive, long-term basic pattern of clothing. In comparison with our fitted clothing, Greek and Roman clothing was draped on the body. While this statement is not wholly exact, it is true comparatively. Sleeves were little developed, trousers lacking, the waist of clothing was not fitted in to follow the body, the general effect accentuated the fall of drapery and flowing line. The Roman toga was a wrap-around blanket. One did not slip into it like a coat, one adjusted it to hang in proper folds. . . .

Of course dress is notoriously subject to fashion change. But it is remarkable how virtually all changes of fashion, alike in Classical, Western, and East Asiatic costume, have consistently operated each within the basic dress pattern of its own civilization. Fashion creates a thousand bizarre forms and extravagances; but it never has produced, among Occidentals, a man's type of dress based on toga instead of trousers, nor a woman's with a Japanese silhouette. The matter of fashion changes, which represent a minor sort of restless and anonymous innovation or invention, is discussed elsewhere, with emphasis on a concealed rhythm or regularity much greater than the participants in a fashion are ordinarily aware of. But there is another aspect of fashion change—what may be called the intensity of its alteration, its momentary degree of variability—that both defines the basic pattern and helps to explain variation from it. Variability is high when the fashion of one year differs considerably from that of the year before; it is still more so when a series of particular dresses, all of the same year, differ considerably from one another. Low variability of course is marked by small differences of this sort. Such variabilities are easily expressed statistically.

The underlying fashion swings or trends change what might be called the total silhouette of dress rather than its details. These minor features may come and go quite rapidly, and are what give the impression nearly everyone has that dress fashions are highly unstable. On the contrary, the total silhouette shifts rather steadily for perhaps fifty years toward one extreme of proportion, such as a narrow skirt for women, and then for about fifty years toward the opposite, giving a wavelength of close to a century for the periodicity, which seems to be adhered to with fair consistency in case after case.

It might be thought that the basic pattern (for Occidental women's dress during the last hundred and fifty years) would lie somewhere between these proportion extremes. Occasionally it does. But mostly the basic pattern proves to coincide with one of the extremes. The other extreme then represents a sort of opposition or aberration from the pattern. One might describe these aberrant extremes as the proportions still just inside the pattern but as far away as possible from its center of gravity. Or one might say the aberrant extreme is antithetical—almost perversely antithetical—to the ideal or saturation point of the pattern, though still barely remaining within its range. Thus, as the permanent Western pattern aims at amplitude from the hips down but slenderness above, the silhouette-extremes conformable to the pattern would be: full or wide skirt, long or low skirt, narrow waist, and therefore waistline just at the waist proper. The antithetical extremes would be: narrow skirt, short skirt, wide or full waist, and waistline moved from the anatomically narrowest part up toward the broader breast or down toward the broader hips. In this last proportion—position of the waistline—pattern saturation evidently falls at the midpoint between extremes. In the three other proportions, pattern saturation coincides with one of the extremes. . . .

This example may make more concrete the role of patterns—both style patterns and total-culture patterns—in cultural change and stability. Not that patterns are the beginning and end of everything about civilization. But practically everything in culture occurs as part of one or more patterns. Hence whatever happens in the way of accomplishment, alteration, succession, or persistence in any culture is likely to happen through the mechanism of patterns. We do not yet know too much about them, because awareness of patterns is relatively recent in anthropology. But it is already clear that understanding of culture as something more than an endless series of haphazard items is going to be achieved largely through recognition of patterns and our ability to analyze them.

17 PATTERNING AS EXEMPLIFIED IN NAVAHO CULTURE
CLYDE KLUCKHOHN

All cultural behavior is patterned. This is merely a way of saying that many things which an individual does and thinks and feels may be looked upon not merely from the standpoint of the forms of behavior that are proper to himself as a biological

Reprinted by permission of the University of Utah Press from Clyde Kluckhohn, "Patterning as Exemplified in Navaho Culture," in Edward Sapir et al., eds., *Language, Culture, and Personality*, Sapir Memorial Publication Fund, 1941.

organism but from the standpoint of a generalized mode of conduct that is imputed to society rather than to the individual. . . . "Pattern" is a very popular word with contemporary American anthropologists. Unfortunately it has come to be used with considerable looseness of reference. In particular, confusion has resulted from the circumstance that "pattern" has been used to designate both (a) specific modalities of ideals and behavior, and (b) generalized configurations which structure widely varying contexts of culture content. Professor Sapir hinted on more than one occasion that "pattern" and "configuration" were concepts of a different order of abstraction, and put forward other terminological suggestions toward the more precise description of various types of patterning. The purpose of this essay is to follow out and elaborate systematically the leads given by Sapir. In view of the present confusion let us begin *de novo* with two examples.

Introductory

In my field notes are the reports of one or more interviews with 46 different Navaho informants on the subject of witchcraft. In all save 3 cases it is recorded that before the informant for the first time actually gave me some anecdote or bit of the cultural theory on witchcraft he or she remarked "I don't know—I just heard about it." The fact that 43 out of 46 informants uttered the same form of words (translated in precisely the same way—except for pronouns—by 8 different interpreters) makes it clear that we are here dealing with what Professor Sapir has called a "generalized mode of conduct" (in this case linguistic conduct, of course). So striking is the trend to uniformity that we are likely to label the response a "verbal reaction *pattern*." The content of the statement is (approximately) a disavowal of participation in witchcraft and even of direct observation of it. Clearly this content could have been expressed by a variety of linguistic symbols, arranged in a variety of ways. The remarkable fact is that only one of the wide range of potentialities is actualized. The content which the informant communicates is *patterned* in its expression.

Walter Dyk's *Son of Old Man Hat* has for me an overpowering imaginative reality. For me it utterly lacks that necrotic aroma which I find pervasive in the disembodied accounts of most ethnological publications (including my own!). When I read *Son of Old Man Hat* it is as if I were actually hearing living Navahos talk. Now let me leave this slightly romantic exultation in the material to ask coldbloodedly the question: what are the concrete stimuli which provoke in me this extraordinary sense of authenticity? Undoubtedly *one* source is the circumstance that Dyk's interpreter used exactly the same clichés in translating Navaho into English as have numerous interpreters of mine. For example, when the sense is that a person ought to avoid persons, animals, or objects, the preferred English verb is "bother." "Don't bother your wife." (Usually with the meaning: don't have sexual intercourse with your wife). Similarly: "Young boys shouldn't bother the girls." When a helper in a chant was being sent out to gather materials used in the bath a part of the instructions given him was translated, "Then bring it right back to me—don't bother horses, sheep, or herders on the way." Now "avoid" is admittedly far too literary a word to expect as a translation of the Navaho verb in question, but "keep away from," "don't go near," "stay away from," and other words and circumlocutions would be distinctly congruent with the vocabulary of these interpreters. Indeed those I have mentioned are also heard but, in my experience, they are most significantly rarer than "bother." Since the interpreters come from widely separated areas of the Navaho country, went to different schools or learned their English from different whites for whom they worked, the tendency to prefer the term "bother" cannot be set down simply to emulation of a European model. It is evident that here again we have to do with a *patterning* of linguistic expression.

Indeed I was astonished to discover that—with very occasional and trivial substitutions—I could parallel whole groups of sentences as recorded by Dyk with sentences dealing with the same topic as translated by my interpreters. All linguistic material appears to be rich in illustrations of patterning. Conceptions of patterning used in anthropology seem to have been much influenced by linguistics.

Linguistic Concepts in Anthropology

In a period when even some natural scientists considered the systematic study of humanity as fruitless because of the complexities involved or actually denounced it as contravening the conception of God-given free will, the success of comparative philology, perhaps more than any other single fact, encouraged students of man to seek for regularities in human behavior. . . . Even today, though the dialect geographers in Germany and the United States have challenged the *Ausnahmslösigkeitsprinzip* of Brugmann and the rest, the uniformities of phonetic change remain, I think, one of the most striking of human phenomena, the astonishing nature of which we now tend to overlook because the facts are so familiar and accepted.

Equally exciting, if one can look at them with at all fresh eyes, are the implications of phonemes, the principle of phonemic configuration, and Zipf's establishment of "k constant." These discoveries further demonstrate that at least linguistic human behavior is structured to the point where prediction (minimally, in a statistical sense) is possible. Thus, in Navaho, so soon as a single voiceless lenis stop was identified the betting odds became enormous that other sounds in the stop series would turn out to conform to this pattern. Navaho speech organs are physically capable of producing sounds of "b" type as voiceless lenis consonants, sounds of "d" type as voiceless fortis, sounds of "g" type as sonants, etc. But such random actualization of the physical possibilities is just simply not characteristic of actual phonetic systems.

Professor Sapir very early drew explicit attention to the applicability of "prediction in terms of pattern" to nonlinguistic aspects of culture: "The value to social sciences of such comparative study of languages . . . is that it emphasizes the extraordinary persistence in certain cases of complex patterns. It is in virtue of pattern conservatism that it is often possible to foretell the exact form of a specific cultural phenomenon." Undoubtedly it is awareness of "pattern" (often subliminal) which sometimes enables the field worker to "know" how his natives will react to a set of circumstances before he observes the reaction. Familiarity with the Navaho "pattern" of generalized economic reciprocity between clansmen justifies my anticipation that, if a Navaho journeys into a portion of the Navaho Reservation which he has not visited before and where he has no acquaintances, he will seek out a hogan belonging to someone in his (or occasionally his father's) clan and there obtain lodging and food. Observation shows that this is factually the course of action followed in 13 cases out of 15. In one case, however, a man elected to camp alone; in another he looked for a family of whom a friend had told him. Statistically, the prediction was validated. The student of Navaho ceremonialism similarly can attend a chant which he has never before witnessed and have a relatively concrete idea of what is coming next at any given point.

A number of Sapir's articles, but particularly his *Unconscious Patterning of Behavior in Society* and *The Concept of Phonetic Law,* indicated how the concept of "pattern" might be transferred from linguistics to anthropology. An example where the data are primarily verbal but where the reference goes beyond the narrowly linguistic will bring out particularly clearly what is involved. The Navaho have been shown to possess unequivocally the sensory capacity for distinguishing between "blue" and "green." It is also true that when the occasion arises they will distinguish (by compound phrases) between the two. However, the basic fact remains that in general they refer to colors which we would designate as "blue" and "green" by a single Navaho word. This seems to me strictly analogous with a linguistic example of Sapir's: ". . . the naive Frenchman confounds the two sounds 's' of 'sick' and 'th' of 'thick' in a single pattern point—not because he is really unable to hear the difference, but because the setting up of such a difference disturbs his feeling for the necessary configuration of linguistic sounds." Just as the Frenchman fails normally to distinguish what are to us two sounds (though he can do so), so the Navaho normally fails to distinguish what are to us two colors (although once again he can do so).

The Nuclear Conception of Pattern

What is the conceptual core of the category of patterning? The key is the characteristic which Sapir has predicated of speech and culture in general: "inhibition of the randomness of instinctive behavior." So far as organic potentialities are concerned a given act can be carried out, an idea stated, or a specific artifact made in a number of different ways. But in all societies the same mode of disposing of many situations is repeated over and over. There is, precisely, "inhibition of the randomness of instinctive behavior." A determinate organization prevails.

Structure, therefore, is the foremost constituent in the nuclear idea of pattern. The reference is predominantly to form, not content. But a cultural pattern is not merely a structure—it is a structure to which there is some degree of conformance on the part of a number of persons. "Pattern" preserves what is probably historically its dominant meaning "something to be copied." Pattern, then, in its most general meaning is a *structural regularity.* Such conceptions are necessarily conscious constructs, abstractions.

While the conceptual nucleus of "pattern" is clear enough, the serviceability of the term is impaired at present by usage in a variety of disparate ways, by being made, in general, to cover too wide a range of phenomena. Sapir has well described the situation:

> There are certain terms that have a peculiar property. Ostensibly, they mark off specific concepts, concepts that lay claim to a rigorously objective validity. In practice, they label vague terrains of thought that shift or widen with the point of view of whoso makes use of them, embracing within their gamut of significances conceptions that not only do not harmonize but are in part contradictory.

To escape the imprecisions and contradictions inherent in describing the phenomena unsystematically we need a whole hierarchy of concepts. It is convenient, however, to have one word which will designate in inclusive fashion the existence of structuralization (to which there is some degree of conformance in word, or deed, or both) in a range of data. It is suggested that *patterning* is an appropriate designation for this broadest category. We might, for instance, have occasion to speak of "the patterning which exists in Navaho ceremonialism." This is, to be sure, a somewhat loose usage. No distinction is made between the patterning observed in the overt culture and that which is inferred in the covert culture; the ideal and the behavioral is merged; levels of abstraction are not differentiated. But there are contexts in which these finer discriminations are unnecessary. It may, for example, be only pertinent to point out that the Navaho chant system is not quite so stupendously complex as the very large number of named chants would imply. In this connection it is quite sufficient to draw attention to the omnipresence of *patterning* in the system.

But if this broad basic concept is to be usable with a minimum of confusion and with something approaching precision, its territory must for some purposes be divided up among a number of related auxiliary concepts, the terrain of each of which is roughly staked out with reference to general level of abstraction and other differentiae. To accomplish that end without creating further confusion we must first specify certain delimitations of our interest. The behavior of one individual is often demonstrably distinguished from that of another individual (even one who occupies approximately the same ascribed and achieved statuses) in the same society by "patterns" which are characteristic of him as a personality. It might be well, as Sapir has hinted, to reserve the term "personal habit system" for this class of patterning, but in any case we shall deal only with what Hallowell has called "cultural variables" (as opposed to "individual variables"). Hence we shall also not consider the effects of cultural patterning upon the "psychology" of the individual, a question which Goldenweiser has briefly discussed. We shall likewise disregard the part which patterning plays in cultural dynamics and the historical and psychological origin of "patterns." In short, we limit ourselves to the task of providing definitions and classifications suitable to describing phenomena of patterning *statically*. . . .

From the point of view of level of abstraction the most basic distinction in phenomena of patterning is between specific modalities of ideals and behavior (such as the helical design of planted fields) and generalized configurations which structure widely varying contexts of culture content (such as the principles of "imitative and contagious magic"). These are conceptually such different orders of phenomena that if we were to insist on designating both as "patterns" we ought to follow Korzybski and speak of Pattern$_1$ and Pattern$_2$ respectively. Pattern$_1$ is a determinate relationship of various highly concrete pattern-parts. It is inevitably tied to a particular culture content. It is a regularity (a mode) in the structuring of that content in that culture and as such is a portion of the *overt* culture (to borrow a useful conception from Linton). Pattern$_2$ is not tied to only one bit of culture content. It approaches the polarity "concept of pure structure." Of phenomena of Pattern$_2$ there is minimal *articulate* awareness on the part of the culture carriers. These are the "patterns" of the *covert* culture and, to avoid confusion, we shall call them *configurations*. Patterns are specifically oriented; *configurations* have a more generalized orientation. A *configuration* is reducible to a "principle" which is, so to speak, "behind" the structural regularities of the overt culture, which "accounts for" two or more specific patterns.

Patterning of Overt Culture: Patterns

It is suggested, then, that the technical term *pattern* be rigorously restricted to phenomena of patterning of the *overt* culture. This conforms to the usage which is older and more firmly established in anthropology where the reference has more frequently been to rather concrete and specific modalities of stylization. We can further delimit the concept *pattern* in an oblique way: by contrasting it with other technical terms used in anthropology. The imminent anthropological critic would, at this point in our discussion, be perfectly justified in objecting: "You say that 'pattern' is 'a generalization of behavior or of ideals for behavior.' Well, so is a 'custom' and so, often, is a 'trait.' I can think of certain concrete examples which could be equally well called 'customs,' 'traits,' or 'patterns.' Aren't these all just synonyms?"

The distinctions are not perfectly clearcut and satisfactory from an existential or philosophic point of view. That is, the same set of facts of behavior could *in certain cases* justifiably be symbolized by any one of the three words. The *empirical* definition (as opposed to definition from the point of view of traditional philosophy) of concepts rests fundamentally on the use for which they are purposed. When one calls a given set of facts a *pattern* one is looking at the facts from a different point of view than when one calls the same set of facts a "custom" or a "trait"—one is purposing a different sort of analysis.

We can properly say "According to Navaho custom one shakes hands less frequently than in our society." There is no doubt that the behavioral reference is to acts and statements which also constitute a pattern of great interest. It is equally true that both "pattern" and "custom" imply some degree of social restraint tending to produce some conformance on the part of culture carriers. But "custom" accentuates the habitual angle, the "givenness" of the phenomena; pattern the interrelationship of pattern-parts, the fact that one part of the pattern presupposes the others. "Custom" indicates that our attention is upon the usualness, the repetitiveness; is, so to speak, merely upon the *regularity;* while "pattern" implies that our interest is in the *structural* regularity. Sapir has pointed out another subtlety of differentiation. The term "custom" is not altogether purely denotative and objective;" it "has a slightly affective quality indicated by the fact that one uses it more easily to refer to geographically remote, to primitive or bygone societies than to one's own."

As for "trait" and "pattern" there is again unquestionably some overlap between the two concepts. "Pattern" looks more to structure, "trait" more to content. When we talk of "patterns" our question is not primarily: what observable features, what items, traits, and trait complexes appear in this culture? The focus of our question is: what is the arrangement of discrete bits of cultural content? This is, however, not an "all or none" distinction. Indeed we have expressly reserved an entirely different term for the concept which embraces those aspects of patterning which approach the *purely* structural. The difference here is once again primarily that of emphasis. When one speaks of "matrilocal residence" as a trait of Navaho culture, one is mainly interested in the existential import of the various items into which the trait may be decomposed. That is, we are concerned about a discrete set of facts: married daughters with their children remain at the home of their mother; each married daughter (except sometimes in the case of sororal polygyny) usually has her own house, etc. The interrelationships of these isolable facts are secondary from the point of view of the anthropologist who is operating with traits and items. To the anthropologist who is operating with patterns, however, the item is (to paraphrase Sapir) conceived not as a separable unit but as a point in a pattern. When one speaks of matrilocal residence as a pattern one is singling out the circumstance that the parts of the pattern bear a determinate, not a haphazard relationship to one another.

Moreover—not perhaps as a matter of theory, but demonstrably as a matter of practice—the central meaning which is communicated by "trait of matrilocal residence" tends to be limited to only a very few of the items into which the trait could be resolved. Some Berkeley anthropologists have used "traits" in cultural analysis more intensively than any group of anthropologists working in the United States at the present time. In one of their recent publications I find the trait "patrilocal residence" is broken up into only the following items: first residence patrilocal, final (permanent) residence patrilocal, husband's parents' house, own house. To the anthropologist dealing in patterns a much more extensive analysis is obligatory. "The Navaho pattern of matrilocal residence" is indeed a highly elliptical way of referring to a whole network involving such things as the presence of a kinship terminology where a distinction is made between mother's and father's relatives, nursing and care of each other's children by sisters, economic cooperation.

On a trait list "matrilocal residence" among the Navaho and among the Hopi appears as an equivalent. As soon, however, as "pattern" comes into the picture one is careful to differentiate between "the Navaho pattern of matrilocal residence" and "the Hopi pattern of matrilocal residence. "Nor can "trait" and "pattern" be reduced to synonyms on the basis that if the decomposition into items proceeded far enough we should have everything which was present in a complete statement of the pattern. The interest would still be in the discrete items as such, not in their phrasing. Besides, in some cases one can show that exactly the same items of content enter into two different patterns. The order in which the items appear in action may be different; the same item may have a different time duration in the two instances; the same item may in the one case be typically associated with manifestations of affect which are lacking in the other or there may be some other differentiating emphasis.

"Pattern" is today almost invariably restricted to describing the relations between persons or between persons and things. Material culture entities are referred to only as "traits." An arrow is never a "pattern." Actually the arrangement of items in a Navaho arrow is patterned. Navaho arrows bear the imprint of patterning which distinguishes them from Hopi arrows as much as the various patterns which structuralize Navaho dances, in which impersonators of supernaturals participate, distinguishes them from the corresponding Hopi dances. But it is significant that it is a terminological convention to call the one and not the other a "pattern." That is, it is preferred to keep the localization of pattern manifestation in persons, not things.

Ideal and behavioral patterns

Do "patterns" refer to cultural theory or to cultural practice? If I speak simply of "the Navaho pattern that helpers at chants are from the patient's family or clan" it is quite likely that this will be interpreted in two importantly different ways. One group of readers will infer that this is an expected form, enjoined by the ideals of Navaho culture. As a matter of fact, this is not the case. More than 30 informants stated the ideal pattern as "anyone can help." Another group of readers will infer merely that this pattern is the statement of a behavioral modality. In this instance this happens to be factually the correct interpretation. When confronted with concrete facts, 11 informants showed that they recognized the behavioral tendency but made their feeling plain that this "generalized mode of conduct" was not culturally prescribed but arose out of geographical circumstances and other factors of convenience.

On the one hand, a trend toward uniformity in the cultural conception of how a person *ought* to behave in a given situation may be evidenced by regularities of statement and/or manifestations of approval by word and deed. On the other hand, the structural regularity may be of the indicative rather than of the optative or imperative modes—Sapir's "generalized mode of conduct" conceived not as a thematic way in which the culture carriers are *supposed* to respond but as a thematic way in which they do behave in fact. The differential of *ideal pattern* is that one is trying to describe what people would do or say in a defined situation if they conformed completely to ideals accepted in the culture. For purposes of statement of the ideal pattern the degree to which the actual relevant behaviors deviate from the ideal does not matter. On the other hand, in a behavioral pattern the focus of attention is precisely upon some mode of what people do in fact do. A *behavioral pattern* is nothing more nor less than a stylized set of behaviors observed as one modal way of meeting a specified situation. The center of interest here is not upon a standard to be achieved but rather upon a central tendency in a range of behavioral dispersion. It is true, of course, that each conception is to some extent dependent upon the other. As I have heard Professor Linton point out, an ideal pattern which (in a non-literate culture) failed for a long period to serve in any sense as a model for actual behavior would almost inevitably sooner or later cease to be a part of the culture (unless perhaps perpetuated through ritualized verbalization). Similarly, behavioral patterns imply standards of selectivity in most cases. Nevertheless the necessity for a distinction is not just for the sake of conceptual neatness. If an anthropological writer refers to a "pattern" (meaning but not specifying an *ideal pattern*) and certain of those who use his material operate as if he had been talking about a behavioral pattern, inferences are drawn which are more than casually misleading.

Much of the criticism which has been directed against Ruth Benedict's *Patterns of Culture* is based upon the premise that she is talking about behavioral patterns. It is said that she has not counted cases to establish the statistical norms of behavior; that she has in some cases neglected anecdotal and other material in the literature which does not fit her leading ideas, and so forth. But close study of her work makes it fairly plain that she is not so much interested in an inductive analysis of how the Zuñi, for example, do in fact behave as in suggesting a relationship between accepted standards of behavior in Zuñi (*"ideal patterns"*) and cultural *configurations* of which the Zuñi are largely unconscious. The "selected detail of behavior" is presented not toward an inductive demonstration of behavioral pattern but only as the behavioral counterpart of an ideal pattern or as an exemplification of the influence of configuration. It seems unfortunate that this is not explicit in her text.

Idea and action patterns

The dichotomy between ideal patterns and behavioral patterns is partly analogous to that Sapir has made between "idea patterns" and "action patterns." There is, however, a nuance of difference which appears to me important and which leads me to prefer Linton's terms as major categories. "Idea" and "action" suggest that the one class of patterns is manifested only in words, the other only in deeds. The distinction between linguistic and other types of behavior is of course one of which the social scientist should never lose sight. But some recent thinkers have given to this distinction an emphasis which seems exaggerated and calculated to obscure the fact that linguistic *behavior* is inescapably a form of behavior. If one Navaho calls another "son of a coyote" and the epithet is obviously not bestowed in friendly jest, this bit of linguistic behavior is quite likely to find a place in a chain of events similar to that which would be initiated by a physical blow. The first patterns to which we called attention were patterns of linguistic behavior. It is sometimes enlightening to contrast such patterns with patterns observed in non-linguistic action. But in our basic terminology the contrast to be underlined is the contrast between those patterns which are "morally" given high value by the culture carriers and the corresponding thematic regularities of behavior (whether in word or in deed).

That the ideal patterns are not arrived at by abstraction from verbal behavior only is shown by the fact that a shake of the head, a disapproving look, a sudden departure are often essential elements in the observer's building up his conception of the ideal pattern. Conversely, an example will show that *idealized* and *ideological* patterns are not necessarily coterminous. Navaho informants agree that uninitiated children *ought* to believe that the masked impersonators are actually the supernaturals themselves. This is the ideal pattern. But of the 23 Navaho children to whom I have talked on the subject only 5 failed to manifest awareness of the impersonation. Most of these had never seen a chant in which masked men take part. But their "idea," their "belief" was: the dancers in Night Way, etc., are just men wearing masks. This is a structural regularity in the realm of ideas—an idea pattern. But it is unmistakably not the same thing as what Navaho children are *supposed* to believe in this connection. There are approved ideas as well as approved deeds. Hence an idea pattern may be either an ideal pattern or a behavioral pattern.

Awareness of patterns

It is well to remind ourselves of the wide variation in awareness of patterns as such on the part of both the culture carriers and observers. As Sapir has said: "Forms and significances which seem obvious to an outsider will be denied outright by those who carry out the patterns; outlines and implications that are perfectly clear to these may be absent to the eye of the onlooker."

In some cases informants will give quite articulate verbal statements of both types of pattern. The incidence of discrepancy between ideal and behavioral patterns is very high in Navaho culture at the present time—as in most rapidly changing cultures. The conflict between old and new ideas, between traditional and altering modalities of action, tends to bring the contrast of ideal and behavioral patterns into full consciousness for the culture carriers. If you ask an informant who is presenting the ideal pattern of our last example, "Well, do the children really believe this?", almost all of the replies are of the type: "Not many do any more;" "Very few do these days." In fact many informants will volunteer remarks of this kind (as a commentary upon the "degeneracy" of the times) without being specifically questioned. The same thing, however, is true of some instances which need not be connected with acculturation. While the ideal pattern prescribes that a man's wife should not (except in certain defined circumstances) object to his taking a second wife, the observer soon realizes that the Navaho are quite aware that resistance and quarreling bulk very prominently in the apposite behavioral pattern. In other words, in these cases the ethnographer could get from interview material not only statements of the ideal patterns but also descriptions of the behavioral patterns which would not differ markedly from that which he would get by abstracting in an inductive analysis of the relevant behaviors. . . .

By definition, the culture carriers must have some sort of awareness of an ideal pattern. But this does not imply that the ideal pattern will always be stated in an articulate, abstract form. In some realms of culture this polarity is indeed consistently approached. In fact—particularly in the case of ethnographers who have worked with but a few informants—it is almost exclusively the ideal patterns which make up our accounts of some cultures. With respect to some patterns this may matter practically very little, for the goodness of fit between ideal and behavioral pattern is in certain instances almost perfect. In Navaho culture the ideal patterns for mother-in-law avoidance and avoidance of physical contact on the part of siblings of opposite sex (as stated by informants) and the behavioral patterns (as abstracted from observation) are almost identical among Navaho who are little acculturated. But much depends on the extent to which patterns of both types are formalized. The degree of consciousness ranges widely and is indicated by the extent to which one or more highly concrete features of the action are singled out as "right" or "wrong" or, on the other hand, by the extent to which an unspecific indignation or a vague uncomfortableness is manifested toward the action in general. . . .

Subsidiary concepts

Informants who are discussing the behavior proper to a singer during a chant make it clear that the singer is expected to maintain one of several stylized positions while singing. All of these are ideal patterns within the ceremonial ideology. It is recognized that a given singer tends to follow the pattern which his teacher follows but all have equal value status in the cultural ideology. They are *alternative* ideal patterns. In other words, one must not confuse *ideal patterns* with "preferred patterns." For some behavioral networks the Navaho seem to recognize but a single ideal pattern. At the ideal level the pattern is regarded as compulsory and therefore we well may speak of a *compulsory* ideal pattern. In many other cases a number of different traditional solutions are approved. Thus the following ideal patterns prevail with respect to sex: sororal polygyny, non-sororal polygyny, monogamy, transvestite homosexuality. On the whole, the evidence indicates that sororal polygyny was in a sense a *preferred ideal pattern,* but all of the patterns were certainly part of the system of ideal patterns. In cases where one ideal pattern is simply the ideal most frequently expressed (without there being any implication that it is singled out as the object of idealized preference) *typical ideal pattern* suggests itself as an appropriate designation. Hill's data and mine both indicate that transvestite homosexuality was considered a proper solution for some individuals only, and hence it would perhaps be well to call such a pattern a *restricted ideal pattern*.

Ideal patterns, then, may be subdivided into *compulsory, preferred, typical, alternative,* and *restricted* when the context demands such a precise specificity. Always, however, care must be exercised to speak of the ideal pattern only when one is either contrasting a particular ideal pattern with the corresponding behavioral pattern or when one unequivocally means a compulsory ideal pattern. Since there is often more than a single locus around which the data relating to culturally idealized ways of handling a situation pile up, the word "mode" was designedly used in discussing the evidence on the ideal patterns of marriage limitation. For in attempting to define both ideal and behavioral patterns, one's conception is operationally much closer to "mode" than to "mean" or "median."

If we were to attempt to obtain a mean average from the facts and state *the* ideal pattern, we should often have either to accept a form of statement which was cumbersome and imprecise or to neglect the minor mode or modes entirely and, with calm disregard of quite a number of facts, consider the major mode as *the* ideal pattern. While the major mode is likely to be the most representative single value in such material, most cultures (since their historical and biological origins have been highly heterogeneous) will strongly tend to give bi-modal or multi-modal distributions with respect to many of their ideals and behaviors. And a single mode is a notoriously unsatisfactory description of any unsymmetrical curve. If the trend of the distributions were pronouncedly regular in the direction of flatness (in which case the mean would doubtless be the most representative value) this fact would in itself signify unpatterned ideals or behaviors.

It is convenient to distinguish the behavioral patterns by names which are different from those used to categorize the ideal patterns. "Compulsory," for instance, plainly refers to a standard of value and only in the case of an extraordinarily well integrated culture or a culture where the external sanctions were uncommonly efficiently enforced could behavioral patterns empirically be characterized as "compulsory." Conversely, one hardly expects the ideal pattern system to encompass patterns which are *disapproved* or *prohibited*. There can be cognizance of such patterns in the *idea* patterns of the culture but not in the *ideal* patterns. Disapproved and prohibited patterns are inevitably behavioral patterns. For example, adultery is not recognized in the ideal patterns of Navaho culture. Behaviorally, however, adultery is common and the carrying out of adulterous acts is most distinctly patterned in ways of which Navaho are rather explicitly aware. Prostitution has likewise (at least at some times and places) been a disapproved pattern of Navaho culture.

Where the anthropologist is interested only in the behavioral patterns or where he has insufficient knowledge of the ideal patterns, the behavioral patterns may be described simply as modalities without in any way begging the question of conformance to the corresponding ideal patterns. *Major behavioral* pattern will serve as a label for a behavioral mode which is unequivocally the major mode of a set of correlative patterns. *Minor behavioral pattern* is suggested for those modes which are definitely minor. When the interest is in conformance and the necessary information is available, *conformant* and *deviant* behavioral patterns may be distinguished. The two sets of terms must not be regarded as synonyms, for in a changing culture it will be found very frequently that the deviant patterns are also the major behavioral patterns.

Pattern assemblages and sub-patterns

We have now proposed an horizontal dichotomy (with possible internal subdivisions) of the patterns of the overt culture. This classification was based upon what I believe to be the conceptually central distinction of ideal and behavioral patterns. It remains to set forth a vertical sub-classification which applies equally well to both ideal and behavioral patterns, but is designed to assist in keeping our levels of abstraction straight. For this purpose I propose using Sapir's terms *pattern assemblage* (to designate a complex of patterns associated with a major cultural function) and *sub-pattern* (to isolate the more concrete patterns within a broader, more general pattern).

In the *pattern assemblage* which centers on marriage there are, on both the ideal and behavioral levels, a host of patterns which interact with each other in a complex state of mutual interdependence. A few of these, labeled according to the outstanding feature of content, are: limitation of choice by clan exogamy, etc.; economic and other qualifications of prospective spouses; role of the relatives in arranging the marriage; the actual marriage ceremony; polygyny; interference of biological and clan relatives in the married life of the couple; mother-in-law avoidance. All of these save the last-named and perhaps "marriage ceremony" can be broken down into various *sub-patterns*.

For example, "qualification of spouses" includes a sub-pattern relating to the virginity of a girl at marriage. On the ideal level this sub-pattern is made up of (at least) the following *pattern-parts*: (1) a girl should be a virgin at her first marriage; (2) a young man's first wife should be a virgin; (3) if a girl is known not to be a virgin, this rightly affects her prospects in general; (4) the gifts of the groom's family may properly be less valuable where the girl has lost her virginity; (5) if a groom finds that his bride is not a virgin (and this is her first marriage) he is justified in returning her to her parents and demanding a return of the marriage gifts; (6) the marriage ceremony ought to be held only over a girl who is a virgin. On the behavioral level the "role of relatives" pattern encompasses such sub-patterns as consulting or informing various relatives, arrangement of economic exchanges between the two families, a particular relative acting as a go-between. (Here, for brevity, I have again used "labels" rather than specifying pattern-parts in detail.) The pattern of polygyny may be resolved into the sub-patterns of sororal polygyny, non-sororal polygyny, mother-daughter (by another marriage, of course) polygyny.

In each of these cases a particular behavioral sub-pattern tends to be (in one locality at a given time) the major one. Among the corresponding ideal sub-patterns *preferred*, *alternative*, and other forms are distinguishable. Thus the preferred ideal sub-pattern is that the mother's brother (now among some groups the father) should be the go-between; "any relative" is, however, an alternative ideal sub-pattern. It is also to be noted that the same sub-pattern may appear in more than one pattern and the same pattern in more than one pattern assemblage. Thus the pattern of clan exogamy and preference is a component of the pattern assemblage structuralizing the marriage activity and also of the pattern assemblage clustering around the role which clan plays in Navaho culture. And into the assemblage which defines the status of "singer" in Navaho culture enter a number of sub-patterns and patterns which are familiar in other pattern assemblages.

Discussion

The terminology for classifying and describing structural features of overt culture shows crude correspondence with Linton's terminology for the content of culture. Thus *item* and *pattern-part*, *sub-pattern* and *trait*, *pattern* and *trait-complex*, *pattern-assemblage* and *activity* tend in a very general way to be correlative conceptual hierarchies suited to describing approximately the same behavioral phenomena *from different angles of interest*. The parallelism must not be pushed too far or interpreted too rigidly. Thus, from the point of view of logical coherence one *could* distinguish sub-patterns within "arrangement of economic exchanges." Moreover, whether one treats "marriage ceremony" as "pattern" or breaks it up into "sub-patterns" or again whether one considers mother-daughter polygyny an independent sub-pattern or merely a set of pattern-parts in the non-sororal polygyny sub-pattern is altogether a matter of empirical convenience.

The choice therefore must not be phrased as being between "no classification" and "a classification which works in every concrete instance without a hitch." It is a question of having a terminology which affords an ordering of the data roughly consistent with the factual range of levels of abstraction and which permits classification as coarse or as fine as the purpose in hand suggests. In certain rather general discussions or in treatments where patterning is of only incidental interest the anthropologist might justifiably utilize only a few of the conceptual differentiations which have been made here. On the other hand, an intensive analysis of all the structural details of a body of cultural material would require all of the concepts and perhaps others. For example, in a complete description the degree of flexibility of particular patterns would need to be specified.

Patterning of Covert Culture: Configurations

To phenomena of patterning in the *covert* culture it is proposed to apply the term *configuration* as a master concept comparable to "pattern" in the overt culture. The contrast between these two master concepts can best be seen through a consideration of concrete data from which examples of both can be abstracted. At a time when I was naive enough to suppose that I could get substantial bodies of anecdotal material on witchcraft from Navaho who knew me only casually, I approached 11 persons independently with the request that they tell me what they knew about witchcraft. In 7 cases the first verbal response which I received to my preliminary remarks was "Who told you that I knew about witchcraft?" Here plainly is a trend toward a structural uniformity. The presentation of the stimulus, "Tell me what you know about witchcraft," is not followed by a random assortment of responses: "I don't know anything about it;" "Why do you want to find out about witchcraft?" "That is a very dangerous thing to talk about; I can't do it;" "How much will you pay me if I tell you about witchcraft?" This past summer (with no expectation of learning anything substantial about witchcraft as such, but purely for purposes of this experiment) I repeated the question—with a standardized technique of presentation—to 25 informants. In 16 cases almost identical verbal responses were manifested. They varied only in this fashion: "Who told you to talk to me about witchcraft?" "Who said I knew anything about witchcraft," and "Why do you come to me to ask about this—who told you I knew about it?" Here we have a behavioral pattern of the overt culture, for the structure consists in a determinate interdigitation of linguistic symbols as a response to a verbal (and situational) stimulus.

Suppose now, however, that we juxtapose this and other behavioral patterns which have no extrinsic interconnection. Unacculturated Navaho are uniformly careful to hide their faeces and to see to it that no other person obtains possession of their hair, nails, sputum, or any other bodily part or product. They are likewise characteristically secretive about their personal names. All three of these patterns (as well as many others which might be mentioned) are manifestations of an abstracted *configuration* which may be intellectualized as "fear of the malevolent intentions of other persons." Only most exceptionally would a Navaho make this abstract generalization, saying, in effect, "These are all ways of showing our anxiety about the activities of others." Nevertheless, this principle does order all sorts of concrete Navaho behaviors and, although *covert*, is as much a part of Navaho culture as the overt pattern of verbal symbols. Similarly, I have never heard "distrust of extremes" verbalized as an overt part of Navaho ideology. In terms of this covert configuration, however, one can understand such patterns as the Navaho tendency to project accusations of witchcraft against persons who are either very poor or very rich. One more example: if any one of the concrete pattern-parts of the "spirit outlet" (a break in design found in weaving, pottery, basketry, etc.) is missing or "wrong" in any respect, Navaho are sensitive to the pattern transgression. But of the configuration as such there is minimal awareness. Configurations are Sapir's "unconscious system of meanings," Benedict's "unconscious canons of choice."

Possibly *sub-configuration* would serve to designate the more specific entities into which a configuration may sometimes be resolved. I have noticed that the replies which an ethnographer receives when he asks questions about various ceremonial subjects which the Navaho show reluctance to discuss are not *verbally* patterned as are those in the case of questions about witchcraft. The responses seemed to take such a wide variety of verbal forms that even an experienced observer could hardly hope to predict in any significant way. I tried this experimentally the past season (using the same 25 informants as in my experiment on witchcraft). While 6 of the 10 arrangements of words which entered into my predictions did occur (in approximately the same form) one or more times in the answers, 5 replies which had not appeared at all in my predictions were given, and in only 2 cases out of 25 did a particular informant make the response predicted specifically of him. While no *verbal pattern* was manifested, there was nevertheless a consistency in the "intent" of the replies, for all showed a disposition to "hedge," to make excuses for not directly answering my questions. It was put as a matter of other engagements, of insufficient pay, of doubt as to my motives, etc. This negativistic pattern may be associated with behavioral patterns toward strangers who travel in the Navaho country and with other behavioral patterns. The principle configurating these patterns may be phrased as "suspicion of any outsider." This, however, is surely but a special instance, a sub-configuration, of the configuration "anxiety as to the activities of others," of which "distrust of extremes" would seem to be another sub-configuration.

A pattern is a generalization *of* behavior or of ideals for behavior. A configuration is a generalization *from* behavior. Both patterns and configurations are thus abstractions. They are not the actual behaviors. For, as Sapir so tenaciously insisted, culture is not behavior—it is an abstraction from behavior. Thus when we abstract the behavioral pattern "sibling-of-opposite sex avoidance" we pay attention to things of this sort in our field notes: "X did not hand the cup directly to his sister, Y. He put it on the ground between them." "Whenever I could hear the conversations at the 'squaw dance' I noted that each man who asked a girl to dance inquired her clan first." We neglect for operations of arriving at the behavioral pattern many details of the specific situations in which the actual behaviors in all their concreteness are imbedded in everyday life. We disregard the observation in our notes that at the moment when the brother put the cup on the ground the sister was wearing a turquoise necklace, the brother had a cold, etc. But when we abstract a configuration we depart even further from the actual behaviors. The recurrent form of words "I don't know—I just heard about it," constitutes a pattern in arriving at which, to be sure, we take each such statement out of its total context and overlook small differences in pronouns, etc. But implicit in these data and others which could be related to it is the *configuration* "Navaho tend to be scrupulous about differentiating what they have themselves seen or done from what they know merely by verbal report." Here it is plain that we are remote from even a generalized statement of the verbal behaviors from which the *pattern* was abstracted.

Any *cultural* conception is an abstraction. It is of cardinal importance that these abstractions should be based upon adequate data. Descriptions of actual behaviors (in more than anecdotal proportions) should find a place in our ethnographics and the ethnographer should provide quantitative materials in terms of which his abstractions can be controlled by the reader. But the point I wish to make here is that a configuration is a conception at a much higher level of abstraction than a pattern. Likewise, inference predominates much more in the operations of deriving configurations. To a considerable extent patterns are arrived at by simple abstraction from trends toward uniformity in statement and deed. Inference enters principally where it is a case of interpreting approval or disapproval. Configurations, on the other hand tend to be purely inferential constructs. Configuration looks to an *inner* coherence in terms of the large structuralizing principles which prevail in the *covert* culture. Patterns are forms; configurations are, so to speak, interrelationships between forms.

It is for such reasons that the term "configuration" seems appropriate. "Configuration" as a technical term in psychology carries with it the implication that "the whole is more than the sum of its parts." A pattern, however, can be defined by listing the pattern-parts in a determinate sequence (and perhaps indicating the duration or accentuation of each). A *configuration* states the principle "behind" a group of patterns—it is only implicit in them and must be inferred out. A pattern is a generalization of what people do or should do; a configuration is in a sense a generalization of "why" they do or should do certain things. Configurations are the abstract principles in terms of which patterns are themselves configurated.

It was, I think, because anthropologists have long realized that there was more to culture than its overt content that Sapir's transfer to configurational principles from linguistics was seized upon so avidly. Examples of this sort confirmed suspicions of the limitations of functional analysis: "If the plural were to be understood functionally alone, we should find it difficult to explain why we use plural forms with numerals and other words that in themselves imply plurality. 'Five man' or 'several house' would be just as adequate as 'five men' or 'several houses.' "

The substantive aspects of a culture may alter in important features, but to the observer with experience of that culture even the new overt content somehow has a familiar tone. The same holds in a synchronic plane for different sectors of the same culture. One may be attending the Navaho chant "Beauty Way" for the first time, but if one has had a fairly rich experience of other chants one feels quite at home. The sandpaintings may be quite new to one, various articles of ceremonial equipment different, many of the patterns different, yet one has a sense that—to borrow Demoulin's phrase—*"plus ça change, plus cèst la même chose."*

It is to these perdurable cultural features, the configurations (which are not dissimilar to Pareto's "residues") that Ruth Benedict has given her major attention. To follow out some of the major misunderstandings which appear to have arisen with regard to her work will further clarify our conception of configuration. Many of her critics have been guilty of the fallacy of misplaced concreteness. They have tacitly assumed that she was talking of behavioral patterns, whereas even ideal patterns enter into her schema far less than configurations. Configurations, as we have suggested, come nearer to dealing with the "whyness" than the "whatness" of a culture. We find Dr Benedict writing of "characteristic purposes" and of "the motives, and emotions and values that are institutionalized in that culture." To some anthropologists Dr Benedict has appeared to treat "pattern" as the equivalent of "the outstanding emotional principle of a culture." One hears objections of a sort which may be generalized and paraphrased as follows: "Benedict calls the dominant affects of a culture its patterns. This is a confusing procedure, for culture is, by definition, affect-less. Individuals have affect, yes—but not a culture. Culture is an abstraction from the behavior of individuals. It is illogical to impute emotion to an abstraction. Emotional expression on the part of individuals is usually patterned, but patterns are not emotions." But Benedict is not really identifying her "patterns of culture" with affects. She is attempting to describe what Talcott Parsons has called "ultimate value-attitudes." From the point of view *of the observer* configurations do constitute (largely unconscious) "motivations" for the culture carriers. The locus of emotion remains in the individual, of course, but "pattern" and "configuration" are very useful conceptual tools in attempting to dissect out the emotional structure of a society. For the behavior of individuals with respect to pattern or configuration, conformance on their own part or that of others is, typically, affective. One may generally expect neutral attitudes only toward those areas of behavior where patterning does not prevail. Hence the emotions which are most frequently expressed by the individuals of a particular society or which are characteristic manifestations in certain situations assuredly do bear a determinate relationship to pattern assemblages and configurations. It is for this reason that one finds such a pronounced association between the language of emotion and configurations in Dr Benedict's writings.

That remarkable convergence (which Professor Parsons has so magnificently documented) in social theory upon conceptions of the order of "residue," "value-attitude," and "configuration" suggests that Dr Benedict has raised for anthropologists a series of problems of the greatest significance to their science. But when she designates both types of "pattern" and more than one type of "configuration" by the same term she invites confusion. Sometimes she is talking of different principles of the covert culture; at other times she seems to have in mind a single over-summative principle: "Order is due to the circumstance that in these societies a principle has been set up according to which the assembled cultural material is made over into consistent patterns. . . ." Would it not be well to designate this broadest type of configuration by a special term, say, *integration?* Even though we recognize that "integration" is a polar concept which is seldom if ever fully realized in any culture it is a useful conception just as "health" is useful, although few higher organisms are completely normal. If there be an *integrating principle* in Navaho culture it is, I suspect, subsumed under the root *hoźą́*—. But this is only a highly provisional suggestion. The question needs intensive and extensive examination if a determination is to be arrived at inductively rather than by a kind of synthetic apperception.

Conclusion

Someone has said "The primary task of science is the detection and description of uniform modes of relationships between things." It is only in the hope that it may be an aid in this task that a somewhat involved terminology (summarized in the accompanying chart) has been set forth. But a science of human behavior could not be content with even the most perfect statement of patterns and configurations. There are too many meaningful descriptions of observable behavior which do not get into such statements. For example, one individual manifests affect in actualizing a pattern; another carrier of the same culture does not. But Professor Sapir has too brilliantly urged the necessity for studying actual behavior as well as patterns and configurations for the point to need elaboration in this volume.

Summary

Patterning—a structural regularity
    A. Pattern—structural regularity in overt culture
        1. Ideal Pattern—optative and imperative mode
            a. Compulsory ideal pattern—one only recognized
            b. Preferred ideal pattern—one usually selected
            c. Typical ideal pattern—one most frequently expressed
            d. Alternative ideal pattern—one which may be selected
            e. Restricted ideal pattern—proper for some individuals only
        2. Behavioral Pattern—indicative mode
            a. Major behavioral pattern—major mode of a set
            b. Minor behavioral pattern—minor mode of a set
                aa. Conformant behavioral pattern—conforms with ideal pattern
                bb. Deviant behavioral pattern—does not conform with ideal pattern
    AA. Pattern Assemblage—complex of patterns (activity)
        AA^1. Pattern (trait complex)
        AA^2. Sub-Pattern (trait)
            AA^3. Pattern-Part (item)
    B. Configuration—a structural regularity in covert culture
        a. Sub-Configuration—part of a configuration
    BB. Integration—guiding principle of configurations
"Idea pattern"—manifest in words—may be either ideal or behavioral
"Action pattern"—manifest in deeds—may be either ideal or behavioral.
"Custom"—emphasis on regularity (rather than structural regularity).
"Trait"—emphasis on content rather than structure (things as well as persons).
"Personal habit system"—patterns characteristic of individual as a personality.
Configuration roughly correlative with "residue," "value-attitude," "unconscious canon of choice."

SECTION INTRODUCTION REFERENCES* AND SUGGESTIONS FOR FURTHER STUDY

Barnouw, Victor, 1949, "Ruth Benedict: Apollonian and Dionysian." *University of Toronto Quarterly* 3:241–253.
*Benedict, Ruth, 1928, "Psychological Types in the Cultures of the Southwest."*In Proceedings of the Twenty-third International Congress of Americanists,* pp. 572–581.
*———, 1934, *Patterns of Culture*. New York: Houghton Mifflin.

Berrien, F. Kenneth, 1968, *General and Social Systems*. New Brunswick, N.J.: Rutgers University Press.

Bertalanffy, Ludwig von, 1962, "General Systems Theory: A Critical Review." *General Systems* 7:1–20.

Ford, Clellan S. and Frank A. Beach, 1951, *Patterns of Sexual Behavior*. New York: Harper and Hoeber.

Gillin, John, 1936, "The Configuration Problem in Culture." *American Sociological Review* 1:373–386.

Hoyt, Elizabeth E., 1961, "Integration of Culture: A Review of Concepts." *Current Anthropology* 2:407–426.

Kluckhohn, Clyde, 1943, "Covert Culture and Administrative Problems." *American Anthropologist* 45:213–229.

_____, 1946, "Review of A. L. Kroeber, Configurations of Cultural Growth." *American Anthropologist* 51:336–341.

Kroeber, Alfred L., 1919, "On the Principle of Order in Civilization as Exemplified by Changes of Fashion." *American Anthropologist* 21:235–263.

_____, 1944, *Configurations of Culture Growth*. Berkeley: University of California Press.

Kroeber, Alfred L. and J. Richardson, 1940, "Three Centuries of Women's Dress Fashions: A Quantitative Analysis." *University of California Anthropological Records* 5:111–154.

Opler, Morris E., 1945, "Themes as Dynamic Forces in Culture." *American Journal of Sociology* 51:198–206.

_____, 1946, "An Application of the Theory of Themes in Culture." *Journal of the Washington Academy of Sciences* 36:137–166.

Wissler, Clark, 1926, *The Relation of Nature to Man in Aboriginal North America*. New York: Oxford University Press.

See also references in Section VII, on cognitive systems (and their structures), and in Section XI, on functions (and structures) in culture. Other references to conceptions of pattern in culture, society, and personality are found in Sections IV, VI, IX.

section VI

Personality as Culture

Aristotle observed that man is by nature a social animal, a view with which anthropologists have always agreed. Social living requires understanding of the actions and reactions of other members of one's social group. This understanding is gained by every normal human being in the process of learning and adjustment called enculturation, that is, learning the patterned rules and symbols of one's native culture. As we mature, we learn that social norms of behavior exist, that these differ according to age, sex, and social status, and also that they differ idiosyncratically among individuals in ways that cannot be related to differences in age, sex, or social status. When our social life brings us into contact with members of foreign societies, we soon see complete sets of norms of behavior that differ from our own, varying in extent from slight to great.

Modern scholarly attempts to account for similarities and differences in human behavior have used the term *personality* to label characteristic behavior of both individuals and groups. Protoscientific explanations of the nature of personality are recorded by philosophers of classical Greece and Rome, who explained differences in the behavior of foreigners on the basis of innate qualities of temperament and differences in physical environments. The fierceness of the barbarians of the north, for example, was seen by the Romans to be a result of the harsh, wild climate in which they lived. Patterns of folk thought remaining strongly alive in most of the world today offer similar explanations of differences in personality, often laying greatest stress on presumed racial differences regarded as genetically transmitted or, in considering differences of behavior among individuals, upon genetically transmitted idiosyncracies.

The scientific study of personality is a development of the twentieth century that first became an anthropological interest in the 1930s. In view of the importance of the concept of culture in modern studies of personality, it seems surprising that anthropology was so tardy in concerning itself with this subject. As with many other topics of anthropological interest, recognition of this subject as an anthropological concern appears to have depended upon the growth of the social sciences in general, and the principal stimuli for the study of personality came from developments in psychiatry, clinical and other branches of psychology, anthropologically oriented linguistics, and sociology. The modern anthropological study of personality is then a composite with many roots, a combination which is nevertheless distinctive because of the elements which anthropology has added.

Current studies of the formation of personality, in psychiatry, social psychology, and sociology as well as in anthropology, consider many factors as influential in producing distinctive conformations of personality. These may be classified simply in four major categories, *geographical-environmental, biological* or *somatic, biosocial,* and *cultural,* to which an indefinite number of subclassifications may be added. In considering the personalities of individuals, a fifth category, *situational factors,* may be added.

The first two of these categories are recognizable as the ancient ideas once used by the Greeks, although both have undergone modification in modern times. Characteristics of the geographic environment that affect man, such as climate and mineral and nutritional resources, must of course be considered in attempts to understand human behavior, but environmental determinism—the idea that traits of personality are the result of the physical environment alone—has long been discredited.

Biological factors affecting personality include as a major component genetically inherited physical traits, but these, like the influence of the geographic environment, are no longer regarded as lone determinants of personality. Traits of the human physical makeup that affect behavior or personality are also acquired in the course of life through the joint influence of culture and other factors. Examples include obesity, slimness, malnutrition, vigor, weakness, and deliberate modifications of the body such as binding the feet of females and castrating males. These acquired physical traits may be the effects of the geographic environment or the goals of cultural practices, and they may be either planned or unplanned. However induced, these conditions are physical or biological conditions that may have important influence on behavior. Since they differ in genesis from biologically inherited physical features, this class of biological conditions is sometimes distinguished by the name of *constitutional factors*—features of the physical makeup at any given point in time, however they may have been derived, that affect personality.

As the name implies, *biosocial factors* influencing personality combine biological and sociocultural factors. They consist of any physical traits to which cultural value is attached—values such as ideas of beauty or ugliness, desirability or undesirability, and superiority or inferiority. Familiar examples are height, weight, bodily form, skin color, the form and color of eyes, nasal form, and the color, texture, and distribution of hair. This class of factors affecting personality has as yet had little study, but it seems probable that future investigations will point up their importance. From personal observation any reader can provide illustrative examples of the effects on the personalities of individuals of our own society of having physical features that are regarded as desirable or undesirable. Under modern conditions of intersocietal contact, the entire world provides abundant examples of ideas of superiority of physical features that have developed as peoples of different racial strains have come together in positions of political, economic, and military dominance and inferiority. One article on this subject (Norbeck), referring particularly to attitudes toward skin color, is included among our readings.

Situational factors influencing personality may also combine biological and cultural matters. Relating to the study of the individual rather than of social groups, these are conditions unique to individuals, such as being the eldest child or the only child, and idiosyncratic experiences of any kind. Each status in society has a different role, and no two persons holding the same status have identical experiences. Moreover, few if any roles give access to all information and events in a culture. Thus, in studying the personality of individuals, each set of conditioning factors may be seen as unique.

An additional category of influence, derived from psychiatric and psychological ideas, principally those of Sigmund Freud, bears no standardized label. These are psychic "dynamisms" said to inhere in human nature, such as the Oedipus complex and the castration complex, which are associated with human sexuality. These ideas have never been in the mainstream of anthropological studies, however, and perhaps the greatest importance of Sigmund Freud to anthropology has been through acceptance of his views of the role of the unconscious. The unconscious patterns of behavior outlined by Freud and Carl Jung are treated in a somewhat similar way by structural anthropologists such as Claude Lévi-Strauss (see Section VII). In the study of personality as well as of other subjects, anthropologists have become aware of the existence of covert as well as overt patterns of behavior.

As might reasonably be expected, the emphasis laid on particular categories of factors that influence personality reflects the general interests and goals of the individual disciplines of study. Vested scholarly interests are also evident, for example, in the human subjects selected for study by the various disciplines and the ways in which the different fields define personality. Psychiatry and much of psychology have concerned themselves with abnormal, or aberrant, individuals, with aims of providing remedial therapy. Anthropology, sociology, and, in lesser degree, social psychology have most commonly studied groups. Anthropology has given little attention to deviants from group or societal norms, whereas sociology, in accord with its traditional interest in bringing about social reforms, has studied socially abnormal (sometimes labeled alternative) as well as normal groups of people.

Definitions of personality tend to differ accordingly. Reflecting their concern with groups rather than individuals, anthropologists and sociologists most commonly define personality modally, using such names as *modal personality, basic personality structure, status personality,* and *national character.* These formulations of personality types are abstractions of the characteristic behavior of identifiable social groups, including entire societies, social classes, occupational groups, social deviants, and subdivisions by sex of these various social categories. Psychiatrists and many psychologists commonly define personality as the characteristic behavior of individuals. The numerous definitions of personality may, however, be reduced simply to the two words "characteristic behavior," to which the phrases "of an individual person" or "of a class or category of people" might be added, or inferred as additions, to represent the two trends of thought and interest in the social sciences.

Factors which influence the modal personality and the personality of the individual overlap; that is, the same categories of factors may be influential but they do not exert influence in identical ways. For example, whether acquired or innate, biological traits must be considered in attempting to understand the personality of the individual as it differs from that of other individuals. Except as they are used to formulate the mode or type, however, all individual differences, biological or cultural, are irrelevant to the interpretation of factors directly influencing the typical or modal personality. In most studies of modal personality, in fact, biological factors are regarded as constants and omitted entirely from consideration. Comparisons are often involved in studies of modal personalities, but these comparisons are not of individuals. They are instead intertypical or intersocietal.

As the preceding paragraphs illustrate, the study of personality has shown that the formation of personality is a complex process. Rather than leading to any simple explanation of the factors molding personality, research on this subject has been heuristically fertile, progressively stimulating the formulation of questions that could not have been asked at an earlier time and thus leading to new avenues of investigation. What stands out most prominently in an overall review of studies of personality is the great importance accorded to culture as a determinant of personality. Cultural anthropology might reasonably be expected to emphasize cultural factors, but it is especially noteworthy that all of the social sciences concerned with the study of personality have also given increasing attention to cultural influences, sometimes using other names. The prevailing interpretations of socially aberrant types of personality of our own society, for example, were formulated principally by social psychologists and sociologists, and these interpretations give attention almost exclusively to cultural factors that foster the kinds of behavior characterizing the types of social aberration. Criminals, alcoholics, sexual deviants, drug addicts, and juvenile delinquents are seen primarily as "the products of society," that is, as the result of certain combinations of cultural factors with unintended effects upon human life. Studies of socially normal types of personality conducted by all fields of the social sciences similarly tend strongly to reflect the anthropological view that personality is largely a mirror of culture.

Without ignoring noncultural influences on personality, cultural anthropology has seen culture as the most important category of such factors, particularly in the formation of modal or typical personalities. Largely without conscious awareness of the role of cultural anthropology in developing the concept of culture, this view has been widely accepted by other social sciences and the educated world in general. A specific contribution to the study of personality made by cultural anthropology has been indicating many categories of cultural influences, including customs of childhood socialization, cultural influences in later life, the size, composition, and nature of relationships in the family and other participatory social groups, and associated ideals, values, and sanctions.

A second major contribution, stemming from anthropological tradition, is cross-cultural research in personality. Most of the studies of personality in foreign societies and almost all such studies of primitive societies have been the work of anthropology. A summation by John J. Honigmann (1968:266–267) lists fifty-four primitive societies "for which major studies of personality are available"; a figure that may seem impressive but which, if considered in relation to the total number of societies in the world, indicates that research on personality is still in a pioneering stage. As another indication of the pioneering status of the study of personality, we may note that no systematic classification of the range of cultural factors that are thought to influence personality has met general acceptance, and few attempts have been made to formulate such a comprehensive classification.

Certain additional trends in the history of the anthropological study of personality merit attention. Early studies, conducted at a time when many of the cultural factors that are now seen to bear on personality were not discernible, sometimes presented interpretations attributing profound influence upon the adult personality to certain specific customs or sets of customs of child training, such as toilet training, nursing and weaning, and swaddling. These interpretations, inspired in large part by Sigmund Freud, have long been regarded as naive and oversimplified. The study of early socialization remains a major interest in modern studies, but the scope has long been broadened to the investigations of who, what, when, where, and how in connection with child rearing, and to dominant or pervasive attitudes, values, and patterns of thought and action that prevail in child training. Modern studies also give attention to cultural influences in the lives of adults throughout life. Reflecting the demographic trend throughout most of the world toward an increasing proportion of aged people, a small beginning has been made in the study of the aged.

As we have noted, anthropological studies of personality have abstracted modes representing whole societies or various distinguishable social classes. Some of these studies have formulated ideal personality types thought to reflect the salient themes or patterns of culture, and many others have sought to formulate modal concepts without special or exclusive regard for ideal types. Whatever the focus of study, the underlying assumption is that differences in culture produce differences in behavior and that the characteristic behavior—the personality—of members of different societies, social groups, and social statuses is distinctive.

The progress of the anthropological study of personality may be indicated by the awareness that a large and ever growing number of cultural factors that influence personality have been pointed out and comparative studies have increased in number. Future research will undoubtedly point to additional influencing factors and increase the scope of cross-cultural studies. Although consensus probably exists in the judgment that cultural experiences of childhood have the greatest influence on the adult personality, no effective techniques have yet been devised to assess with assurance the relative importance in the formation of personality of the many kinds of cultural factors that now appear to be influential.

18 THE PSYCHOLOGICAL APPROACH IN ANTHROPOLOGY
EDWARD M. BRUNER

The field that I am reporting upon here, culture and personality, is one of the most controversial in contemporary American anthropology. The reasons usually offered in explanation of the controversy are that the field is relatively new—systematic studies by psychologically oriented anthropologists were not initiated until the late 1920's—and that the early work of some of these scholars was lacking in scientific rigor. But this explanation is not entirely satisfactory.

The more fundamental reason is that culture and personality presents a seemingly irreconcilable impasse to some social and cultural anthropologists, such as A. R. Radcliffe-Brown and Leslie White, who take the position that we should study only social and cultural systems. They say that anthropologists should not be concerned with either psychology, personality, or individuals, even in a cross-cultural framework. They fear that the psychological anthropologist will offer naïve explanations of social institutions and events in terms of individual motivation—for example, that war is caused by man's aggressive instinct—without reference to the complex historical, political, and economic factors which precipitate warfare in any given instance.

The modern student of culture and personality, on the other hand, well aware of the excesses of his predecessors and of the cautions of his critics, contends that the psychological dimension is an essential component of human existence, and further, that adequate understanding of relationships among men or their cultural institutions must include statements about what goes on within an individual's mind—about what he thinks and feels—with due attention to irrational unconscious processes as well as to the rational conscious ones. It is the acknowledgment of the importance of unconscious and cognitive processes which characterizes culture and personality research.

Psychiatrists also study unconscious processes, and it was, in fact, "the encounter of anthropology . . . with psychoanalysis that gave rise to culture and personality studies." Many contemporary workers in the field today do rely upon one or another variant of the Freudian psychoanalytic model. But there are basic differences in objective and approach between psychiatry, and culture and personality. Our discipline is not a mere extension of psychology applied cross-culturally, and we are not clinically oriented, in that no attempt is made to help or cure the mentally ill. Nor are we primarily interested in any particular person in all his uniqueness; individuals are studied for the light they shed on regularities in the social process. Indeed, psychological anthropology takes as its field of investigation the study of culture as such, only it does so from a special point of view and with reference to a limited number of problems.

Reprinted from Sol Tax, editor, *Horizons of Anthropology* (Chicago: Aldine Publishing Company, 1964); Copyright © 1964 by Aldine Publishing Company. Reprinted by permission of the author and Aldine Publishing Company.

In this paper we shall examine some of the premises of the psychological approach starting with universal aspects of the human condition and ending with the analysis of specific cultures. Let us begin by viewing the origins of man and culture in evolutionary perspective. As Clifford Geertz and Clark Howell have pointed out in earlier papers in this series, the emergence of modern man from the lower animals did not occur all at once, as if by divine or legislative act, but was a slow, gradual, possibly painful process that took place over many hundreds of centuries during and even before the ice ages. In some respects, the hominization of our species is relived, or recapitulated, by every one of us and our children, as each newborn infant is slowly, gradually, and painfully transformed from an animal-like being into a more or less fully socialized adult member of some particular human society. For at birth, children have much in common with our primate ancestors in that neither can talk, love, laugh, believe in ghosts or gods, nor reflect upon themselves in relation to the larger environment that surrounds them. The frustrations and joys of childhood are, in a very real sense, the residue and inheritance of man's imperfect and incomplete biological and cultural development in the past.

I do not wish to push too far the analogy between the hominization of our species and the socialization of children, as the mechanisms involved, the time depth, and other aspects of the two processes are certainly different. A basic difference is that the genetic potential for humanization, acquired over the last few hundreds of thousands of years, is immediately present in every human infant, and the infant is ready and eager to actualize this potential in the family context. The essential similarity, however, is that evolution made us human phylogenetically and culture makes us human ontogenetically. But culture was not a gift from the gods, nor did it just grow by itself. It was achieved at great psychic cost. All of us, all humanity, past, present, and future, pay the price of civilization.

Let us be more specific about those universal aspects of a cultural mode of adaptation which exact this psychic cost. Infants are helpless at birth and immature for a relatively long period; and they are born with or soon develop aggressive, sexual, and acquisitive desires which must be controlled in the socialization process. There is no known human society in which men can kill, rape, or rob at will, and there is no known human society in which children and adults, at one time or another, and in one way or another, have not experienced such desires. Every culture must control the expression of aggression; otherwise society would be disrupted. And every culture must regulate the allocation of women and property, simply because there are never enough of these scarce commodities to satisfy everyone. Individuals who cannot adequately control their aggressive, sexual and acquisitive needs can never adjust to any human society. Persons who approach this extreme are either killed, ostracized, or placed in mental or penal institutions.

On the other hand, it is difficult to imagine a society in which all personal desires of all individuals were gratified. Such a hypothetical society would probably be without suicide, or neurosis, or crime as we know it, but it would also lack passion, creativity, and change. Our imaginary culture would, I think, be a rather dull place, inhabited by fully satisfied vegetable-like beings instead of by human beings. But to return to this, the real, world: if all the aggressive, sexual, and acquisitive needs of an individual were immediately and completely gratified, then that individual would never become fully human. We develop ego strength, self-awareness, and a sense of reality as a consequence of external controls and inhibitions. Some degree of frustration is necessary for survival and maturity.

The psychic cost to which we have referred, the inherent frustration associated with the socialization process, is even more specific. There is a necessary delay between wish and gratification, the wishes and desires themselves may be ambivalent, and cultural goals are often contradictory. Children are universally reared in a nuclear family unit or in some culturally stipulated substitute, and the transition from complete dependence upon the parents or parental surrogates to independence in the larger community is often difficult and awkward. This is so because prolonged intimate association in the family context leads to extremely complicated interpersonal bonds. From the point of view of the child, "the beloved person is the frustrating agent, and the pleasure-giving object inflicts pain." The child develops strong sexual and aggressive feelings toward one or both parents, feelings which are frequently reciprocated and which are only partially controlled by the incest taboo. Further, family units are never exact duplicates of one another. Thus what the child learns at an early age from his parents may be in conflict with what he learns at a later age from his peers.

The inherent conflict between personal desires and cultural demands is resolved in slightly different ways by each individual and by each society, although there are some universally human regularities in the process and in the techniques of resolution. One means is by a variety of unconscious defensive mechanisms. We repress culturally unacceptable desires by banning them from consciousness; we project and displace some by attributing our own desires to outsiders or to scapegoats in our own society; we deny the existence of other desires or sublimate them, thereby placing the released energy to work for the benefit of society. We may reverse incompatible wishes, for example, by expressing approval when we really feel hate, or we may direct an aggressive impulse against ourselves with a consequent loss of self-esteem.

Society provides disguised means of gratification in fantasy, literature, drama, folk tales, play, or religious ritual. Such forms of fantasy have a variety of social and individual functions, but by directing potentially harmful impulses into approved or at least acceptable channels, some measure of vicarious satisfaction is provided for the participants. Satire, cartoons, and jokes almost universally perform similar functions. For the individual, the content of dreams both reflects and expresses culturally patterned stress.

Society must, of course, directly fulfill some personal needs, but in every instance it rigidly defines the appropriate objects, goals, and techniques of gratification. Most societies carefully define those persons whom it is proper to hate, precisely specify approved sexual objects, and develop a complex series of rules regulating the acquisition of wealth and property. It is indeed remarkable how elaborate are cultural norms governing aggressive, sexual, and acquisitive aspects of human behavior.

We have some comments to make about the means of resolving the basic human conflict between personal and cultural needs. The first is that these varied mechanisms, taken together, must be investigated on the individual and on the societal level simultaneously. The nature of the problem is such that it cannot be adequately studied entirely from the perspective of individual psychology, without regard for the socio-cultural context in which the individual develops and in which his needs are expressed, nor can it be studied entirely from the perspective of the cultural system, without regard for the individual and the mechanisms he employs to adjust to his society. Neither the psychiatrist nor the cultural anthropologist alone can satisfactorily handle all dimensions of the problem within the framework of one single discipline. It is such problems that give rise to psychological anthropology, to anthropologically-oriented psychology, and to coöperative inter-disciplinary research.

Our second comment merely gives emphasis to what has already been implied. We have seen that a major function of the emergence of culture was to direct, channel, and prescribe how our aggressive, sexual, acquisitive, and other needs were to be gratified. From the point of view of our species, man is more flexible than any other animal in that his behavior is more dependent upon learning than upon biology or inherited predisposition. But this potential variability is never allowed free spontaneous expression within the boundaries of any given society. Human behavior is universally patterned by cultural norms and prohibitions. Man may be infinitely plastic but particular cultures are not. Each culture has its own special variant of what it means to be fully human and civilized, its unique ways of handling children and of socializing them, and its own model of the good life. This variety of present-day cultures and social structure proves that the human experiment is a continuing process.

The members of a society do not, of course, reconstruct or recreate their culture every generation. They are born into an existing system and they inherit a cultural tradition from their parents and elders. Psychological anthropologists are very much interested in the process by which culture is transmitted from one generation to the next. One means by which this is accomplished is through the application of social and supernatural sanctions. Children who conform to their culture are rewarded and those who do not are punished. The agents of punishment in addition to the parents may incude other relatives, neighbors, peers, teachers, or political authorities. They may utilize a variety of techniques including beatings and other forms of physical punishment, threats of bodily harm by supernatural beings, the withdrawal of food or love, and the inculcation of guilt or anxiety. As a consequence of these and other techniques the child internalizes some, but not all, cultural norms; he develops a conscience which serves as a constant reminder of parental and cultural prohibitions. In the later years it is the internalized anticipation of punishment which serves as a substitute for sanctions applied by the real parents or other authority figures.

This process is not completely negative, however, in that it is not dependent entirely upon frustration, sanction, and punishment. In the course of growing up children come to identify with their parents or with others who serve as models of the cultural ideal. They emulate the behavior of these models, and they evaluate themselves with reference to the standards established by them. To paraphrase Erich Fromm, eventually the members of a society want to act as they have to act; they come to desire what is socially necessary. Most people in most societies most of the time strive to achieve their particular culture's definition of the good life, because they find it personally and socially rewarding.

But not all people do so. Thus far in this paper we have dealt with particular cultures as if they were constant monolithic entities, and we have talked as if the personality structures of all members of a given society were relatively uniform. These are obvious oversimplifications, and it is now time to correct them. Many of us, in popular speech, commit a similar error when we say, for example, that Americans are materialistic, Englishmen are formal, or Italians volatile. Irrespective of whatever element of truth there may be to these stereotypes, it is perfectly clear that not all Americans are equally materialistic, and undoubtedly there are informal Englishmen and passive Italians. The problem we have raised is this: how can we make statements about those aspects of personality shared by an entire group or nation in view of the personality differences that exist between individuals and subgroups within the society? The more fundamental question here concerns the nature of the correspondence between culture on the one hand and personality on the other.

In a short but incisive book, Anthony F. C. Wallace has contributed to our understanding of this problem. He does so by contrasting two different points of view which he calls the replication of uniformity and the organization of diversity. In the first view, the aim is to describe how the character structure of one group differs from that of another, and the emphasis is on the uniqueness of each. The members of a society are considered to have learned the "same things" because of similar early experiences and because of common participation in the same cultural system. The culture is considered relatively homogeneous, individuals are thought to share a uniform personality organization, and one expects to find a nearly perfect correspondence between culture type and personality type. Industrialization, urbanization, revolution, and other forms of rapid culture change are seen as leading to personal breakdown and social disorganization. It is assumed that each new generation becomes a replica of the preceding one in both cultural tradition and character structure. The research problem is to investigate the mechanisms of socialization by which this is accomplished.

In the second view, which is Wallace's own, culture is, in fact, characterized by diversity of individuals and groups, each acting to further their own interests, and socialization is not considered to be a perfect mechanism for ensuring the replication of either culture or character from one generation to the next. Individuals differ because of variations in genetic constitution and because of unique experiences in the life career. Society is stratified, regimented, and diversified due to age-sex differences, occupational specialization, the necessary inequality in social life, and differential participation in the total culture. Rapid culture change does not necessarily lead to disintegration; as Wallace says, it is the natural condition of man. In view of the above, the research problem is to investigate the basis of orderly social life. How do diverse individuals organize themselves so as to maintain a cultural system which is itself constantly changing, shifting, and oscillating?

The crucial distinction is between behavior and motivation. To take an example from my own profession, the students who attend my lectures behave in strikingly similar ways. All are dressed more or less alike, all arrive and leave at approximately the same time, most prepare their reading assignments, and unfortunately, even their answers to the examination questions are quite similar. But it is a commonplace of university life in America and probably elsewhere that the underlying motivations of the students are highly variable. One man comes to the university because of an inner compulsion to learn; another because of parental pressure; a third out of expediency—he hopes to make contacts which eventually will be beneficial in his later business or political life; and a fourth, because of social expectation, comes to college because his friends do. Of course, the motivation in any given case would be much more complex than I have indicated, but the general point should be clear; common participation in a social institution does not imply psychological uniformity among the participants. Individuals may conform to their culture because of a wide variety of different motives. In other words, the same behavior may satisfy different personal needs, and the same needs may be satisfied by different behavior.

In Wallace's view, the basis of societal functioning is complementarity, not uniformity. In any social interaction it is not necessary that motivation be shared or even that one party understands the motives of the other; it is only necessary that the behavior of each be more or less predictable. To paraphrase Wallace, the relationship between professor and student does not depend on mutual conformity to one role, but on a complementarity of different roles. Complex human social systems are able to function precisely because each person is relieved of the burden of understanding the motivations of others and of acquiring the appropriate skills and knowledge necessary for the performance of others' roles. Nor is it necessary for him to reveal many aspects of his own personality to those with whom he interacts. To some extent, each of us lives in our own private world.

As we have seen, it cannot be assumed that the members of a society share a common social character. But does this imply that each individual is unique? Certainly not. In the words of Clyde Kluckhohn and Henry A. Murray, every man is in certain respects like all other men, like some other men, like no other man. There may not be a perfect one-to-one correspondence between the culture of a society and the personality of its members, but some correspondences do exist. In order to study them, as well as the areas in which no correspondences occur, we must make detailed analyses of subgroups within a society and of the primary social units which have significance in personality formation and cultural transmission. We cannot infer personality from social institutions or overt behavior alone, but must investigate the shared aspects of emotional and cognitive patterning based upon detailed study of individuals and of their significant social relationships. We must continue to study the varied means by which culture structures and channels the expression of universal human needs, and we must turn our attention to the bases of conformity and change in social life. These are complex problems, but they are among those that will be of crucial importance for psychological anthropology in the next decade.

19 PSYCHOLOGICAL ANTHROPOLOGY
JOHN J. HONIGMANN

Culture, either in the sense of constructs that constitute models of reality* or in Tylor's far more inclusive sense ("that complex whole which includes knowledge, belief, art, law, morals, custom, and any other capacities and habits acquired by man as a member of society"), remains the central interest of anthropology. This review is concerned mainly with work appearing from 1964 to 1968, wherein a psychological or psychiatric vantage point is used (often with a certain degree of unavoidable naïveté[2]) to illuminate cultural phenomena, as well as with work that develops psychological concepts through employing the vantage point afforded by data from other cultures. "Psychocultural analysis" characterizes the first approach,[3] and "cross-cultural psychology" describes the preoccupation of some psychologists with the latter.[4] Formerly, both would have been subsumed under the label "culture and personality," a name that had the virtue of not identifying the field with any specific discipline. However, "psychological anthropology" has come to be increasingly favored to designate any psychological attention paid to cultural materials. We might now redefine "culture and personality" to designate that fairly coherent tradition that developed in American anthropology in the 1930's under the aegis of Edward Sapir, Ruth Benedict, A. I. Hallowell, and Margaret Mead, and that exhausted its initial vitality in the middle 1950's.[5] Compared to that tradition, psychological anthropology is a far broader, more eclectic, and still viable field, as several recent reviews of the literature testify.[6] Yet, controversy continues over the legitimacy and wisdom of applying a psychological viewpoint to social phenomena,[7] and over what such a viewpoint encompasses.[8]

General Works

Collections of readings,[9] texts like *Personality in Culture*,[10] and chapters in texts[11] are means of introducing college students to psychological anthropology. They also serve to maintain the continuity of this intellectual tradition and, through incorporating criticism and reconsiderations periodically, reorient interest and direct attention into new directions of research. Increased reliance on a phenomenological perspective for understanding people in society is one such reorientation that has

Reprinted by permission of the author and The American Academy of Political and Social Science. Copyright © 1969 by The American Academy of Political and Social Science.
*See pp. 332–339 for notes.

been urged,[12] but as a recent encyclopedia article indicates,[13] an opposite tendency to utilize causal or functional explanations for understanding personality in theoretical terms enjoys much greater current vogue.

Social Personality

The best-known genre of psychological anthropology consists of accounts describing members of societies by major obvious (or modal—in the truly statistical sense of the word) psychological characteristics. In contrast to the way in which anthropologists and psychoanalysts have tended to make global generalizations, based on no acknowledged sampling process, about the personality characteristics of groups, cross-culturally-oriented psychologists base their conclusions on highly restrictive samples.

Recent years have produced few works competing with such classics as Margaret Mead's *Sex and Temperament* or Abram Kardiner's *Psychological Frontiers of Society*. It is a pleasure at last to have, in Leighton and Adair's study of the Zuni Indians,[14] the final one of a series of tribal monographs that began appearing in 1944, with results of the Indian Education Research Project. Another noteworthy book-length account deals with a village on St. Kitts, British West Indies.[15] A number of special features distinguish the work, including use of A. H. Maslow's psychological theory and skillful use of controlled comparison for testing. Less ambitious is a psychiatrist's report of the basic personality of the Caribou Eskimo, which continues where Kardiner left off.[16] Psychoanalytical perspectives also loom large in Boyer's continuing publications on Mescalero Apache Indians and their psychological—especially identity—problems, stemming in part from the tribes' subjugation by the United States government.[17] Psychiatrists, like Lubart and Boyer, who turn their attention to culture rely heavily on psychoanalytic concepts. Other social scientists have come to prefer concentrating on the overt features of personal adaptation, an approach appearing, for example, in recent work done on the Eskimos of Frobisher Bay,[18] and on Indians and Metis in northern Saskatchewan.[19]

Every anthropologist has been fascinated by the possibility that different observers may formulate contradictory characterizations of the same people or culture. Such contradictions may, in fact, reflect different aspects of behavior in the society being studied, like, for example, what Seymour Parker calls the "dramatic dichotomy between the cooperative 'social' and the competitive, violent 'ceremonial' " aspects of Kwakiutl culture and behavior.[20] Without unduly stressing contradictions, Colby sums up Meso-American psychological orientations anew; John Gillin pioneered in the study of this area.[21]

Turning to work done outside the Americas, we note a monograph that deals with *Thai Peasant Personality*.[22] Several observers look at the psychological features of the Lebanese,[23] and factor analysis demonstrates Westernization to be associated with lowered anxiety and less insecurity in Sinhalese students.[24]

Rorschach test data on Ghanaian children provide a welcome contribution to our knowledge of Africans' social personalities, and this one is all the more welcome because the author compares his subjects with an age-mated control group of American youngsters.[25] A book on the Burakumin, a Japanese outcaste community,[26] adds itself to what has already been written about Japanese national character.[27] Substantive work on other national characters is rare, for this is obviously not currently an active field of research.[28] However, critical and programmatic essays, mostly by nonanthropologists, testify to a lingering fascination with the topic.[29]

Psychological Traits and Processes in Cultural Settings

We have already noted the current popularity of achievement theory in psychocultural research,[30] the theory being especially promising for its ability to explain the capacity of indigenous people for economic development.[31] Under standard research conditions projective techniques, like the Thematic Apperception Test and story-composition, test for achievement motive.[32] Occupational preferences in a developing country, Ghana, provided one investigator with an index to what must surely be a related construct—"aspiration."[33]

Competence, another, but possibly more remotely related, trait, has likewise been employed to understand social change in Africa.[34] In quite a different context, an anthropologist writes on the incompetent adaptation of mentally retarded Americans, following their discharge from hospitals.[35] Adaptation can be approached as readily from a psychological as from a purely sociocultural point of view,[36] the topic being inclusive enough to embrace almost all the psychological traits mentioned in this review.[37] A recently devised projective test, the Instrumental Activities Inventory, is designed to discover how individuals choose means for adapting, especially when several alternative paths confront them under conditions of culture change.[38] Adaptation in aging highland Maya, and in a control group of American males, is studied by David Gutman, utilizing the Thematic Apperception Test.[39]

Explorations of cognition by anthropologists have mostly been executed several steps removed from actual people behaving in the real world, and have paid little attention to the genetic development of cognitive abilities in other cultures. An exceptional piece of work, a comparison of Apache "learners" and "nonlearners," has been done, chiefly under a psychiatrist's leadership.[40] Anthropologists tend to rely on linguistic and formal semantic analysis in studying cognition, which leaves their work without a clear-cut psychological orientation.[41] Psychologists, on the other hand, take cultural factors for granted, and that makes their work comparatively uninteresting for anyone concerned with in the interplay of cognition and culture.[42] We shall have to wait to see if cognitive processes ever achieve a place in psychocultural analysis comparable to that of motivation studies, which still dominate the field. Several cross-cultural studies of creativity by sociologists similarly fail to dwell on cultural context to any significant extent,[43] and the same criticism holds for many investigations of ethnic differences in pain-tolerance.[44] By way of comparison, two small-scale, cross-cultural experimental comparisons, one on sex-role-identification among the Yoruba and Gusii[45] and the other on conformity-independence among West African Temne and Baffin Island Eskimo,[46] do heed cultural factors when they explain their findings. Such research suggests that anthropology might profitably supplement large-scale, cross-cultural studies of psychological and other traits by smaller, field-based comparative studies, planned to test significant psychological problems.[47]

What other psychological traits or processes have anthropologists examined? The current popularity of the identity concept expectedly shows up in recent literature.[48] Other concepts, like psychological atomism[49] and the image of limited good,[50] have been created by anthropologists, and are not yet listed in the indexes of psychology texts. Not long ago, values promised to be a fruitful concept for understanding how individuals participate in culture, but the final report of Harvard's "Rimrock Study" of values in five southwestern United States cultures, with chapters by E. Z. Vogt, John W. L. Whiting, M. S. Edmonson, Clyde Kluckhohn, and others,[51] is curiously flat, at least to someone who recalls the excitement generated in the 1950's by the first monographs to issue from the project. It is strange that, despite so much research on values, social scientists should still disagree on the extent to which the American poor hold values in common with the country's dominant social strata.[52]

Cultural Patterns and Social Behavior in Psychological Perspective

From research that focuses on psychological traits and processes as they operate in cultural context, we turn to essays that interpret *cultural* traits or institutions and social behavior in terms of underlying psychological dynamics. Psychoanalysts with ethnological leanings continue to pursue such research,[53] as they have since Freud interpreted religion and wit psychodynamically. Seemingly, they do so with little trepidation. For many social scientists, the question which they find difficult to answer is whether, generally speaking, cultural patterns—say, for example, economic development and its component activities—are determined more by internal psychological states or by external situational factors.[54] The famous "sentiments controversy," which has, by now, about run its course, provided a dramatic publication of the problem.[55]

What Kardiner calls "secondary institutions," and views as derivatives of the basic personality's projective system—institutions like folklore and religion—continue to invite the greatest share of attention from psychologically minded social researchers.[56] A number of psychological interpretations of religious and more or less related phenomena, like witchcraft and divination, appear in the new edition of a comprehensive reader,[57] while two recent texts on the anthropology of religion combine several similar approaches eclectically.[58] Other recent publications view religious systems as culturally standardized defense mechanisms,[59] examine taboo[60] and spirit possession,[61] and reconsider that Cree Indian and anthropologists' bogey, Windigo psychosis.[62] A spate of articles explain how cultural institutions, like confession, various ceremonies, magic, shamanism, and similar practices operate psychotherapeutically among the Eskimo, the Apache, and other cultural groups.[63] The normal as well as the deviant uses of alcohol also continue to attract researchers, the constant stream of literature making periodic reviews of the topic, like David Mandelbaum's, very useful.[64]

The psychological vantage point figures prominently in research, some of it comparative, that John Roberts and associates are carrying out on ticktacktoe and other games.[65] Psychological interest in such more serious matters as political behavior and the sources of war has not been notably insightful in either psychology or anthropology, and has not gone far beyond the stage of very broad generalization.[66] Jerome Frank has written an ambitious book that applies concepts and experimental findings from psychology in an attempt to understand military planning and other types of behavior which can lead a nation to war or to the conference table.[67] Durkheim's pioneer work on the social dynamics of suicide continues to be followed by attempts to link self-destruction with cultural conditions, and anthropologists share this interest with other social scientists.[68]

Social and Cultural Change

The psychological consequences of accultural and other social change have comprised a subject of long-standing interest and consistent productivity in psychological anthropology. In recent work pursuing the trend, a Nigerian psychiatrist points out the effects which change has had on his countrymen's mental health,[69] and an anthropologist reports that young unmarried, "educated" Peruvian men adapt better to change than older folk.[70] The Rorschach test helps in comparing two Apache groups, one that underwent quick, forced acculturation and the other, permitted to change at its own pace.[71] Another projective picture technique enables Parker to discern evidence of frustration and hostility in acculturated Alaskan Eskimo.[72] Erik Erikson's dedication to historical psychology is revealed in portions of a new book that examine identity conflict in adolescents,[73] and another report notes accommodations made by Japanese youth to social change.[74]

The psychological dynamics of change can be inferred from the vantage point of culture when, for some reason, it is inconvenient clinically to seek them in individuals, who are the source of change and bear its consequences. William Madsen's account of value conflict in Mexican-Americans mostly remains on a cultural, nonclinical level of inference,[75] and so does the work of Homer Barnett (who followed the same practice in his book *Innovation*, published in 1953), along with that of other contributors to a recent pertinent volume.[76]

Individual in Culture

Biographical data in social research, as L. L. Langness points out in his systematic treatment of life-history materials in anthropology,[77] allow the fieldworker to experience vicariously cultural events that he himself never witnessed. Biographical accounts vary in how extensively they employ psychological concepts and theory, but they are always concerned with specific individuals' behavior, sometimes abnormal behavior.[78] So are extended analyses of particular "cases" observed by a fieldworker, but in those, the interacting persons may be only briefly identified by a few crucial status characteristics.[79]

Oscar Lewis—author of a number of well-known individual-life and family histories, the latest having taken him from Mexico to Puerto Rico and New York[80]—is the single most active exponent of the biographical method that the social sciences have ever seen. Other significant ethnological accounts, mostly concerned with the subject's experience of culture change, represent Nigeria;[81] a Mexican agrarian leader;[82] several other American Indians,[83] including a Mackenzie River Eskimo and Washo shaman;[84] and a Papuan who has become a pathologist and political leader.[85] A case-analysis of a Venezuelan revolutionary is considerably more psychodynamic and interpretative than most of the anthropological accounts.[86]

Childhood and Socialization

Because disciplinary specialization, while encouraging rapid growth of a field, increasingly restricts specialized knowledge to small groups of well-trained professionals, one notes with mixed feelings how sociology and the psychology of child development have come to dominate socialization theory and research on child-rearing. Young anthropologists and other social scientists, already burdened with reading in their own specialties, will not, without special effort, regularly encounter many new materials dealing with socialization. Hence danger arises either that they will increasingly neglect the study of socialization or that their work in the field will embody archaic concepts and methods, making it of negligible significance to other scholars. On the other hand, much that is written by psychologists and sociologists about childhood and adult socialization uses, mainly, data from the United States, a fact which limits the significance of what they say.[87]

A number of the publications that we have already noted touch on socialization or enculturation[88] (efforts to clarify the distinction have been slow to take hold). Many more works are exclusively concerned with the process, including a cross-culturally oriented review of childhood influences on personality-formation.[89] The social-learning approach (familiar to readers of *Patterns of Child-Rearing* by R. R. Sears, E. E. Maccoby, and H. Levin)' has been applied to the Philippines;[90] effects of institutional child-rearing are explored in Israeli *kibbutzim*;[91] and a book notes how Marxist ideology besets education and child-rearing in the Soviet Union.[92] The substantial re-evaluation of psychoanalytic theory that has occurred in the social sciences is indicated in Murray Straus' re-examination of his Sinhalese data.[93] Where he was once puzzled by the failure of schedule-feeding and severe toilet training to induce anxiety, as he had expected, in his sample of children, he now sees those features of child-rearing as providing elements of stability in the loosely structured society of Ceylon. Search for antecedents of socialization lying outside socialization itself[94] and attention to the way in which socialization functions to meet the role needs of particular social systems[95] likewise reflect shifts in thought away from early psychoanalysis. Yehudi Cohen offers an original explanation of the function of initiation rites for creating a sense of identity and individuality in certain kinds of societies, and also deals with "the socialization of sexuality."[96] *The Field Guide to the Study of Socialization* directs attention to many variables that fieldworkers interested in personality-formation should note.[97]

Formal education has begun to receive zealous attention from social scientists. Referring only to work possessing an anthropological cast, there are studies of schools among the Pine Ridge Sioux Indians,[98] in United States cities,[99] among Kwakiutl Indians,[100] in Germany,[101] and in Japan.[102] The last three monographs appear in the new series of "Case Studies in Education and Culture," edited by George and Louise Spindler, a series that also narrates how the new mathematics is being learned by Kpelle children in Liberia.[103]

The culture of childhood has long had a place in anthropological research, and continues to be represented.[104] Book-length ethnographic reports often contain chapters that, in varying degrees of intensity, touch on childhood, socialization, and even formal education, as they occur within the culture being studied. The number of such works is too large to attempt a complete listing.[105]

Rarely are we informed how culture change is effected through adult socialization; hence the importance of a story of government-fostered co-operatives among eastern Arctic and Quebec Eskimo.[106]

Social Psychiatry

The term "social psychiatry" usually denotes examination of psychiatrically abnormal behavior in its social and cultural contexts. Often the concept of stress is used to help explain the quality of interaction between person and culture that leads to psychiatric disorder.[107] We believe that we are warranted in extending the term to include certain socially abnormal behavior, or deviance, especially when some psychodynamic theory serves to explain how sociocultural conditions motivate deviance.

Publication of the interdisciplinary Tri-Ethnic Project's final report represents one of the most significant events in the period being reviewed.[108] The report, comparing Indian, Spanish-American, and Anglo-Saxon subjects living in the same Colorado community, presents impressive, but not altogether consistent, support for a complex "field theory" that integrates psychological and sociocultural variables deriving from the thought of many social scientists since Durkheim. The three ethnic groups differ in deviant behavior as well as in those antecedent characteristics which, the theory predicts, will instigate deviance. Deviance (in adults) is indicated by markers like excessive drinking, heavy use of alcohol to cope with frustration, and offenses that land the person in court, as well as (in the high school subjects) poor academic performance. Indians and Spanish-Americans are more deviance-prone than Anglo-Saxons. Members of the former two groups also enjoy relatively poorer opportunities to achieve personal goals, live under greater anomie, and are more often exposed to deviant role models.[109] Obviously, the question of cultural relativity poses little difficulty in research of this type, nor does it give much trouble to psychiatrists who identify psychiatric disorder cross-culturally,[110] though here danger lies in overestimating the severity of symptoms in a culturally exotic group.[111]

Other cross-cultural research dealing with deviance examines juvenile delinquency in Japan,[112] among Japanese-Americans,[113] among Chinese-Americans,[114] and in Ghana.[115]

Recent publications in more conventional social psychiatry include reviews of the field's problems and methods,[116] and many specific studies devoted, for example, to mental illness among the poor,[117] forms of schizophrenia in Japanese and Americans,[118] hysterical forms of behavior among Ainu and in Southeast Asia,[119] emotional disorder and indigenous psychotherapy among Mexican-Americans,[120] and native conceptions of psychiatric disorder.[121] Sentiments in two socially disintegrated communities, Stirling County in Nova Scotia and the Navaho Indians, are compared,[122] and five far-northern Canadian communities are re-examined with respect to the degree of patterning of social integration.[123] Norman Chance reviews his North Alaskan Eskimo data in the light of a similar Formosan study of how disjunction between aspiration ("identification") and opportunity relates directly to personality maladjustment,[124] and a questionnaire (similar to the one that Chance used), designed to elicit symptoms of psychiatric disorder, is assessed for its effectiveness in an Eskimo community. Finally the vexing question recurs: When and to what degree are shamans psychiatrically disturbed?[125] The question calls for a careful, theoretically informed review as well as for more fieldwork while opportunities to study shamans remain.

20 BIOSOCIAL INFLUENCES ON CULTURE—A NEGLECTED CATEGORY
EDWARD NORBECK

Anthropological interpretations of similarities and differences in culture among societies of the world have concerned three major classes of factors that are seen to influence or "determine" the nature of culture—the culture of mankind in general, specific cultures, and the unique cultures of individual human beings. In simplest terms, these three categories may be called *biological, environmental,* and *cultural* factors.

Biological factors are traits characteristic of *Homo sapiens* as a biological species that foster, permit, or require certain cultural activities and limit or prohibit others. They are analogous with the innate traits of beavers, kangaroos, earthworms, and all other forms of life. Culture would obviously be quite different if human beings were aquatic or herbivorous, or reproduced themselves by laying eggs. The "cultures" of any two individuals are obviously also influenced by their unique and hereditary physical traits.

Anthropological ideas and arguments about the influence upon culture of environmental factors and the influence of culture itself—that is, culture influencing culture—are equally familiar to any anthropologist and require no elaboration.

The concern of this paper is with a category of "influences" to which I have given the name *biosocial factors*. These are values which have biological referents, values that are hierarchically rated and must, therefore, have more than one kind or variety of biological referent as a basis of comparison. I refer here to cultural ideals of such things as human physical beauty, masculinity, and femininity, ideals which set one distinguishable variety of physical trait above its allelomorphs. These values may at first seem to be matters of little consequence, but they may easily be shown to have significance with reference to social problems of minority groups in various nations of the world and to relations among societies and nations of the world whenever physical and racial differences exist among the peoples concerned.

Such values are established on the basis of prestige in the manner described by Gabriel de Tarde in his *Laws of Imitation,** in which he discusses cultural innovations. There is little doubt of the force or value of prestige in establishing traits of culture. "Proper" English, Spanish, and German, for example, represent no inherent structural or semantic superiority over "improper" varieties of these languages. They are instead the varieties of those languages spoken by persons of high social status and are therefore often emulated by others. Standard Japanese owes its position or prestige to the same circumstances, and is in no way structurally or semantically superior to the native speech of northeastern Japan, which is regarded as "bad" Japanese. Examples of what de Tarde called "imitation" are abundant

---

Reprinted by permission of the author from *Proceedings,* VIIIth International Congress of Anthropological and Ethnological Sciences, Vol. II (1968).

*See p. 339 for references.

outside the realm of language. The spread of Buddhism in Japan, for example, was strongly favored by its adoption by members of the Japanese royalty in the sixth century.

Certain values, established in precisely the same way, refer to genetically inherited biological traits that distinguish races, sub-races, and still finer varietal groups of human beings. In both Europe and Japan, for example, rather vague concepts exist of "patrician" physical types, complexes of physical traits that are regarded as desirable or beautiful. Concepts of "peasant" types also exist, and the physical traits they represent are not ordinarily regarded as beautiful or desirable. To the extent that these "patrician" and "peasant" types exist in reality, they are varietal differences among people who regard themselves as a single people or race.

When whole societies or sub-societies differ from each other in physical traits and intersocietal contact among such differing peoples is close, circumstances closely resembling those described by de Tarde also obtain. To residents of the United States, a thoroughly familiar example is provided by Negro-White relations and related Negro ideals of physical beauty. I refer to American Negro practices of applying facial bleaches to lighten dark skin and other practices—costly, time-consuming and sometimes painful—of straightening hair of the head to simulate Caucasian hair form. To be sure, a small counter trend presently exists among some Negroes of the United States that may be seen as an attempt to seek social and psychological identity by idealizing physical traits innate to Negroes. The slogan "Black is beautiful" has some currency today, and natural, unstraightened hair is favored by a few Negroes. If personal observation and the advertisements in *Ebony* and other magazines published for Negro readers are indicative, however, the prevailing trend continues to be simulation, insofar as possible, of the physical traits of the white population.

Citizens of nations of the world other than the United States may doubtless easily supply similar examples from observation of the circumstances in their own societies. Referring to Japan, an example is provided by the relations and attitudes that apply between Japanese from the principal islands of Japan and the Ryukyuans.

I wish especially to discuss this phenomenon as it exists between nations rather than between sub-societies of a single nation. This is a subject about which few people think it appropriate to express themselves in print and on which documentary information is therefore scarce. I shall take as my example the relations between Japan and the Western world—that is, Europe and the United States—confining my remarks principally to a discussion of Japanese concepts of male and female beauty.

Evidence points to a clear trend in Japan during the past century of change in conceptions of male and female beauty toward the model of European physical characteristics. Historical records of the sixteenth and seventeenth centuries, when Europeans first came to Japan, reveal that Europeans were not admired for their physical beauty and that they were often regarded as physically repulsive. European fairness of skin is something of an exception. Fair skin was a common value, for the Japanese had also long placed a premium on whiteness of skin. But it is interesting to note that in Japanese eyes the skin of Europeans appears to have become more admirably white as the centuries have passed, and as the prestige of Western culture has risen.

The great changes in Japanese concepts of beauty occurred during the past century, the only period of Japan's history in which it has had close contact with Europeans. Periods of heightened change seem evident during the 1920's and since the end of World War II. No reactionary trend seems yet in sight, and current ideals of beauty appear to trend more than ever in the past to Western models. It is my strong impression that this trend is clearly evident in Japanese magazine photographs of the 1920's and since World War II. Photographers' models and other professional female beauties in particular tend increasingly to be women with Western physical features, facial and other. The Japanese emulation of Western fashion in curling hair is a truly remarkable departure from the past, for straight, black hair was the ideal for centuries. For a time after World War II, permanent waves were even popular among some young Japanese males as well as females. Straight hair is presently once again fashionable among young women—as it is in the West.

Other Japanese practices of altering or attempting to alter physical characteristics after the Western model are abundant. Bleaching the hair to a brown or auburn shade had a temporary vogue, at its height perhaps ten years ago, and is still practiced by a few women. Although white skin continues to be valued and perhaps more highly valued than formerly, a lesser trend of Japanese opinion finds attractiveness in sun-tanned skin, a value that appears surely to have been derived from the West. Japanese recipes for beauty have in the past stressed avoidance of exposure to the sun and consequent tanning. Perhaps the most remarkable example of striving to reach the Western ideal is the current practice among professional female beauties and some of their male counterparts of altering the eyes surgically to produce what the Japanese called the "double fold," that is, to produce eyelids and "round" eyes resembling those of Europeans. Cosmetic surgery also less commonly includes today nasal alterations to produce a high-bridged nose, a trait that is European and also traditionally valued by the Japanese provided the nose is not large.

These practices and the values they represent should not, I think, be brushed aside as the foolish vanities of empty-headed people. The Japanese female entertainer who runs the entire gamut of surgery and other means of Westernizing her appearance may be regarded as the apogee of values that permeate the entire society in varying degree. Her professional stock in trade is her appearance, and her artifice has enlarged the capital stock.

I am well aware that I have been discussing a subject that is likely to evoke hostile reactions. I am also aware that many conceptions of beauty exist in Japan, but the trend of which I have spoken seems nevertheless unquestionable. My aim is not to brand the Japanese in this respect as slavish imitators of the West. The Japanese are probably no more imitative than any other people who have had to face societies that seemed overwhelmingly superior in economic and military power and in scientific and technological knowledge. Changing concepts of beauty in Japan appear to me to be but one manifestation of a trend of change in Japanese attitudes that has much broader significance, a trend toward viewing the self at reduced value that has come as a result of Japanese experiences with the West.

And here I shall take refuge in the printed words of two perceptive Japanese social scientists, one a young psychologist and the other a senior anthropologist. In a recent writing,[2] Hiroshi Wagatsuma presents a detailed account of changing conceptions of beauty, especially of skin color, toward Western physical features. He observes that the degree of admiration of Western physical features varies according to the degree of the individual's identification with Western culture. A writing by the anthropologist Eiichiro Ishida is a remarkable account of personal reactions to Western culture and, what is most relevant here, to Western physical features. Ishida gives in the most candid terms a statement of feelings of inferiority. His reaction upon return to Japan after a stay in the West is expressed by the statement (I quote): "Why, I thought we were better-looking than *this*." Like Wagatsuma, he refers to national identity, stating: "Before the tide of Westernization, self-confidence, pride, and assurance all went by the board . . . Japanese . . . have not been able to conquer the inferiority complex toward the West that has persisted since Meiji times."

Circumstances such as I have briefly described with reference to Japan and the West very likely exist elsewhere in the world, in Russia, Africa, India and in other countries. The bearing such values have upon problems of social and psychological identity for minority groups or whole societies in their relations with other societies seems obvious, but the implications of these values with regard to international relations is hard to appraise. These values appear to become established in precisely the way described by de Tarde in his discussion of cultural "imitation." But, let us note, there is a signal and insurmountable difference. Unlike other traits of culture, which may be acquired by all races and varieties of *Homo sapiens,* these values with biological referents rest upon matters quite beyond cultural control by man. "Acquiring" these ideal attributes is limited principally to crude simulation. Anthropology and the entire realm of science presently can offer no effective remedy for the implied problems.

In conclusion, I shall note a modern trend of Western attitude that further illustrates the subject of this discussion and indicates the prestige which Japan presently holds among nations of the world. As described by Hiroshi Wagatsuma, this trend also illustrates the Japanese view of themselves which I have discussed. Wagatsuma refers to a new perception of beauty growing in the West that includes Japanese aesthetic standards in art, and architecture, and (I quote Wagatsuma) ". . . *even* in Mongoloid beauty" (emphasis mine).

SECTION INTRODUCTION REFERENCES* AND SUGGESTIONS FOR FURTHER STUDY

Barker, Roger, and Herbert Wright, 1955, *Midwest and its Children, the Psychological Ecology of an American Town.* New York: Harper & Row.

Benedict, Ruth, 1946, *The Chrysanthemum and the Sword: Patterns of Japanese Culture.* Boston: Houghton Mifflin.

Beidelman, T. O., 1966, "The Ox and Nuer Sacrifice: Some Freudian Hypotheses About Neur Symbolism." *Man* 1:453–467.

Burger, Henry G., 1972, "Behavior Modification and Operant Psychology: An Anthropological Critique." *American Educational Research Journal* 9:343–360.

Buros, Oscar, 1970, *Personality: Tests and Reviews*. Highland Park, N.J.: Gryphon Press.

Child, Irvin L., 1968, "Personality in Culture." In E. F. Borgatta and W. W. Lambert, eds., *Handbook of Personality Theory and Research*. Chicago: Rand McNally, pp. 82–145.

De Vos, George A., 1968, "Achievement and Innovation in Culture and Personality." In Edward Norbeck et al., eds., *The Study of Personality: An Interdisciplinary Appraisal*. New York: Holt, Rinehart and Winston, pp. 348–370.

De Vos, George A., and Arthur E. Hippler, 1969, "Cultural Psychology: Comparative Studies of Human Behavior." In G. Lindzey and E. Aronson, eds., *Handbook of Social Psychology*, 2nd ed. Reading, Mass.: Addison-Wesley, pp. 323–417.

Du Bois, Cora, 1960, *The People of Alor*. Cambridge: Harvard University Press.

Erikson, E. H., 1968, "Life Cycle." *International Encyclopedia of the Social Sciences* 9:286–292.

Goodman, Mary Ellen, 1967, *The Individual and Culture*. Homewood, Ill.: The Dorsey Press.

Honigmann, John J., 1967, *Personality in Culture*. New York: Harper & Row.

*———, 1968, "The Study of Personality in Primitive Societies." In Edward Norbeck et al., eds., *The Study of Personality: An Interdisciplinary Appraisal*. New York: Holt, Rinehart and Winston, pp. 246–276.

Hsu, Francis L. K., ed., 1972, *Psychological Anthropology*. Cambridge, Mass.: Schenkman.

Jung, Carl G., 1968, *Man and His Symbols*. New York: Dell.

Kaplan, Bert, ed., 1961, *Studying Personality Cross-culturally*. New York: Harper & Row.

Kardiner, A., 1950, *The Psychological Frontiers of Society*. New York: Columbia University Press.

Kroeber, Alfred L., 1948, "Cultural Psychology." In *Anthropology*. New York: Harcourt, Brace, pp. 572–621.

LeVine, Robert A., 1973, *Culture, Behavior, and Personality*. Chicago: Aldine.

Linton, Ralph, 1945, *The Cultural Background of Personality*. New York: Appleton-Century-Crofts.

McClelland, David C., and David G. Winter, 1969, *Motivating Economic Achievement*. New York: Free Press.

Mead, Margaret, 1928, *Coming of Age in Samoa*. New York: Morrow.

———, 1935, *Sex and Temperament in Three Primitive Societies*. New York: Morrow.

Norbeck, Edward, D. Price-Williams, and W. M. McCord, 1968, *The Study of Personality: An Interdisciplinary Appraisal*. New York: Holt, Rinehart and Winston.

Norbeck, Edward, Donald E. Walker, and Mimi Cohen, 1962, "The Interpretation of Data: Puberty Rites." *American Anthropologist* 64:463–485.

Price-Williams, Douglas R., 1968, "Ethnopsychology I: Comparative Psychological Processes," "Ethnopsychology II: Comparative Personality Processes." In J. A. Clifton, ed., *Introduction to Cultural Anthropology*. Boston: Houghton Mifflin, pp. 305–315, 317–335.

Roheim, Geza, 1950, *Psychoanalysis and Anthropology*. New York: International Universities Press.

Sapir, Edward, 1938, "Why Cultural Anthropology Needs the Psychiatrist." *Psychiatry* 1:7–12.

Segall, M. H., D. T. Campbell, and M. J. Herskovits, 1966, *The Influence of Culture on Visual Perception*. Indianapolis: Bobbs-Merrill.

Skinner, B. F., 1971, *Beyond Freedom and Dignity*. New York: Knopf.

Spindler, George, and Louise Spindler, 1963, "Psychology in Anthropology: Applications to Culture Change." In S. Koch, ed., *Psychology: A Study in Science,* Vol. 6. New York: McGraw-Hill, pp. 510–551.

Spiro, M. E., 1951, "Culture and Personality: The Natural History of a False Dichotomy." *Psychiatry* 14:19–46.

―――, 1972, "An Overview and Suggested Reorientation." In F. L. K. Hsu, ed., *Psychological Anthropology*. Cambridge, Mass.: Schenkman.

Wallace, Anthony F. C., 1961, *Culture and Personality*. New York: Random House.

White, Leslie A., 1947, "Culturological vs. Psychological Interpretations of Human Behavior." *American Sociological Review* 12:686–689.

Whiting, J., and I. Child, 1953, *Child Training and Personality: A Cross-cultural Study*. New Haven, Conn.: Yale University Press.

section VII

Culture as a Cognitive System

The view that man's intellectual or cognitive perceptions of the universe form subconscious systems, patterns, or structures that follow panhuman principles of thought is widespread in the social sciences and has been an important or guiding assumption of studies known by a great variety of names. These include ethnoscience, ethnosemantics, ethno/psycho/socio/linguistics, formal semantic analysis, componential analysis, new ethnography, new structuralism, French structuralism, and cognitive anthropology. As our inventory of titles suggests, the idea of universal principles of thought has interested sociologists, psychologists, and linguists, many of whom are anthropologists specializing in linguistics, as well as ethnologists. The most common label for studies of this kind in anthropology today is *cognitive anthropology*, a recent term.

Most studies that might reasonably be placed under the heading of cognitive anthropology are recent or fairly recent, but the central concept and the interests it implies have a long if shadowy history. The idea of "psychic unity" of all mankind held by Adolph Bastian, an early German pioneer in anthropology of the middle of the nineteenth century, is an early episode in this history. Some later scholars, such as Lucien Lévy-Bruhl, held that "primitive mentality," the manner of thinking of primitive societies, was less highly evolved than the manner of thought of civilized folk, an idea which did not meet general acceptance in anthropology and which has now long been discredited. If anything at all, Lévy-Bruhl's contribution was to stimulate interest in the subject and to revive or fortify the assumption of psychic unity. The background of the modern anthropological interest in cognitive analysis certainly reaches back to the writings of Franz Boas and, especially, Bronislaw Malinowski, who repeatedly stressed the importance of gaining knowledge of the native view of reality. "The final goal, of which an Ethnographer should never lose sight . . . is, briefly, to grasp the native's point of view, his relation to life, to realize *his* vision of *his* world" (Malinowski 1961:25). An early writing by A. L. Kroeber on kinship (1909), still useful today, treats terms of kinship as primarily cognitive rather than genealogical categories.

Other forerunners of modern views of "structured patterns of thought" appear in the writings of linguists and anthropological linguists, such as Edward Sapir (1927, 1934). The prime movers in modern cognitive anthropology, which began to take form in the mid-1950s, have also been anthropological linguists. The development of precise methods of classifying, describing and analyzing the phonological and structural features and patterns of language and their relationships had earlier made linguistics the most exact of the social sciences. These analytic constructs and associated working procedures were then adapted to the study of cognition, which may be regarded as semantics placed in an ethnological framework. The tie with linguistics continues to be strong in modern anthropological studies of cognition and, although some ethnologists concerned with cognition reject the ideas and methods derived from linguistics, most studies are either conducted by anthropological linguists or make use of linguistic ideas and procedures.

Cognitive anthropology aims to understand native concepts of the universe, how they are formulated or organized and how they are used. This goal involves another goal, of developing a mode of study free from the ethnocentrism imposed by the cognitive processes and interpretations of the culture of the investigator, which are thought to distort or mask the realities of foreign cultures. Thus, ideally, studies of cognition provide unbiased ethnography for multiple uses. However, as the stated aim of understanding "native systems of classification" or "folk taxonomies" suggests, the primary concern of cognitive studies is not the acquisition of ethnographic information. It is instead attaining an understanding of the systems, patterns, or structures involved in cognition, the regularities in the ways in which human beings segregate and classify the phenomena of the universe and perceive relations between the categories of phenomena. Attempts to see the ordering principles have relied upon comparing and contrasting categories with other categories, which might or might not bear categorical labels in the native language.

Thus far, the classes or categories studied in cognitive anthropology have been principally terminologies or taxonomies of kinship, colors, cuisine, botany, and disease. The intra- and inter-cultural comparison of systems of classification relates to an ultimate goal which, although seemingly perceived only hazily in early studies of cognition, is now explicitly stated. Through comparative study, cognitive anthropology seeks insights about the cognitive unity of mankind. Continuity with the anthropological past is clearly evident in this goal since "cognitive unity" may be seen as a modern version of the idea of psychic unity. Still another idea that may be traced to the beginnings of anthropology is evident in the word "unity." The view that human neurology is such that members of different societies and races perceive and categorize in panhuman ways is part of the enduring anthropological view that man, as a single species, is everywhere essentially alike in innate attributes. The study of differences—in cognitive categories as well as in other matters—is at the same time the study of similarities.

The general aim of understanding principles or structures that are assumed to underlie human thought is shared by studies of symbolism generally placed under the loose labels of "new structuralism" or "French structuralism," as exemplified particularly by certain of the writings of Claude Lévi-Strauss. None of these writings, which are generally lengthy, is here reproduced. Far more intuitively based than studies of cognition stemming directly from linguistics, these studies have explicitly or implicitly emphasized as a structural feature of thought the concept of binary opposition, which appears to be so common among societies of the world. Although many examples of pairs of conceptions that are seen as opposing each other, such as black-white, good-evil, dark-light, and perhaps male-female, may be so regarded in native thought, not all phenomena labeled in these studies as opposing pairs are consciously so regarded in the native view. Perhaps some oppositions are so conceived by the scholarly observers because of the cognitive patterns of the scholars themselves. A group of somewhat similar studies of the nature and significance of symbols, among which the writings of Lévi-Strauss are sometimes included, are ordinarily referred to as studies of "symbolism." As exemplified by the writings of Victor W. Turner (1967, 1968, 1969), these studies relate symbols principally to social features of the societies studied but also make use of the ideas of binary opposition and complementarity. Some of these writings, for example those of Mary Douglas (1966, 1970), have been commended for their ingenuity and chided for being vague and intuitive (Spiro 1968).

The ideas of the linguist Noam Chomsky have influenced some anthropologists interested in the subject of cognition. In the following essay, his views resemble in certain respects those of Lévi-Strauss but differ in other respects (Chomsky 1968:64–66). Chomsky and other linguists (e.g., Lenneberg 1967) proceed on the basis of the hypothesis that the ability to create and use language is uniquely human and genetically transmitted, depending upon organic structures, principally neurophysiological, that underly particular language functions. One line of their research, also followed by some cognitive anthropologists, is to attempt to understand the nature of these innate structures and thereby to gain understanding of language and other cultural behavior. No firm conclusions have yet been offered by these studies, and the extension of linguistic theory to nonlinguistic behavior is beset with many problems (Keesing 1972). Although the principal goal of this research is to describe universal patterns of thinking, the actual studies appear to focus primarily on what is genetically innate, and their concern with culture relates only to intersocietal variations from the common master pattern. From the viewpoint of cultural anthropology, however, this linguistically oriented research nevertheless concerns the subject of culture.

21 INTRODUCTION TO COGNITIVE ANTHROPOLOGY
STEPHEN A. TYLER

The Old and the New

. . . Cognitive anthropology constitutes a new theoretical orientation. It focuses on *discovering* how different peoples organize and use their cultures. This is not so much a search for some generalized unit of behavioral analysis as it is an attempt to understand the *organizing principles underlying* behavior. It is assumed that each people has a unique system for perceiving and organizing material phenomena—things, events, behavior, and emotions. The object of study is not these material phenomena themselves, but the way they are organized in the minds of men. Cultures then are not material phenomena; they are cognitive organizations of material phenomena. Consequently, cultures are neither described by mere arbitrary lists of anatomical traits and institutions such as house type, family type, kinship type, economic type, and personality type, nor are they necessarily equated with some over-all integrative pattern of these phenomena. Such descriptions may tell us something about the way an anthropologist thinks about a culture, but there is little, if any, reason to believe that they tell us anything of how the people of some culture think about their culture.

In essence, cognitive anthropology seeks to answer two questions: What material phenomena are significant for the people of some culture; and, how do they organize these phenomena? Not only do cultures differ among one another in their organization of material phenomena, they differ as well in the kinds of material phenomena they organize. The people of different cultures may not recognize the same kinds of material phenomena as relevant, even though from an outsider's point of view the same material phenomena may be present in every case. For example,

From *Cognitive Anthropology*, edited by Stephen A. Tyler. Copyright © 1969 by Holt, Rinehart and Winston, Inc. Reprinted by permission of Holt, Rinehart and Winston, Inc.

we distinguish between dew, fog, ice, and snow, but the Koyas of South India do not. They call all of these *mancu*. Even though they can perceive the differences among these if asked to do so, these differences are not significant to them. On the other hand, they recognize and name at least seven different kinds of bamboo, six more than I am accustomed to distinguish. Similarly, even though I know that my cousin George is the son of my mother's sister, while my cousin Paul is the son of my mother's brother, this objective difference is irrelevant to my system of classification. They are both "cousins." If I were a Koya, however, this difference would be highly important. I would call my mother's brother's son *baaTo* and my mother's sister's son *annaal*. Even though the same material phenomena are objectively present, they are subjectively perceived and organized differently by Koyas than they are by Americans. Furthermore, there is no apparent over-all integrative pattern which relates the classification of bamboo to the classification of relatives. These are separate classes of phenomena with distinctive and unrelated principles of organization.

Not only may the same phenomena be organized differently from culture to culture, they may also be organized in more than one way in the same culture. There is, then, *intracultural* variation as well as *intercultural* variation. Some intracultural variations may be idiosyncratic, but more important from the anthropologist's point of view are those variations which are used by different classes of people and/or occur in different situations and contexts. For example, if we are interested in describing the way people classify colors we may discover that there are variant patterns dependent upon the sex or age of our informant as well as his general experience with colors. Thus, females in our culture can generally discriminate and name more colors than males. Or, to take another example, the classification of relatives may be partially dependent on the social statuses of the people talking about relatives, the relationship between them, and the social context in which they are conversing. A Telugu refers to his younger sister as *celli* when talking to another member of his family, but when speaking to a person outside his family group, he uses the term *cellelu,* which may mean younger sister, or mother's sister's daughter, or father's brother's daughter.

A consequence of this interest in variation is the idea that cultures are not unitary phenomena, that is, they cannot be described by only one set of organizing principles. For each class of relevant phenomena there may be several alternative organizations. The realization or choice of one alternative to the exclusion of some other is dependent upon a variety of factors. For example, some people have more or less knowledge of some phenomena, or certain alternatives may be acceptable only in particular contexts. If these variants are used only in certain identified situations, or if there is a hierarchy of choice so that variants are ordered on the basis of their relative desirability, we can say that they are in complementary distribution and do not conflict with one another. In such a situation it is possible for a large number of variants to coexist. But, if these variants conflict in their organization and the situations in which they occur, there must be some means of harmonizing the contrast. This can be achieved by some change in the principles of organization or in the situations in which they occur. For example, among the Koyas, the pig is classed as an edible animal, but among neighboring Muslims the pig is classed as inedible and defiling. Suppose a Koya woman were married to a Muslim man. While in her husband's home she could not act on her classification of the pig as an edible by eating pork; while visiting her parents in the absence of her husband she could. So long as the two systems of classification can be realized in these isolated contexts there is no necessary conflict between them, and both may persist. If these contexts were not in complementary distribution, some rearrangement of the two contrasting systems of classification would have to take place if the marriage were to persist.

In fact, this is an argument for a different kind of unitary description which sees unity as emerging from the ordered relations between variants and contexts. Variants are not mere deviations from some assumed basic organization; with their rules of occurrence *they are the organization*. It must be emphasized, however, that such a unitary description can be achieved only by the anthropologist. It is highly unlikely that the members of a culture ever see their culture as *this kind of* unitary phenomenon. Each individual member may have a unique, unitary model of his culture, but is not necessarily cognizant of all the unique, unitary models held by other members of his culture. He will be aware of and use some, but it is only the anthropologist who completely transcends these particular models and constructs a single, unitary model. This cognitive organization exists solely in the mind of the anthropologist. Yet, to the extent that it will generate conceptual models used by the people of a particular culture, it is a model of their cognitive systems.

The "theory" here is not so much a THEORY OF CULTURE as it is *theories of cultures,* or a theory of descriptions. The aim of such a theory is to provide answers to the questions: How would the people of some other culture expect me to behave if I were a member of their culture; and what are the rules of appropriate behavior in their culture? Answers to these questions are provided by an adequate description of the rules used by the people in that culture. Consequently, this description itself constitutes the "theory" for that culture, for it represents the conceptual model of organization used by its members. Such a theory is validated by our ability to predict how these people would expect us to behave if we were members of their culture.

Order out of Chaos

In a sense, cognitive anthropology is not a new departure. Many anthropologists have expressed an interest in how the natives see their world. Yet, there is a difference of focus between the old and the new. Where earlier anthropologists sought categories of description in their native language, cognitive anthropologists seek categories of description in the language of their natives. Ultimately, this is the old problem of what do we describe and how do we describe it? Obviously, we are interested in the mental codes of other peoples, but how do we infer these mental processes? Thus far, it has been assumed that the easiest entry to such processes is through language, and most of the recent studies have sought to discover codes that are mapped in language. Nearly all of this work has been concerned with how other peoples "name" the "things" in their environment and how these names are organized into larger groupings. These names are thus both an index to what is significant in the environment of some other people, and a means of discovering how these people organize their perceptions of the environment. Naming is seen as one of the chief methods for imposing order on perception.

In a very real sense, the anthropologist's problem is to discover how other people create order out of what appears to him to be utter chaos. Imagine, for a moment, a being from another planet equipped with all our sensory apparatus who perceives for the first time the infinite variety of sight and sound in which we live. Suppose further that he is attempting to describe this world in a scientific report for his colleagues at home. At first, everything would be chaotic. Each sound and object would seem to be unlike any other. His experience would be similar to what we feel the first time we hear a language we have never heard before. But, with infinite time and patience, let us assume that he is able to describe everything he perceives—that is, the total environment of earth. Probably he would eventually be able to organize his report around concepts acceptable to his world or devise new ones as he saw fit. Yet, would anyone of us accept his report as an accurate account of the world as we see and live in it? If he in fact describes everything, we would not. Nor would we accept his organization of the things he perceived, for they would almost certainly not fit our own system of organization. Unlike this mythical creature, we do not live in a world in which we discriminate among all the possible sensory stimuli in our environment, nor do we react to each stimulus as if it were totally new and foreign. In effect, we choose to ignore many of those perceptual differences which make each object unique. In large part, we do this by naming. By naming we classify and put objects which to us are similar into the same category, even though we can perceive differences among them. For example, the chair in which I sit has a nick in the left leg, yet I class it as a "straight chair" no different from others like it in the room.

We classify because life in a world where nothing was the same would be intolerable. It is through naming and classification that the whole rich world of infinite variability shrinks to manipulable size and becomes bearable. Our methods of classification are entirely arbitrary and subjective. There is nothing in the external world which demands that certain things go together and others do not. It is our perception of similarities and differences together with a set of hierarchical cues that determine which things go together. We not only react to certain discriminable stimuli as if they were the same, we name them and organize them into groupings. Thus, for example, there are objects with a seat, a back and four legs which we label *chairs,* even though no two of these objects are exactly alike. The word *chair* then stands as a sign for a whole class of objects with a seat, a back, and four legs. This sign, too, is arbitrary—we might as well call these objects *argoboos.* Just as there is no inherent quality in an object that forces us to perceive it in exactly one way, neither is there an intrinsic characteristic associating an object with its name. Consequently, with the passage of time, a class of objects may be renamed, but the class of objects denoted by this name does not change, or, conversely, the class of objects denoted by a name may change, but the name does not.

Thus, we subjectively group the phenomena of our perceptual world into named classes. These classes are not disparate and singular. They are organized into larger groupings. To the extent that these groupings are hierarchically arranged by a process of inclusion, they form a *taxonomy*. To continue the example of chairs, there are other objects in our homes which are not chairs. There are sofas, tables, desks, cabinets, and the like. Each of these constitutes a separate class, some with many subclasses. For example there are end tables, dining tables, and coffee tables, but each of these is also a member of some more inclusive class—the class of things called "furniture." A portion of this taxonomy is shown in Figure 21-1.

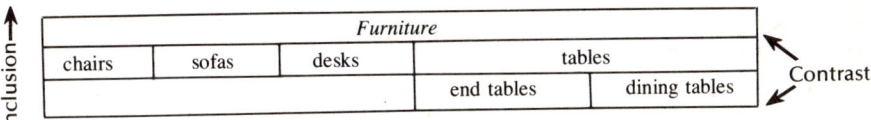

FIGURE 21-1 Taxonomy of furniture.

Figure 21-1 illustrates two processes characteristic of taxonomies: (1) items at the same level contrast with one another; (2) items at different levels are related by inclusion. At the bottom level are the more highly discriminated classes, at the top is the most inclusive class. Thus, end tables are kinds of tables as tables are kinds of furniture; end tables are not the same as dining tables just as tables are not the same as chairs. These relationships could also be represented in a branching diagram as in Figure 21-2.

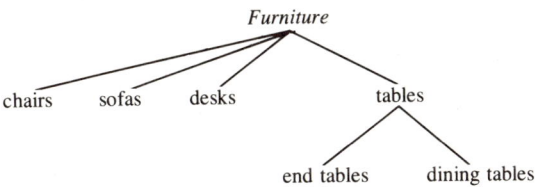

FIGURE 21-2 Branching diagram.

This particular taxonomy constitutes one *semantic domain* in our culture. A sematic domain consists of a class of objects all of which share at least one feature in common which differentiates them from other semantic domains. Chairs, sofas, desks, end tables, and dining tables have in common the designation *furniture*.

Note that Figure 21-2 tells us nothing of the things which distinguish a chair from a table. It tells us only that they are different. Suppose you had to tell someone how you know that one object is a chair and the other is a table. In the process of doing this, you might describe certain underlying features, some of which both chairs and tables share and some of which they do not. For example, you might say a chair has four legs, a seat, and a back, but a table has four legs and a top. Chairs would thus differ from tables by the presence of two features—a seat and a back, and the absence of one feature—a top. These underlying features are *components* or *features* of meaning. They are some of the dimensions of meaning underlying the general domain of *furniture*. That these are not the only dimensions is apparent in the contrasts between desk and table. Both pieces of furniture have four legs and a top. Using only the two features you have isolated, it is not possible to say how a table differs from a desk. Should you wish to show how each of these items differs from the other you would have to discover other features of meaning.

Semantic features, like labels, are also organized. A part of the taxonomy of "animals" in American English consists of the following lexemes: cow, bull, heifer, calf, steer, mare, stallion, filly, foal, colt, gelding, sow, boar, gilt, barrow, shoat, piglet, ewe, ram, wether, lamb, livestock, cattle, swine, horse, sheep. This taxonomy is arranged in Table 21–1.

On even casual examination the items occurring in the lowest level of Table 21–1 seem to be related in some way. Closer inspection reveals that similar distinc-

Table 21–1 Taxonomy of "Livestock"

	Animal		
		Livestock	
cattle	horse	sheep	swine
cow	mare	ewe	sow
bull	stallion	ram	boar
steer	gelding	wether	barrow
heifer	filly	lamb	gilt
calf	colt		shoat
	foal		piglet

tions are made under each major category of livestock. The contrast between cow and bull, for example, is the same as the contrast between boar and sow; ram and ewe; stallion and mare. We can readily identify this contrast as one of sex or gender, male versus female. Similarly, there is an identical contrast between bull and steer; ram and wether; stallion and gelding; boar and barrow. Again, we would identify this as a contrast between male animals versus neutered animals. In addition to this sex contrast there is a further contrast between mature and immature animals. A calf is an immature cow or bull and a heifer is an "adolescent" cow. All the lexemes in the lowest level of Table 21–1 reflect the two semantic features of sex and maturity. Each of these has three values: sex (male, female, neuter); maturity (adult, adolescent, child). Note, however, that horse and pig have an additional feature of maturity denoting "newborn" or "baby" (piglet and foal).

Using symbols: ♂—male; ♀—female; ∅—neuter; M^{-1}—adult; M^{-2}—adolescent; M^{-3}—child; M^{-4}—baby; H—horse; P—swine; C—cattle; S—sheep; the distribution of features for each label can be stated in formulae as follows:

stallion	H ♂ M⁻¹	boar	P ♂ M⁻¹
mare	H ♀ M⁻¹	sow	P ♀ M⁻¹
gelding	H ∅ M⁻¹M⁻²	barrow	P ∅ M⁻¹M⁻²
filly	H ♀ M⁻²	gilt	P ♀ M⁻²
colt	H ♂ ♀ M⁻³	shoat	P ♂ ♀ M⁻³
foal	H ♂ ♀ M⁻⁴	piglet	P ♂ ♀ M⁻⁴

The first formula reads: a stallion is a horse, male, adult, or more appropriately, a stallion is an adult male horse. Such formulae are simply expressions of the distribution of features for each separate label. A box figure shows how these features distribute across the whole set of labels.

Reading from the diagram, a stallion is an adult male horse and a mare is an adult female horse. The features "adult" and "male" *intersect* at the space containing the label "stallion," while the features "adult" and "female" intersect at the space containing the label "mare." Since this diagram has two major features (maturity and sex) which cut across (intersect) one another, it is a *paradigm*. Features are paradigmatically arranged when they are: (1) multiple; (2) intersect.

Paradigms and taxonomies are different kinds of semantic arrangements. In contrast to a paradigm, a taxonomy orders its labels by contrast and inclusion. A taxonomy typically asserts that items in lower levels are *kinds of* items in higher levels. A horse, for example, is a *kind* of livestock. A paradigm makes no such assertion. In Figure 21-3 for example, a shoat is not necessarily a kind of boar.

		Sex		
		male ♂	female ♀	neuter ∅
Maturity	adult M-1	stallion boar	mare sow	gelding barrow
	adolescent M-2		filly gilt	
	child M-3	colt shoat		
	baby M-4	foal piglet		

FIGURE 21-3 Paradigm of features for "horse" and "swine." For cattle and sheep the contrast between baby and child would be omitted. Sheep also omits the adolescent distinction. There is however an archaic form for newborn sheep *viz.* "Yeanling."

In addition to taxonomies and paradigms semantic features may be arranged on a branching diagram called a *tree*. Features in a tree are ordered by sequential contrast of only one feature at a time. Trees are thus based on successive choices between only two alternatives. Such a semantic arrangement is most frequently encountered in zoological or botanical texts. Figure 21-4 is a simplified example of a tree.

A reading of Figure 21-4 would be: Are the flowers spurred? If yes, are the flowers regular? If they are regular, then this is a delphinium. Unlike a paradigm, the features of a tree do not intersect, and unlike a taxonomy items at lower levels are not included in higher levels. Consequently, paradigms, taxonomies and trees are fundamentally different kinds of semantic arrangements. Each semantic domain of a culture may be ordered by one or more of these arrangements.

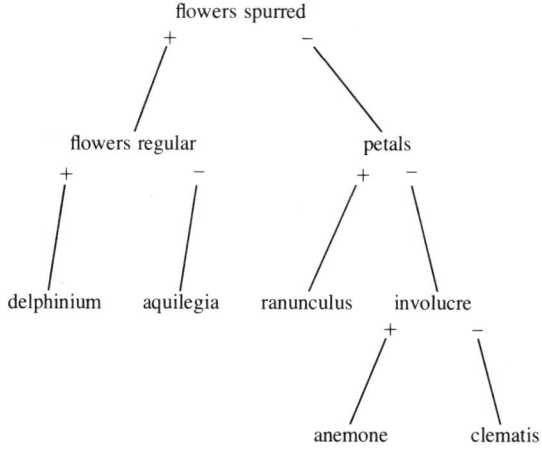

FIGURE 21-4 A tree arrangement. Plus (+) indicates presence of the feature, minus (-) its absence. Thus, if a flower is not spurred, has no petals, and no involucre, it is a clematis.

A culture consists of many semantic domains organized around numerous features of meaning, and no two cultures share the same set of semantic domains or features of meaning, nor do they share the same methods of organizing these features. The problem for the anthropologist is to discover these semantic domains and their features, for an anthropologist in the field is much like our interplanetary visitor. There is no familiar order to the way these strange people organize their world. But, unlike our visitor, the anthropologist must avoid imposing his own semantic categories on what he perceives. He must attempt to discover the semantic world in which these people live. There are, then, two ways of bringing order out of apparent chaos—*impose* a preexisting order on it, or *discover* the order underlying it. Nearly all of earlier anthropology was characterized by the first method. By contrast, cognitive anthropology seeks to develop methods which can be used for discovering and describing these principles of organization.

Since such semantic systems are implicit in our use of language, they constitute one of the most significant features of human communication. Yet, what can be communicated and how it is communicated is not solely determined by this kind of semantic feature. Other semantic features deriving from the context of communication are equally important. Context includes the manner of communication (for example, verbal and written), the social setting, and the linguistic repertoires of speaker and hearer. Contextual semantic features and their mutual interdependence are as much a part of the cognitive system as taxonomies and semantic domains.

There still remains the question of how we discover features in cultures other than our own. If you will attempt to complete the statement of semantic features for the taxonomy of furniture, you will see that the discovery of these features is difficult enough in your native language. It is even more difficult in a strange language. As a consequence, new fieldwork techniques and methods have had to be devised. Most important among these are techniques of *controlled eliciting* and methods of *formal analysis*.

Controlled eliciting utilizes sentence frames derived from the language of the people being studied. The aim of such eliciting is to enable the ethnographer to behave linguistically in ways appropriate to the culture he is studying. This involves the use of linguistically correct questions which relate concepts meaningful in that culture. Suppose you are a foreigner attempting to learn something about American culture. On seeing an object for which you do not know an English term, one possible sequence of related questions and responses might be:

Q. What is this?
A. This is a sow.
Q. Is that a sow, too?
A. No, that's a boar.
Q. Is a boar a kind of sow?
A. No, a boar is a kind of livestock.
Q. Is a sow a kind of livestock?
A. Yes.
Q. How many kinds of livestock are there?
A. There are pigs, horses, mules, sheep, goats and others.

This sequence indicates that sows and boars are conceptually linked and that there are numerous other things grouped with them in the taxonomy of livestock. Note that decisions concerning the inclusion of items within this taxonomy are made by the informant, not by the investigator. Contrast this procedure with a familiar questionnaire technique derived from handbooks on social science methodology. Is the cow __very like; __somewhat like; __only a little like; __not at all like a god (check one). Aside from the spurious scaling, this question would be meaningful only in societies of English speakers in which there were: (a) cows, (b) gods, (c) some evidence that gods and cows were conceptually linked, or (d) sociologists. In this technique, the investigator has already made all the decisions about conceptual relevance. The informant's responses can only be replications in one way or another of the investigator's judgments about conceptual relevance. In a sense, such a method merely tells you what you already know. Controlled eliciting, on the other hand, is designed to provide the ethnographer with not only the answers, but also to assist him in discovering the relevant questions. It clearly derives from the fact that the questioning process is itself the dominant factor in scientific investigation.

Where the procedures and results of controlled eliciting are contained in the report, two things are achieved: (1) there is an explicit record of how the data were gathered; (2) a public record of the results is available.

Formal analysis is simply one method of stating the results of such controlled eliciting. It differs from other methods in its emphasis on internal consistency, completeness, and form. A particular set of data relating to some semantic domain must be explained by the relationship between units comprising that domain—not by determinants outside it. The problem of external determinants is delayed until internal determinants are analyzed. For example, the question of whether I call my mother's sister's son "cousin" because he is outside my nuclear family cannot be determined until I know the system of relations between cousin, brother, and all the other kin terms in the English system. A formal analysis is complete when the relations among all the units comprising a semantic domain are described.

The New Order

The aims and methods of cognitive anthropology have important implications for cultural anthropology. They entail a rethinking of the culture concept, the comparative method, and of ethnography.

In this discussion culture has been identified with cognition. This must strike some cultural anthropologists as a truncated version of the culture concept, for it neglects many of their traditional interests. They might well ask, What about process? What about behavior? What about motivation? Implicit in these questions is an assumption that in addition to cognitive systems a theory of culture must explain cultures as systems emerging from patterned frequencies of observed behavior and processes of development and change. *As a general statement of anthropological goals, these are relevant considerations, but they are not relevant to a theory of culture.* There is no necessity to assume that the cognitive order is either systematically a derivative of or a predictor of substantive actions. Just as the grammar of a language provides no information on what an individual speaker will say on any given occasion, so too a cognitive description of a culture does not pretend to predict the actual behavior of any individual. The formal analysis of culture, like a grammar, is concerned only with what is expected and appropriate. And just as an adequate grammar is neither contingent upon prior assumptions concerning developmental processes nor necessarily explains them, a grammar of culture need make no assumptions about nor attempt to explain these processes. So construed, neither prediction of actual events nor specification of developmental process is a necessary component of a theory of culture. To paraphrase Collingwood, cultural anthropology is not a description of events or an account of change. The cultural anthropologist is only concerned with those events which are expressions of underlying thoughts. His aim is to penetrate beyond mere material representation to the logical nexus of underlying concepts.

Culture, conceived as the totality of human behavior, ideas, history, institutions and artifacts has never been particularly useful as a meaningful method of explaining ethnographic facts. Such a conception merely asserts that culture is equivalent to the whole of human knowledge. As a device which purports to explain all of man's learned behavior, motivations, pre-historic record, ecological adaptations, biological limitations, and evolution it attempts too much. What we need is a more limited notion of culture which stresses *theories of culture*. Rather than attempt to develop a general THEORY OF CULTURE, the best we can hope for at present is particular theories of cultures. These theories will constitute complete, accurate descriptions of particular cognitive systems. Only when such particular descriptions are expressed in a single metalanguage with known logical properties will we have arrived at a general theory of culture. Such a general theory will be equivalent to the language in which we describe cultures. In effect we already have a pseudometalanguage. It is for this reason that nearly all ethnographies have similar chapter headings. The problem with this metalanguage is that it assumes universality without prior demonstration. Its universality inheres in the language of description and not necessarily in the object being described.

At issue here are two contrasting views of cultural anthropology. The central issue is, Is cultural anthropology a *natural* or a *formal* science? Traditional cultural anthropology is based on the assumption that its data are discrete material phenomena which can be analyzed like the material phenomena of any other natural science. Cognitive anthropology is based on the assumption that its data are mental phenomena which can be analyzed by formal methods similar to those of mathematics and logic. Each particular culture consists of a set of logical principles which order relevant material phenomena. To the cognitive anthropologist these logical principles rather than the material phenomena are the object of investigation. For the cognitive anthropologist cultural anthropology is a formal science. It seems likely that the logical operations underlying principles of ordering are finite and universal, but capable of generating an infinite number of possible specific orderings. In this limited sense, cognitive anthropology constitutes a return to Bastian's search for the "psychic unity of mankind."

The implications for the comparative method follow directly from the above. The central issue in comparative analysis is, What is the unit of comparison? There have been many attempts to specifically delimit the unit of comparison. Yet most so-called cross-cultural comparisons have really been nothing more than cross-tribal or cross-community comparisons. Obviously, if a culture is the unit of comparison, then we must compare whole systems which are bounded in space and time or demonstrate that the parts of systems we are comparing are justifiably isolable. Since most ethnographies are not sufficiently complete for either of these possibilities, the whole comparative approach based on substantive variables must be abandoned if our aim is indeed cultural comparison. Those who insist that no fact has meaning except by comparison are right, but the implication that comparison can occur only between similar facts from different systems does not follow. It is much more pertinent to compare similar, but not identical facts within the same system. This is not so much a total abandonment of the comparative method; it is a matter of priorities. Comparisons between systems can only be useful if the facts compared are truly comparable, and we cannot know what facts are comparable until the facts themselves are adequately described. When this is achieved, the units of comparison will be formal features rather than substantive variables.

22 LANGUAGE AND THE MIND
NOAM CHOMSKY

How does the mind work? To answer this question we must look at some of the work performed by the mind. One of its main functions is the acquisition of knowledge. The two major factors in acquisition of knowledge, perception and learning, have been the subject of study and speculation for centuries. It would not, I think, be misleading to characterize the major positions that have developed as outgrowths of classical rationalism and empiricism. The rationalist theories are marked by the importance they assign to *intrinsic* structures in mental operations—to central processes and organizing principles in perception, and to innate ideas and principles in learning. The empiricist approach, in contrast, has stressed the role of experience and control by environmental factors.

The classical empiricist view is that sensory images are transmitted to the brain as impressions. They remain as ideas that will be associated in various ways, depending on the fortuitous character of experience. In this view a language is merely a collection of words, phrases, and sentences, a habit system, acquired accidentally and extrinsically. In the formulation of Williard Quine, knowledge of a language (and, in fact, knowledge in general) can be represented as "a fabric of sentences variously associated to one another and to nonverbal stimuli by the mechanism of conditioned response." Acquisition of knowledge is only a matter of the gradual construction of this fabric. When sensory experience is interpreted, the already established network may be activated in some fashion. In its essentials, this view has been predominant in modern behavioral science, and it has been accepted with little question by many philosophers as well.

The classical rationalist view is quite different. In this view the mind contains a system of "common notions" that enable it to interpret the scattered and incoherent data of sense in terms of objects and their relations, cause and effect, whole and part, symmetry, gestalt properties, functions, and so on. Sensation, providing only fleeting and meaningless images, is degenerate and particular. Knowledge, much of it beyond immediate awareness, is rich in structure, involves universals, and is highly organized. The innate general principles that underlie and organize this knowledge, according to Leibniz, "enter into our thoughts, of which they form the soul and the connection . . . although we do not at all think of them."

Reprinted from *Psychology Today* Magazine, February 1968, Copyright © Ziff-Davis Publishing Company.

This "active" rationalist view of the acquisition of knowledge persisted through the romantic period in its essentials. With respect to language, it achieves its most illuminating expression in the profound investigations of Wilhelm von Humboldt. His theory of speech perception supposes a generative system of rules that underlies speech production as well as its interpretation. The system is generative in that it makes infinite use of finite means. He regards a language as a structure of forms and concepts based on a system of rules that determine their interrelations, arrangement, and organization. But these finite materials can be combined to make a never-ending product.

In the rationalist and romantic tradition of linguistic theory, the normal use of language is regarded as characteristically innovative. We construct sentences that are entirely new to us. There is no substantive notion of "analogy" or "generalization" that accounts for this creative aspect of language use. It is equally erroneous to describe language as a "habit structure" or as a network of associated responses. The innovative element in normal use of language quickly exceeds the bounds of such marginal principles as analogy or generalization (under any substantive interpretation of these notions). It is important to emphasize this fact because the insight has been lost under the impact of the behaviorist assumptions that have dominated speculation and research in the twentieth century.

In Humboldt's view, acquisition of language is largely a matter of maturation of an innate language capacity. The maturation is guided by internal factors, by an innate "form of language" that is sharpened, differentiated, and given its specific realization through experience. Language is thus a kind of latent structure in the human mind, developed and fixed by exposure to specific linguistic experience. Humboldt believes that all languages will be found to be very similar in their grammatical form, similar not on the surface but in their deeper inner structures. The innate organizing principles severely limit the class of possible languages, and these principles determine the properties of the language that is learned in the normal way.

The active and passive views of perception and learning have elaborated with varying degrees of clarity since the seventeenth century. These views can be confronted with empirical evidence in a variety of ways. Some recent work in psychology and neurophysiology is highly suggestive in this regard. There is evidence for the existence of central processes in perception, specifically for control over the functioning of sensory neurons by the brain-stem reticular system. Behavioral counterparts of this central control have been under investigation for several years. Furthermore, there is evidence for innate organization of the perceptual system of a highly specific sort at every level of biological organization. Studies of the visual system of the frog, the discovery of specialized cells responding to angle and motion in the lower cortical centers of cats and rabbits, and the somewhat comparable investigations of the auditory system of frogs—all are relevant to the classical questions of intrinsic structure mentioned earlier. These studies suggest that there are highly organized, innately determined perceptual systems that are adapted closely to the animal's "life space" and that provide the basis for what we might call "acquisition of knowledge." Also relevant are certain behavioral studies of human infants, for example those showing the preference for faces over other complex stimuli.

These and other studies make it reasonable to inquire into the possibility that complex intellectual structures are determined narrowly by innate mental organization. What is perceived may be determined by mental processes of considerable depth. As far as language learning is concerned, it seems to me that a rather convincing argument can be made for the view that certain principles intrinsic to the mind provide invariant structures that are a precondition for linguistic experience. In the course of this article I would like to sketch some of the ways such conclusions might be clarified and firmly established.

There are several ways linguistic evidence can be used to reveal properties of human perception and learning. In this section we consider one research strategy that might take us nearer to this goal.

Let us say that in interpreting a certain physical stimulus a person constructs a "percept." This percept represents some of his conclusions (in general, unconscious) about the stimulus. To the extent that we can characterize such percepts, we can go on to investigate the mechanisms that relate stimulus and percept. Imagine a model of perception that takes stimuli as inputs and arrives at percepts as "outputs." The model might contain a system of beliefs, strategies for interpreting stimuli, and other factors, such as the organization of memory. We would then have a perceptual model that might be represented graphically (Figure 22–1).

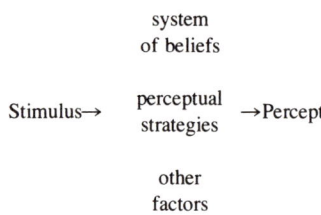

FIGURE 22–1 Model for perception. Each physical stimulus, after interpretation by the mental processes, will result in a percept.

Consider next the system of beliefs that is a component of the perceptual model. How was this acquired? To study this problem, we must investigate a second model, which takes certain data as input and gives as "output" (again, internally represented) the system of beliefs operating in the perceptual model. This second model, a model of learning, would have its own intrinsic structure, as did the first. This structure might consist of conditions on the nature of the system of beliefs that can be acquired, of innate inductive strategies, and again, of other factors such as the organization of memory (Figure 22–2).

Under further conditions, which are interesting but not relevant here, we can take these perceptual and learning models as theories of the acquisition of knowledge, rather than of belief. How then would the models apply to language? The

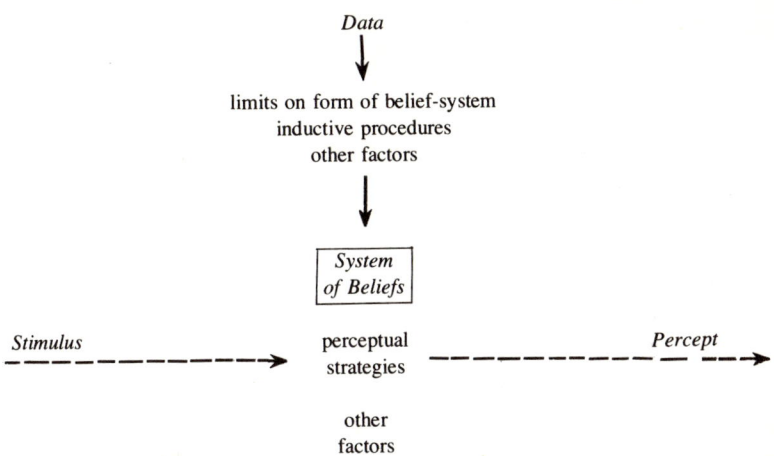

FIGURE 22-2 Model for learning. One's system of beliefs, a part of the perception model, is acquired from data as shown above.

input stimulus to the perceptual model is a speech signal, and the percept is a representation of the utterance that the hearer takes the signal to be and of the interpretation he assigns to it. We can think of the percept as the structural description of a linguistic expression which contains certain phonetic, semantic, and syntactic information. Most interesting is the syntactic information, which best can be discussed by examining a few typical cases.

The three sentences in the example seem to be the same syntactic structure [*see Figure 22-3 below*]. Each contains the subject *I*, and the predicate of each consists of a verb (*told, expected, persuaded*), a noun phrase (*John*), and an embedded predicate phrase (*to leave*). This similarity is only superficial, however—a similarity in what we may call the "surface structure" of these sentences, which differ in important ways when we consider them with somewhat greater care.

The differences can be seen when the sentences are paraphrased or subjected to certain grammatical operations, such as the conversion from active to passive forms. For example, in normal conversation the sentence "I told John to leave" can be roughly paraphrased as "What I told John was to leave." But the other two sentences cannot be paraphrased as "What I persuaded John was to leave" or "What I expected John was to leave." Sentence 2 can be paraphrased as: "It was expected by me that John would leave." But the other two sentences cannot undergo a corresponding formal operation, yielding: "It was persuaded by me that John would leave" or "It was told by me that John should leave."

Sentences 2 and 3 differ more subtly. In Sentence 3 *John* is the direct object of *persuade*, but in Sentence 2 *John* is not the direct object of *expect*. We can show this by using these verbs in slightly more complex sentences: "I persuaded the doctor to examine John" and "I expected the doctor to examine John." If we replace the embedded proposition *the doctor to examine John* with its passive form *John to be examined by the doctor,* the change to the passive does not, in itself, change the meaning. We can accept as paraphrases "I expected the doctor to examine John" and "I expected John to be examined by the doctor." But we cannot accept as paraphrases "I persuaded the doctor to examine John" and "I persuaded John to be examined by the doctor."

(1) I told John to leave
(2) I expected John to leave
(3) I persuaded John to leave

First Paraphrase

(1a) What I told John was to leave (ACCEPTABLE)
(2a) What I expected John was to leave (UNACCEPTABLE)
(3a) What I persuaded John was to leave (UNACCEPTABLE)

Second Paraphrase

(1b) It was told by me that John would leave (UNACCEPTABLE)
(2b) It was expected by me that John would leave (ACCEPTABLE)
(3b) It was persuaded by me that John would leave (UNACCEPTABLE)

(4) I expected the doctor to examine John
(5) I persuaded the doctor to examine John

Passive replacement as paraphrase

(4a) I expected John to be examined by the doctor (MEANING RETAINED)
(5a) I persuaded John to be examined by the doctor (MEANING CHANGED)

FIGURE 22-3 Superficial similarity. When the sentences above are paraphrased or are converted from active to passive forms, differences in their deep structure appear.

The parts of these sentences differ in their grammatical functions. In "I persuaded John to leave" *John* is both the object of *persuade* and the subject of *leave*. These facts must be represented in the percept since they are known, intuitively, to the hearer of the speech signal. No special training or instruction is necessary to enable the native speaker to understand these examples, to know which are "wrong" and which "right," although they may all be quite new to him. They are interpreted by the native speaker instantaneously and uniformly, in accordance with structural principles that are known tacitly, intuitively, and unconsciously.

These examples illustrate two significant points. First, the surface structure of a sentence, its organization into various phrases, may not reveal or immediately reflect its deep syntactic structure. The deep structure is not represented directly in the form of the speech signal; it is abstract. Second, the rules that determine deep and surface structure and their interrelation in particular cases must themselves be highly abstract. They are surely remote from consciousness, and in all likelihood they cannot be brought to consciousness.

A study of such examples, examples characteristic of all human languages that have been carefully studied, constitutes the first stage of the linguistic investigation outlined above, namely the study of the percept. The percept contains phonetic and semantic information related through the medium of syntactic structure. There are two aspects to this syntactic structure. It consists of a surface directly related to the phonetic form, and a deep structure that underlies the semantic interpretation. The deep structure is represented in the mind and rarely is indicated directly in the physical signal.

A language, then, involves a set of semantic-phonetic percepts, of sound-meaning correlations, the correlations being determined by the kind of intervening syntactic structure just illustrated. The English language correlates sound and meaning in one way, Japanese in another, and so on. But the general properties of percepts, their forms and mechanisms, are remarkably similar for all languages that have been carefully studied.

Returning to our models of perception and learning, we can now take up the problem of formulating the system of beliefs that is a central component in perceptual processes. In the case of language, the "system of beliefs" would now be called the "generative grammar," the system of rules that specifies the sound-meaning correlation and generates the class of structural descriptions (percepts) that constitute the language in question. The generative grammar, then, represents the speaker-hearer's knowledge of his language. We can use the term *grammar of a language* ambiguously, as referring not only to the speaker's internalized, subconscious knowledge but to the professional linguist's representation of this internalized and intuitive system of rules as well.

How is this generative grammar acquired? Or, using our learning model, what is the internal structure of the device that could develop a generative grammar?

We can think of every normal human's internalized grammar as, in effect, a theory of his language. This theory provides a sound-meaning correlation for an infinite number of sentences. It provides an infinite set of structural descriptions; each contains a surface structure that determines phonetic form and a deep structure that determines semantic content.

In formal terms, then, we can describe the child's acquisition of language as a kind of theory construction. The child discovers the theory of his language with only small amounts of data from that language. Not only does his "theory of the language" have an enormous predictive scope, but it also enables the child to reject a great deal of the very data on which the theory has been constructed. Normal speech consists, in large part, of fragments, false starts, blends, and other distortions of the underlying idealized forms. Nevertheless, as is evident from a study of the mature use of language, what the child learns is the underlying ideal theory. This is a remarkable fact. We must also bear in mind that the child constructs this ideal theory without explicit instruction, that he acquires this knowledge at a time when he is not capable of complex intellectual achievements in many other domains, and that this achievement is relatively independent of intelligence or the particular course of experience. These are facts that a theory of learning must face.

A scientist who approaches phenomena of this sort without prejudice or dogma would conclude that the acquired knowledge must be determined in a rather specific way by intrinsic properties of mental organization. He would then set himself the task of discovering the innate ideas and principles that make such acquisition of knowledge possible.

It is unimaginable that a highly specific, abstract, and tightly organized language comes by accident into the mind of every four-year-old child. If there were not an innate restriction on the form of grammar, then the child could employ innumerable theories to account for his linguistic experience, and no one system, or even small class of systems, would be found exclusively acceptable or even preferable. The child could not possibly acquire knowledge of a language. This restriction on the form of grammar is a precondition for linguistic experience, and it is surely the critical factor in determining the course and result of language learning. The child cannot know at birth which language he is going to learn. But he must "know" that its grammar must be of a predetermined form that excludes many imaginable languages.

The child's task is to select the appropriate hypothesis from this restricted class. Having selected it, he can confirm his choice with the evidence further available to him. But neither the evidence nor any process of induction (in any well-defined sense) could in themselves have led to this choice. Once the hypothesis is sufficiently well confirmed, the child knows the language defined by this hypothesis; consequently, his knowledge extends vastly beyond his linguistic experience, and he can reject much of the experience as imperfect, as resulting from the interaction of many factors, only one of which is the ideal grammar that determines a sound-meaning connection for an infinite class of linguistic expressions. Along such lines as these one might outline a theory to explain the acquisition of language.

As has been pointed out, both the form and meaning of a sentence are determined by syntactic structures that are not represented directly in the signal and that are related to the signal only at a distance, through a long sequence of interpretive rules. This property of abstractness in grammatical structure is of primary importance, and it is on this property that our inferences about mental processes are based. Let us examine this abstractness a little more closely.

Not many years ago, the process of sentence interpretation might have been described approximately along the following lines. A speech signal is received and segmented into successive units (overlapping at the borders). These units are analyzed in terms of their invariant phonetic properties and assigned to "phonemes." The sequence of phonemes, so constructed, is then segmented into minimal grammatically functioning units (morphemes and words). These are again categorized. Successive operations of segmentation and classification will lead to what I have called "surface structure"—an analysis of a sentence into phrases, which can be represented as a proper bracketing of the sentence, with the bracketed units assigned to various categories (Figure 22-3). Each segment—phonetic, syntactic or semantic—would be identified in terms of certain invariant properties. This would be an exhaustive analysis of the structure of the sentence.

With such a conception of language structure, it made good sense to look forward hopefully to certain engineering applications of linguistics—for example, to voice-operated typewriters capable of segmenting an expression into its successive phonetic units and identifying these, so that speech could be converted to some form of phonetic writing in a mechanical way; to mechanical analysis of sentence structure by fairly straight-forward and well-understood computational techniques; and perhaps even beyond to such projects as machine translation. But these hopes have by now been largely abandoned with the realization that this conception of grammatical structure is inadequate at every level, semantic, phonetic, and syntactic. Most important, at the level of syntactic organization, the surface structure indicates semantically significant relations only in extremely simple cases. In general, the deeper aspects of syntactic organization are representable by labeled bracketing, but of a very different sort from that seen in surface structure.

There is evidence of various sorts, both from phonetics and from experimental psychology, that labeled bracketing is an adequate representation of surface structure. It would go beyond the bounds of this paper to survey the phonetic evidence. A good deal of it is presented in a forthcoming book, *Sound Pattern of English,* by myself and Morris Halle. Similarly, very interesting experimental work by Jerry Fodor and his colleagues, based on earlier observations by D. E. Broadbent and Peter Ladefoged, has shown that the disruption of a speech signal (for example, by a superimposed click) tends to be perceived at the boundaries of phrases rather than at the point where the disruption actually occurred, and that in many cases the bracketing of surface structure can be read directly from the data on perceptual displacement. I think the evidence is rather good that labeled bracketing serves to represent the surface structure that is related to the perceived form of physical signals.

Deep structures are related to surface structures by a sequence of certain formal operations, operations now generally called "grammatical transformations." At the levels of sound, meaning, and syntax, the significant structural features of sentences are highly abstract. For this reason they cannot be recovered by elementary data-processing techniques. This fact lies behind the search for central processes in speech perception and the search for intrinsic, innate structure as the basis for language learning.

How can we represent deep structure? To answer this question we must consider the grammatical transformations that link surface structure to the underlying deep structure that is not always apparent.

Consider, for example, the operations of passivization and interrogation. In the sentences (1) John was examined by the doctor, and (2) did the doctor examine John, both have a deep structure similar to the paraphrase of Sentence 1, (3) the doctor examined John. The same network of grammatical relations determines the semantic interpretation in each case. Thus two of the grammatical transformations of English must be the operations of passivization and interrogation that form such surface structures as Sentences 1 and 2 from a deeper structure which in its essentials also underlies Sentence 3. Since the transformations ultimately produce surface structures, they must produce labeled bracketings [*see illustration below*]. But notice that these operations can apply in sequence: we can form the passive question "was John examined by the doctor" by passivization followed by interrogation. Since the result of passivization is a labeled bracketing, it follows that the interrogative transformation operates on a labeled bracketing and forms a new labeled bracketing. Thus a transformation such as interrogation maps a labeled bracketing into a labeled bracketing.

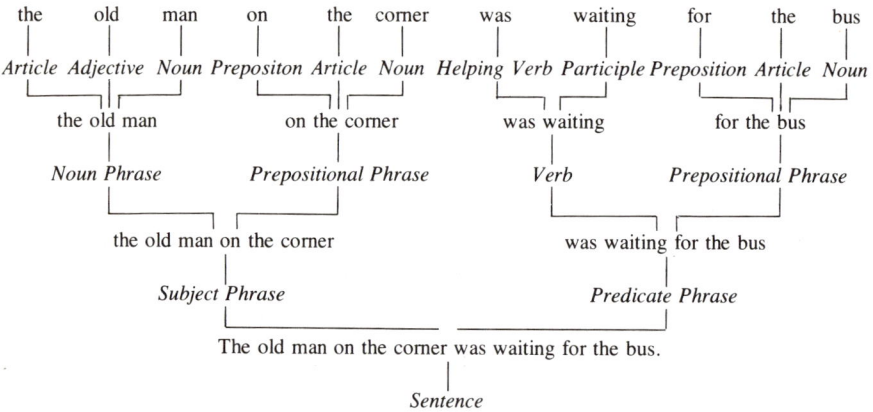

FIGURE 22–4 Surface structure analysis. A type of sentence analysis now abandoned as inadequate at every level is this labeled bracketing which analyzes the sentence by successive division into larger units with each unit assigned to its own category.

By similar argument, we can show that all grammatical transformations are structure-dependent mappings of this sort and that the deep structures which underlie all sentences must themselves be labeled bracketings. Of course, the labeled bracketing that constitutes deep structure will in general be quite different from that representing the surface structure of a sentence. Our argument is somewhat oversimplified, but it is roughly correct. When made precise and fully accurate it strongly supports the view that deep structures, like surface structures, are formally to be taken as labeled bracketings, and that grammatical transformations are mappings of such structures onto other similar structures.

Recent studies have sought to explore the ways in which grammatical structure of the sort just described enters into mental operations. Much of this work has been based on a proposal formulated by George Miller as a first approximation, namely, that the amount of memory used to store a sentence should reflect the number of transformations used in deriving it. For example, H. B. Savin and E. Perchonock investigated this assumption in the following way: they presented to subjects a sentence followed by a sequence of unrelated words. They then determined the number of these unrelated words recalled when the subject attempted to repeat the sentence and the sequence of words. The more words recalled, the less memory used to store the sentence. The fewer words recalled, the more memory used to store the sentence. The results showed a remarkable correlation of amount of memory and number of transformations in certain simple cases. In fact, in their experimental material, shorter sentences with more transformations took up more "space in memory" than longer sentences that involved fewer transformations.

Savin has extended this work and has shown that the effects of deep structure and surface structure can be differentiated by a similar technique. He considered paired sentences with approximately the same deep structure but with one of the pair being more complex in surface structure. He showed that, under the experimental conditions just described, the paired sentences were indistinguishable. But if the sequence of unrelated words precedes, rather than follows, the sentence being tested, then the more complex (in surface structure) of the pair is more difficult to repeat correctly than the simpler member. Savin's very plausible inference is that sentences are coded in memory in terms of deep structure. When the unrelated words precede the test sentence, these words use up a certain amount of short-term memory, and the sentence that is more complex in surface structure cannot be analyzed with the amount of memory remaining. But if the test sentence precedes the unrelated words, it is, once understood, stored in terms of deep structure, which is about the same in both cases. Therefore the same amount of memory remains, in the paired cases, for recall of the following words. This is a beautiful example of the way creative experimental studies can interweave with theoretical work in the study of language and of mental processes.

In speaking of mental processes we have returned to our original problem. We can now see why it is reasonable to maintain that the linguistic evidence supports an "active" theory of acquisition of knowledge. The study of sentences and of speech perception, it seems to me, leads to a perceptual theory of a classical rationalist sort. Representative of this school, among others, were the seventeenth-century Cambridge Platonists, who developed the idea that our perception is guided by notions that originate from the mind and that provide the framework for the interpretation of sensory stimuli. It is not sufficient to suggest that this framework is a store of "neural models" or "schemata" which are in some manner applied to perception (as is postulated in some current theories of perception). We must go well beyond this assumption and return to the view of Wilhelm von Humboldt, who attributed to the mind a system of rules that generates such models and schemata under the stimulation of the senses. The system of rules itself determines the content of the percept that is formed.

We can offer more than this vague and metaphoric account. A generative grammar and an associated theory of speech perception provide a concrete example of the rules that operate and of the mental objects that they construct and manipulate. Physiology cannot yet explain the physical mechanisms that affect these abstract functions. But neither physiology nor psychology provides evidence that calls this account into question or that suggests an alternative. As mentioned earlier, the most exciting current work in the physiology of perception shows that even the peripheral systems analyze stimuli into the complex properties of objects, and that central processes may significantly affect the information transmitted by the receptor organs.

The study of language, it seems to me, offers strong empirical evidence that empiricist theories of learning are quite inadequate. Serious efforts have been made in recent years to develop principles of induction, generalization, and data analysis that would account for knowledge of a language. These efforts have been a total failure. The methods and principles fail not for any superficial reason such as lack of time or data. They fail because they are intrinsically incapable of giving rise to the system of rules that underlies the normal use of language. What evidence is now available supports the view that all human languages share deep-seated properties of organization and structure. These properties—these linguistic universals—can be plausibly assumed to be an innate mental endowment rather than the result of learning. If this is true, then the study of language sheds light on certain long-standing issues in the theory of knowledge. Once again, I see little reason to doubt that what is true of language is true of other forms of human knowledge as well.

There is one further question that might be raised at this point. How does the human mind come to have the innate properties that underlie acquisition of knowledge? Here linguistic evidence obviously provides no information at all. The process by which the human mind has achieved its present state of complexity and its particular form of innate organization are a complete mystery, as much of a mystery as the analogous questions that can be asked about the processes leading to the physical and mental organization of any other complex organism. It is perfectly safe to attribute this to evolution, so long as we bear in mind that there is no substance to this assertion—it amounts to nothing more than the belief that there is surely some naturalistic explanation for these phenomena.

There are, however, important aspects of the problem of language and mind that can be studied sensibly within the limitations of present understanding and technique. I think that, for the moment, the most productive investigations are those dealing with the nature of particular grammars and with the universal conditions met by all human languages. I have tried to suggest how one can move, in successive steps of increasing abstractness, from the study of percepts to the study of grammar and perceptual mechanisms, and from the study of grammar to the study of universal grammar and the mechanism of learning.

In this area of convergence of linguistics, psychology, and philosophy, we can look forward to much exciting work in coming years.

23 AMERICAN KINSHIP TERMS ONCE MORE
ROBBINS BURLING

Introduction

Several times in the last decade American anthropologists have turned to their own kinship terminology as a testing ground for their varied theories. Though these studies have hardly had uniform goals, I think it is fair to note that two themes, in

Reprinted by permission of the author and the *Journal of Anthropological Research*. From the *Southwestern Journal of Anthropology, 26,* 1, 15–24, 1970.

varying proportions and with varying explicitness, have been woven through many of them. One is the ideal of providing a formal analysis, and this seems to have meant an analysis with a sort of mathematical look. No hesitation has been shown in using special symbols that could be carefully defined, that could provide parsimony and precision to one's treatment, and that might even overawe one's less formally inclined or more gullible colleagues. Formal analyses have varied from the purely componential approach of Goodenough (1965),* through Wallace's suggestions for the use of "relative products" (Wallace and Atkins 1960; Wallace MS), to the generative approach of Bock (1968). The other theme found in much of the work on American kinship has been a search for some sort of psychological reality, or an attempt to decide which among various formal analyses is closest to the way in which Americans actually conceive of their own terms (Romney and D'Andrade 1964; Sanday 1968; as well as some of the articles already cited). The possibility that these two goals might be in conflict (as would be the case if the psychologically real solution turned out not to be the most formal or abstract) does not seem to have caused concern.

The analyses of Bock, Goodenough, Wallace, Atkins, and Romney and D'Andrade appear, superficially at least, to be rather different from one another. A good deal of this variation is little more than notational, but the variation must make us inquire what sort of criteria could help us choose among alternatives. The obvious answer is to call upon additional data that might be better explained by one alternative than by another. Thus, when Wallace or Romney and D'Andrade have presented speakers with various sorting or listing tasks, they have, in effect, sought data beyond a formal list of appropriate kin types to help choose among alternatives. Some other investigators seem to have assumed that simply by tightening the formality of their solution they would, in some way unclear to me, automatically approach psychological reality. It strikes me, however, that several additional sources of data that are a bit less artificial than the results of sorting or listing tests, sources which previous analysts have touched upon only tangentially, might be added to the standard lists of kin types to help us reach a satisfactory solution. These additional sources of data are the following:

> 1. Most analysts have taken for granted that they could operate with the assumption that terminological usage was fairly well fixed and consistent at least within a single dialect. Even the most thorough and complete analysis yet offered, that of Goodenough, inevitably suffers most severely from the overrigidity which comes from ignoring alternative and variable usage. Readers like myself who have somewhat different usages must occasionally be bothered by the assurance with which Goodenough states his various principles. It is not quite enough for him to appeal to the standard "that is the way it is in my dialect" because, after all, Goodenough and I can discuss our kinsmen and understand each other with very little difficulty. Goodenough claims to use expressions as "first cousin once removed" (for instance) which I do not use, but this variability hardly interferes with our conversation. In some sense, expressions like "once removed" are at the periphery of American kinship terminology and deserve a different treatment from the more central expressions which we all share. Any realistic

*See pp. 339–340 for references.

description of American kinship terminology ought to leave a place for the slightly varying patterns used by different speakers. Since people with alternative usage can communicate so easily, it is a distortion of our system to dismiss all alternative patterns as irrelevant.

2. Children who have not yet mastered the full scope of adult terminology offer other examples of alternative usage. All analyses of American kinship terms that I have seen have been limited to a fully developed adult system and have disregarded the obvious fact that these must have been gradually built from the simpler systems of a child. One might hope that the ideal treatment even of adult kinship usage might somehow be understandable as the end product of an ontogenetic process.

3. It ought to be obvious to all that speakers can easily define some kinship terms by means of other terms. We can define *grandfather* as "parent's father," *father* as "male parent," *parent* as "either father or mother," and so forth. Our ability to give verbal definitions surely reflects our understanding of our kinship system, but this ability has been only very imperfectly reflected in the analyses of anthropologists. The suggestion that we use relative product definitions goes part way toward meeting this challenge. A number of writers have suggested that it might be more reasonable to define *uncle* as "parent's brother" than to define the word by some such cluster of components as "male, first ascending generation, non-lineal, first collateral line." However even those who have advocated relative product definitions seem to have preferred building up their definitions out of a string of abstract symbols rather than from previously defined words. Thus, Romney and D'Andrade offer "a+a+m" as a definition of *grandfather*. These symbols mean: speaker of either sex's (a)/ parent (+)/ of either sex's (a)/ parent (+)/ who is male (m). Wallace, after listing the meaning of *step-brother* as "child of spouse of parent of ego," seems to feel that he has produced a more elegant or formal analysis by converting this into a symbolic notation "a d c" where a is defined as "child of," d as "spouse of," c as "parent of." I think that if I wanted to produce a "psychologically real" model of American kinship terminology I would be entirely content to leave the definitions in words and forget the symbols. The words strike me as closer to the way ordinary mortal Americans talk, and perhaps they are also closer to the way that Americans think.

It may be useful to take yet another look at American kinship terminology and see whether we cannot give an account that will be compatible with children's usage as well as with adult alternatives and also with our ability to give verbal definitions. I feel that American kinship terminology can be usefully looked upon as if it were a sequence of principles which reflect the route by which we must all have learned our system. I will outline a possible sequence here, and suggest that it is the early principles which in some degree are central to our system and the ones most universally held by all speakers. The later principles are more peripheral. They are more variable from speaker to speaker and even from time to time for the same speaker. Without trying to be exhaustive I think that I can still suggest the skeleton of a description, one which accounts in a rather natural way not only for the terminology of one adult idiolect but also reflects the alternatives used by children, which can be easily adjusted to adult alternatives, and which incorporates natural verbal definitions.

Principles

1. Sex and age

Many amused parents and a few anthropologists have noticed that children first use kinship terms in a way that deviates from adult usage. Their system is not only incomplete; it is wrong. The four terms which a child is likely to need first are those for the other members of his own nuclear family: *mother, father* (or intimate equivalents for these such as *mommy, daddy,* etc.), *brother, and sister.* Typically, the other four terms used within the nuclear family (*wife, husband, son,* and *daughter*) are in the beginning accepted as synonyms of the first four. My own daughter would not only describe me as her "mommy's papa" but would unhesitatingly point to her mother when asked who her *wife* was, and to her brother when asked to designate her *son*. What she grasped at this early age, and what many other children grasp, were the two cross-cutting distinctions of sex and age. The people in her own family, and in the families of her friends and neighbors, were divided into adults and children, and into males and females. She had no tendency to confuse these categories, and she would never, for instance, have called a boy by the term *sister* or called an adult man by the term *brother;* but even after all eight terms were thoroughly familiar, the more subtle distinction that separated *father* from *husband, brother* from *son, mother* from *wife,* and *sister* from *daughter* escaped her. *Father, brother, mother,* and *sister* were probably the more commonly used set, but the other members of each pair were also known and were simply accepted as synonyms. Diagrammatically the terms could be shown as follows:

age	father/husband	mother/wife
	brother/son	sister/daughter
	sex	

2. Egocentricity

To shift this system to a more adult pattern, a child must grasp a subtle relational principle. A table is a table from whatever point of view one considers it, but a mother is only a mother with respect to particular people. A child must learn that the woman who is a *mommy* to him is a *wife* to his father and that his *brother* is not his mother's *brother* at all. It must be learned, in other words, that kinship terms are different from most of our vocabulary in being used only with respect to some understood ego, often but not necessarily the speaker. Once this is learned, the earlier synonyms can be differentiated, and the reciprocity of kinship terms then becomes evident. It is the egocentric nature of kinship terms that produces reciprocals. *Brother* and *sister* now become reciprocals as do *husband* and *wife*. It may be that age remains the primary feature which discriminates *husband, father, wife,* and *mother* from *son, brother, daughter,* and *sister*. The first four terms are never used for children, and their early experience may lead children to conclude that the latter four can never be used for grownups. The application of these terms to adults may come a bit later. Recognition of the relational aspect of these terms, however, alters and refines their use, and the following diagram may be a reasonable representation of the understanding that children at this stage have of these eight terms.

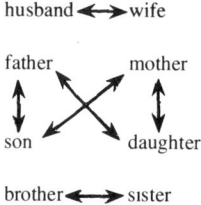

3. Consanguinity and generation

To bring these eight terms into final alignment with adult usage, a child must learn one more thing: a recognition of the special status of *husband* and *wife*. In early usage these hardly stand out as different from the other six terms, but children eventually learn that the *husband-wife* relationship is of a different sort from that of *brother* and *sister* or *parent* and *child*. It is contractual, not the automatic result of birth; or in colloquial terms it is a relationship of "marriage" rather than of "blood." Once the unique status of *husband* and *wife* is recognized, the remaining six terms fall most naturally into a somewhat revised arrangement in which the initially obvious feature of absolute age is replaced by the more abstract principle of generation. The distinction of sex, which is never obscured, is now cross-cut by the three-way distinction of higher, own, and lower generation. The natural way to diagram the kinship terms has now come closer to adult usage and to the usual anthropological conventions, though it obviously includes only a small proportion of all possible terms.

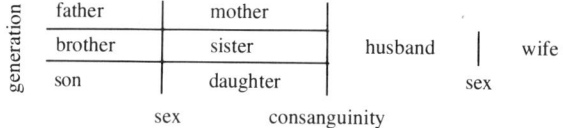

4. Cover terms

At some point a child learns to use the terms *parent* and *child,* and he learns that they embrace the combined meaning of two other terms simply by overriding the distinction of sex. I do not know whether these cover terms are learned at the precise point where I have placed them in the sequence of acquiring kinship terms. Perhaps children learn them before they learn the consanguineal/affinal distinction or even before grasping the egocentric principle. On the other hand, they may wait until later, after they learn the principle of relative product definitions, and in all likelihood different children follow different sequences. For present purposes it is convenient to suppose they are learned here, for these cover terms are useful in the succeeding steps. Adult English, of course, has two additional cover terms, *spouse* and, at least for some speakers, *sibling,* but they are less common and probably not learned so early.

Up to this point, terms have been distinguished from one another by an essentially componential analysis. Each of the ten terms used so far (including *parent* and *child*) can be understood as having a meaning built up from several semantic components. The dimensions of semantic contrast that have been recognized are 1) sex, 2) generation, and 3) consanguinity. Age has been eliminated and replaced by generation. Thus *husband* is an affinal male. *Daughter* is a consanguineal female of the lower generation. *Parent* is a consanguineal of the ascending generation. Except for *parent* and *child* (which Goodenough omits from his analysis) these are also the terms which Goodenough designates as lying at the first degree of genealogical distance. They designate the closest kinsmen, and they are the terms likely to be learned first. After this stage, I will go beyond the resources of simple componential analysis and introduce the remaining terms by differing principles. I will assume that the meaning of the first ten terms can now be taken as known, and that these terms can be used as elements in defining further terms.

5. Relative products

Eventually a child discovers that his immediate kinsmen have other kinsmen. A child learns about these secondary kinsmen later than he learns to differentiate among his primary kinsmen. After he has come to understand that the term *brother* cannot be used by his father for anyone within the child's own nuclear family (stage two, above), he still must learn that his father may have a brother after all, even if that brother is a grownup and lives far away. This is not an easy principle to grasp; but once it is acquired, several new terms can be used with understanding. The knowledge that one's own primary kinsmen may themselves have other kinsmen is beyond the grasp of young children when they first begin to use kin terms within their own nuclear family, but the knowledge is surely available by the time they learn a term like *uncle*. Relative products allow easy definitions of the various terms which Goodenough groups together as standing at the second degree of genealogical distance:

Grandfather:	Parent's father
Grandmother:	Parent's mother
Grandparent:	Parent's parent
Uncle:	Parent's brother
Aunt:	Parent's sister
Nephew:	Brother's or sister's son
Niece:	Brother's or sister's daughter
Grandson:	Child's son
Granddaughter:	Child's daughter
Grandchild	Child's child

If the cover terms *parent* and *child* have not yet been learned, of course, a term like *uncle* can still be explained as "mother's or father's brother." To me it seems manifest that such a definition comes closer to colloquial practice than such a cumbersome definition as "consanguineal, male, non-lineal, first-degree collateral, of the first ascending generation," and I do not see how it lacks in precision. I believe that the relative product definition reflects the manner in which terms are explained to children and the manner in which they are learned, and I would even imagine that anyone who felt concerned to produce a "cognitively real" analysis would be far happier with a version that uses colloquial words than with one that uses esoteric terms and symbols.

Relative products can also easily provide definitions of terms for some more distant kinsmen:

Cousin:	Uncle's or aunt's child
Uncle:	Aunt's husband
Aunt:	Uncle's wife
Nephew:	Husband's or wife's nephew
Niece:	Husband's or wife's niece

These are tertiary relatives, and except for *cousin* the definitions are needed to expand the scope of terms which have already been defined in a more limited sense. They cover the spouses of "blood" aunts and uncles, and nephews and nieces of one's spouse. These four terms, when applied to affinals, have a somewhat marginal status as kinship terms. Although we regularly use *uncle* and *aunt* for the spouses of our "blood" aunts and uncles, the terms are not quite so literally applicable to them as to parent's own siblings. As Schneider has pointed out, we can also use *aunt* and *uncle* for friends of our parents who are in no way related, and this demonstrates that the use of the term cannot be taken as proof that a man or woman is in fact a kinsman. We may be doubtful about applying the term *uncle* to a man who marries our aunt late in life, after we have long known our aunt, especially if we have been accustomed to addressing her earlier husband as *uncle*. We seem, however, to be slightly more confident about applying the terms *uncle* and *aunt* to these affinal kinsmen than in applying *nephew* and *niece* to their reciprocals. Occasionally someone will argue that his father's sister's husband is indeed his *uncle,* but that his wife's brother's son is nevertheless not his *nephew*. I once rather upset a student who was arguing this way by pointing out that these kintypes were reciprocals and that this would mean that he would not be the *nephew* of his own *uncle*. The basis of this peculiar lack of symmetry is presumably our earlier need for the *uncle* and *aunt* terms in their affinal use. When, later in life, we acquire a spouse with nieces and nephews, we may find other ways to refer to them; and by then we are more vividly aware of the separation between our own kinsmen and those of our spouse than we are of the consanguineal/affinal distinction as children.

With the exception of the affinal *aunts, uncles, nieces,* and *nephews,* the definitions given up to this point are probably uniform for all Americans. This is the common core of our kinship system, and it is this core that allows us all to talk to each other so easily. After this point in the sequence a few variables begin to creep in which make for some variation in usage at the peripheries of the system, but these variables do not touch the common core upon which they are built.

6. Operators

The basic English kinship terms that have now been defined can all be modified by one or more operators. It seems likely that learning these operators is the last stage in the acquisition of our kinship terminology, and it is the area in which there is the greatest variation from speaker to speaker. I will not attempt to give a complete or formal account of all these operators but will be content to list them briefly in approximately the order of their importance or of their acquisition, pointing out some of the ways in which their use is variable.

great (grand): These can be preposed to any of the secondary terms to increase by one generation the distance between ego and kinsman, and of course they can be applied recursively. The fact that *great* is learned as a recursively applicable operator, and that terms like *great grandfather, great uncle,* etc. are not all learned as separate terms is suggested by the delight children take in stringing together long series of *greats* when speculating about such ancestors as a *great great great great grandfather.* There is variability in the use of *grand* as a substitute for *great* in the first position preceding *uncle* and *aunt,* and *grand* is especially likely to be used with *niece* and *nephew.*

-in-law: This form is added to the six primary consanguineal terms and, at least in my usage, to the cover terms *parent* and *child.* It designates the corresponding kinsmen of one's spouse, or their reciprocals. There is variability or uncertainty in the applicability of *-in-law* terms to such kinsmen as WiBrWi and adult Americans can be provoked into lengthy discussions about whether such a person really deserves to be called a *sister-in-law.* The *-in-law* terms are not all learned individually, but rather the entire set is learned together by some such rule as this: "call your wife's (or husband's) immediate relatives by the same term she (he) uses but add *-in-law.*" The fact that this should be stated as a general rule is suggested by the ease with which people accept the idea that if there were such a thing as an *uncle-in-law* he would be one's wife's uncle. Of course, *-in-law* is usually applicable only to the terms for primary kinsmen, but its extension beyond them requires no great stretch of the system but only the crossing out of "immediate" from the rule as I have given it.

half-, full-: These can be prefixed only to *brother* and *sister* (and probably to *sibling* if that term is known), and they distinguish siblings who share only one parent from those who share two. There seems little variability in the application of these terms.

step-, foster: Like *-in-law,* these forms can be attached to any of the terms for primary kinsmen. I find that Goodenough's characterization of the *step-* relatives as "structurally equivalent" to the primary kinsmen to be a useful way of viewing the application of these terms. It is our cultural expectation that one's mother's husband will also be one's father and that the mother's husband's son will also be a brother. When, as a result of secondary marriages, such expectations are not fulfilled, the *step-* terms are appropriate. *Foster* can be used with the same terms, but the "foster" relationship is probably considered by many Americans to be only marginally within kinship bounds; it seems likely that many Americans hardly ever use the term, though they may have a vague idea that it stands for some sort of adoptive relationship.

first, second, etc.: These are applicable only to the term *cousin.* Americans vary in their exact use of these modifiers. All agree that *first cousins* are the children of one's aunts and uncles. Certainly *second cousins* are more distantly related, and *third cousins* are still further. A good many Americans are not quite clear about exactly which of their "distant cousins" deserves which term, however, and they may be in some doubt about whether generation distance or only collateral distance must be counted in determining which cousin rates what. For any speaker who, like Goodenough, has consistent usage, it would not be difficult to write a rule that would build upon previously defined terms to characterize his practices. The more interesting point to be made about these terms, however, is that they are *not* consistently used. Many speakers are likely to dismiss the matter by saying "he is some sort of cousin"; or, if they need to be more precise, they describe the particular chain of relationship which ties them to that individual.

once removed, twice removed, etc.: These unquestionably constitute the most variable and inconsistent niche of our terminological system. Most speakers know about these terms but a majority probably never uses them, and indeed they freely express their ignorance of "correct" usage. Those who do use the terms probably learn them very late in the acquisition of their terminology. Possibly they are used primarily by those who take it upon themselves to assume a sort of expert stance toward the phenomenon of kinship. As in the case of *first, second,* etc. it would not be difficult to construct a rule which, by building upon previously defined terms, would account for the usage of anyone who used these terms consistently; but whether or not one defines the periphery of his system with a refinement like "twice removed" makes very little difference to the rest of his terminology.

7. Extension

One final refinement of the use of kinship terms deserves brief mention: the extension to non-kinship domains, as when we speak of a *fraternity brother* or a *mother superior.* I find it hard to shake my faith that such usages are indeed extensions, and I cannot help feeling that the primary reference of the terms lies in the domain of kinship and that they are extended outward to analogous individuals who play a role that can in some way be made to seem kinship-like. It seems reasonable, therefore, to place this final extension of kinship terms last in the sequence; there is surely considerable variability in the manner in which terms are extended beyond the kinship domain.

Conclusions

My account of English kinship terminology is hardly startling. Possibly it will even seem rather banal when compared to the more sophisticated and symbolically more elaborate treatments given by others, but I think it has a number of advantages. First, it seems to harmonize with the ontogenetic development, or at least to be more readily harmonizable with it than is a simple componential analysis. Second, by recognizing some areas of kinship as being more central than others, we gain a reasonable way of dealing with the fact that parts of our terminology are very uniform while others are much more variable. We can see how people can agree completely about the core of their kinship system and easily understand each other even when they differ considerably in the more peripheral parts of their systems. A componential analysis which places all terms at the same level and defines them all by the same procedures gives us little basis for supporting our intuitive feeling that *mother* is, in some way, a more standard, central, and basic term than *second cousin once removed*. Third, it is difficult not to feel that this treatment is rather more natural, possibly even more "cognitively real," than other more symbolically elaborate treatments. We need no fancy notions like "ablineal" or "colineal" or even "first degree of collaterality" or "second degree of genealogical distance." Such concepts have little place in American culture except for the esoteric subculture of the anthropologist, and one would suppose that kinship terminology ought to be describable in the terms that the natives use themselves. Recognition of "sex," "generation," "blood," and "marriage," and the ability to string together a sequence of kinship terms to define other terms are well entrenched within general American culture. I see no difficulty in capitalizing upon these native concepts in providing a description of American kin terms.

I have one final point, though it may be of more interest to linguists than to anthropologists. I have used two essentially different techniques of definition. The early terms were defined referentially, using devices of componential analysis to show how the terms were related to observable characteristics of kinsmen. These terms were then used to build verbal definitions of the remaining terms. Curiously, when linguists have dealt with semantics, they have tended to concentrate upon verbal definitions and have been most reluctant to consider referential definitions; anthropologists have generally limited themselves to referential definitions and seem to have ignored the possibility of giving verbal definitions. I am convinced that both kinds are essential and that neither one alone can give us a satisfying description of the way in which we use words.

SECTION INTRODUCTION REFERENCES* AND SUGGESTIONS FOR FURTHER STUDY

Agar, Michael, 1974, *Ethnography and Cognition*. Minneapolis: Burgess.

Barker, Roger G., 1965, "Explorations in Ecological Psychology." *American Psychologist* 20:1–14.

Berlin, B., D. E. Breedlove, and P. H. Raven, 1968, "Covert Categories and Folk Taxonomies." *American Anthropologist* 70:290–299.

Berlin, B. and P. Kay, 1969, *Basic Color Terms: Their Universality and Evolution*. Berkeley: University of California Press.

Berreman, Gerald, 1966, "Anemic and Emetic Analysis in Social Anthropology." *American Anthropologist* 68:346–354.

Birdwhistell, Ray L., 1970, *Kinesics and Context: Essay on Body Motion Communication*. Philadelphia: University of Pennsylvania Press.

Black, Mary B., 1973, "Belief Systems." In J. J. Honigmann, ed., *Handbook of Social and Cultural Anthropology*. Chicago: Rand McNally, pp. 509–578.

Bright, Jane O., and William Bright, 1965, "Semantic Structures in Northwestern California and the Sapir-Whorf Hypothesis." *American Anthropologist* 67:249–258.

Burling, Robbins, 1964, "Cognition and Componential Analysis: God's Truth or Hocus-Pocus?" *American Anthropologist* 66:20–28.

———, 1969, "Linguistics and Ethnographic Description." *American Anthropologist* 71:817–827.

Carroll, J. B., ed., 1956, *Language, Thought, and Reality: Selected Writings of Benjamin Lee Whorf*. Cambridge, Mass.: The M.I.T. Press.

Chomsky, Noam, 1957, *Syntactic Structures*. The Hague: Mouton.

———, 1959, "Review of: *Verbal Behavior*, by B. F. Skinner." *Language* 35:26–58.

*———, 1968, *Language and Mind*. New York: Harcourt.

Cole, Michael, and J. S. Bruner, 1972, "Preliminaries to a Theory of Cultural Differences." In *Yearbook of the National Society for the Study of Education*, No. 71.2. Chicago: University of Chicago Press, pp. 161–179.

Cole, Michael, et al., 1971, *The Cultural Context of Learning and Thinking: An Exploration in Experimental Anthropology*. New York: Basic Books.

Diamond, Stanley, 1974, "The Inauthenticity of Anthropology: The Myth of Structuralism." In *In Search of the Primitive*. New Brunswick, N.J.: Transaction Books, pp. 292–331.

Dineen, Francis P., 1967, "Noam Chomsky: Transformational Grammar and Linguistic Universals." In *An Introduction to General Linguistics*. New York: Holt, Rinehart & Winston, pp. 355–399.

*Douglas, Mary, 1966, *Purity and Danger: An Analysis of Pollution and Taboo*. London: Routledge & Kegan Paul.

———, 1967, "The Meaning of Myth." In E. Leach, ed., *The Structural Study of Myth and Totemism*. ASA Monograph No. 5:49–69. London: Tavistock.

*———, 1970, *Natural Symbols: Explorations in Cosmology*. New York: Pantheon.

Durbin, Marshall, 1973, "Cognitive Anthropology." In J. J. Honigmann, ed., *Handbook of Social and Cultural Anthropology*. Chicago: Rand McNally, pp. 447–478.

Fishman, Joshua A., 1964, "A Systematization of the Whorfian Hypothesis." In E. E. Sampson, ed., *Approaches, Contexts, and Problems of Social Psychology*. Englewood Cliffs, N.J.: Prentice-Hall, pp. 27–43.

Frake, Charles O., 1964, "Notes on Queries in Ethnography." *American Anthropologist* 66:132–145.

French, David, 1963, "The Relationship of Anthropology to Studies in Perception and Cognition." In S. Koch, ed., *Psychology: A Study in Science*, Vol. 6. New York: McGraw-Hill, pp. 388–428.

Garfinkel, H., 1967, *Studies in Ethnomethodology*. Englewood Cliffs, N.J.: Prentice-Hall.

Garvin, P. L., ed., 1970, *Cognition: A Multiple View*. New York: Spartan.

Gladwin, T., and W. G. Sturtevant, eds., 1962, *Anthropology and Human Behavior*. Washington, D.C.: Anthropological Society of Washington.

Goodenough, Ward H., 1967, "Componential Analysis." *Science* 156:1203–1209.

Hall, Edward T., 1968, "Proxemics." *Current Anthropology* 9:83–95, 105–108.

Hammel, Eugene A., 1972, *The Myth of Structural Analysis: Lévi-Strauss and The Three Bears*. Addison-Wesley Modular Publications, Module No. 25.

Harris, Marvin, 1968, "Emics, Etics, and the New Ethnography." In *The Rise of Anthropological Theory: A History of Theories of Culture*. New York: Crowell, pp. 568–604.

Hebb, B. O., W. E. Lambert, and G. R. Tucker, 1971, "Language, Thought and Experience." *Modern Language Journal* 55:212–222.

Henderson, Richard N., 1967, "Onitsha Ibo Kinship Terminology: A Formal Analysis and Its Functional Applications." *Southwestern Journal of Anthropology* 23:15–51.

Hockett, Charles F., 1968, *The State of the Art*. Janua Linguarum, Series Minor, 73. The Hague: Mouton.

Hoijer, Harry, 1954, "The Sapir-Whorf Hypothesis." In *Language in Culture*. Chicago: University of Chicago Press, pp. 92–105.

Horton, Robin, 1968, "Neo-Tylorianism: Sound Sense or Sinister Prejudice?" *Man* 3:625–634.

Joos, Martin, 1958, "Semology: A Linguistic Theory of Meaning." *Studies in Linguistics* 13:53–70.

*Keesing, Roger M., 1972, "Paradigms Lost: The New Ethnography and the New Linguistics." *Southwestern Journal of Anthropology* 28:299–332.

*Kroeber, A. L., 1909, "Classificatory Systems of Relationship." *Journal of the Royal Anthropological Institute* 39:77–84.

Leach, Edmund, 1970, *Claude Lévi-Strauss*. New York: The Viking Press.

———, 1972, "The Structure of Symbolism." In J. LaFontaine, ed., *The Interpretation of Ritual*. New York: Harper & Row, pp. 239–275.

Lees, Robert B., 1957, "Review of: *Syntactic Structures*, by Noam Chomsky." *Language* 33:374–408.

*Lenneberg, Eric H., 1967, *Biological Foundations of Language*. New York: Wiley.

Lévi-Strauss, Claude, 1966, *From Honey to Ashes*. New York: Harper & Row. (First published in French in 1966.)

Lévy-Bruhl, Lucien, 1923, *Primitive Mentality*. New York: Macmillan. (First published in 1910.)

———, 1966, *The "Soul" of the Primitive*. (Trans. by L. Clare). New York: Praeger. (First published in 1928.)

Lyons, John, 1970, *Noam Chomsky*. New York: Viking.

*Malinowski, Bronislaw, 1961, *Argonauts of the Western Pacific*. New York: Dutton. (First published in 1922.)

Munn, Nancy D., 1973, "Symbolism in a Ritual Context: Aspects of Symbolic Action." In J. J. Honigmann, ed., *Handbook of Social and Cultural Anthropology*. Chicago: Rand McNally, pp. 579–612.

Murphy, Robert F., 1963, "On Zen Marxism: Filiation and Alliance." *Man* 63:17–19.

Pears, David, 1970, *Ludwig Wittgenstein*. New York: Viking.

Peng, Fred C. C., 1969, "Review of: *Aspects of the Theory of Syntax*, by Noam Chomsky." *Linguistics* 49:91–128.

Piaget, Jean, 1970, *Structuralism*. New York: Basic Books.

Pitt-Rivers, Julian, 1967, "Contextual Analysis and the Locus of the Model." Archives Europeennes de Sociologie. *European Journal of Sociology* 8:15–34.

Prattis, J. I., 1972, "Science, Ideology, and False Demons: A Commentary on Lévi-Strauss Critiques." *American Anthropologist* 74:1323–1325.

Ricoeur, Paul, 1963, "Structure et Herméneutique." *Esprit* No. 332:598–627.

Robins, R. H., 1968, "Linguistics in the Present Century." In *A Short History of Linguistics*, Indiana University Series in the History and Theory of Linguistics. Bloomington, Ind.: Indiana University Press, pp. 198–240.

*Sapir, Edward, 1927, "The Unconscious Patterning of Behavior in Society." In E. S. Drummer, ed., *The Unconscious: A Symposium*. New York: Knopf, pp. 114–142.

*———, 1934, "The Emergence of the Concept of Personality in a Study of Cultures." *Journal of Social Psychology* 5:408–415.

Scheffler, H. W., 1966, "Structuralism in Anthropology." In *Structuralism*. Yale French Studies 36–37:66–80.

Scholte, Bob, 1973, "The Structural Anthropology of Claude Lévi-Strauss." In J. J. Honigmann, ed., *Handbook of Social and Cultural Anthropology*. Chicago: Rand McNally, pp. 637–716.

Schneider, David M., 1965, "American Kin Terms and Terms for Kinsmen: A Critique of Goodenough's Componential Analysis of Yankee Kinship Terminology." *American Anthropologist* 67:288–308.

———, 1968, *American Kinship: A Cultural Account*. Englewood Cliffs, N.J.: Prentice-Hall.

*Spiro, Melford, 1968, "Review of: *Purity and Danger: An Analysis of Pollution and Taboo*, by Mary Douglas." *American Anthropologist* 70:391–392.

Sturtevant, William C., 1964, "Studies in Ethnoscience." *American Anthropologist* 66:99–131.

*Turner, Victor, 1967, *The Forest of Symbols*. Ithaca, N.Y.: Cornell University Press.

*———, 1968, "Myth and Symbol." *International Encyclopedia of the Social Sciences* 10:576–582.

*———, 1969, *The Ritual Process: Structure and Anti-Structure*. Chicago: Aldine.

Werner, Oswald, 1966, "Pragmatics and Ethnoscience." *Anthropological Linguistics* 8:42–65.

———, 1969, "The Basic Assumptions of Ethnoscience." *Semiotica* 1:329–338.

DYNAMIC ASPECTS OF CULTURE

PART

section VIII

Culture and Biology

Anthropological studies of the relationship between culture and the human organism have followed several discernible lines, some of which have already been discussed briefly under other headings. One of the main concerns has been the question of the nature of the relationship between race and culture, a subject that has been surrounded by dissension and contention in our nation although not often markedly so among anthropologists. Our selections of readings do not concern this subject, which we shall here dismiss with a few brief statements representing general views in anthropology. We have earlier noted that the prevailing trend in the anthropological study of culture has been to regard all varieties of man as essentially alike biologically so that, for most goals of study, physical differences may or should be set aside as irrelevant. During the century since this view was set forth by Edward Tylor, no scientific data or interpretations have been presented that have altered it. The problem of understanding the relationship between race and culture is beset by unsolved and seemingly insoluble problems of devising an adequate classification of human races and objective instruments for comparatively measuring cultural achievements and innate intellectual potentials. It is quite clear that any variety of human being may acquire any culture, given the opportunity, and that such understanding as we now have of differences in cultural attainments among societies of the world has come only from examination of the cultures themselves, in their geographic environments and in their relationships to other cultures.

Currently active trends of anthropological study relating culture to physical traits of man have followed two main lines, which are the subjects of the readings included in this section: the role of culture in the biological evolution of man, and the effects of beliefs and practices of modern societies upon the physical traits of their members.

Speech and the manufacture and use of tools have long been regarded as cultural innovations of evolutionary significance, that is, innovations that have been involved in the process of biological evolution leading to the formation of the species *Homo sapiens*. More recently, this importance has been attributed to a complex of additional interrelated cultural innovations that are presumed to be early human inventions. Much attention has been given to the human control of sexual activities, in such ways as practices of exogamy, customs of periodic celibacy, rules of marriage, and incest prohibitions. Opinions about the importance and the nature of human control of sexual behavior have diversified and changed. According to certain current opinion, for example, the evolutionary importance accorded to the control of sex is an overstatement. No one, however, doubts that the cultural control of sex is powerful and that it has had significance in the biological evolution of man. Other early cultural developments of similar significance discussed in the selections by Buettner-Janusch and Hulse include sharing, especially of food, a trait which has only incipient development among some species of nonhuman primates; the division of labor by sex and age; the creation of kinship; and the control of physical aggression against others, a development which has sometimes been called "softened dominance."

The key to understanding the hypothesized biological significance of such cultural innovations is the idea of feedback, which means that the biological developments complementarily foster the development of culture by favoring the survival of human beings with the physical traits best suited for the cultural activities in question. Any one of the cultural traits we have mentioned is seen to have multiple effects and to relate in complex ways to the other cultural innovations as well as to a train of biological developments. For example, sharing and the division of labor by sex and age both create dependance, between males and females and between the mature and the immature. These conditions foster the development of the genetically transmitted trait of prolonged immaturity, which in turn fosters increasing dependance of the immature upon the mature and at the same time fosters the growth of culture through the long period of human immaturity and plasticity. This period of many years provides favorable circumstances for the transmission from the mature to the immature of an elaborate inventory of culture and its absorption by the immature. Among nonhuman species, a long period of helplessness means extinction of the species; among human beings, whose existence and continuation depends upon culture, it is a biological advantage. The evolutionary result of the various early cultural innovations has been the creation of an unconsciously self-domesticated social animal, dependant for existence upon culture and also upon other human beings.

Many modern studies in medicine and genetics as well as in anthropology involve genetic and other biological effects of certain customs and values, especially those which seem to be biologically harmful or undesirable. An example is the concern with the societal protection of people with gross, genetically determined physical maladies (such as those of the blood or of body chemistry) who are protected to the extent that they can reproduce and perpetuate their maladies in the gene pool. These studies cannot have bearing on the emergence of the human species, but they often express concern about the human genetic condition in the future. A well-known example of this trend of thought is included in the philosophy of eugenics, which questions the genetic fate of man as the result of such human customs as the preservation of members of society who are regarded as sub-par physically or mentally. Writings on this subject are abundant in the popular press as well as in scholarly works and for this reason are well enough known so that omission of them in this volume seems appropriate. (For a cogent treatment of the topic, see Curt Stern 1960:630–679.) Our two selections by the anthropologist Frederick S. Hulse concern the subjects of the influence of culture upon human physical traits and genetics with no special reference to eugenics. These discussions make clear that culture affects biological traits in many ways, even influencing our conception of race, a presumably biological concept.

Culture and biology relate to each other in various other ways which are discussed here and there in preceding and following sections. We shall call attention to earlier discussions of cultural universals relating to biological traits such as the human needs for food and sleep, the importance of considering biological differences when attempting to understand differences in the cultures or personalities of individuals, and the social and psychological significance of biological features in relations among societies and subsocieties when differences exist in biological traits, such as skin color and bodily conformation, that are given social values of superiority and inferiority. Still other instances of relationships between culture and biology are touched upon in the section that follows concerning culture and the geographic environment.

24 SOCIETY
ELMAN R. SERVICE

The peoples at the band level of social integration make up the smallest as well as the simplest of all human societies. That they stand, therefore, in marked contrast to a modern industrial nation, and live apparently closer to nature because of technological and economic simplicity, may suggest that hunting-gathering bands are in some ways closer to ape society than any other. Biologically, the great apes are more like human beings than any other animals. It is therefore natural to think that there are also similarities between ape and human societies, especially when the latter are small and lack the so-called refinements of civilization.

Of course there are some similarities between the social behavior of apes and that of human beings. These are normally the elementary and largely biological and psychological aspects of social life: a mother petting or feeding a baby, the jealousy of siblings, youngsters playing together. But these are common to all levels of human and ape society. If we speak now of culturally determined modes of social behavior, however, we find ourselves on another plane entirely, with no similarity or even far-fetched analogy, between the social life of apes and that of the simplest hunting-gathering groups.

Subhuman Primate Society

Different species of subhuman primates have different kinds of social organization, but each particular species has its own characteristic type. This is because the social life is set by hereditary biological needs and there are, therefore, very definite limits to the variations in responses that can be induced by different situations and environments. The forms of human society, on the other hand, are tremendously variable in size, complexity, style, and rules of behavior, which demonstrates their adaptability to varying circumstances and environments. This flexibility is possible because human society is structured more by cultural rules and norms than by the biological needs and urges that are common to both apes and men.

Many normal biological traits, of both apes and humans, are prejudicial to social order. The significance of cultural rules and their great power becomes apparent when we notice that at many points these rules create the exact opposite kind of behavior from that which is governed by biological heredity alone. In these respects all human societies are very different from all ape societies; the small rudimentary societies of hunters and gatherers are just as distinct from ape society as are higher societies, and in some respects perhaps more so. Let us take a quick look at a few of these contrasts.

From Elman R. Service, *The Hunters*, © 1966, pp. 27–32. Reprinted by permission of Prentice-Hall, Inc., Englewood Cliffs, New Jersey.

Sexual behavior

We think of sexual behavior as preeminently biological, probably correctly. And certainly the sex act itself seems similar among both apes and humans, as are apparently the physiological urges that lead to it. But sex is channeled, sublimated, restricted, and tabooed in human society in ways which strikingly modify the social dangers that are inherent in its free manifestation.

Ape society is strongly affected by sex. Many other kinds of animals experience seasonal sexuality only and form families or herds part of the year and are dispersed the rest of it. Ape society is a year-round organization, however, and even though sexual activity may be somewhat seasonal or cyclical between particular pairs, the group association continues.

Sex as practiced by the great apes has both positive and negative effects on group life. The attraction between male and female is, of course, the positive effect and moreover is absolutely basic to society, especially to its continuity. The negative or anti-social aspect of sex is created mostly by male competition in the quest for mates. Ape society is limited in scope and in the kinds of things it can do because this omnipresent disruptive factor is curbed only by the ephemeral victory of one of the contestants. At any given time when there is no actual fighting, therefore, a male despot is ruling over several females and their young, while several other younger or weaker males remain on the fringes of this elementary group.

Food

Apes compete for a limited amount of food, even when they are members of the same horde. Just as they attempt to usurp the females, the strongest animals dominate the taking of food. There is of course one difference: The dominant male (or female dominant over other females) will permit others to eat once he is sated, a privilege not extended to sexual matters. At any rate, individuals compete, and by force or threat of force establish dominance patterns until a complete hierarchy of dominance and submission characterizes the social order of the horde. There is little evidence of friendly sharing or of cooperation among apes except for the collective defense of the group.

Territoriality

The primate horde is a closed social group. Like many other kinds of animals, monkeys and apes (with the possible exception of the mountain gorilla) forage in a territory which they undertake to defend against all competition, and especially against other groups of their own species (because of competition for exactly the same resources). Primates, including man, are cowardly, though blustering, animals, and do not seem to seek battle for the fun of it. The apes do, however, defend their territories even if mostly with belligerent cries, chest-thumping, or minor skirmishes. The point is that the group, whatever its size, is territorially closed, and this is another significant contrast with human hunting-gathering societies, for even when human societies are strongly territorially based, as we shall see, they are never completely exclusive.

Rudimentary Human Society

Equipped with approximately the same biologically determined urges and needs as apes, human beings at the simplest level of society contrast most strikingly with apes in social behavior because the expression of those urges have been so thoroughly repressed or channeled in the interests of society. Each one of the characteristics of subhuman primates discussed above contrasts with human behavior generally and particularly with the simple hunting-gathering peoples.

With respect to sexual behavior, the contrast between apes and humans is apparent in several respects. Most general is the human repression of sex urges in terms of taboos: in all human societies sexual activity is normally private; all regulate exposure of the genitalia in various ways; all limit the age and relationship of partners; and so on. Perhaps the most interesting of all is the so-called incest taboo. All human societies prohibit sexual relations between parents and children, between siblings (except for certain ancient emperors), and in some cases between cousins, or some cousins. This taboo is not always an explicit law or rule, for some peoples simply regard incest as so horrible that they cannot imagine the necessity of having a rule against it. (One of the most interesting things about the incest taboo is the inability of any social scientists or psychologists to explain it—or at least to agree on an explanation.)

Related to the repression and channeling of sex is the institution of marriage. Apes mate, but only humans marry. Marriage is a special kind of pairing arrangement, different from anything found in ape society; it involves social recognition, the acquiescence of society to the arrangement—the opposite of the apes' dominance by threat of force. A marriage, in other words, is in some important sense an *agreement* between groups of people. The agreement, of course, particularly in primitive society, involves a great many matters besides sex. But sexual rights and restrictions are normally included among the others, and for this reason the institution of marriage is one of the more usual of the ways in which sexual urges are modified by cultural rules and taboos. We shall see in later pages that marriage rules have explicit political functions in primitive society, and in this respect sex is often involved directly in peacemaking rather than being the purely disruptive agent that it is in ape society.

Food in primitive society also functions to enhance sociability rather than to be the cause of friction and competition. As we have seen in the preceding chapter, the act of sharing is so frequently a matter of polity as well as etiquette that even when food is scarce and hunger is acute generosity is more likely to prevail over hoarding simply because the maintenance or strengthening of social bonds is so important in rudimentary societies.

In the same way that food is shared in primitive society, so is territory. There are variations in hunting-gathering societies in the degree of territoriality—that is, in the explicitness of boundaries—but in all cases there is some, and in most a rather strict, definition of the band in terms of the general locality it occupies even when boundaries are not specific. But the territory is never occupied exclusively, defended against all outsiders. Normally, the band's territory is closed to strangers and enemies and open to friends and allies. Friends and allies are typically secured by marriages so that eventually they become kinsmen of various kinds and degrees. As we shall see in greater detail in subsequent pages, marriage rules can be created that tie a few bands into even tighter and closer relationships, or they can be so dispersed and attenuated that they include a great many people in the web of kinship. Thus territoriality itself becomes, in human society, variable and adaptable to political situations, only *more or less* closed as environmental-political circumstances require.

In all these points of contrast between human and ape societies it is possible to pinpoint one general characteristic of the apes. Ape society is composed of selfish, "anti-social" beings—an apparent verbal contradiction that reflects a real contradiction. If the positive bonds of attraction are merely sexual, and if many apes are deprived of sex by the dominance of others, then what keeps the society together? Apparently the apes that remain in the horde, even though dominated, do so because of their greater fear of being alone. This may be in some measure a psychobiological deprivation—that apes, like many other animals, seem naturally to require companionship—but it might also be due to real environmental circumstances. S. L. Washburn, an investigator of baboon social life put it this way: "The troop is a survival mechanism. To not be a social animal is to be a dead animal." Thus the dominance-submission hierarchy, the primate "pecking order," characterizes the social life within the horde and relations among hordes remain antagonistic. A refugee from one group is not accepted into another.

Hunting-gathering bands differ more completely from the apes in this matter of dominance than do any other kinds of human society. There is no peck-order based on physical dominance at all, nor is there any superior-inferior ordering based on other sources of power such as wealth, hereditary classes, military or political office. The only consistent supremacy of any kind is that of a person of greater age and wisdom who might lead a ceremony.

Even when individuals possess greater status or prestige than others, the manifestation of the high status and the prerogatives are the opposite of ape-like dominance. Generosity and modesty are required of persons of high status in primitive society, and the rewards they receive are merely the love or attentiveness of others. A man, for example, might be stronger, faster, braver, and more intelligent than any other member of the band. Will he have higher status than the others? Not necessarily. Prestige will be accorded him only if these qualities are put to work in the service of the group—in hunting, let us say—and if he therefore produces more game to give away, and if he does it properly, modestly. Thus, to simplify a bit, greater strength in ape society results in greater dominance, which results in more food and mates and any other things desired by the dominant one; in primitive human society greater strength must be used in the service of the community, and the person, to earn prestige, must literally sacrifice to do so, working harder for less food. As for mates, he ordinarily has but one wife just like the other men.

It seems that the most primitive human societies are at the same time the most egalitarian. This must be related to the fact that because of rudimentary technology this kind of society depends on cooperation more fully more of the time than any other. Apes do not regularly cooperate and share, human beings do—that is the essential difference.

In selective adaptation to the perils of the Stone Age, human society overcame or subordinated such primate propensities as selfishness, indiscriminate sexuality, dominance and brute competition. It substituted kinship and cooperation for conflict, placed solidarity over sex, morality over might. In its earliest days it accomplished the greatest reform in history, the overthrow of human primate nature, and thereby secured the evolutionary future of the species.*

But as some apes became *homo sapiens* and lived in human-like society it was not simply that somehow a gene for altruism overcame the gene for selfishness, thus changing the character of social life. Individual humans are as self-serving as any other animals. The difference lies in the fact that human societies have systems of rewards and punishments and associated joys and fears that can make service to one's fellows become simultaneously a self-service.

The evolution of culture has involved an evolution of technology, and thus an increasing mastery over hostile nature. Just as necessary, just as difficult, but not always so obvious, has been the mastery of man's own nature. The social inventions that have enabled societies to become larger, more complex, and stronger all have something to do with remaking or channeling man's biological needs and propensities, most of all with redirecting his selfishness.

*Marshall D. Sahlins, "The Origin of Society" *Scientific American,* 203, No. 3 (1960), 86.

25 MAN'S CAPACITY FOR CULTURE
JOHN BUETTNER-JANUSCH

Culture

The first subject to which we turn our attention is the transition from an anthropoid to a human way of life. We have already discussed the evolution of language as an essential functional part of this transition. We now must consider the origin and differentiation of culture. The evolutionary divergence of *Homo sapiens* introduced this new factor to the evolution of life on this planet. Man is unique in the possession of culture, and we must evaluate the evidence that bears upon its origin. In the scheme of evolution, culture is a new kind of biological adaptation with a nongenetic mode of inheritance. The mode of inheritance of culture depends

From John Buettner-Janusch, *Origins of Man,* Copyright © 1966 by John Wiley & Sons, Inc. Reprinted by permission of John Wiley & Sons, Inc.

upon symbolic contact and transmission rather than upon the fusion of gametes. To some extent its evolution has supplemented the organic evolution of man.

Culture is a biological event; it is a product of the evolutionary process. It is a trait which only one genus of the order Primates developed, and the reasons it developed must be sought in the evolutionary history of that genus—*Homo*. . . . Once culture developed, it differentiated, grew, and changed much as if it were independent of organic man; indeed the expression "superorganic" was applied to culture by Kroeber. There is no question that culture is man-made, but individuals have hardly any control over it. Culture is one of the most impressive adaptations achieved by any evolving organism. Every human individual is born into a culture of some kind or other. This culture determines the language he will speak, the kinds of clothes he will wear, the rules for choosing a mate, the rituals he will participate in, the musical scale he will consider normal, the standards of interpersonal behavior he must achieve.

Culture is a word much used by anthropologists. It is a word which stands for a concept of fundamental importance in the science of anthropology. There are many ways in which culture, or a particular culture, is learned by individuals. There are many ways in which culture is transmitted from generation to generation. Culture is closely related to behavior, for human behavior is conditioned by and is a function of culture. It is quite possible to develop a sound and useful concept of culture by considering it the sum of all behavior that is uniquely human as opposed to the parts of man's behavior that are instinctual and physiological. We prefer to view culture in its most general form, as a universal biological adaptation of the genus *Homo*. A nonorganic, a superorganic, adaptation was developed by a particular evolving lineage. Culture added a significant factor to this lineage's evolutionary potential, and the subsequent development of this lineage was to a great extent due to the elaboration and evolution of culture.

Culture is based upon an ability, a trait, which appeared during the course of primate evolution, the ability to symbol. A symbol is a thing with physical form that is given meaning by those who use it. The physical form can be a wavelength of light, a frequency of sound, a nod of the head. The physical sensation is transmitted to the brain. It is in this organized neurological tissue that a meaning is attached to the physical sensation. Symbols are given meanings arbitrarily. . . .

An important problem in evolutionary biology is the determination of what it is that makes it possible for man to associate arbitrary meaning with physical objects. The obvious structure to examine is the brain, the center for association and voluntary control. Unfortunately there are no living animals that are in any way transitional between the primates that do not and the one that does use symbols. Neurological evolution obviously proceeded in the primate line to the point where a primate, which we would unquestionably recognize as a member of the genus *Homo*, was able to symbol. This ability made possible the accumulation and transmission of information from one generation to the next. Culture and symboling, closely connected in their origins, the former dependent upon the latter, may be seen as the consequence of certain characteristics that *Homo sapiens* developed, characteristics not present in other primates.

The distinction between man and other primates lies in the use of tools. Some nonhuman primates make tools even if they do so in a most rudimentary way, and they use tools on many occasions. But there is a fundamental difference between man and the other primates in the use of tools and their manufacture. The use of tools by *Homo sapiens* is a cumulative process, progressive from one generation to another. Among the apes tool-using, toolmaking, does not perceptibly change or progress from one generation to another. The human species, by virtue of its symbolic faculty, can store up information about tools and pass it on to the next generation.

We pointed out that primate evolution may be viewed, in one way, as the development and refinement of erect posture, bipedal locomotion, and manual dexterity. The faculty to symbol and the development of culture are closely associated with man's erect posture, bipedal locomotion, opposable thumb, and gregariousness or sociability. Although animals other than primates are gregarious (sea lions, cattle, and elephants are examples), the social behavior of primates and primate social groups are more complex and more highly structured than those of other mammals. The organ of association and control, the cerebral cortex, developed rapidly as the visual sense grew more complex and refined. At the same time, a fine control over the limbs and digits developed to a greater extent as did voluntary control of the muscles. Man comes from a stock preadapted for symboling and culture.

These brief words on culture are far from all that can be said on this subject. Some of the references listed at the end of this chapter will introduce the reader to the enormous literature about what culture is and about the validity and usefulness of the culture concept in anthropology. We agree with Simpson that many polemics and resulting confusions would be eliminated if, at least for some purposes, culture were viewed as a biological phenomenon. Indeed it seems obvious that it is. For an understanding of human evolution, the cultural evolutionists' view of culture as an extrasomatic trait, which developed out of certain biological characteristics unique to man, is less confusing and more useful than any of the other views of culture. And it is quite valid. Culture, since its invention and differentiation, has had profound effects upon human evolution.

We must ask a number of questions. How do we determine when culture first differentiated; in other words, how do we determine when man first became a toolmaker? What critical changes in the primate nervous system accompanied this change in behavior? Neither of these questions can be answered conclusively, but they can be discussed, and we can make some speculations about the origin of tools, the development of the primate nervous system, and the advent of culture.

Tools and Intelligence

It is unlikely that the earliest appearance of the ability to make tools will be precisely correlated with a specific fossil. By the time symboling had developed and culture had differentiated sufficiently for recognizable tools to appear in the archeological record, the associated primate fossil was far past that stage in his lineage at which the earliest tools were made. Some of the evidence that these abilities are part of man's general primate heritage comes from the work by Goodall, who showed that chimpanzees use objects as tools and appear to pass on some rudimentary information about their use from one animal to another. This does not invalidate our contention that man makes and uses tools in a distinctly different way than chimpanzees.

Most of the evolution of human behavior is based upon the ability to symbol, which in turn is a product of neuroanatomical evolution. During primate evolution the cerebral cortex increased in size. The major trend, which we have repeatedly emphasized, was the development and elaboration of the special senses and the expansion of those centers of the brain, particularly in the cortex, concerned with conscious control over complex behavior and voluntary control over the muscles. Therefore it is believed that areas of association (areas receiving and sorting complex sensory impressions) and areas of control over voluntary actions have increased in size.

We suggested that cranial volume is a trait not especially useful in distinguishing various taxa of the Hominidae after the middle Pliocene. Our point was that by the time of development of the toolmaking capacity, which is the consequence of the capacity to use symbols, the size of the brain was not the critical factor. Once there is evidence that the making of tools to a particular plan has developed, we must assume that symbolic communication and education were part of the repertoire of traits possessed by the primate whose fossil bones are associated with the tools. If a small-brained animal, for example an australopithecine, with a brain volume of about 600 cc is found in association with tools, we must assume that the brain volume was large enough for symbolic communication. We also assume that archeologists can tell us whether the fossil primate made the tools. Stone tools are prima facie evidence that there was sufficient neurological material for culture. Incidentally the earliest tools were not necessarily made of stone. Indeed it is unlikely that they were, but stone tools have the greatest likelihood of being preserved. The absence of tools from a site in which early hominids are recovered does not mean the hominid did not use wood or bone tools or that tools were not made.

But this does not answer all the questions we need to ask about evolution of the brain and its consequent effect upon the evolution of symboling and culture. What is there in the fossil record of primates that we can use to make deductions about the increasing capacity for association, control, and, eventually, symboling? All we have are fossil crania. The volume of an endocranial cast is such a gross measure that it is very difficult for us to deduce specific neurological functions from it. In recent years this problem has intrigued a number of competent students, and progress has been made in developing a way of answering this question.

Jerison has proposed a theory which can be used to distinguish major groups of primates. His theory is based on estimates of body weight and brain volume. From the estimates he calculates the total number of neurons in the cerebral cortex. The number of neurons associated with the body weight and the number of neurons associated with the adaptive capacity of the animal are then calculated. The calculation that is important here is the one that gives an estimate of the adaptive capacity of the animal. For simplicity let us call this the number of adaptive neurons. It is not possible to make very refined distinctions among the various primates by using methods based upon this theory, and distinctions between any two closely related species or genera are not possible at present. But the eight major taxa may be distinguished from each other with this method.

. . . [T]he number of adaptive neurons has increased markedly in hominid evolution. Even the australopithecines, with only 4.4 billion adaptive neurons (on the average), were toolmakers. Perhaps the development of more elaborate or at least more distinctive stone tools depended upon the increase in adaptive neurons from 4.4 to 6 or 7 billion. Yet we must remember that astonishingly rapid advances and changes in culture took place after the 8.5 billion neuron level was achieved. Perhaps there was a minimum number of these neurons associated with adaptive capacity necessary for great diversity and elaboration of cultural artifacts. There is a relationship between brain size and body size—as the body size increases, brain size generally increases. The size of the brain relative to the size of the body is a different matter. Very small mammals tend to have a larger relative brain size than might be expected. This is probably because of the need for a certain minimum number of neurons for muscular coordination and other important functions. We noted earlier that the living primates have a brain-to-body ratio that is larger than that of other mammals. The "typical primate brain" is about twice the size of the "typical mammalian brain" for any given body size.

We suggested that there are different levels of capacity for social behavior and for problem solving among various groups of nonhuman primates. But the exact neuroanatomical features associated with such differing levels are, as we stated, not well known. Gross brain size appears to be associated with differing capacities, and this is the only neurological trait that can be determined, even if crudely, for some fossil primates. Jerison's methods of analysis show that gross brain size may be analyzed in such a way that more adaptive neurons are predicted among more capable primates. *Homo sapiens* has the largest number of adaptive neurons.

It so happens that both the porpoise and the elephant have at least as many adaptive neurons as man. How do we explain this? Although there is a rich mythology about the incredibly advanced capacities of elephants for memory and porpoises for speech, there is little evidence to support these stories. Neither the elephant nor the porpoise has the symbolic faculty of man. Yet within the econiche each occupies, each is remarkably successful and well-adapted. There is no need to postulate complex elephant societies with special burial customs or porpoise vocal language to account for what they do with all their neurons. The size of the brain and the number of adaptive neurons cannot be considered outside of the adaptive zone in which the brain must function. As research on elephants and porpoises continues, we have faith that the relationship between the demands of the environment and the neurological adaptations of these mammals will be better understood.

The increase in size of the brain of *Homo* has often been considered the result of increasing manipulative skill (greater effectiveness in making tools) or increasing intelligence. But it does not seem reasonable that the apparent average increase in size of brain from the pithecanthropines to modern man can be accounted for on the grounds that manual dexterity became so great. Since we cannot administer intelligence tests to a pithecanthropine, and since we do not have a very precise notion of what intelligence is in contemporary sapiens, it is not profitable to pursue the evolution of brain size as a concomitant of the evolution of intelligence. Evolution of the larger brain of *Homo* may be related to the evolution of culture. Once the neurological capacity to symbol and to make culture evolved, the differentiation and rapid development of culture itself very likely put severe demands upon the brain. The cultural part of the environment of man grew more and more elaborate, and the need grew to sort the messages (symbols) coming into the brain. It became necessary to separate those messages that were important from all the sensory information coming through the ears and the eyes. This probably required elaboration of the cerebral cortex, a larger set of association neurons and interconnections between them. As Garn put it,

... it may be that our vaunted intelligence is merely an indirect product of the kind of brain that can discern meaningful signals in a complex social context generating a heavy static of informational or, rather, misinformational noise.

Hypotheses about the course of neurological evolution in the hominids are without substance unless material evidence of the products of the evolving nervous system are available. Fortunately there are many tools in the archeological record, products of the evolving hominid nervous system and good evidence for the hominid capacity for culture. Once tools are found in the archeological record and fossil hominids are found associated with these tools, it is clear that the capacity for culture, culture itself, is already developed. The degree to which there is a correlation between neurological evolution and the manufacture of tools is difficult to determine with any kind of certainty today. It appears, from the archeological and fossil records that there were very long periods when there was little or no change in the tool kit of man. During all of the lower Pleistocene, the same kinds of rather crude tools, stone choppers, were made. In later periods very rapid, abrupt, changes in the catalog of tools occurred. The rate at which tools developed, changed, improved, and became complex increased remarkably during the upper Pleistocene and early Recent epochs. The rapidity of change and the rapid rate of the evolution of culture is an important feature of human evolution. Certain other significant advances, such as the development of agriculture, led to what seems to be an explosive development of cultural inventions.

The archeological record suggests that there was a very long period when tools were extremely simple, merely pebble tools. The tool kit of man is quite simple until the latter part of the lower or the early part of the middle Pleistocene. At this time tools of several different kinds appear. There seemed to be a rapid increase in cultural developments. But there is no evidence at all that there was a large discrete increase in cranial capacity and, hence, in adaptive neurons of the cerebral cortex.

The changes in the brain appear to have been gradual. The rather abrupt change in the tool kit of man, if it was abrupt, is not associated with an abrupt change in the physical dimensions of the brain.

It is true that the archeological record may be biased. It very likely represents only a fragment of the material artifacts used by the earliest members of the genus *Homo*. Nevertheless there are some interesting features of the archeological record that can be related to the evolution of the brain. The stone tool kit of man, until the latter part of the lower Pleistocene, consisted of artifacts just a bit above the level of rocks or sticks picked up by a primate for the immediate task at hand. The first stones seen by the primate were seized and used to pound, dig, and cut. The stone and bone tools were made to a plan and imply that the primate who made and used them was a symboling animal. But they do not imply that very detailed blueprints were used in their manufacture. Dart believes that the earliest tools were bones, long bones and mandibles of common antelopes. He proposes that the long bones were used by early man, or by a prehuman ancestor, for clubbing and killing other animals and that the mandibles functioned as knives.

There is another factor which may have influenced the kinds of tools made. Man was restricted to the tropics during the entire early period of his development. The earliest fossil man in Europe is *Homo sapiens;* there is as yet no evidence from Europe of earlier forms such as the australopithecines. Fossil men are not found in Europe until the brain reached what is essentially modern size. The interpretations by archeologists stress the observation that more elaborate and complex tools are found in Europe than in Africa and Asia. Africa is almost devoid of flint and other raw materials from which were made the complex and diverse stone tools found in Europe in the middle and upper Pleistocene. It is reasonable to suggest that the elaborate flint tools, which occur about the time that hominid fossils appear with brains of modern size, partly depended upon the availability of raw materials. Quartz and quartzite, common in Africa, are, as Rouse points out, excellent materials from which to make pounding tools—choppers—but poor materials for sharp cutting tools—blades. Good, sharp blades can be made of obsidian (volcanic glass), and obsidian is found in Africa. But obsidian tools are not found in sites of the lower Pleistocene. Obsidian is brittle but not much more difficult to work than flint. However the process of working obsidian is more complex than the process of working quartzite to obtain pounding, chopping tools. It is not only the brain and what goes on in the brain that is important, but also what materials are available for it to think about.

The earliest stone tools are called pebble tools. The shape of the original pebble is still present in the tool. Pebble tools are, essentially, stones that have been worked a little at one end, with a few chips knocked off. Such a slightly sharpened stone is a most useful tool, and a new one can be made quickly as the old one wears out. The pebble tool tradition persisted through out the lower Pleistocene. Pebble tools, often called choppers, are also found throughout the middle and upper Pleistocene in parts of Asia. The effectiveness of such tools was recently demonstrated by Leakey when he skinned and butchered a small antelope in less than 20 minutes by using a pebble tool found at Olduvai.

The next tools in the kit, the flakes and bifaces, may be viewed as by-products of pebble tools and logical extensions conceived by toolmakers. If the chips knocked off the pebble tool are used and worked, the flake tool results. At its highest development in Europe, it culminated in elegant blade tools. If the pebble itself continues to be worked, the biface or handaxe results. Rouse has suggested that the records of tool types in the Pleistocene can be interpreted as a function of increasing elaboration in conceptual thought. Biface and flake tools are not found until the time when fossil men with relatively large brains are found—brains of almost modern size. It is clear that to make biface or flake tools man must have gone through a more complex intellectual process than the process necessary for making pebble tools. The manufacture of flake and biface tools is an abstract and highly intellectual activity. There are several conceptual stages between the finished flake or biface and the original pebble from which it is made. In comparison the manufacture of the simpler pebble and bone tools found in earlier horizons of earlier strata in the tropics is little more than the utilization of objects at hand.

Man's capacity for culture depended upon the evolutionary development of a brain of sufficient size and complexity to enable him to symbol. The interpretation of fossil and archeological records suggests that brain and tools developed together. Yet there is no clear evidence that the rather rapid increase in diversity and complexity of tools was a function of a brain of a certain critical size. Neither is there evidence that tools had a direct influence on the evolution of a large brain. The availability of raw materials for the hands to use and for the brain to imagine using was also a critical factor. The development of culture also depended upon culture itself. The filling of the tool kit depended on the cultural traditions, on raw materials, and on the brain.

Sex and Society

An important aspect of the evolution of primate societies is the nature of sexual behavior among the various primates, particularly the apes and man. In many species of mammals, sexual behavior is closely tied to cyclical changes in the physiology and anatomy of the female and the male. There is considerable variation in the mammalian reproductive or estrous cycle. Estrous cycle is the term used to describe the reproductive cycle of sexually mature females of many mammalian species. An estrus occurs only during the breeding season, if the species has a breeding season, and it is usually of short duration. During the estrous cycle there is a period of sexual receptiveness or "heat" in the female. During this period of heat (estrus) the female will copulate with the male. The female will copulate at no other time in species with a full estrous cycle. Ovulation coincides with estrus as do other physiological and anatomical changes. Among the higher primates—monkeys, apes, and man—a menstrual cycle occurs. The menstrual cycle is considered a modified estrous cycle; it does not coincide with a breeding season, and there is no definite estrus, i.e., "heat." However among the monkeys some aspects of a typical mammalian estrus exist. For example female baboons develop a large, brilliant red swelling near the base of the tail. This appears at the time of ovulation. This may be a kind of signal to the males that copulation should occur. There is little evidence that a physiologically determined breeding season exists among monkeys, but there does appear to be a periodicity in the fertility of some species. There does not appear to be any cyclical periodicity in the sexual receptiveness of female macaques or baboons. Mounting occurs, and copulation occurs (or appears to occur) throughout the time between observed menstruations in the females. There may be intensification of sexual behavior at the time of estrus, but among the terrestrial monkeys of the Old World this is not the only time when copulation takes place. There is considerable evidence that the copulatory behavior of monkeys is more independent of sexual physiology than that of lower mammals and of prosimian primates.

There is an important question which must be introduced and answered here. How did the cyclical differences in external genitalia and the periodic sexual receptiveness of the females come to be deemphasized? One of the critical factors probably was the development of social life. Solitary primates, such as *Microcebus*, unquestionably are well served by very marked cyclical changes in sexuality. The reproduction of the species is ensured by automatic physiological and anatomical changes which serve to bring males and females together. Continuous contact between males and females, as among baboons, may have reduced the importance of cyclical sexual signals in maintaining the species. But some substitute for cyclical signals must have developed. The marked sexual dimorphism of *Homo sapiens* very likely was substituted for a marked sexual cycle. Sexual dimorphism in man involves characters of both males and females. The most obvious male characters involve the pattern of distribution of the hair—presence of facial hair, baldness at the temples, extension of pubic hair to the navel. The more notable female characteristics are the broadening of the hips by deposits of fat and the development of breasts. The nipples are not placed on obvious permanent prominences in other primates. There are no very noticeable external physical changes in human females during the 25- to 30-day menstrual cycle. If fertilization is to occur, something must stimulate and signal frequent, regular copulation. Characters which are obviously female and sufficiently attractive to males have evolved so that copulation will be regular and frequent. These female traits would have affected the copulatory behavior of the species and reduced the importance of any cyclical differences in the external genitalia or the sexual receptiveness of females. Sexual stimuli, sexual attractiveness, sexual behavior would gradually come to be like that of modern man—dependent upon factors that have no cyclical variation.

Copulation is elicited in many lower primates and other mammals by the cyclical changes in the gonadal hormones. Copulatory behavior can sometimes be prevented in many of these animals by appropriate hormonal injections or by gonadectomy. In chimpanzees and in man, gonadectomy of adults will not prevent copulation. Their sexual behavior is under much greater control of the cerebral cortex. It seems reasonable to argue that a selective advantage would be gained by increased cortical control over sexual behavior and other behavioral activities such as play and sleep. The neurological advances related to this increased cortical control over behavior might have preceded the capacity for culture, the capacity to symbol.

The cortical, hence to a large extent voluntary, control of sexual receptivity of females may not have been essential in forming the family or social units of the first hominids, but voluntary control of sex is relevant to the function of these social units. The family unit in nonhuman primates is, functionally, concerned with sex and reproduction. The human family's dominant function was and is subsistence, and the change in control of sexual behavior may have made this possible. There is a fundamental distinction between nonhuman primate social groupings and human societies. The society of nonhuman primates is wholly dependent upon anatomy and physiology; the society of man is largely governed by culture. Differences among human societies are not the concomitant expressions of variations in the biology of the organism. They are largely, if not entirely, independent of them. Variations in nonhuman primate societies on the contrary are the concomitants of variations in physiology and anatomy.

The principal determinants of primate sociality are probably, as Zuckerman said in 1932, ". . . search for food, search for mates, avoidance of enemies." We base our view on the reasonable assumption that primate social groups are part of the adaptive responses primates developed in order to survive. The capacity to copulate and mate throughout most if not all of the reproductive cycle and throughout all seasons of the year led to the formation of the various kinds of heterosexual groups found among monkeys and apes. Prosimii which have a definite estrus do not have the same kinds of social groups as monkeys and apes. Mammals with short, single mating seasons each year have more transitory heterosexual groups. A new level of social integration developed among the primates as the sexual physiology and receptiveness of females changed. The process of group integration through sex behavior establishes and reinforces heterosexual social bonds.

Defense against predators and avoidance of enemies is certainly a much less significant determinant of primate social order than sex. The search for food is less significant as a dominant force determining sociality in nonhuman primates than it is in man. Among men, even sex has been subordinated to subsistence, to economics, as a determinant. Sahlins points out that primate sexual behavior is used to reinforce economic bonds in human societies.

The reproductive consequences of primate sexual behavior, the helpless offspring which the primate female must carry with her, may have had an important effect upon emerging human social structure. Females with young are handicapped in societies that have a subsistence based on hunting. Carrying the young about at all times would be no great hindrance, as far as we can see, if insects, fruit, flowers, or foliage are gathered. But to hunt even small animals with a helpless clinging infant would be most difficult. A female with young who has a mate that brings her back part of the kill would no longer be at a disadvantage. Permanent pair formation would be an advantage. Among wolves permanent pair formation occurs, and both male and female provide food for the young. This would be a marked advantage to any primate which used hunting as a principal means of subsistance.

Baboons, chimpanzees, and monkeys are relatively successful primates that do not need to hunt other mammals. But let us consider a Miocene hominid like *Ramapithecus*. This creature is a medium-sized anthropoid, with rather smaller front teeth and cleverer hands than most others. It was faced with a massive change in ecozone. It seems likely that this hominid was able to respond by developing a posture and a mode of locomotion that enabled it to see over tall savanna grass and to follow herds of ungulates for long distances over the African, and probably Asian, veldts. The ecological conditions, most likely, were among the primary factors in conferring a selective advantage on an erect biped.

But what was the selection pressure that was the major factor in all this development? Clearly a new adaptive zone was open to the hominids. What was this adaptive zone? It included a change in ecology, from thick forest cover to open bush and savanna, and a change in primate social structure, from a food-gathering group to an organized hunting group. The development of cooperative hunting groups very likely provided the selection pressure, the selective advantage, which emphasized erect bipedalism, skillful use of the hands, symboling, and humanoid social structure. Formation of hunting groups probably emphasized toolmaking, an ability which depends on the unique faculty of symboling. It is our opinion that the recent and often most impressive demonstrations of the use of tools by chimpanzees and baboons do not alter, in any way, our earlier views that this is not the same as human tool-using. Among chimpanzees and baboons use of tools is clearly subject to the restriction, "out of sight is out of mind." Similarly the often dramatic illustrations of meat-eating by chimpanzees and baboons do not suggest in any way an organized hunting party. The chimpanzees, now famous for the capture and eating of a colobus monkey recorded in Goodall's superb films, are gathering food. This activity is not one whit more organized or complex than the banana collecting done by the same animals.

Under the pressure of selection, erect bipeds, with small anterior dentition and skillful hands, still could not create cooperative hunting groups without modifications of the existing social structure. It seems clear that organized hunting as a characteristic of a species requires social differentiation of the roles of those who care for the infants (females) and those who hunt (males). Cooperation among males must develop, and family groups must be permanent and well integrated. While these changes in social structure are developing, certain faculties of the brain are also changing. An ability or mentality must develop that allows for discussion of objects and animals not present, for example, the tools needed for hunting at some future time. The lineage of primates in which all of these capacities were presumably developing would be under strong selection pressure to continue to develop and refine such traits, in an environment rapidly changing from forest to open bush and plains.

George Bernard Shaw once wrote that religion, politics, and sex were the only possible subjects for intelligent conversation. The purely *hominid* way of life became the *human* way of life when our ancestors developed the capacity to make intelligent conversation that met the standards of GBS. Out of sight, out of mind is one way to characterize the quality of prehuman life. Symboling and social life made it possible for the emerging human hominid to plan, to manipulate objects imaginatively, and to convey the results of such imaginative manipulations to his fellows. (Sometimes this ability is called the time-binding ability, an unnecessarily obfuscating phrase.) Let us consider an early human hominid hunting group as it rests after the day's activities. The males are planning the next day's hunt. They ask for the support of supernatural entities; they decide which animals to hunt and how to divide the carcasses among the hunters and their families; and they conclude their planning session by talking about the females who are not present. Of course we dare not speculate about what the females were doing. After this human condition was achieved, nothing could stop the evolutionary success and progress of this fortunate primate, except himself.

26 HOW CULTURE AFFECTS GENETICS
FREDERICK S. HULSE

The profound effect of human culture upon human genetics is well indicated by the example of the sickle cell. There are other examples in later chapters, but a statement of some of the more obvious ways in which culture is capable of skewing the relative frequency of contrasting alleles should be made here. All human sexual behavior is subject to cortical control, and all human societies place restraints upon it. . . . Such restraints may be imposed for a variety of reasons. Many of these reasons have to do with social structure, especially with kinship, and they tend to interfere with the random mating postulated by the Hardy-Weinberg Law. A certain amount of skewing in the distribution of alleles may be expected because of this, even without the action of natural selection. Consequently, students of human genetics, when studying any population, must take into account the social regulations concerning mating habits within that population.

The Incest Tabu

The most widespread of these cultural practices is the incest tabu, which in one form or another is found in all human societies. Intercourse between mother and son is invariably outlawed: this is one of the few cultural universals. Probably this is an exceedingly ancient tabu, and it may have evolved from prehuman social structure. We find that the incest tabu is commonly extended to forbid other sexual relations in

Fom *The Human Species: An Introduction to Physical Anthropology,* 2nd edition, by Frederick S. Hulse.
Copyright © 1971, by Frederick S. Hulse. Copyright © 1963, 1971 by Random House, Inc. Reprinted by permission of the publisher.

almost all societies. Father-daughter and brother-sister matings are permitted in only a few cases, and still further prohibitions are very common, as well as quite varied. In general, however, mating with individuals who are thought of as close relatives is abhorred. The effect of the incest tabu has been to promote gene flow. If the local group is numerous enough, appropriate mates may be found within the neighborhood; otherwise, young males may have to look elsewhere for sexual gratification.

Available data, such as that provided by Washburn and DeVore, indicate that other primates mate within their group of origin. They observed only two successful cases of intergroup migration in months of field observation. It is quite clear that human breeding habits, due to the effects of culture, have become quite different. There is among us a far greater amount of pressure favoring the exchange of genes between different groups than exists among nonhuman primates. The lines of genetic communication within the human species have been kept open because of this universal habit, and the result must have been to minimize differences which would otherwise have developed between populations.

Exogamy and Endogamy

The practice of mating or of marriage outside of one's group of origin is known as exogamy. Mating and marriage within the group are called endogamy. It is very common for human societies to have rules concerning both. Some peoples consider first cousin marriage to be incestuous; others believe that a mother's brother's offspring or perhaps a father's sister's are not really close relatives at all. They may, in fact, be preferred as spouses; this is known as cross-cousin marriage. Still other societies forbid marriage between people of the same surname or between people who belong to the same clan, even though the genetic relationship may be remote. These are exogamous practices which carry further the pressure which favors gene flow.

In contrast, we find that in some societies the best possible mate is the father's brother's child. This has been traditional since biblical times in the Near East and is still very common there. Bonné in her study of the Jewish isolate from Habban, found that 56 percent of the marriages were between first cousins, of this sort, and that marriages between individuals of different surnames were most unusual. In other societies it has been regarded as very bad form to marry outside of one's village, even though first cousins are tabu as mates. In Switzerland, for instance, I found that in many villages during the nineteenth century 90 percent or more of the recorded marriages were between fellow villagers. These are examples of rather close endogamy, which tends to restrict ene flow.

Social stratification also affects the mating habits of at least 99 percent of the world's population, in one way or another. Most marriages are between people of more or less the same status in their societies; mating is by no means random between the rich and the poor. In many cultures, to be sure, rich men have been given and have taken the opportunity to beget children upon several or many women of the poorer classes as well as upon their legal wives. But rich women are less frequently encouraged to bear the children of poor fathers. Among other societies men who are ambitious to raise their social status have found it advantageous to father very few offspring or none at all. Caste barriers, which are much more rigid than those which separate socioeconomic classes, act as even stronger barriers to gene flow.

Differences in religious preference and in ethnic origin have become, during the past hundred generations at least, still further obstacles to random mating in many societies. This is, of course, especially noticeable in countries in which a variety of ecclesiastical organizations coexist or to which migrants from many other countries have come, such as the United States. Very few localities in this country can be thought of as comprising a single breeding population, although there are some communities of a religious nature which are in fact genetic isolates. . . .

Marriage

Perhaps in spite of or, perhaps because of the lack of a breeding season in the human species, the vast majority of children are conceived as a result of intercourse between a married couple. Marriage need not be religiously sanctioned or even legally recognized to be real in the eyes of the couple and their social peers; in any case it serves to reduce the random flow of genes within a group, as well as between groups. Nor need marriage be lifelong; by far the greater number of societies recognize divorce. A student of human genetics attempting to account for the distribution of alleles in a population must pay attention to the local beliefs and practices of the people concerning the institutions and obligations of matrimony. But he had better not assume that these beliefs and practices resemble those of his homeland, because a great deal of cultural diversity exists.

Polygyny, for those who can afford more than one wife, is highly approved of in many societies, as is concubinage. Dorjahn found that in one tribe, at least, husbands with several wives fathered more children than did monogamous husbands. This result might have been expected, but Dorjahn also found that a co-wife did not bear as many offspring as a sole wife. Allele frequencies might be expected to shift from one generation to the next under these circumstances.

Polyandry, although rare, is also found. Sometimes a group of brothers will share a single wife, as in Tibet; the social father is the oldest brother. Sometimes younger brothers are permitted access to an older brother's wife or wives; the social father is the official husband. Arrangements of this sort can confuse geneticists who are accustomed to the European forms of marriage, leading them to suppose that promiscuity exists, when, in fact, genes are channeled in an orderly way from one generation to the next. . . .

Human geneticists must also ascertain, if they can, the frequency of adoption and the rules concerning it in any society under study. Where kinship bonds are strong, as in Japan for instance, cousins are often adopted, especially if a wife has not provided the family with a son. Close questioning may be required to ascertain genetic rather than social relationships. Estimates of the degree of consanguinity, or of the mode of inheritance of a trait, or of the amount of differential fertility depend upon precise knowledge of biological parenthood.

27 BIOLOGICAL ADAPTATIONS TO CULTURE
FREDERICK S. HULSE

Instead of one's ancestral race determining one's cultural characteristics, it is often the other way around. The cultural behavior of one's ancestors may determine many of one's own biological characteristics. Sometimes their behavior will affect the phenotype only, but in many cases it will have brought about genetic changes as well. Since culture is the ecological plateau to which the human species has had to adapt, this is not strange. It is, however, a reversal of the opinion maintained by the greater number of scholars during the nineteenth century. It also contradicts the deeply felt emotions of a vast number of people today.

We have already mentioned some of the ways in which the fossil record of human evolution reveals adaptation to the exacting requirements of culture. The difference between an ape's hand and a person's is the result of selection working over thousands of generations: the ape's hand has become adapted to grasping branches, the man's to manipulating tools. Selection against small brains continued to operate among our ancestors until a few thousand generations ago or less. Brains of at least a certain minimum size are needed to cope with the demands of culture and of life with other people. It is perfectly possible that complexity of organization of the brain and consequent improvements of its operating efficiency have continued to be selected for during the past few tens of thousands of years. The fossil record cannot tell us. But human societies make such complex demands, even when technology is poorly developed, that we can be sure that our ancestors needed just as good brains to cope with their problems 10,000 years ago as we need to cope with the problems of the modern world.

Growing plasticity of response characterizes the evolution of vertebrates, of mammals from reptiles, of primates among the mammals, and of man from his primate ancestors. The development of social organization among primates put a premium upon such mental traits as emotional adjustability and educability to one's social role. The further development of society among our early ancestors increased the premium, adding further complexities. Ability to communicate meaning through language has had survival value for any group which practices such a technique in contrast to competitive groups. This ability demands a far more powerful intellect

From *The Human Species: An Introduction to Physical Anthropology,* 2nd edition, by Frederick S. Hulse. Copyright © 1971 by Frederick S. Hulse. Copyright © 1963, 1971 by Random House, Inc. Reprinted by permission of the publisher.

than any other creatures possess, yet it is an absolute necessity for human culture. And this ability is equally characteristic of all known peoples. No language can be called a better instrument for communication than any other language, nor is any language more difficult to learn than another. Each has its own complexities and subtleties, yet very young children in every society learn to speak with ease. Long ago, selection eliminated those whose genes did not grant this potentiality.

Language is but a single example of the intricacy of cultural behavior. In all fields of human activity, those who display fixity of response suffer in contrast to those who are supple and aware, who can learn rapidly to do what a new situation requires. A genetic constitution which enables educability is appropriate to a species which, like our own, must adapt to constantly changing conditions. The activities of human beings continually alter the natural environment. These alterations take place too rapidly for useful fixed responses to evolve. Selection favors plasticity or educability.

In all societies with which ethnographers are acquainted such characteristics as wisdom, poise, and ability to get along with others are favored. These seem to be pretty basic. The manner of their expression may differ with time and place, and additional characteristics may have survival value, too, but the Pygmies' culture calls for such personalities as strongly as the Englishmen's. It is for such reasons that we must be dubious about the notion that selection could have led to different psychic traits in different breeding populations. In not one of them is it profitable to be stupid.

You will recall from the example of balanced polymorphism at the sickle-cell locus that alleles are selected with reference to the advantage of the breeding population rather than of any individual within it. Some individuals are bound to suffer from anemia, and some individuals suffer from stupidity, too. Intelligence tests have been given to millions of people in many countries and to members of many different ethnic groups and genetic isolates. It has been debated whether intelligence is a single entity which can be measured with any degree of validity. The tests which have been given attempt to ascertain the effectiveness of a person's mental response to a variety of problems. They do show a very considerable range in ability within any large group. Some people are certainly much brighter than others, and the variability within all groups as shown by the standard deviation is rather high. The conditions of life in any form of human society involve so much communication that not all of us have to be geniuses.

Differences have been noted in the average scores of different ethnic groups, social classes, and breeding populations. The meaning of such findings depends upon a number of factors. We can safely draw one conclusion immediately: we cannot properly stereotype anyone as stupid or brilliant on grounds of group membership. . . .

Other conclusions are less certain. It would appear that the culture of the group as such greatly affects average scores. Tests which are suitable in one culture may be ridiculous in another. Motivation to do well depends upon social circumstances. Members of one group may seek personal distinction, whereas members of another group may evade it. A pretense of stupidity often has survival value for members of a lower caste. Malnourished subjects do more poorly than well-nourished ones. On the whole, any attempt to relate the results of intelligence tests to human genetics seems premature. There are too many intervening variables, and culture obviously is one of the major factors affecting the mental phenotype.

During the past few years, attempts have been made by a few scientists who lack any degree of anthropological sophistication to show that the American Colored are unable to learn as readily or as rapidly as are members of other racial groups and that their alleged lack of ability must be attributed to an inferior genetic endowment. It should be noted that two quite separate and distinct propositions are advanced: proof of inability to learn is by no means proof that the genetic endowment is involved, as the first part of this chapter should have made clear. But in fact the most recent data submitted to support the opinion that American Colored children cannot learn is no more convincing than earlier data: it still takes no account of the motivation, the vocabulary, the family and social backgrounds, the state of health or the tensions suffered by the children who were tested. Conclusions which depend upon evidence which is so tainted are of no scientific importance at all.

Caste Divisions and Social Selection

The fact that outsiders—however an outsider may be defined—have been so commonly thought of as inferior in some sense is an aspect of culture which has affected the distribution of genes in the human species. In the same way, the fact that inferiors are considered unworthy of equal treatment has had effects upon both genotype and phenotype. Slavery is an example.

This peculiar social institution dates from antiquity but attained real economic significance only twice: during the classical period in the Mediterranean area and again much more recently in the warmer parts of the Americas. Slavery far from their homeland was the best fate which war prisoners might expect in classical times. Sometimes whole populations were enslaved and transported far from home. The use of slaves for all sorts of unskilled or even highly skilled labor was well established by the time that the Romans began to extend their dominion throughout the Mediterranean basin. As their empire expanded, the slave markets were constantly replenished by fresh supplies of captives from all directions.

Slaves were given the most perilous tasks as well as the most arduous, so their life expectancy was low. Even those lucky enough to escape such a fate almost never succeeded in rejoining their own societies; and they must have been unable to breed rapidly enough to supply the next generation's demands for slave labor, since new captives were constantly being sought. Whatever genes they contributed to later generations were left among populations foreign to their own, since Syrians were transported to Britain and Berbers to Romania to suit the convenience of their owners.

Improvements in shipping led to the transportation of slaves, and their genes, to far greater distances during recent centuries. The tropical African origin of approximately one gene out of eight in the present population of the Americas—as we noted in Chapter Twelve—is entirely due to slavery. Whether or not this shifted allele frequencies in Africa we can never know, but it has certainly done so in the whole area from the United States to Brazil. Here, too, the death rate has been exceptionally high, and the reproductive potential consequently low. Although freed or escaped Negro slaves competed successfully with Indians in many parts of tropical America, any natural advantages due to climatic adaptation which they may have possessed were more than counterbalanced by their unfavorable economic and social status in competition with populations of European ancestry. Since the abolition of slavery, improvements in public sanitation and nutrition have begun to change this situation—again demonstrating the importance of culture in determining allele frequencies.

Slavery is perhaps the most extreme example of the caste divisions which human culture has created and which have served as barriers to gene flow, for caste endogamy is standard practice. In places such as India, where many castes exist, the barriers must be strong, for Sanghvi and Khanolkar (1949)* have found that marked differences at several loci separate such endogamous groups, all sharing the same territory. Despite the fact that selection by means of disease should be equivalent for all the castes concerned, blood groups A and B varied from 20 to 30 percent and the sickle-cell trait from 0 to 17 percent among these castes. In observable morphological traits, caste differences are just as great. Females especially are restrained from mating with males of a lower caste; sometimes the sanctions employed are quite violent. Males, on the other hand, are less easily restrained; in some cultures society pretends not to notice their breaches of etiquette. The genetic barrier is far from absolute, and as a result of this there is often a tendency for lower caste allele frequencies to approximate those of the upper caste.

Members of a dominant caste set aesthetic ideals, so that individuals showing physical features thought to be typical of that caste are likely to be regarded as desirable matches. Henriques (1953) illustrates this situation with an example from Jamaica. Only 3 percent of that island's population are of purely European ancestry, yet more than 25 percent display enough European characteristics to be classified as Colored rather than Negro. Children with such features have a higher survival rate than children who lack them, as well as opportunities for better jobs, so that they in turn can raise more children of their own than their darker cousins. Social selection supplements, if it does not replace, natural selection, for the social environment has become at least as important as the natural environment. . . .

Religious Barriers

More or less endogamous castes, like those of India and those which are the leftover relics of past slavery in North and South America, are not the only breeding

*See p. 341 for references.

populations which owe their boundaries to social rules. Differences in religion have often served as barriers to gene flow in areas where several religious organizations coexist. Here in the United States there are some religious isolates, such as the Dunkers, which have allele frequencies at some loci which are quite distinctive not only from their neighbors but from the populations from which they originated. Blood group B, for instance, has been almost lost from the Dunker gene pool although their ancestors came from central Europe. This is very probably the result of chance or genetic drift, for the Dunkers are a small group and do not intermarry with people of other faiths.

Members of many denominations are often encouraged to marry only within their group, but the extent to which this fact may be correlated with varied allele frequencies has rarely been examined in the United States. The Jewish isolate of Rome, however, is the subject of a classic study by Dunn (1959). This community has been in existence for a very long time, possibly as much as 2,000 years. It has been largely endogamous for at least several hundred years. And like the Dunkers, it has some distinctive allele frequencies, notably a very high incidence of the alleler' of the Rh system.

Religion, occupation, and ethnic origin have been quite likely to be associated in many Balkan and Near Eastern countries. Each city contained several communities, each organized about a certain denomination and tending to follow specified trades. Craft skills as well as religious membership are handed down from one generation to the next, and endogamy is strictly adhered to, since marriages are arranged by the elders of the families. As might be expected, allele frequencies at various loci differ from one community to another. In Cairo, for instance, the percentage of tasters of PTC is greater among Moslems than among native Christians, whereas the Christians are much more likely to have hair on the central segment of their fingers. Since communities of the same faith in different cities differ from one another too, it seems probable that genetic drift, rather than the retention of some ancient racial trait, is responsible for the allele frequencies which have been noted.

Even within a single community, different inbred lineages may vary in allele frequencies. Among the Jews from Habban in southern Arabia, Bonné (1969) found that the Sameach family has a distinctly higher frequency of the V, Sutter, and Duffy-amorph alleles than the other three families studied. In the same group I found that the Matoof family are distinctly light in skin color. Marriage to someone of the same surname is widely practiced in this isolate; presumably the founder effect is responsible for the genetic differences found at the loci responsible for these traits.

Occupational Barriers

In a few cases occupation alone sets people apart from their neighbors, leading to reproductive isolation. The Gypsies in Europe have remained wandering traders and repairmen of household utensils since they first entered the continent six centuries or more ago. The idea that their original homeland was India is supported by analysis of blood-group frequencies as well as by observation of their external physical features. In both they resemble certain lower caste groups of northwestern India rather than the Europeans among whom they dwell. The professional Sumo wrestlers of Japan are quite a bit taller and very much fatter than almost all other Japanese. Wrestlers almost always marry the daughters of other wrestlers. It is possible to become a wrestler, but one must be very big to succeed in this trade. Alleles for large size continue to enter this occupational group, but occupational endogamy serves as a selective force to maintain the appropriate physical type.

Linguistic Barriers

Linguistic barriers to gene flow have been noted in a number of cases. Such barriers tend to preserve ethnic identity in circumstances where it would otherwise be lost. The Basques, who live both in France and Spain at the western end of the Pyrenees, are a case in point. This ethnic group shares the religion and the occupations of their neighbors and have no political status of their own. Their bond of unity is their language, which is quite unrelated to any other so far as anyone has been able to discover. Yet it has long been noted that the frequency of certain distinctive features, such as the combination of broad foreheads and narrow jaws, is most unusually high among them. They are equally unique in the incidence of various blood type alleles, as examination of the maps in Chapter Eleven shows. Their exclusiveness, expressed in their retention of their mother tongue, has led to a retention of genetic distinctiveness.

There are similar examples on the other side of the world and in another cultural context. Tribes of the Athapaskan linguistic stock, whether in Arizona or Canada, differ from their neighbors in a standard fashion. They have a higher frequency of blood group A, a lower frequency of blood type N, and a greater variety of Rh types. Apparently they have mated very little with the members of other tribes. In South America allele frequencies at the Diego locus differ very considerably between tribes of Arawak and Carib linguistic affiliation for the same reason.

Since there is no causal correlation between the cultural phenomenon of language on the one hand and the genetic phenomenon of blood types on the other, these findings must be regarded as signifying the importance of mating preferences in the flow of genes. A person's racial characteristics are incapable of determining the language which he speaks. The language which he learned as a child, however, is a most vital part of the culture in which he lives, and it influences his behavior profoundly. In most cases, he learned how to speak from his biological parents from whom he derived whatever genes he has. In most cases, too, it is convenient to be able to talk with one's husband or wife. Casual mating, to be sure, does not require speech, but most children are born of married couples. Cultural differences are the cause rather than the result of genetic differences. This is just as true of language as it is of economic circumstance.

Miscegenation

Despite all the barriers to gene flow which exist, mating between members of different groups has been constant for as long as we have any evidence concerning human sexual behavior. There is no reason to suppose that once upon a time all races were "pure," just as there is no evidence that human diversity is a recent phenomenon. Certainly, throughout recorded history all sorts of groups have been forming, mingling, and vanishing. Miscegenation is the term applied to the genetic mixing of groups which had been distinct, but like the word inheritance, this word has been used in several different ways and applied to at least three totally distinct processes. Sometimes it is used in reference to matings between members of different castes; sometimes with reference to mating between members of ethnic groups; and sometimes with reference to mating between members of genetically distinct breeding populations. This is very natural, although it is unfortunate, because these three sorts of human groupings are very likely to overlap in their composition. It is very unfortunate, although it is natural, because this overlapping makes it possible to claim that the results of one sort of mixture are really due to another sort of mixture. Since explanations of this sort are often emotionally comforting, they have been readily accepted and form part of the common folklore.

A caste is a socioeconomic group which is set apart rather rigidly from other groups living in the same geographic area. Ritual sanctions are applied to enforce the separation. Often the members of a caste are engaged in specified occupations, or their ancestors were. As a rule, different castes within a society are hierarchically arranged; at least some are regarded as better than others. As a rule, matings between members of different castes are forbidden by custom or even by law; although in some cases females may marry males of a higher caste, and in some cases males may take lower caste females for their pleasure. Sanctions against a male who attempts to mate upward are frequently ferocious. Consequently, gene flow between different castes tends to be minimized. Yet different castes need not be genetically distinguishable. The Eta of Japan have been called "Japan's Invisible Race" (DeVos and Wagatsuma, 1966) since, despite segregation, there is no way to spot a member of this group by physical appearance. The keymarks of caste are rank and rigidity.

An ethnic group is a recognizable sociocultural unit based upon some form of national or tribal distinction, which lives among other people rather than in its own country. The unity is one of sentiment and tradition and need not involve economic factors or hierarchical status. Both its own members and their neighbors recognize the existence of an ethnic group. Yet it is not rigid, nor even necessarily stable. In a New England town only the members of old families of eighteenth-century vintage are thought of as Yankees. In New York and further west all New Englanders are thought of as Yankees. In the ex-Confederate States all northerners are thought of as Yankees. In Europe all people from the United States are thought of as Yankees. Nor need an ethnic group be in any sense a genetic group. In Hawaii the Portuguese comprise an ethnic group of whom some members are from the Cape Verde Islands and are obviously dark, while others are from the Azores and are obviously light. Neither physical appearance nor allele frequencies are useful criteria for distinguishing the Yankees from the Irish at Newburyport. But all the neighbors know who belongs to which group.

A genetically distinct breeding population is an entity of a thoroughly different sort, since it may be characterized in biological terms. Castes and ethnic groups are found only in the human species, but breeding populations exist in most if not all bisexual animal species. The barriers between castes and ethnic groups are the result of human culture and human imagination. The barriers between breeding populations may be oceans, mountains, deserts, and climatic zones as well. Society often determines the composition of a breeding population, but it is less able to determine its genetic characteristics. In many cases, at least within the human species, social regulations may be effective in causing genetic distinctions to be retained, but it is far more doubtful that social regulations caused them to originate. . . .

In summary, we can say with complete confidence that all statements alleging disadvantageous effects from miscegenation refer either to caste or to ethnic miscegenation. Most of them concern caste miscegenation and simply reflect the speakers' prejudices in regard to status. There is no indication that genetics is concerned in any way. The essential mistake made by those who assert disadvantageous effects has been a total disregard of cultural factors and an assumption that all human behavior is genetically determined.

There are, of course, scientists, scholars, and publicists who assert that miscegenation is beneficial rather than unfortunate. The high birth rates noted earlier have been taken to indicate hybrid vigor, or heterosis, for instance, and Shapiro (1929) goes on to proclaim that the Pitcairn Islanders created a social structure superior to that of either Tahiti or England. Rodenwaldt (1927) praised the vigor of the "Mestizen auf Kisar" whom he studied, and Williams (1931) wrote of the vitality of the Maya-Spanish crosses in Yucatan. Many historically minded scholars have noted cultural efflorescence after two groups of people have merged, and they have attributed this to the beneficial effects of introducing "new blood" into the population. Certainly cultural interchange can have a stimulating effect, but this is true whether genes are exchanged or not. The Japanese, whose island country has taken in a smaller proportion of immigrants during the last 1,500 years than any other nation I know of, have been as stimulated by culture contact as any people in the world.

Hybrid vigor has been claimed as one of the chief virtues resulting from miscegenation, but this is almost certainly due to a misunderstanding. Mendel (1866) noted that, in the F_1 generation of some of his hybrid peas, the plants grew extra large. As a phenomenon of the first filial generation after crossing of two genetically distinct strains, many later investigators have noted such hybrid vigor as well. Biologically, however, this is evanescent. Later generations, if inbred, do not continue to manifest this characteristic. If indeed extra vigor is noted among such groups as those studied by Shapiro and Fischer, it can scarcely be termed hybrid vigor, and in any case Trevor (1953), in reviewing a number of studies of miscegenation, was unable to confirm its existence in any of them. As Penrose (1955) has pointed out, the classic studies of race mixture have described cases of hybridization between groups neither of which were in fact genetically pure strains like Mendel's peas.

Another, but possibly related, advantage attributed to miscegenation is the lessened frequency of appearance in the phenotype of harmful recessives. This is a reasonable expectation in accordance with genetic knowledge and theory. One has to remember, however, that not all genetic recessives can be described as harmful, nor are all deleterious alleles recessive. Let us consider the case of blue eyes, which are found among about half of northwestern Europeans—so that the allele frequency may be calculated at about 70 percent—but not at all among aboriginal North American Indians. A good deal of miscegenation has taken place between these two groups during the last few hundred years, and it has been genetic as well as ethnic miscegenation. The allele frequencies in a population of hybrids would then be about 35 percent, and, if they mated only with one another, the phenotype frequency of blue eyes would be one in eight. Is this advantageous, disadvantageous, or simply irrelevant except aesthetically? We would expect the allele frequency of Rh negatives to be halved in such a mixed group, too, so that the phenotypic incidence would drop to one-fourth of that found in West European populations. This might be considered advantageous from the European point of view, but an American Indian might become indignant at the introduction of a new hazard into his population.

In the malarial regions of Africa a mulatto population would, at first, have a lower frequency of sickle-cell alleles and, consequently, a lower incidence of heterozygotes useful as a buffer against malaria than a Negro population long resident in the area. But natural selection might remedy this misfortune within a few generations. In the United States or England, on the other hand, since malaria is a minor hazard in these countries at the present time, the allele Hb^s is properly considered deleterious. Whether a certain genetic factor is harmful or not depends upon the environmental stresses to which a population is subject. It is rash and prejudicial to consider it a matter of absolute good or bad. We may conclude, however, that extensive outbreeding, whether or not it involves caste or ethnic miscegenation, does serve to retain recessives in the gene pool, and this is good insurance against possible environmental changes in the future. What we deplore now may serve as useful functions for later generations.

Heterozygote advantage, which seems to have been pretty well demonstrated in the case of the sickle-cell locus, has been another of the arguments advanced in favor of miscegenation. There may well be many cases in which heterozygotes do enjoy an advantage of some sort. At any rate it is difficult to explain the numerous cases of balanced polymorphism in any other way, and the excess of the phenotype MN over expectation in so many family studies supports this opinion too. But, in fact, genetic polymorphism is so common at so many loci within each caste or ethnic group which has been studied that intermarriage between members of different social groups is not required to ensure its continuance.

Studies of miscegenation, as distinct from polemics, date at least as far back as Boas's (1894) publication, "The Half Blood Indian." As our understanding of the mechanisms of biological inheritance and of the relationships between genetics and environment have improved, investigators have turned more and more to the analysis of special problems rather than all-embracing population surveys. This has permitted more precise analysis of the particular problem chosen but has sometimes resulted in a neglect of factors which are relevant to the dynamics of miscegenation. Stuckert (1958) published a provocative paper on "African Ancestry of the White American Population" which neglected to take into account the fact that most of the American Colored were concentrated in a relatively small area within the United States, the fact that about 40 percent of American Whites are of quite recent European extraction, the fact that sanctions against Colored males mating with White females have been of the utmost ferocity, and the fact that "passing" as White has been exceedingly difficult. In any study of genetic miscegenation both cultural and geographical circumstances have to be considered.

Mating is never at random in the human species, and among those who mate across the barriers of caste or ethnic group it is clearly less random than among those who mate within their own social group. Slave owners have been more likely to mate with slaves than have members of the slave owners' stocks who do not own slaves. Wandering fur traders were more likely to mate with American Indians than were their kinsmen who remained at home. Sailors whose ships took them to the South Seas were almost the only Europeans to mate with Polynesians. There is no reason to suppose that the Indonesians and Africans who became the ancestors of the Malagasy were a random sample of the populations from which they were derived. We have very little information on the physical, let alone the genetic, characteristics of those particular European males who were the ancestors of the hybrid groups which have been analyzed in the classic studies of race mixture. Nor do we know much about their consorts. We can imagine that slave owners picked the girls who pleased them most, but we do not know what standards they used.

Futher more, since, in cases of ethnic miscegenation, at least one of the participating groups must have come from another region, they may be subject and their offspring may be subject to unfamiliar selective stresses which would result in shifts in allele frequencies whether or not race mixture took place. This was found to be the case by Workman, Blumberg, and Cooper (1963): the incidence of Hb^s among the Colored in Georgia had declined much more than it would have if hybridization with North Europeans alone had been responsible. When we are dealing with populations which have resulted from miscegenation several centuries ago, it becomes very difficult to estimate the relative proportions of alleles contributed by each of the ancestral stocks concerned. Pollitzer in a beautifully designed study of "The Negroes of Charleston, South Carolina" compared this population with West Africans, American Whites, and the larger group of American Colored for serological and morphological traits. He found that in blood-type frequencies both the Charleston Negroes and the United States Colored as a whole resemble West Africans more closely than they do in morphology. Manuila (1956) noted a higher incidence of blood type B in those parts of eastern Europe overrun by the Mongols than in neighboring areas, yet the inhabitants do not look in the least Mongoloid. It is quite possible that social selection has been operative in both these cases, inasmuch as humans have not yet developed such prejudices about blood types as they have about external anatomical features. Further studies are needed, of course, to confirm or deny this guess of mine.

Harrison and Owen (1964) in Liverpool studied the skin color of a group of mixed European-West African ancestry and many of their European and West African parents. Since there is no overlapping at all in the degree of pigmentation of the unexposed skin in West Africans and North Europeans, a study of this sort is most suitable to determine the number of loci involved in the inheritance of skin color. Much more precise genetic analyses can be made in a situation such as this: here we see the essential difference between cultural and genetic inheritance. Cultural characteristics are transmitted from one generation to the next at large; genetic characteristics are transmitted only from biological parents to their own personal offspring. Thus it was possible in the Liverpool study to compare children with their own parents and reach conclusions concerning the number of loci involved in the determination of pigmentation. Only by a study of genetic miscegenation conducted in this manner can this sort of information be uncovered. Caste and ethnic factors are eliminated, and selection can scarcely have had time to operate in the course of two generations.

During the present and the coming generation it seems to me that the best place in the world to study genetic miscegenation will be Israel. Populations of Jews from many different parts of the world have just been gathered together into this state. Many of these populations have been highly inbred for centuries, and they differ from one another in a great number of sets of allele frequencies. They are just beginning to interbreed with one another. Parental as well as first and second filial generations will all be available for study during the next two or three decades. Ethnic and even castelike differences exist but are minimized and can readily be factored out by careful analysis. The cultural atmosphere of the nation favors scientific research, and its compact size makes field work easy. It can therefore be hoped that many important discoveries concerning the consequences of miscegenation will be made by physical anthropologists and human geneticists working in unison in the natural laboratory of Israel.

We have already mentioned that diet, which is determined by culture, has observable effects upon the biological characteristics of human beings and that agriculture sometimes benefits mosquitoes as well as men. Food preferences and changes in food preferences have effects as well. Too great dependence upon one staple crop may lead to vitamin deficiencies, and these in turn may act as selective forces within a population. Maize appears to be associated with pellagra, which is due to niacin deficiency, and rice with beri-beri, caused by thiamine deficiency. Any diet very low in protein, as diets of grains and roots are likely to be, may result in kwashiorkor. All of these deficiency diseases eliminate large numbers of children from the population, and in almost all places where they have been endemic the average body size of adults is small. It is apparent that nonlethal cases delay growth and strongly suspected that permanent stunting is a common result. It would be logical to expect that certain genotypes may be favored at the expense of others in environments which include vitamin or protein deficiency as standard hazards to life; but we cannot be at all sure that alleles leading to short stature or light weight would be those selected.

Changes in diet have had a variety of interesting results. The potato was introduced into Europe only a few hundred years ago, for it had previously been cultivated only in the Andes. It does well in damp, cool climates, and therefore proved a most suitable crop for northern Europe. Agricultural improvements, including the provision of much winter fodder for farm animals, were being made at the time that the cultivation of the potato was spreading. With more and better food available human health improved and population increased. This increase was especially marked in the areas where the incidence of alleles for blondness and for blood group B were high. The result, of course, has been an increase in the frequency of both of these characteristics among Europeans. This increased frequency has nothing whatever to do with any possible adaptive value of the alleles concerned. It is the fortuitous consequence of cultural change. It should serve as another reminder to caution in attributing cultural achievements to the possession of one set of alleles rather than another.

SECTION INTRODUCTION REFERENCES* AND SUGGESTIONS FOR FURTHER STUDY

Alland, Alexander, Jr., 1966, "Medical Anthropology and the Study of Biological and Cultural Adaptation." *American Anthropologist* 68:40–51.
———, 1967, *Evolution and Human Behavior*. Garden City, N.Y.: The Natural History Press.
———, 1972, *The Human Imperative*. New York: Columbia University Press.
Aquili, Eugene G. d', 1972, *The Biopsychological Determinants of Culture*. Addison-Wesley Modular Publications, Module 13.
Baker, Paul T., 1960, "Climate, Culture, and Evolution." *Human Biology* 32:3–16.
Bateson, Gregory, 1967, "Cybernetic Explanation." *American Behavioral Scientist* 10:29–32.
Campbell, Bernard, 1974, *Human Evolution: An Introduction to Man's Adaptations*, 2nd ed. Chicago: Aldine.
Dobzhansky, Th. G., and Gordon Allen, 1956, "Does Natural Selection Continue to Operate in Modern Mankind?" *American Anthropologist* 58:591–604.
Dobzhansky, Th., 1963a, "Cultural Direction of Human Evolution." *Human Biology* 35:311–316.
———, 1963b, "Evolution: Organic and Superorganic." *The Rockefeller Institute Review* 1:1–9.
Fox, Robin, 1967, "In the Beginning: Aspects of Hominid Behavioral Evolution." *Man* 2:415–433.

———, 1973, *Encounter with Anthropology*. New York: Harcourt Brace Jovanovich.
Freeman, Daniel G., 1967, "A Biological View of Man's Social Behavior." In W. Etkin, ed., *Social Behavior from Fish to Man*. Chicago: University of Chicago Press, pp. 152–188.
Giles, Eugene, 1970, "Culture and Genetics." In *Current Directions in Anthropology*, Ann Fisher, ed. Bulletins of the American Anthropological Association 3(3, part 2):87–98.
Gluckman, Max, 1972, "A Bandwagonload of Monkeys." *New York Review of Books*, Nov. 16, pp. 39–41.
Hailman, Jack P., 1969, "How an Instinct Is Learned." *Scientific American* 221 (6):98–106.
Hallowell, A. Irving, 1963, "Personality, Culture and Society in Behavioral Evolution." In S. Koch. ed., *Psychology: A Study of Science*. New York: McGraw-Hill, pp. 429–509.
Hamburg, D. A., 1963, "Emotions in the Perspective of Human Evolution." In *Expression of the Emotions in Man*. New York: International Universities Press.
Hockett, C. F. , and R. Ascher, 1964, "The Human Revolution." *Current Anthropology* 5:135–168.
Huxley, Julian S., 1956, "Evolution, Cultural and Biological." In W. L. Thomas, Jr., ed., *Current Anthropology*. Chicago: University of Chicago Press, pp. 3–25.
Klopfer, Peter H. and Jack P. Hailman, 1967, *An Introduction to Animal Behavior*. Englewood Cliffs, N.J.: Prentice-Hall.
LaBarre, Weston, 1957, *The Human Animal*. Chicago: University of Chicago Press.
Lenneberg, E. H., 1967, *Biological Foundations of Language*. New York: Wiley.
Lerner, I. Michael, 1968, *Heredity, Evolution and Society*. San Francisco: Freeman.
Lorenz, Konrad, 1970–1971, *Studies in Animal and Human Behavior* (2 Vols.). (Trans. by R. Martin.) Cambridge, Mass.: Harvard University Press.
Montagu, M. F. Ashley, ed., 1962, *Culture and the Evolution of Man*. New York: Oxford University Press.
Muller, Hermann J., 1960, "The Guidance of Human Evolution." In Sol Tax, ed., *The Evolution of Man: Mind, Culture, and Society*, (Vol. 2) of *Evolution After Darwin*. Chicago: University of Chicago Press, pp. 423–462.
Norbeck, Edward, 1969, "Human Play and Its Cultural Expression." *Humanitas* 5:43–55.
Provine, William B., 1973, "Geneticists and the Biology of Race Crossing." *Science* 182:790–796.
Sahlins, Marshall, 1959, "The Social Life of Monkeys, Apes and Primitive Men." *Human Biology* 31:54–73.
*———, 1960, "The Origin of Society." *Scientific American* 203 (3):76–87.
Spuhler, J. N. 1959, *The Evolution of Man's Capacity for Culture*. Ann Arbor, Mich.: University of Michigan Press.
Spuhler, J. N., and G. Lindzey, 1967, "Racial Differences in Behavior." In J. Hirsch, ed., *Behavior–Genetic Analysis*. New York: McGraw-Hill, pp. 366–414.
*Stern, Curt, 1960, *Principles of Human Genetics*, 2nd ed. San Francisco: Freeman.
Thorpe, W. H., 1956, *Learning and Instinct in Animals*. Cambridge, Mass.: Harvard University Press.
Washburn, Sherwood L., 1960, "Tools and Human Evolution." *Scientific American* 203:62–75,276.

section IX

Culture and Geographic Environment

As we have earlier noted, the effect of the geographic environment upon culture is an ancient subject of speculative thought. Popular thought today continues to entertain similar ideas, of which perhaps the most common during the twentieth century has been the view that the development of culture is intimately linked with climate. According to one such interpretation the emergence of elaborate civilizations has been possible only in regions of the earth with temperate climates. Extreme views of this kind have been called "geographic determinism," and have generally been unacceptable to anthropologists, who base their interpretations upon cross-cultural observations of ideally very broad scope that have not permitted such interpretations.

Anthropological interest in the relationship between culture and the geographic environment may be traced to the earliest of the pioneer anthropologists of the nineteenth century, especially to the writings of the German anthropologist Friedrich Ratzel, who used the term "anthropogeographie." The history of anthropological concern since the time of Ratzel has been one of varying interest. Developments include one moderate change of opinion, and, since the 1950s, an identification of the subject by the name "cultural ecology."

Cultural evolutionists of the second half of the nineteenth century generally showed little interest in the topic, and this lack of interest continued into the twentieth century until the 1920s and 1930s. Concern with the subject was then stimulated by the process of formulating and refining the concept of culture area, which may be briefly defined as a geographic region in which the cultures are alike and distinctive enough to set them apart from other cultures. The contributions of Clark Wissler and A. L. Kroeber toward formulating the concept of culture area and their efforts to define culture areas of aboriginal North America are especially noteworthy. These studies made it evident that correlations existed between the distinctive conformations of culture of each of the areas and their differing geographic environments. The first reading in this section is a group of excerpts on this subject from Kroeber's book *Cultural and Natural Areas of Native North America*, first published in 1939 and one of the forerunners of the modern study of cultural ecology.

In part as a reaction against the extravagant statements of geographic determinists, anthropologists had been pointing out the variety of relationships between the geographic environment and culture in their studies. Opinion had generally set in the view that the geographic environment exerted limiting and permissive influence upon culture but that its influence could not be regarded as determining culture. This opinion, which prevailed until the 1950s, is well expressed by C. Darryl Forde in his still useful book *Habitat, Economy and Society* (1934), which compares the utilization of the environments by societies of similar technological development living in similar geographic environments. Forde gives special attention to the influence of culture itself, in the form of attitudes and values, upon ways of utilizing natural resources. Implicit in the anthropological opinion about the relationship generally held at this time was the more or less tautological idea that the limiting influence of the physical environment diminished as technology developed. If restated, this view reasons circularly that the influence of the physical environment wanes as human control over it increases. Studies of the varieties of modes of exploiting the physical environment and the strongly conditioning influence of attitudes and values upon these modes were nevertheless informative.

In the past two decades interest has heightened in the subject of links between culture and geographic environment (Hatch 1973), a trend stimulated by the writings of Julian H. Steward, whose concern with cultural ecology goes back at least twenty years before the date of publication (1955) of his essay which is here reproduced in part. Steward's views, which stem from his earlier investigations of ecological aspects of culturally simple American Indian societies of the interior of the far western United States, may be regarded as the forefront of a changed current of opinion that has never in fact represented drastic revision of older views. Steward held that under certain technologic conditions, as exemplified by the ways of life of certain simple hunting and gathering societies, the influence of the geographic environment might be so forceful as to mold the social organization. Rather than being merely culturally limiting and permissive, the geographic environment is thus seen as being in some sense a determinant of culture. Since 1955, some of Steward's data and specific interpretations have been questioned, but his central idea has not been set aside.

Interest in cultural ecology is currently at its most lively, and has undoubtedly been sparked in some degree by the great national concern with immediate problems of ecology such as environmental pollution and the troublesome alterations of flora, fauna, and climate brought about by modern technology. Modern times also provide many striking examples of man's increasing technologic control over environmental conditions, such as the successful construction of air-conditioned, domed stadiums that seat many thousands of spectators and the use of weather modification as a weapon of war. Knowledge of apiculture and the availability of airplanes have made it possible to conduct profitably the formerly inconceivable commercial enterprise of raising honey in the short six weeks of summer in the sub-arctic, where domesticated honey bees cannot survive throughout the year.

Current anthropological investigations in cultural ecology cover a much broader range than formerly and often relate to the interests of physical anthropology and archeology, fields of anthropology which have histories of concern with ecology that appear to be equally as old as that in cultural and social anthropology. Thematically, several of the writings in Section VIII of this book, for example, may be included in cultural ecology, although their principal considerations are biological aspects of man. Physical anthropology has for many decades considered the relationships among culture, the physical environment, and the genetically transmitted characteristics of man. Similarly, archeology relates to cultural ecology by attempting to deal with such archeological topics as the circumstances leading to the domestication of plants and animals, the effects of irrigation, and the complex of factors involved in the emergence of early civilizations. Many modern investigations may readily bridge the subfields of archeology, physical anthropology, and cultural anthropology. A study (Livingstone 1958) which links swidden agriculture with the incidence of malaria and sickle-cell anemia through the effects of this technique of agronomy upon populations of mosquitoes, for example, has relevance to all subfields of anthropology as well as to medicine. The article by Leslie A. White on the human control of sources of energy which appears in Section X has much relevance to cultural ecology although its primary focus is cultural evolution. Present indications suggest that cultural ecology will increasingly concern the special interests and make use of the competences of the subfields of anthropology but will at the same time have generalized goals and become a cooperative concern of the entire field.

28 CULTURAL AND NATURAL AREAS OF NATIVE NORTH AMERICA
A. L. KROEBER

Objectives

This study has two objectives. It aims, first, to review the environmental relations of the native cultures of North America. Its second purpose is to examine the historic relations of the culture areas, or geographical units of cultures.

Three points are best stated explicitly at the outset, to prevent possible misconception.

The first is that the present work in no sense represents a relapse toward the old environmentalism which believed it could find the causes of culture in environment. While it is true that cultures are rooted in nature, and can therefore never be completely understood except with reference to that piece of nature in which they occur, they are no more produced by that nature than a plant is produced or caused by the soil in which it is rooted. The immediate causes of cultural phenomena are other cultural phenomena. At any rate, no anthropologist can assume anything else as his specific working basis. But this does not prevent the recognition of relations between nature and culture, nor the importance of these relations to the full understanding of culture.

The second point is to guard against the possible misconception that the determination of culture areas is here considered an end in itself. The concept of a culture area is a means to an end. The end may be the understanding of culture processes as such, or of the historic events of culture.

The study of processes tends to be analytic, and therefore to disregard time and space relations except so far as they condition the particular phenomena whose processes are being examined. In proportion as the study advances and learns to deal more directly with cultural processes as such, the time and space relations become a sort of frame. They remain factors that for scientific purposes must be controlled, but this control becomes a limitation, almost an encumbrance. This type of study is akin to the dissecting technique of the laboratory, even though cultural anthropology has neither laboratory nor experiment. . . .

. . . The conception on which the present monograph is based is that space and time factors are sufficiently interrelated in culture history to make the culture area a valuable mechanism, rather than a distraction, in the penetration of the time perspective of the growth of cultures so relatively undocumented as are those of native America.

The third point to be kept in mind is that the present study deals with culture wholes, and not, except incidentally, with culture elements or "traits," nor with those associations of elements which are sometimes called "culture complexes" but which always constitute only a fraction of the entirety of any one culture. Culture wholes as a concept correspond in many ways to regional floras and faunas, which are accumulations of species but can also be viewed as summation entities. . . .

Reprinted from University of California Publications in American Archeology and Ethnology, Vol. 38 (1939) (1947). Originally published by the University of California Press; reprinted by permission of the Regents of the University of California.

History of Concepts

For a generation American anthropologists have given less and less attention to environmental factors. In part this represents a healthy reaction against the older naïve view that culture could be "explained" or derived from the environment. For the rest, it is the result of a sharpening of specific anthropological method and the consequent clearer perception of culture forms, patterns, and processes as such: the recognition of the importance of diffusion, for instance, and of the nature of the association of culture elements into "complexes." Most attention came to be paid, accordingly, to those parts of culture which readily show self-sufficient forms: ceremonial, social organization, art, mythology; somewhat less to technology and material culture; still less to economics and politics, and problems of subsistence. Much of the anthropology practiced in this country in the present century has been virtually a sociology of native American culture; strictly historic and geographic interests have receded into the background, except where archaeological preoccupation kept them alive. We have had intensive studies of the internal social grouping of peoples of whom we did not know whether they constituted one or several national units; analyses of the patterns of maize- or acorn-utilization complexes, rather than consideration of whether such a complex provided a tenth, a half, or four-fifths of the subsistence of the various tribes who adhered to it; and so on. This diversion of attention to cultural forms was necessary and desirable; the attendant shift of interest away from historical and subsistence problems was probably inevitable. There is also often a readier productivity in work along the formal lines, especially among Indians on reservations. An old informant can sometimes give exact data on the sequence of details of a ritual that has been abandoned for forty years, but is vague about the proportion of acorns or salmon in his father's diet, or the months of each year spent by his group on the river or in the mountains. However, such facts are also of consequence in their relation to culture, since every culture is conditioned by its subsistence basis. The culminations of culture obviously rest on a certain degree of economic surplus, for instance. Such a surplus will not explain why the lines in a given art are curved instead of straight, or why a people derives the origin of mankind from below ground rather than from the sky. But it may help to explain why Haida art is esthetically richer than Kwakiutl, or Pueblo ritual more complex than Havasupai. And these are also legitimate problems; and strictly historical ones. We need not edge away from them because they involve qualitative judgments or a concern with culture wholes. Anthropology does not have to be exclusively analytic in order to be valid.

Relations of Environmental and Cultural Factors

The assumption upon which the discussions in this section rest is that on the one hand culture can be understood primarily only in terms of cultural factors, but that on the other hand no culture is wholly intelligible without reference to the noncultural or so-called environmental factors with which it is in relation and which condition it.

An example will illustrate. Six American states stretching in a belt from Ohio to Nebraska today produce nearly half the world's maize crop. This is a region in which the Indians also farmed maize, but with less intensity than in many other regions; and their population remained scant. The difference is not in the plant, nor fundamentally in methods of farming it. It is factors extrinsic to the cultivation itself which have changed an area of below-average maize-growing into one of most successful specialization. These factors are cultural: domesticated animals, economic demand and distribution facilities, methods of transportation, improved machinery. The natural environment remained the same.

However, maize-farming of itself, like other subsistence and economic activities, and through these all cultural activities, is obviously conditioned by "natural" factors such as climate, soil, and drainage. The frostless season must be warm and long enough, the precipitation within it sufficient, and so on. Where these conditions fail, the limits of maize-growing are reached. This inability tends to affect the whole of a culture unable to farm; but quite differently according to situation: in California and eastern Canada, for instance. The difference in effect is due to both environmental and cultural causes, which vary areally. In California, nature provided other food to make population in the nonfarming territory denser rather than lighter. The local cultures thus were able to flourish with some vigor and with considerable independence of the farming ones near them. In the East, there was no comparable natural food supply, and the hunting population remained light. This put it in a position of dependence, culturally, on the adjacent farming populations. And at the same time the cultural medium was so much thinned by the smaller subsistence possibilities that many elements of the farming culture failed to obtain a foothold to the north.

It is in this way that the interactions of culture and environment become exceedingly complex when followed out. And this complexity makes generalization unprofitable, on the whole. In each situation or area different natural factors are likely to be impinging on culture with different intensity.

It does seem worth while to review briefly the more striking cases of influence of the various environmental factors, as indicated by the degree of agreement between cultural areas and natural ones of various kinds. The intent is not so much to evaluate in general terms the strength of each environmental factor as to recognize specific cases where environment is of importance.

Physiography

Natural areas, in the sense of geologic or physiographic units, have already been compared at length with cultural and ethnic areas, and the more striking correspondences listed. These correspondences are more numerous and definite on the Pacific than on the Atlantic side of the continent, with Mexico possibly promising to fall rather with the Pacific side when it shall be well enough known.

Under "Population" it has been noted that the more decisive differentiation and variegation of local landscapes on and near the Pacific is probably connected both with a greater sessility of population and a stronger tendency toward speech diversification there.

Natural vegetation

Plant cover is obviously almost always likely to stand in relation to culture. It largely expresses climate; it tends heavily to determine the fauna; and it enters directly into subsistence, besides at times affecting travel and transport. It is rather surprising, in fact, that culture is not therefore a function of natural vegetation to a greater degree than actually obtains. That it is not, suggests the preponderant strength of purely cultural forces. However, there are a number of neat correspondences of areas of plant cover and culture. Among the principal of these are the following:

The Northwest Coast culture tallies almost perfectly with the Northwestern Hygrophytic Forest.

Within this, the area appearing most aberrant culturally, the Williamette Valley, is also aberrant phytogeographically, being classed as forest by some authorities, as grassland by others.

In the Southwest, the historically primary line of cleavage between cultures of Pueblo and of Sonora-Gila-Yuma type is closely paralleled by a division of the area into semidesert and true desert.

The Pueblo semidesert is part of the sagebrush-juniper semidesert of the Great Basin, into which both Basket Maker and Pueblo culture proliferated.

Snake River drainage affiliates not with the Columbia but with the Great Basin in prevailing plant cover, speech and, apparently, culture.

The short-grass plains and tall-grass prairies, before the introduction of the horse, probably harbored cultures respectively of prevailing western mountain and eastern forest affiliations.

The Wind River Shoshone, basically a Basin tribe with a recent overlay of Plains culture, lived in a sagebrush habitat even though this drains into the Mississippi system.

The tropical region of southern Florida corresponds to a local variant of the general Southeastern culture.

The northern Iroquoian territory is characteristically one of Northeastern Hardwood forest.

The classic Maya culture is situated in tropical rain forest, the sub-Maya culture of the other Mayan tribes in more open plant cover.

The Pacific Nicaragua or Chorotegan culture lay in a region of relatively arid vegetation.

East of the Mississippi, correspondences are less definite than elsewhere. The varieties both of culture and of plant cover differ from one another by small intervals, so that conditions are more nearly uniform on both scores. Mexico, on the other hand, presents sharp contrasts, but knowledge of the ecology is too imperfect, and that of the cultures too little organized, to make most classifications and correlations more than tentative.

Climate

Climate has been incidentally rather than systematically considered in this work. It is not an easy thing to deal with; partly because of its compositeness. Temperature, precipitation, seasonal régime, besides minor factors, are all of varying influence. Here one component and there another becomes specifically influential upon culture. Temperature may be uniform in two regions and yet the precipitation cause them to vary enormously as cultural habitats; or the reverse. A climatic classification taking cognizance of all factors is obviously the desideratum. . . .

Native California failed to become agricultural because of its dry summers, for which, so far as maize was concerned, no amount of winter precipitation could compensate. In most of the eastern United States cold winters and winter precipitation did not matter, because low elevation permitted the summer to be hot and long enough, and the considerable and relatively even precipitation contained summer rainfall enough, for maize to thrive. Obviously, these conditions have also determined modern maize distribution: California today is not notably a corn-raising state. As between the summer-showered hot desert of southern New Mexico-Arizona and the dry-summer hot steppe climate of southern California, Pueblo culture evidently could and did cling to its maize foundation and persist somewhat precariously in the former, but was not able even to become established in the latter. The country between—roughly, central and western Arizona—in general suffered from too great absolute aridity and evaporation to make primary maize subsistence possible except where local natural flood conditions as on the lower Colorado, or specialized technique as in the Gila-Salt Valley, made irrigation on a fair-sized scale possible.

The idea that seasonal distribution of rainfall largely controlled both the successful functioning of Pueblo culture and the nonagriculture of California, I owe to my colleague Sauer. Russell's careful maps render possible the more precise application of the idea. . . .

Water

Water is obviously a factor to which culture tends to effect a strong adaptation, primarily in regard to subsistence, also to settlement and transportation. So far as food supply is concerned, water, whether fresh or salt, normally comes in only as providing a fauna, not a flora. The chief exception is shallow lakes and lake marshes bearing wild rice or water lilies.

The greatest effect of water on culture in most of native North America seems to be through population increase, which in turn is brought about by the added subsistence opportunity. The ocean with its shore may sometimes provide actually more food than the land; the two together will normally provide more than the land alone. This tendency has been abundantly exemplified in the discussion of native population densities. However, there are some unexplained and surprising variations of the densities on certain length of coast line.

On the Pacific side, the higher concentration of coast population resulted, in most areas, in a corresponding intensification as well as specialization of culture. On the Atlantic coast, such an effect is scarcely noticeable. The reason probably is the general narrowness of Pacific coast land, which often is wholly restricted to beach, coupled with long ranges beginning to rise almost from the beach and sharply dividing shore from interior. The wide, gentle, Atlantic coastal plain, on the contrary, tends to keep shore and inland linked by its almost insensible gradation.

Along and near the Arctic Ocean the sea provides more food than the land, so that the Eskimo, who generally have also some land-hunting opportunities, are more populous than the Athabascans and Algonkins of the interior. It might be disputed whether this has led to a higher culture level, but it has certainly resulted in marked diversification of culture between coast and inland.

Besides the sea, its concomitant in the North, ice, has been a factor of greatest importance in Eskimo economy. The presence of rough pack ice, smooth sea ice, and open sea determines the presence or absence of mammalian and other species, and the opportunities for taking them, as Boas and Steensby have shown. The ice in turn depends not only on temperature but also on depth of shore waters, indentation of the coast line, and winds and currents. The results of these variations are a number of essentially equivalent but well differentiated forms of the Eskimo economy, reflected in material culture, technology, and habits of life. The principal of these forms have been listed in the discussion of the Eskimo culture area. Roughly, it might be said that it is shore residence which makes Eskimo culture distinct from adjacent Indian, ice which primarily determines what form the Eskimo culture of any locality assumes.

In Mexico and Central America the coast as such seems to have exerted little influence. The reasons for this condition are not clear. . . .

Beyond Mexico also, on the Gulf eastward as far as the Mississippi, and again in southern Florida, the coast seems to have effected little condensation of population or intensification of culture. But here the causes were probably different from those in Mexico, since the interior was nonagricultural.

In the development of the Northwest Coast culture, the original environmental factor of importance, as has been noted above in the detailed consideration of this culture, is likely to have been the rivers rather than the sea. The streams are relatively numerous, fairly large in volume even when short, sometimes great in both volume and length, and carrying salmon and other fish that come in enormous runs. There was high seasonal variation, but it was essentially in the fish, rather than in the rivers as in Mexico. This condition allowed the population to reside, travel, and in large measure feed itself by means of the streams, without cutting itself off from land subsistence or habits. Later, relative stillness of salt water in regions like Puget Sound, Georgian Bay, and numerous large fjord "inlets," farther north, tended to coax and train local groups for the sea, finally ending by giving some of them a more maritime aspect, with an attendant shift in climax habitat and cultural values and intensification within the Northwest Coast frame as a whole. This is hypothesis, but so far as it may hold it affords an exemplification of one type of relation between natural environment and culture.

In more complex ways, too, water has been a factor through a combination of influences on subsistence, transportation, and other aspects of culture which cannot always be clearly analyzed. It can scarcely be an accident, for instance, that such culture focusing as is discernible in the Southeast existed on the lower Mississippi, with the coast cultures on both sides rather below average level. Added subsistence from the river was scarcely the important factor in the determination of the Natchez center; nor does the river seem to have served as a serious defense barrier. Also not wholly clear are the causes for the localization of Californian focal culture on the lower Sacramento. On the lower Colorado the chief determining element evidently was the easy utilization of flood lands for farming, but fishing and facility of communication along the stream probably contributed. East of the Mississippi the cultures show little tendency to intensify on the lower courses of streams. There are in this region many rivers rather than outstanding ones, excepting the Ohio and St. Lawrence. But there were evidently other and obscurer factors involved besides relative stream size. . . .

Drainage

Drainage areas ought also to be considered at least briefly. Basically, of course, they express geology rather than distribution or supply of water. But, also obviously, they do not conform at all regularly with the recognized physiographic areas reviewed [previously]. Successive levels of a drainage may include coast plain, interior plain, and the flanks of several mountain systems. Geological structure, as embodied sometimes in a very long history, is the primary factor in the production of physiographic areas. Erosion is the next most important. The extent of a drainage system is determined by these factors, but remains a geographical rather than geological expression of them.

Both speech and culture show some tendency to conform to drainage areas; but this brute fact seems to mean primarily that conditions tend to be more uniform, and communications easier, within a basin. Where drainages are connected by nearly level country, they are often rather similar to each other in speech or culture or both, even where the distances involved are great: Orinoco and Amazon, for instance, Mississippi and Great Lakes, Indus and Ganges, Vistula and Dnieper. Conversely, where the course of a stream is so long that it flows through markedly different altitudes, climates, and vegetations, the cultures along it are likely to differ fundamentally. The Nile, Danube, and Amazon are obvious examples. It is difficult to see how the situation of a culture in corresponding parts of one rather than another drainage could of itself affect culture. The culture adaptation must be primarily to the factors most relevant to the culture, such as plant cover or perhaps climate; and to these, drainage areas as such are not necessarily fundamental.

When larger culture and speech groups characterize drainage areas, it is usually "typically" rather than exactly. The Shoshonean language and Basin culture of the Great Basin serve as an example. The speech as well as the culture extend both northward into Columbia and southward into Colorado River drainage. The interior drainage area of the Great Basin is only the heart, the characterizing portion, of the total territory covered by the culture and language. And it will be recalled that in both physiography and plant cover the same thing holds: the Basin-and-Range province and the Sagebrush Semi-desert area also center in the great landlocked Basin, but stretch out into Columbia and Colorado drainage. It is of secondary moment to geological structure and vegetation, as well as to human activities, where the available water of an area comes to rest. How much water there is, how it is distributed, and how it functions, are of far more significance for all these otherwise so diverse points of view. . . .

In one respect drainage is often a good indicator: of tribal boundaries. Except where streams are very large and the country of relatively uniform height, watersheds and not rivers tend to form native ethnic or political frontiers. This is expectable. The headwaters are usually the least habitable and valuable parts of a territory. Native settlement, being on the whole extremely light, concentrated in the valleys and along larger streams. The uplands were hunted in, visited, and claimed, but actually little utilized. Since frontiers were therefore unimportant, they tended to remain vague or general, and were not literally demarked. Crests and watersheds, which are almost always easily observed, thus sufficed. The divide might be a high range or a spur between tributaries; the principle was the same. The chief exceptions occur where uplanders are contrasted with lowlanders; and here of course the alignment is without reference to drainage—rather than violating it by a partition according to sides of a stream.

In a similar way, culture boundaries not infrequently follow watersheds. But, cultural groups being usually much larger than tribes, it is generally only pronounced ranges that serve in this way—especially the Rockies and main Pacific Coast systems.

29 THE ECOLOGICAL APPROACH IN ANTHROPOLOGY
JUNE HELM

The purpose of this paper* is to survey the development and the ramifications of the ecological perspective in anthropology. Excluding those inquiries limited to hominoid animal ecology, the seeming diversity within that perspective can be resolved into those problems that involve relationships between environment, technology, population, and other sectors of sociocultural life (adapting Duncan's delineation of the human "ecological complex"[2]).

Early Trends in Anthropology

In the era before the turn of the century, when anthropology was forming as a distinct discipline, there were at least two major lines of inquiry relevant to the development of an ecological point of view. First, the two great evolutionists of anthropology, Tylor and Morgan, both set forth *technological advance* as a major referent for stages of cultural development,* and it remains a viable and enduring theme in contemporary longitudinal ecological views in anthropology. The second

Reprinted by permission of The University of Chicago Press from June Helm, "The Ecological Approach in Anthropology," *American Journal of Sociology* 67 (1962): 630–639.
*See pp. 340–344 for notes.

enduring orientation is exemplified in the stress by the German "anthropogeographer" Ratzel[4] and by his American contemporary Otis T. Mason[5] on the importance of *habitat* in effecting cultural diversity and distributions. In American anthropology, the geographical orientation continued with the development of the "culture-area" concept.[6] It was the view of "culture-area" proponents (who were essentially adherents of geographical "possibilism") that particular environments, especially as "food areas," tend to set the bounds of and to stabilize resident cultures. But, in point of fact, in "culture-area" studies environment was converted into *space* as answers to historical problems were sought in the spatial distribution of culture traits and complexes.

It was those ethnologists who concentrated on the primitive cultures in harsh and epecially limiting environments who developed a pragmatic ecological outlook. In this vein the circumpolar area and, as a specific cultural group, the Eskimo, received perhaps the richest treatment.[7] The aims of these scholars, however, remained particularizing and historical.

In the thirties, there came three influential, emphatically ecological works that evinced a contextual, "natural-history" approach to the peoples and cultures under study. One was C. Daryll Forde's survey of food gatherers, cultivators, and pastoralists throughout the world,[8] another was Kroeber's delineation of the cultural and natural areas of native North America, in which he chided "a generation of American anthropologists" for their inattention to the *whole* culture in its environmental setting.[9] Kroeber's demands were met by the avowedly functional *cum* ecological studies begun in this period by Julian Steward. Steward's attention to the particularities of specific habitats, especially the nature of the biota available for exploitation under primitive hunting and gathering technologies, allowed him to identify related types of exploitative and demographic patterns that in turn shaped band and kinship organization of primitive societies.[10]

During this period two eminent British archeologists published popular syntheses of the aims and understandings of archeology, stressing efficiency in food procurement as the base upon which population density and elaboration of social organization rest.[11] Nevertheless, ten years later, Walter Taylor felt justified in attacking American archeologists for limiting the goals of their discipline to the establishment of the distribution and chronology of culture traits and assemblages, instead of "thinking of a culture history consisting of events against their backgrounds of local human culture and local natural environment."[12] Times were ripe, however, for within the next ten years the ecologically contextual study had become an established model in American archeology.[13]

The Ecological Outlook in Contemporary Cultural Anthropology

Whether the raw materials of investigation be archeological or ethnographic, a functionalist spirit pervades the formulation and pursuit of problems in contemporary cultural anthropology.[14] This overview has contributed heavily to the rise in emphasis on ecology that is evidenced jointly in studies by archeologists and by ethnologists and social anthropologists. The following paragraphs present a selective survey of ecological studies in these fields of anthropology, made during roughly the past twelve years.

Archeology

That the specific character of certain environmental zones may determine the distribution of ancient traditions of material culture is receiving sophisticated delineation in regional studies by archeologists.[15] More broadly, an encompassing typology from the archeological purview of causal factors in cultural stability and change sets forth one class as environmental, offering "polar concepts of 'ecologically bound' and 'ecologically free' " traditions.[16]

Other archeological studies appraise habitat as a stimulus-deterrent to technological innovation and sociocultural development. These range from the efforts of Braidwood and his collaborators to comprehend the earliest developments of "primary village farming efficiency" through detailed inquiry into conditions of natural habitat[17] to Meggers "law," treating most broadly of habitat as the ultimate limiting factor, that "the level to which a culture can develop is dependent upon the agricultural potentiality of the environment it occupies."[18]

The contextual-functional stance of contemporary archeology has brought significant changes in field techniques and analysis as new kinds of data are now taken into account. Biotal remains, for example, are rich in climatic and in environmental-technological implications and are being subjected to a scrutiny not known in the past.[19] Furthermore, attention to evidence bearing on population and settlement patterns has become paramount to the archeologist who seeks clues concerning the economic and social organization of extinct societies.[20] For example, the coverage in time and space that archeology allows has revealed that different civilizations or urban societies present variant city patterns even to the extent that the formal demographic requirements of urbanism may not be present.[21] Some typologies and inquiries attempt to comprehend this condition.[22] Another delineates neolithic community patterns.[23] And archeologists in seminars have set forth an all-inclusive typology of societies based on differential community mobility, in which they explicitly seek functional and evolutionary implications.[24]

Ethnology: exploitative patterns

It is not the gross categories "environment" and "technology" per se that are often critical in the ecological inquiry, but rather the significant reticulation composed from them—the exploitative pattern.[25] In Northern Amerind ethnology, for example, focus upon the primitive exploitative pattern in its relation to the total ecological complex has revealed the role of the exploitative resources of variant habitats in sociocultural differentiation between contiguous Eskimo bands, the effect of an assymetrical sex ratio on residence patterns of Ojibway hunting-trapping units, and the consequences of new, introduced exploitative activities for Montagnais systems of land use and tenure.[26]

Ecological niche and "oecumene"

Barth has shown how the varying economic and political organizations of contiguous ethnic groups may operate to delimit a specific and distinct "ecological niche" for each society within the same "natural area."[27] This concept of the ecological niche, "the place of a group in the total environment, its relation to resources and competitors"[28] accommodates the "cultural type" that has been identified as "the predatory band."[29] In this case part of the resources of the band consist of other societal groups within its spatial exploitative range. Such cases suggest that we look at environment in yet another dimension—namely, environment as *oecumene*, comprehending not only space and habitat but the sociocultural resources and groups beyond the society but within its experiential field.[30] Especially may the concept of an altered and expanding oecumene serve as a useful perspective when the focus of inquiry is the local or regional society undergoing culture change through culture contact.[31]

Population and culture patterns

That the nature and effectiveness of exploitative patterns are a prime factor in population size, density, and distribution has been documented in anthropological literature,[32] and anthropologists have sketched in broad outline the social-organizational consequences of population growth in the history of civilizations.[33] But there has been little inquiry into the specific "fit" or integration between the size of population and the particular cultural patterns of a society. It may be that this focus is readily rewarding only when the data make it possible to perceive significant demographic *change*, thus providing horizons for comparison through time within the society. C. Wagley has provided a striking account of the shattering effects of heavy depopulation on the social organization of the Tapirapé Indians of Brazil, a depopulation that created severe imbalances between numbers of appropriate personnel and number of traditional statuses.[34] In a later paper he proceeded fom the other end of the spectrum, setting forth the thesis that "each culture has a population policy—an implicit or explicit set of cultural values relating to population size," and in these terms explains the social and physical extinction of the Tapirapé in contrast with the survival of a neighboring tribe.[35]

World view and the balanced "ecocultural structure"

The latter paper by Wagley contains implications of feedback from the "integrative imperatives"[36] of human cultures upon the "realities" of physical existence. This consideration may most broadly be subsumed under "world view"—what peoples perceive as their universe, the meanings and values they find in it, and how they define their relations to it. The ecological aspects and consequences of world view are too broad to be pursued here. Some contributions are overviews of cultural differences in interpretation of the world and its resources by primitive and modern man[37] and, conversely, the concept that a society's environmental setting may shape cultural concepts of time, space, and cosmogeny.[38]

There are also leads concerning the ultimate implications of a society's subsistence base for normative and ideational patterns, enculturation technique and goals, and personality formation.[39] From these ecological aspects of world view we are led to the encompassing conception of cultural stability being based in an ecosystem of human population, culture, and habitat in equilibrium. This overview has been a point of intellectual departure for archeologists and physical anthropologists as well as ethnologists.[40]

Comparative studies: social organization

Over forty years ago the British scholars Hobhouse, Wheeler, and Ginsberg essayed a comparative inquiry into the functional dependence of social organization, or certain sectors of it, on exploitative pattern and attendant demographic characteristics.[41] On the whole, American anthropologists evinced lamentable inattention to the possibilities of such studies until recent decades. Today, however, such inquiries represent one of the more notable advances of contemporary social anthropology. "Controlled comparisons"[42] of contiguous and/or related North American Indian societies[43] have corroborated and advanced Steward's earlier inquiry into ecologic factors in the formation of unilineal descent groups.[44] Forde has drawn comparative conclusions from British studies of African social organization that are broadly consonant with the conclusions of the American scholars:

> Where the combinations of available resources and exploitative techniques reach higher levels, the stability and size of local groups and the regularity of interaction among them all tend to increase. In such societies, the fundamental tendency to transmit rights and status from parent to child and for them to be shared among siblings of one or other sex has wider scope. In combination with the equally fundamental dichotomy of the sexes in economic and political roles, this leads to the emergence of more stable groups of kin according to a principle of unilineal affiliation"[45]

To choose but one further example of the ecologically conceived controlled comparison, there is Sahlins' recent effort to demonstrate that the form and the degree of social stratification in each of fourteen Polynesian cultures are essentially functions of adaptation to environmental setting and of food productivity, respectively.[46]

A complementary method to the smaller scale, rigorously detailed controlled comparison is the broad-scale statistical inquiry. Here may be cited the gross correlation of independent versus extended family systems with success of exploitative pattern.[47] And the results of an inclusive comparison of the social organization of the North American Indian tribes "overwhelmingly" confirm a chain-of-effects sequence from the sexual division of labor in subsistence pursuits to postnuptial residence, to land tenure, to method of reckoning descent, to kinship terminology.[48]

The ecologic foundations of sociocultural development are clearly expressed in recent comparative efforts to assess and quantify social complexity. Naroll[49] and Edmonson[50] establish, by different methods, number of statuses per society, which they find to be positively associated with selected demographic measures. Aginsky argues that the amount of total cultural content per society is proportional to its quantity of "PAM"—that is, population, area (including geopolitical and geocultural environment), and mobility (comprising all modes of communication).[51]

"Cultural ecology" and sociocultural evolution

For the purpose of studying change in the "longest run," that is, in terms of sociocultural development or evolution, Julian Steward has recently brought his studies of two decades together in the most explicit formulation of the ecological domain to be found in contemporary cultural anthropology.[52] He proceeds from the concept of "*cultural* ecology" which refers to "the adaptive processes by which the nature of society and an unpredictable number of features of culture are affected by the basic adjustment through which man utilizes a given environment."[53] In any culture, therefore, it is "the constellation of features which are most closely related to subsistence activities and economic arrangements" that command primary attention as the "culture core."[54] It is part of the problem of "culture ecology" to assess the latitude in the total cultural patterns allowed by the productive arrangements. Beginning with analysis of particular societies in these terms, one objective is to ascertain the cross-cultural regularities which arise from similar adaptive processes in similar environments. For this concept Steward has coined the term "multilinear evolution." Cultural development is "conceptualized not only as a matter of increasing complexity but also as one of the emergence of successive *levels of sociocultural integration*,"[55] and Steward has analyzed and compared selected societies in these terms.[56]

Relevant Studies in Physical Anthropology

The present-day approach in physical anthropology has been characterized as one in which "human populations are regarded as constituting a widespread network of more or less interrelated, ecologically adapted and functional entities."[57] Two related lines of investigation in physical anthropology are pertinent to our present interests: inquiries into the sociocultural consequences of the "animal ecology" of man and inquiries concerning the effects of sociocultural ecological adaptation upon the physical being and life chances of men as organisms. For example, in the latter category are those studies of the effect of technological level[58] and of cultural usages (such as band endogamy[59]) on such biological evolutionary processes as natural selection and genetic drift. With reference to the sociocultural consequences of man's animal ecology, there is Slater's bold hypothesis regarding "ecological factors in the origin of incest," which argues that values follow action, and hence postulates that under primordial conditions the vital statistics of human populations precluded the practice of nuclear family incest.[60]

Concluding Remarks

The anthropological outlook

Perhaps the way in which the anthropologist tends to look at the human ecological complex can be pointed up first by a brief contrast with the approaches used in studies of animal ecology. Proceeding from Duncan's identification of "four referential concepts" in the human ecological complex—environment, technology, population, and organization—animal ecology must be described as involving three of these factors: environment, population, and organization. In animal ecology, while environment belongs to the realm of the inorganic (and organic), organization as well as population must be subsumed under organic. In human ecology, on the other hand, organization and technology are aspects of the *superorganic,* a term adapted by Kroeber from Spencer to refer to culture.[61]

The "organization of conventional understandings manifest in act and artifact"[62] which we call a culture may be posited as essentially an adaptive system whereby human beings in a social aggregate order their relations with their physical world and among themselves and, we might go on to say, to the realm of the superempirical as it is a reality by cultural definition.[63] The ecological approach in anthropology proceeds from the first aspect or level of the adaptive system—man in adjustive and exploitative interaction, through the agency of technology, with his inorganic and biotal milieu. But this level had immediate implications for the second aspect of the adaptive system, that of the relations between men. Economic activities bracket man-nature and man-man relationships, but, as Steward has indicated by means of the concept of the "cultural core," other organized areas of social life may be more or less directly involved. The ultimate implications of and for the third level tend to be only peripherally pursued in the ecological approach.

The empirical definition of human ecology in anthropology that is emerging here is that it is concerned with the adaptive ordering of the relations of human groups to the natural environment and with the demographic and sociocultural conditions and consequences thereof. It is a truism in anthropology as in other social sciences that the immediate effects of environment recede from the total picture as technological control increases. Traditional anthropological emphasis on "primitive culture" has tended to keep environment in the fore. When, however, the touchstone of "adaptation to environment" is lost from view, the anthropologist ceases to speak of his concerns as "ecological." In this respect, Steward's viewpoint and uses are consonant with those of other anthropologists: the concept of ecology is for the anthropologist a "heuristic device," "an operational tool rather than an end [or "sub-discipline"] in itself."[64]

Ecological perspectives in anthropology

Traditionally the ethnologist has gone into the "little community" for his cultural data. However, in the last few decades many anthropologists have come to focus explicitly upon the "little community," be it band, village, or town, as the total "natural" unit of investigation.[65] One result has been a sharpened awareness of the role of the natural setting in shaping the physical and societal attributes of the community.[66] The same benefits have brought American archeologists to an ecological view in pursuit of their rephrased goal of conjunctive interpretation of the material remains of human cultures. An eminent British archeologist has summed up the potentialities and the limits of archeology in this respect when he states that inferences about the sociocultural unit from archeological data are reliable to the extent to which they are about matters explicitly ecological.[67]

Anthropologists have generally acknowledged population size and/or density as indicative of exploitative success, but only recently have they begun to rectify their neglect of attributes of population as covariants and possibly determinants of aspects of social organization. So far, the size and arrangement of the population cluster which constitutes the local group community seems especially promising as a correlate of type of social organization and of degree of social differentiation and ramification.[68]

The ecological approach has provided one way to get beyond the tendency of the anthropological school of "sociological functionalism" to treat all aspects of a sociocultual configuration as mutually dependent variables.[69] Barth and Wagley's papers, for example, demonstrate that the "organic," population, or various aspects of the "superorganic"—sociopolitical organization, values—may emerge as immediate explanatory factors in a particular changing ecological complex. In the long view of the human condition, however, there is increasing evidence that environmental-technological (especially, subsistence) factors take primacy as determinants.[70] In this respect typologies based on attributes of sociocultural structures which correlate and covary with attributes of exploitative patterns lend themselves to the attack on problems of social change or evolution, insofar as we may wish to reserve the latter term to refer to degrees or levels of social coaptation.

Anthropological perspectives for human ecology

I have not touched on the question of the legitimacy of "human ecology" as a separate discipline. We need only grant its existence as an orientation that cuts across several established disciplines to inquire into anthropology's contribution, present and potential, to the ecological sphere. The traditional anthropological attention to small communities and relatively simple societies has allowed total sociocultural systems and their ecological aspects to be perceived and encompassed. This is undoubtedly why anthropologists dealing with small societies with primitive technology are emboldened to speak holistically of an ecosystem composed of the human culture-bearing population in adaptive interrelation with the natural setting.[71]

The avowed interest of anthropology in all societies and their cultures across space and through time has, especially in recent years, turned methodological concern toward the refining and disciplining of the comparative method. Efforts at establishing classifications, be they regarding range of exploitative patterns, types of social structure, or levels of sociocultural integration, provide a preliminary ordering of data potentially useful to social scientists in general, and, as we have observed, in some cases typologies have been directly predicated upon ecological viewpoint and definition.

In its greatest scope anthropology attends to man's course, in all its variance and incrementation, from proto-hominid to his present condition. The ecological point of view has been a unifying and fruitful theme in these efforts and may eventually provide a bridge between the precultural and the cultural animal. Whether the immediate contribution of inquiry in this area is toward the natural history of man or toward the demonstration of evolutionary processes is mainly a matter of level of analysis and of degree of abstraction and generalization employed. In the broadest perspective the following observations can be made: (1) there are infra-human populations in interaction with habitat; and (2) through the span of hominid existence there has been the increasing intrusion of the cultural variable which has continually defined and redefined the oecumene of human societies and which has had continuing consequences for human population aggregates in terms of distribution, size, density, differentiation, and diversification of activities and roles within them. By means of culture man has increasingly structured his own environment and his orderly relations—operational and ideational—to it, even as he structures his relations with his own kind. The "Chicago school" of urban ecology, dealing with twentieth century *Homo sapiens* in his most recently emergent aspect as "urban man" took both the biological makeup of the species and the varying qualities of habitat and of culture essentially as givens, attending only to limited properties of certain population aggregates. If this is the view through the microscope at a speck plucked from a totality, the anthropological perspective is through the telescope. The anthropological view is as yet exploratory and, in general, unsystematic, but it may be sketching the broadest outline of the ecological cosmos.

30 THE CONCEPT AND METHOD OF CULTURAL ECOLOGY
JULIAN H. STEWARD

Objectives in Ecological Studies

At the risk of adding further confusion to an already obscure term, this chapter undertakes to develop the concept of ecology in relation to human beings as an heuristic device for understanding the effect of environment upon culture. In order to distinguish the present purpose and method from those implied in the concepts of biological, human, and social ecology, the term *cultural ecology* is used. Since cultural ecology is not generally understood, it is necessary to begin by showing wherein it differs from the other concepts of ecology and then to demonstrate how it must supplement the usual historical approach of anthropology in order to determine the creative processes involved in the adaptation of culture to its environment.

The principal meaning of ecology is "adaptation to environment." Since the time of Darwin, environment has been conceived as the total web of life wherein all

Reprinted from Julian H. Steward, *Theory of Culture Change* (1955) by permission of the University of Illinois Press.

plant and animal species interact with one another and with physical features in a particular unit of territory. According to Webster, the biological meaning of ecology is "the mutual relations between organisms and their environment." The concept of adaptive interaction is used to explain the origin of new genotypes in evolution; to explain phenotypical variations; and to describe the web of life itself in terms of competition, succession, climaxes, gradients, and other auxiliary concepts.

Although initially employed with reference to biotic assemblages, the concept of ecology has naturally been extended to include human beings since they are part of the web of life in most parts of the world. Man enters the ecological scene, however, not merely as another organism which is related to other organisms in terms of his physical characteristics. He introduces the super-organic factor of culture, which also affects and is affected by the total web of life. What to do about this cultural factor in ecological studies has raised many methodological difficulties, as most human and social ecologists have recognized. The principal difficulty lies in the lack of clarity as to the purpose of using the concept of ecology. The interaction of physical, biological, and cultural features within a locale or unit of territory is usually the ultimate objective of study. Human or social ecology is regarded as a subdiscipline of its own right and not as means to some further scientific end. Essentially descriptive, the analysis lacks the clear objectives of biology, which has used ecology heuristically to explain several kinds of biological phenomena. If human or social ecology is considered an operational tool rather than an end in itself, two quite different objectives are suggested: first, an understanding of the organic functions and genetic variations of man as a purely biological species; second, a determination of how culture is affected by its adaptation to environment. Each requires its own concepts and methods.

The first, or biological objective, involves several somewhat different problems, all of which, however, must view man in the web of life. Since man is a domesticated animal, he is affected physically by all his cultural activities. The evolution of the Hominidae is closely related to the emergence of culture, while the appearance of *Homo sapiens* is probably more the result of cultural causes than of physical causes. The use of tools, fire, shelter, clothing, new foods, and other material adjuncts of existence were obviously important in evolution, but social customs should not be overlooked. Social groups as determined by marriage customs as well as by economic activities in particular environments have undoubtedly been crucial in the differentiations of local populations and may even have contributed to the emergence of varieties and subraces of men.

The problem of explaining man's cultural behavior is of a different order than that of explaining his biological evolution. Cultural patterns are not genetically derived and, therefore, cannot be analyzed in the same way as organic features. Although social ecologists are paying more and more attention to culture in their enquiries, an explanation of culture per se has not, so far as I can see, become their major objective. Culture has merely acquired greater emphasis as one of many features of the local web of life, and the tools of analysis are still predominantly borrowed from biology. Since one of the principal concepts of biological ecology is the community—the assemblage of plants and animals which interact within a locality—social or human ecology emphasizes the human community as the unit of study. But "community" is a very general and meaningless abstraction. If it is conceived in cultural terms, it may have many different characteristics depending upon the purpose for which it is defined. The tendency, however, has been to conceive of human and biological communities in terms of the biological concepts of competition, succession, territorial organization, migration, gradients, and the like. All of these derived fundamentally from the fact that underlying biological ecology is a relentless and raw struggle for existence both within and between species—a competition which is ultimately determined by the genetic potentials for adaptation and survival in particular biotic-environmental situations. Biological co-operation, such as in many forms of symbiosis, is strictly auxiliary to survival of the species.

Human beings do not react to the web of life solely through their genetically-derived organic equipment. Culture, rather than genetic potential for adaptation, accommodation, and survival, explains the nature of human societies. Moreover, the web of life of any local human society may extend far beyond the immediate physical environment and biotic assemblage. In states, nations, and empires, the nature of the local group is determined by these larger institutions no less than by its local adaptations. Competition of one sort or another may be present, but it is always culturally determined and as often as not co-operation rather than competition may be prescribed. If, therefore, the nature of human communities is the objective of analysis, explanations will be found through use of cultural historical concepts and methods rather than biological concepts, although, as we shall show, historical methods alone are insufficient.

Many writers on social or human ecology have sensed the need to distinguish between biological and cultural phenomena and methods, but they have not yet drawn clear distinctions. Thus, Hollingshead recognizes a difference between an "ecological order [which] is primarily rooted in competition" and "social organization [which] has evolved out of communication." This attempt to conceptualize competition as a category wholly distinct from other aspects of culturally determined behavior is, of course, artificial. Bates, a human biologist, recognizes the importance of culture in determining the nature of communities, but he does not make clear whether he would use human ecology to explain the range of man's biological adaptation under environmental-cultural situations or whether he is interested in man's culture. The so-called Chicago school of Park, Burgess, and their followers were also primarily interested in communities of human beings, especially urban communities. Their methodology as applied to Chicago and other cities treat the components of each as if they were genetically determined species. In analyzing the zoning of a modern city, such categories as retail businesses, wholesale houses, manufacturing firms, and residences of various kinds, and even such additional features as rate of delinquency, are considered as if each were a biological species in competition with one another for zones within the urban area. Such studies are extremely enlightening as descriptive analysis of spacial distributions of kinds of activities within a modern Euro-American city. They do not, however, necessarily throw any light on world-wide ecological urban adaptations, for in other cultures and periods city zoning followed very different culturally prescribed principles. For example, most of the cities of ancient civilizations were rather carefully planned by a central authority for defensive, administrative, and religious functions. Free enterprise, which might have allowed competition for zones between the institutions and subsocieties arising from these functions, was precluded by the culture.

A fundamental scientific problem is involved in these different meanings attached to ecology. Is the objective to find universal laws or processes, or is it to explain special phenomena? In biology, the law of evolution and the auxiliary principles of ecology are applicable to all webs of life regardless of the species and physical environments involved. In social science studies, there is a similar effort to discover universal processes of cultural change. But such processes cannot be conceptualized in biological terms. The social science problem of explaining the origin of unlike behavior patterns found among different societies of the human species is very different from the problems of biological evolution. Analyzing environmental adaptations to show how new cultural patterns arise is a very different matter than seeking universal similarities in such adaptation. Until the processes of cultural ecology are understood in the many particulars exemplified by different cultures in different parts of the world a formulation of universal processes will be impossible.

Hawley, who has given the most recent and comprehensive statement of social ecology, takes cultural phenomena into account far more than his predecessors. He states that man reacts to the web of life as a cultural animal rather than as a biological species. "Each acquisition of a new technique or a new use for an old technique, regardless of the source of its origin, alters man's relations with the organisms about him and changes his position in the biotic community." But, preoccupied with the totality of phenomena within the locale and apparently with a search for universal relationships, Hawley makes the local community the focus of interest. The kinds of generalizations which might be found are indicated by the statement: "If we had sufficient knowledge of a preliterate peoples to enable us to compare the structure of residence groups arranged in order of size from smallest to largest, we should undoubtedly observe the same phenomena—each increment in size is accompanied by an advance in the complexity of organization." This is the kind of self-evident generalization made by the unilinear evolutionists: cultural progress is manifest in increasing populations, internal specialization, over-all state controls, and other general features.

Hawley is uncertain in his position regarding the effect of environmental adaptations on culture. He states: "The weight of evidence forces the conclusion that the physical environment exerts but a permissive and limiting effect," but he also says that "each habitat not only permits but to a certain extent necessitates a distinctive mode of life" (Hawley, 1950:190). The first statement closely conforms with the widely accepted anthropological position that historical factors are more important than environmental factors, which may be permissive or prohibitive of culture change but are never causative. The second is nearer to the thesis of this paper that cultural ecological adaptations constitute creative processes. . . .

Cultural Ecology

Cultural ecology differs from human and social ecology in seeking to explain the origin of particular cultural features and patterns which characterize different areas rather than to derive general principles applicable to any cultural-environmental situation. It differs from the relativistic and neo-evolutionist conceptions of culture history in that it introduces the local environment as the extracultural factor in the fruitless assumption that culture comes from culture. Thus, cultural ecology presents both a problem and a method. The problem is to ascertain whether the adjustments of human societies to their environments require particular modes of behavior or whether they permit latitude for a certain range of possible behavior patterns. Phrased in this way, the problem also distinguishes cultural ecology from "environmental determinism" and its related theory "economic determinism" which are generally understood to contain their conclusions within the problem.

The problem of cultural ecology must be further qualified, however, through use of a supplementary conception of culture. According to the holistic view, all aspects of culture are functionally interdependent upon one another. The degree and kind of interdependency, however, are not the same with all features. Elsewhere, I have offered the concept of *cultural core*—the constellation of features which are most closely related to subsistence activities and economic arrangements. The core includes such social, political, and religious patterns as are empirically determined to be closely connected with these arrangements. Innumerable other features may have great potential variability because they are less strongly tied to the core. These latter, or secondary features, are determined to a greater extent by purely cultural-historical factors—by random innovations or by diffusion—and they give the appearance of outward distinctiveness to cultures with similar cores. Cultural ecology pays primary attention to those features which empirical analysis shows to be most closely involved in the utilization of environment in culturally prescribed ways. . . .

The Methodological Place of Cultural Ecology

Cultural ecology has been described as a methodological tool for ascertaining how the adaptation of a culture to its environment may entail certain changes. In a larger sense, the problem is to determine whether similar adjustments occur in similar environments. Since in any given environment, culture may develop through a succession of very unlike periods, it is sometimes pointed out that environment, the constant, obviously has no relationship to cultural type. This difficulty disappears, however, if the level of sociocultural integration represented by each period is taken into account. Cultural types therefore, must be conceived as constellations of core features which arise out of environmental adaptations and which represent similar levels of integrations.

Cultural diffusion, of course, always operates, but in view of the seeming importance of ecological adaptations its role in explaining culture has been greatly overestimated. The extent to which the large variety of world cultures can be systematized in categories of types and explained through cross-cultural regularities of developmental process is purely an empirical matter. Hunches arising out of comparative studies suggest that there are many regularities which can be formulated in terms of similar levels and similar adaptations.

31 CULTURAL ECOLOGY AND ETHNOGRAPHY
CHARLES O. FRAKE

Ecology is the study of the workings of ecosystems, of the behavioral interdependences of different kinds of organisms with respect to one another and to their nonbiotic environment. *Cultural* ecology is the study of the role of culture as a dynamic component of any ecosystem of which man is a part. Unique among organisms, man carves his ecological niches primarily with cultural tools of his own invention rather than with biological specializations. This niche-carving activity of man not only remolds existing biotic communities but also has a shaping effect on the tools—that is on man's cultural knowledge and equipment—themselves. In addition, man constantly devises new tools for carving out more effective places in the ecosystem surrounding him. Because of this progressive cultural adaptation and specialization to environmental conditions, the study of cultural ecology, under one name or another, has been closely linked with theoretical interest in culture history and culture evolution. Steward, who framed the present designation of the subject, construes cultural ecology largely as a methodology for building evolutionary theory (Steward 1955:30–42).

Although the utility of ecological studies for such pursuits is undeniable, it is not necessary to regard cultural ecology simply as a methodological adjunct to nobler tasks. Cultural ecology, in that it refers to a delimitable system of phenomena, is a legitimate field of anthropological interests in its own right, as legitimate as the study of social systems which has so absorbed the efforts of many of us. If the social system be envisioned as a network of relationships among persons of a *social* community, then the ecological system is a network of relationships between man,

Reproduced by permission of the American Anthropological Association from the *American Anthropologist*, vol. 64, no. 1, 1962.

the other organisms of his *biotic* community, and the constituents of his physical environment. In both cases the net is woven of cultural threads, and the two networks are, of course, inter-connected at many points.

But before the possibilities for general theory inherent in a study of cultural ecological systems are fully realized, the problem of describing these systems, the ethnographic problem, must, I think, be taken more seriously. As Hymes (1960:343) has remarked of linguistics, "One need not stop with the individual systems, but one must pass through them." The comparative method, whether on the scale of a Murdock (1949), a Steward (1955), or a Gulliver (1955), cannot yield results of greater validity than that of the data being compared. This paper has the purpose of assessing cultural ecology as an ethnographic endeavor. First, I will present some notions of what constitutes an ethnographic description, then I will suggest some ways in which ecological studies might be encompassed within the framework of these notions, giving a brief example from my field work.

Following Goodenough (1957), this paper proposes that a description of cultural behavior is attained by a formulation of what one must know in order to respond in a culturally appropriate manner in a given socio-ecological context. Such a description, like a linguist's grammar, is productive in that it can generate new acts which will be considered appropriate responses by the members of the society being described. A successful strategy for writing productive ethnographies must tap the cognitive world of one's informants. It must discover those features of objects and events which they regard as significant for defining concepts, formulating propositions, and making decisions. This conception of an ethnography requires that the units by which the data of observation are segmented, ordered, and interrelated be delimited and defined according to contrasts inherent in the data themselves and not according to a priori notions of pertinent descriptive categories.

The necessity of coming to terms with one's informants' concepts is well recognized in some ethnographic endeavors, kinship studies providing the most notable example. No ethnographer describes social relations in an alien society by referring to the doings of "uncles," "aunts," and "cousins." Many ethnographers do, however, describe the pots and pans, the trees and shrubs, the soils and rocks of a culture's environment solely in terms of categories projected from the investigator's culture. In comparison with studying religious conceptions or kinship relations, the description of the tangible objects of a culture's ecosystem is usually regarded as one of the ethnographer's simpler tasks. If he does not know a word for a specimen of fauna, flora, or soil, he can always ship it off to a specialist for "identification." However, if one insists that no specimen has been described *ethnographically* until one has stated the rules for its identification in the culture being studied, then the problem of describing a tangible object such as a plant may become rather more complex than the relatively simple task of defining contrasts between categories of kinsmen. Consider, for example, the problem of identifying plants according to the Hanunóo system of folk botany (Conklin 1954, 1957). The Hanunóo, tropical-forest agriculturists of the central Philippines, exhaustively partition their plant world into more than 1,600 categories, whereas systematic botanists classify the same flora into less than 1,200 species. To place correctly, by Hanunóo standards, a newly encountered plant specimen in the appropriate one of the 1,600 categories requires rather fine discriminations among plants—and these discriminations rely on features generally remote from the botanist's count of stamens and carpels. By discovering what one must know in order to classify plants and other ecological components in Hanunóo fashion, one learns what the Hanunóo consider worth attending to when making decisions or how to behave within their ecosystem.

An ethnographer, then, cannot be satisfied with a mere cataloguing of the components of a cultural ecosystem according to the categories of Western science. He must also describe the environment as the people themselves construe it according to the categories of their ethnoscience. From a presentation of the rules by which people decide upon the category membership of objects in their experience, an ethnographic ecology can proceed to rules for more complex kinds of behavior: killing game, clearing fields, building houses, etc. Determining the requisite knowledge for such behavior shows the ethnographer the extent to which ecological considerations, in contrast, say, to sociological ones, enter into a person's decision of what to do. The ethnographer learns, in a rather meaningful and precise sense, what role the environment in fact plays in the cultural behavior of the members of a particular society.

A partial description of the settlement pattern of the Eastern Subanun, a Philippine people, will illustrate the notions of cultural ecological description advanced here. This analysis would ideally rest upon a presentation of the pertinent Subanun ethnoscience relating to agriculture and vegetation types. Limitations of time force a rather inadequate and simplified description, but one, which if not a contribution to ethnography, may at least point up some of the desirable features of a legitimate ethnographic contribution to cultural ecology.

The Subanun have carved a niche for themselves in the tropical rain forests of Zamboanga Peninsula, on the island of Mindanao, by swidden agriculture (or "shifting cultivation" Frake 1955, 1960; cf. Conklin 1957). The tropical forest agriculturist must establish a controlled biotic community of sun-loving annuals and perennials in a climatic region whose natural climax community, the tropical rain forest, is radically different in almost every respect from the community agricultural man seeks to foster. The swidden farmer meets this problem by periodically putting the forest through its successional paces. He modifies and operates on an existing ecosystem rather than permanently replacing it with an utterly different kind of biotic and edaphic world, such as that of the wet-rice paddy.

The Subanun settlement pattern is one of clustered new, secondary, and fallow swiddens with individual nuclear family households dispersed within these swidden clusters. This pattern contrasts with that of many other Southeast Asian shifting cultivators who disperse their swiddens around relatively fixed and nucleated settlements.

The Subanun themselves do not have a notion of "settlement pattern" in the sense of an image of spatial relationships among households and settlements to which they must conform. Rather their settlement pattern as seen by an ethnographer is, like their "rule of post-marital residence," the outcome of a large number of individual decisions. These decisions are not made at random, say by flipping a coin, but by evaluation of the immediate circumstances in terms of a set of quite explicit principles about the desirable relations among houses and fields. An ethnographic description of the Subanun settlement pattern as part of their ecological adaptation must consist of more than a map locating house sites and more than a characterization as "neighborhood," "hamlet," or "village." It should comprise a set of rules which state what one must know in order to decide where to live. Ideally the description should be a set of rules which will generate the Subanun settlement pattern appropriate to any given set of conditions.

To simplify the discussion I will take three features of the Subanun ecological adaptation as given, although they too could be derived from further rules of individual decision. The givens are:

1. Swidden agriculture with grain-crop staples, requiring an annual shift in locus of primary agricultural effort.

2. Organization of production and consumption is assigned to the nuclear family. Each family has the responsibility for clearing and cultivating its own swidden and enjoys joint and exclusive control over the distribution of its produce. No social group larger than a nuclear family cultivates a single swidden. Any individual who is not currently a member of a nuclear family is responsible for his or her own support by swidden agriculture.

3. Division of the population at any one time into discrete social groups, here termed *settlements*. Settlements are local groups emerging from alliances formed by a half-dozen or so related families for cooperation in agriculture and other activities. (One basis for settlement groupings, that of swidden clustering, derives from the rules that follow. But this rule, in itself, is not sufficient to account for the division of the population into settlement groups. Here we take these social groups to be given and concern ourselves only with the spatial arrangement of households within a settlement.)

With these givens in mind any arrangement of households found among the Subanun derives from the application of the following rules to particular ecological and sociological situations:

1. Minimum number of "wild-vegetation boundaries" (*gelunan* "to-be watches") of a swidden consistent with other swidden-site requirements.

2. Minimum house to swidden distance ("house" means the residence of those persons responsible for cultivating a swidden).

3. Maximum house to house distance consistent with the above rules.

These rules are explicit in that they are based on informants' discussions of actual and potential residence-site choices as well as on observations of settlement and swidden patterns. Many other factors, of course, enter into individual decisions of where to live—house-site auguries, access to water, relations with neighbors, kinship obligations such as bride service, etc.—but these do not affect, in any systematic way, the *spacing* of households with respect to each other.

In most situations, settlement members can feasibly reduce exposed swidden boundaries by clustering all or almost all of their swiddens and by making new swidden clusters adjacent to previous years' clusters. The first rule, then, has the normal consequence of clustering the fields of a settlement.

Since a swidden work group normally consists of a nuclear family (and is never a larger social group) the second rule, by demanding that each group live as close as possible to its own swidden, yields a norm of nuclear family households. It furthermore requires that new houses must be constructed periodically at new locations. A distance from house to swidden such that a separate field-house would be required as a base for agricultural operations is considered beyond the maximum limits. When this point is reached, if not sooner, a new residence is always constructed. When new houses are constructed they are invariably located at the absolute minimum distance from the current grain swidden; that is, they are placed inside it, situated to overlook as much of current and prospective swidden sites as possible. When a prospective swidden site is too far away to be cleared from one's existing household, cultivators must temporarily reside in someone else's house (since all houses are built within swiddens, and a new house cannot be constructed in a swidden before the swidden has been cleared and burned).

Within the restraints imposed by swidden clustering and location of houses with respect to swiddens, the Subanun explicitly endeavor to maximize the distance between households. Two households are never, for example, placed adjacent to one another across a swidden boundary, though such an arrangement would often be consistent with ecological considerations. Temporary compound households are maintained only so long as ecologically necessary to gain access to a new swidden. Once it is feasible to build a new house of its own, a family will always do so. This rule of household dispersal derives from the sociological facts of Subanun life which make it prudent to live sufficiently far from one's nearest neighbor so that family conversations and arguments cannot be overheard.

The ecological rules (i.e., Nos. 1 and 2) which determine Subanun swidden and household arrangements are explicitly geared to protection of swiddens from animal pests with a minimum expenditure of time and energy in such tasks as fence building, field-house construction, and travel to fields for daily watching. Yet the practice of clearing large areas adjacent to previously cleared areas increases, under certain conditions, the probabilities of succession to grassland instead of forest, thus removing the land from future swidden cycles. The Subanun emphasize the immediate returns of increased swidden protection and accessibility at the cost of some loss of control over the fallowing stages of the swidden cycle. Other swidden farmers of the same part of the world weigh the advantages and disadvantages of alternative techniques for controlling faunal and floral enemies differently with different consequences for swidden arrangements and settlement patterns. The contrasts among the remarkably different settlement patterns exhibited by Southeast Asian swidden farmers will become ecologically interpretable when one compares the factors which generate these patterns in each case rather than forcing ethnographic observations directly into a priori comparative categories. The full ecological and sociological implications of this analysis of Subanun settlement pattern for both internal and cross-cultural studies cannot be explored here. Hopefully, however, this incomplete account has revealed some of the advantages for the study of cultural ecology derivable from ethnographic description ordered according to the principles by which one's informants interpret their environment and make behavioral decisions. We were able to specify to what extent ecological factors determine settlement pattern, to point out significant general features of the Subanun ecological adaptation, and to discover some meaningful dimensions for cross-cultural comparison. These methodological suggestions are not, of course, intended to replace the analysis of an ecosystem that Western biological science can provide. A scientific knowledge of the climate, soils, plants, and animals of a culture's environment is an essential foundation for ecological ethnography—but it does not, of itself, constitute ethnography.

SECTION INTRODUCTION REFERENCES* AND SUGGESTIONS FOR FURTHER STUDY

Albertson, F. W., 1951, "Man's Disorder of Nature's Design in the Great Plains." In *The Smithsonian Report for 1950*. Washington, D.C.: U.S. Government Printing Office, pp. 363–372.

Baker, Paul T., et al., 1962, "Ecology and Anthropology: A Symposium." *American Anthropologist* 64:15–59.

Barth, Fredrik, 1956, "Ecological Relationships of Ethnic Groups in Swat, North Pakistan." *American Anthropologist* 58:1079–1089.

———, 1959–1960, "The Land Use Pattern of Migratory Tribes of South Persia." *Norsk Geografisk Tidsskrift* 17:1–11 (also found in Bobbs-Merrill Reprint Series in Anthropology, No. A–11).

Bates, Marston, 1953, "Human Ecology." In A. L. Kroeber, ed., *Anthropology Today*. Chicago: University of Chicago Press, pp. 700–713.

———, 1961, *Man in Nature*. Englewood Cliffs, N.J.: Prentice-Hall.

Bateson, Gregory, 1972, *Steps to an Ecology of Mind*. New York: Ballantine.

Bennett, John W., 1944, "The Interaction of Culture and Environment in the Smaller Societies." *American Anthropologist* 46:461–478.

———, 1969, *Northern Plainsmen: Adaptive Strategy and Agrarian Life*. Chicago: Aldine.

Carter, George F., 1968, *Man and the Land: A Cultural Geography*, 2nd ed. New York: Holt, Rinehart and Winston.

Conklin, Harold C., 1954, "An Ethnoecological Approach to Shifting Agriculture." *Transactions of the New York Academy of Science* 17 (Series 2):133–142.

Darling, Frank Fraser, and John P. Milton, eds., 1966, *Future Environments of North America; Being the Record of a Conference Convened by the Conservation Foundation in April 1965 at Airlie House Warrenton, Va*. Garden City, N.J.: Natural History Press.

Duncan, Otis Dudley, 1964, "Social Organization and the Ecosystem." In R. E. Faris, ed., *Handbook of Modern Sociology*. Chicago: Rand McNally, pp. 36–82.

*Forde, C. Daryll, 1934, *Habitat, Economy and Society: A Geographical Introduction to Ethnology*. London: Methuen.

Fried, Morton H., 1952, "Land Tenure, Geography and Ecology in the Contact of Cultures." *The American Journal of Economics and Sociology* 11:391–412.

Glacken, Clarence J., 1970, "Man Against Nature: An Outmoded Concept." In H. W. Helfrich, Jr., ed., *The Environmental Crisis.* New Haven, Conn.: Yale University Press, pp. 127–142.

Goldenweiser, Alexander, 1916, "Culture and Environment." *American Journal of Sociology* 21:628–633.

Gould, Peter R., 1963, "Man Against His Environment: A Game Theoretic Framework." *Annals of the Association of American Geographers* 53:290–297.

*Hatch, Elvin, 1973, "The Growth of Economic, Subsistence, and Ecological Studies in American Anthropology." *Journal of Anthropological Research* 29:221–243.

Kemp, William B., 1971, "The Flow of Energy in a Hunting Society." *Scientific American* 224:104–115,244.

Kendeigh, S. C., 1965, "The Ecology of Man, the Animal." *Bioscience* 15:521–523.

Keyfitz, N., 1966, "Population Density and the Style of Social Life." *Bioscience* 16:868–873.

Lattimore, Owen, 1938, "The Geographical Factor in Mongol History." *Geographical Journal* 91:11–16.

*Livingstone, Frank B., 1958, "Anthropological Implications of Sickle Cell Gene Distribution in West Africa." *American Anthropologist* 60:533–562.

Meggers, Betty J., 1954, "Environmental Limitation of the Development of Culture." *American Anthropologist* 56:801–824.

Mikesell, M., 1967, "Geographical Perspectives in Anthropology." *Annals of the Association of American Geographers* 57:617–634.

Netting, Robert McC., 1971, *The Ecological Approach in Cultural Study.* Addison-Wesley Modular Publication.

Odum, Howard T., 1971a, *Environment, Power, and Society.* New York: Wiley-Interscience.

———, 1971b, *Fundamentals of Ecology,* 3rd ed. Philadelphia: Saunders.

Rappaport, Roy A., 1967, *Pigs for the Ancestors: Ritual in the Ecology of a New Guinea People.* New Haven, Conn.: Yale University Press.

———, 1971, "The Flow of Energy in an Agricultural Society." *Scientific American* 224:116–122,127–132,244.

Sahlins, Marshall D., 1964, "Culture and Environment: The Study of Cultural Ecology." In S. Tax, ed., *Horizons of Anthropology.* Chicago: Aldine, pp. 132–147.

Schnore, Leo F., 1961, "The Myth of Human Ecology." *Sociological Inquiry* 31:128–139.

Shapley, Deborah, 1974, "Weather Warfare: Pentagon Concedes 7-year Vietnam Effort." *Science* 184:1059–1061.

Steward, Julian H., 1936, "The Economic and Social Basis of Primitive Bands." In R. H. Lowie, ed., *Essays in Honor of Alfred Louis Kroeber.* Berkeley: University of California Press, pp.331–350.

———, 1937, "Ecological Aspects of Southwestern Society." *Anthropos* 32:87–104.

———, 1949, "Cultural Causality and Law: A Trial Formulation of Early Civilization." *American Anthropologist* 51:1–27.

———, 1968, "Cultural Ecology." *International Encyclopedia of the Social Sciences* 4:337–344.

Stott, D. H., 1962, "Cultural and Natural Checks on Population Growth." In M. F. A. Montagu, ed., *Culture and the Evolution of Man.* New York: Oxford University Press, pp. 355–376.

Taylor, Griffith, 1957, "Environmentalism and Possibilism." In *Geography in the Twentieth Century: A Study of Growth, Fields, Techniques, Aims and Trends,* 3rd ed. New York: Philosophical Library, pp. 128–162.

Thomas, David H., 1974, "An Archaeological Perspective on Shoshonean Bands." *American Anthropologist* 76:11–23.

Toynbee, Arnold J., 1961, "The Relation between Man and His Environment." In *Reconsiderations* (Vol. 12) of *A Study of History.* London: Oxford University Press, pp. 314–327.

Vayda, Andrew P., and Roy A. Rappaport, 1968, "Ecology, Cultural and Non-cultural." In J. A. Clifton, ed., *Introduction to Cultural Anthropology.* Boston: Houghton Mifflin, pp. 477–497.

Watson, Richard A., and Patty Jo Watson, 1969, *Man and Nature: An Anthropological Essay in Human Ecology.* New York: Harcourt, Brace Jovanovich.

Whiting, John, 1964, "Effects of Climate on Certain Cultural Practices." In W. Goodenough, ed., *Explorations in Cultural Anthropology: Essays in Honor of G. P. Murdock.* New York: McGraw-Hill, pp. 511–544.

See also Wissler (1926) in Section V, on pattern.

section X

Cultural Evolution

Historians of anthropological theory have often pointed out that the idea of cultural evolution, like that of biological evolution, may be traced to classic Greece. Other commentators have regarded the idea of cultural evolution as being intimately linked with the theory of biological evolution and have sometimes stated that the ideas of Charles Darwin and other biological evolutionists were the stimulus and model for the formulation of ideas of cultural evolution. The publication date of Darwin's *The Origin of Species*, 1859, was a time of rapid expansion of the sciences in general, and the influence of Darwin's work in stimulating thinking about cultural evolution is for this reason difficult to appraise. It seems reasonable that the similarities between the two theories of evolution are in considerable part the result of similar assumptions and goals, such as those we have already noted in all sciences concerning themselves with systems.

However, an examination of the history of the development of ideas of cultural evolution, as exemplified by the writings of Herbert Spencer and other scholars of the nineteenth century, seems to show a general independence from the ideas of biological evolution. This position is clearly stated by the foremost cultural evolutionist of the nineteenth century, Edward Tylor, who wrote that his interpretation takes little cognizance of Darwin's ideas and proceeds along its own lines of thought. Some of Tylor's ideas, transmitted through intermediaries such as Thomas Malthus, may be traced to the pioneering cultural evolutionist William Robertson, who wrote in the 1770s (Hoebel 1960).

An outline of the history of these lines of thought has already essentially been presented in readings in Section I and Section III, and the selections in this section are intended to serve as amplification. Our discussion here will be limited to a brief summarizing history of the development of the idea of cultural evolution and a discussion of criticisms made of specific theories of cultural evolution.

As a preliminary step, it is useful to look at concepts of evolution in general. Scientific theories of evolution describe it as a continuous development, each stage of which unfolds from a previous stage. This development may exist in inorganic, organic, or superorganic orders of phenomena. A theory of inorganic, astronomic evolution conforms with the second law of thermodynamics, which states that complexity of organization and differentiation of function of matter gradually diminish, moving toward a state of universal, homogeneous distribution of matter and energy. Rather than diminishing, the direction of biological and cultural evolution is toward greater organizational complexity and functional differentiation associated with greater concentrations of energy. At times, individual cultural systems and populations of living forms have evolved in a counter direction, toward simplicity and diminished control of energy, but these specific instances of seeming reversal do not invalidate the hypothesis concerning the direction of cultural and biological evolution in general.

As an organized science, anthropology began with an evolutionary framework. As our selection by Tylor (Section III) shows, the procedure of the evolutionists was that of any science. A distinguishable category of phenomena called culture was first selected as the subject of investigation. Like all other categories, culture is assumed to have a combination of traits unique to its class. Culture is also assumed to constitute a system. An added fundamental assumption is that the system of culture grows and changes or evolves, producing new cultural conformations of greater complexity. The objectives of study were then to formulate generalizations about the sequential order of the evolution of culture and the means by which it evolved.

We have earlier noted that, beginning at the end of the nineteenth century, many criticisms were made of the ideas of evolution and the specific evolutionary schemes of the two foremost cultural evolutionists of the time, E. B. Tylor and L. H. Morgan. From this time until the 1940s, cultural evolution was generally regarded by anthropologists as a useless or misleading way of examining culture. The many criticisms then made of Tylor and Morgan are generally viewed today as being partly unsound. Both scholars were indeed ethnocentric, placing Western culture at the apex of their schemes of evolutionary development, and both, quite understandably, had problems in compiling reliable comparative data. Certain additional charges of failings or weaknesses are also regarded today as valid, and the specific schemes of evolutionary sequence of both scholars have long been regarded as outmoded. The criticism that these scholars presented ideas of unilineal evolution merits special comment.

Upon examination, this charge seems to stem partly from misinterpreting or misunderstanding the views of Tylor and Morgan. Once this misinterpretation is corrected, it becomes evident that the criticism is otherwise meaningless. At the time of the strongest opposition to ideas of cultural evolution, the term "unilineal evolution" meant an hypothesis of a single sequence of stages of cultural evolution *through which all societies must pass in their evolutionary development.* The italicized portion of this statement erroneously expresses a view which Tylor and Morgan did not hold. The charge against them now becomes one of failure because their goal of study was to formulate statements about the path and dynamics of cultural evolution in general. The Darwinian theory of biological evolution similarly concerns general evolution, stating that living forms have developed from other living forms and offering an interpretation of the means by which this evolution occurred. Criticism of the theory of biological evolution as being unilineal seems quite meaningless.

The assumptions and procedures of the mainstream of modern studies of cultural evolution, as exemplified by the selections in this section by Marshall Sahlins and in this and other sections by L. A. White, differ in no essential way from those of the early cultural evolutionists. As in the past, the view of culture as superorganic is an integral part of the whole. Comparative data for use in drawing evolutionary inferences are today more reliable and much more abundant than they were a century ago.

Certain specific interpretations from this time continue to be valid. A familiar example is the view of early evolutionists of the sharp contrasts between simple primitive societies and advanced civilizations that reflect fundamental differences in the basis of social organization of the two types of societies. The nineteenth-century evolutionist Sir Henry Maine, whose ideas on the subject are briefly excerpted in this section, described the contrasts as "status versus contract." Status referred to societies socially organized upon kinship and personal ties (primitive societies), and contract to societies, such as our own, in which the primary bases of social organization are impersonal ties of property, residence, and common interests rather than highly personalized bonds of kinship and friendship. This interpretation has long been acceptable and has, in fact, become standard thinking in cultural anthropology.

Modern cultural evolutionists have attempted to avoid the weakness of early scholars in being overly and thus often inaccurately specific in defining the criteria, such as stone tools, metal tools, plant and animal husbandry, of the hypothesized stages of cultural evolution. The essay by White reproduced here may be considered an attempt of this kind. As an index of evolutionary development and as the principal motive factor in that development, it uses the amount of energy harnessed per capita by whatever means rather than using specific technological developments.

As with other ideas in anthropology, the "energy theory" of cultural evolution has considerable historic depth and has some foreshadowing in the nineteenth-century writings of Tylor and Morgan. Quite independently of anthropology, it may be found in the writings of the distinguished twentieth-century chemist Wilhelm Ostwald (1907), who also wrote on the "science of culture" and used the term "culturology" (1915:165–169). Regarding the evolution of culture from the standpoint of what he called "energetics," he said (1907:510–511):

> Now if all events are defined as transformations of energy as we have seen, their control becomes directly dependent upon the control of the relations of energy, and the history of civilization becomes the history of man's advancing control over energy.

An addition of modern times that might or might not be regarded as a divergent line of evolutionary thought is the idea of multilineal evolution, advanced by Julian H. Steward, which is discussed in some detail in our selection by Sahlins. The main current of modern evolutionary studies does not embrace the concept of multilineal evolution as set forth by Steward (1955). Rather than being evolutionary in a classic sense, Steward's ideas and method of study concern developmental or evolutionary histories of individual societies or, at most, of a few societies treated comparatively. Sahlin's discussion of the ideas of Steward that follows is illuminating, and his distinction between specific and general evolution is informative and useful.

The distinction involved here is that between culture in a generic sense and a culture or specific cultures. The differences are analagous with those in biological evolution between the evolution of plants and animals in general and the evolutionary histories of individual biological species. An analogy is also evident with the distinctions we have earlier noted between modal personalities and variations in the personalities among individuals. Dependant upon whether one is interested in the general or the specific, assumptions and procedures of study will differ. In the formulation of White's theory concerning energy and culture, for example, consideration of the geographical environment is not essential; in studies of the evolutionary history of individual cultures or of a few cultures treated comparatively, physical environment may be a stongly conditioning factor that must be considered. Similarly, in the study of modal personality, no consideration is ordinarily given to biological factors and certainly no consideration to differences in biological traits among the individuals concerned. In trying to understand the formation of the personalities of individuals, however, consideration must be given to the biological traits of individuals as these resemble and differ from the traits of other individuals. A useful exposition of the concept of universal evolution by Leslie A. White, which has relevance to the view of multilineal evolution advanced by Steward, appears in summary form as the concluding paper in Section XI on functionalism.

32 PRIMITIVE SOCIETY AND ANCIENT LAW
HENRY S. MAINE

The movement of the progressive societies has been uniform in one respect. Through all its course it has been distinguished by the gradual dissolution of family dependency and the growth of individual obligation in its place. The individual is steadily substituted for the Family, as the unit of which civil laws take account. The advance has been accomplished at varying rates of celerity, and there are societies not absolutely stationary in which the collapse of the ancient organisation can only be perceived by careful study of the phenomena they present. But, whatever its pace, the change has not been subject to reaction or recoil, and apparent retardations will be found to have been occasioned through the absorption of archaic ideas and customs from some entirely foreign source. Nor is it difficult to see what is the tie between man and man which replaces by degrees those forms of reciprocity in rights and duties which have their orgin in the Family. It is Contract. Starting, as from one terminus of history, from a condition of society in which all the relations of Persons are summed up in the relations of Family, we seem to have steadily moved towards a phase of social order in which all these relations arise from the free agreement of individuals. In Western Europe the progress achieved in this direction has been considerable. Thus the status of the Slave has disappeared—it has been superseded by the contractual relation of the servant to his master. The status of the Female under Tutelage, if the tutelage be understood of persons other than her husband, has also ceased to exist; from her coming of age to her marriage all the relations she may form are relations of contract. So too the status of the Son under Power has no true place in the law of modern European societies. If any civil obligation binds together the Parent and the child of full age, it is one to which only contract gives its legal validity. The apparent exceptions are exceptions of that stamp which illustrate the rule. The child before years of discretion, the orphan under guardianship, the adjudged lunatic, have all their capacities and incapacities regulated by the Law of Persons. But why? The reason is differently expressed in the conventional language of different systems, but in substance it is stated to the same effect by all. The great majority of Jurists are constant to the principle that the classes of persons just mentioned are subject to extrinsic control on the single ground that they do not possess the faculty of forming a judgment on their own interests; in other words, that they are wanting in the first essential of an engagement by Contract.

The word Status may be usefully employed to construct a formula expressing the law of progress thus indicated, which, whatever be its value, seems to me to be sufficiently ascertained. All the forms of Status taken notice of in the Law of Persons were derived from, and to some extent are still coloured by, the powers and privileges anciently residing in the Family. If then we employ Status, agreeably with the usage of the best writers, to signify these personal conditions only, and

Reprinted from Henry S. Maine, *Ancient Society,* 1884, Holt, Rinehart and Winston.

avoid applying the term to such conditions as are the immediate or remote result of agreement, we may say that the movement of the progressive societies has hitherto been a movement *from Status to Contract.*

33 ENERGY AND THE EVOLUTION OF CULTURE
LESLIE A. WHITE

The purpose of culture is to serve the needs of man. These needs are of two kinds: (1) those which can be served or satisfied by drawing upon resources within the human organism alone. Singing, dancing, myth-making, forming clubs or associations for the sake of companionship, etc., illustrate this kind of needs and ways of satisfying them. (2) The second class of needs can be satisfied only by drawing upon the resources of the external world, outside the human organism. Man must get his food from the external world. The tools, weapons, and other materials with which man provides himself with food, shelter from the elements, protection from his enemies, must likewise come from the external world. The satisfaction of spiritual and esthetic needs through singing, dancing, myth-making, etc., is possible, however, only if man's bodily needs for food, shelter, and defense are met. Thus the whole cultural structure depends upon the material, mechanical means with which man articulates himself with the earth. Futhermore, the satisfaction of human needs from "inner resources" may be regarded as a constant, the satisfaction of needs from the outer resources a variable. Therefore, in our discussion of cultural development we may omit consideration of the constant factor and deal only with the variable—the material, mechanical means with which man exploits the resources of nature.

The articulation-of-man-with-the-earth process may be analyzed and resolved into the following five factors: (1) the human organism, (2) the habitat, (3) the amount of energy controlled and expended by man, (4) the ways and means in which energy is expended, and (5) the human-need-serving product which accrues from the expenditure of energy. This is but another way of saying that human beings, like all other living creatures, exploit the resources of their habitat, in one way or another in order to sustain life and to perpetuate their kind.

Of the above factors, we may regard the organic factor as a constant. Although peoples obviously differ from each other physically, we are not able to attribute differences in culture to differences in physique (or "mentality"). In our study of culture, therefore, we may regard the human race as of uniform quality, i.e., as a constant, and, hence, we may eliminate it from our study.

Reproduced by permission of the American Anthropological Association from the *American Anthropologist*, vol. 45, no. 3, 1943.

No two habitats are alike; every habitat varies in time. Yet, in a study of culture as a whole, we may regard the factor of habitat as a constant: we simply reduce the need-serving, welfare-promoting resources of all particular habitats to an average. (In a consideration of particular manifestations of culture we would of course have to deal with their respective particular habitats.) Since we may regard habitat as a constant, we exclude it, along with the human organism, from our study of the development of culture.

This leaves us, then, three factors to be considered in any cultural situation: (1) the amount of energy per capita per unit of time harnessed and put to work within the culture, (2) the technological means with which this energy is expended, and (3) the human need-serving product that accrues from the expenditure of energy. We may express the relationship between these factors in the following simple formula: $E \times T = P$, in which E represents the amount of energy expended per capita per unit of time, T the technological means of its expenditure, and P the magnitude of the product per unit of time. This may be illustrated concretely with the following simple example: A man cuts wood with an axe. Assuming the quality of the wood and the skill of the workman to be constant, the amount of wood cut in a given period of time, an hour say, depends, on the one hand upon the amount of energy the man expends during this time: the more energy expended, the more wood cut. On the other hand, the amount of wood cut in an hour depends upon the kind of axe used. Other things being equal, the amount of wood cut varies with the quality of the axe: the better the axe the more wood cut. Our workman can cut more wood with an iron, or steel, axe than with a stone axe.

The efficiency with which human energy is expended mechanically depends upon the bodily skills of the persons involved, and upon the nature of the tools employed. In the following discussion we shall deal with skill in terms of averages. It is obvious, of course, that, other things being equal, the product of the expenditure of human energy varies directly as the skill employed in the expenditure of this energy. But we may reduce all particular skills, in any given situation, to an average, which, being constant may be eliminated from our consideration of culture growth. Hereafter, then, when we concern ourselves with the efficiency with which human energy is expended mechanically, we shall be dealing with the efficiency of tools only.

With reference to tools, man can increase the efficiency of the expenditure of his bodily energy in two ways: by improving a tool, or by substituting a better tool for an inferior one. But with regard to any given kind of tool, it must be noted that there is a point beyond which it cannot be improved. The efficiency of various tools of a certain kind varies; some bows are better than others. A bow, or any other implement, may vary in efficiency between 0 per cent and 100 per cent. But there is a maximum, theoretically as well as actually, which cannot be exceeded. Thus, the efficiency of a canoe paddle can be raised or lowered by altering its length, breadth, thickness, shape, etc. Certain proportions or dimensions would render it useless, in which case its efficiency would be 0 per cent. But, in the direction of improvement, a point is reached, ideally as well as practically, when no further progress can be made—any further change would be a detriment. Its efficiency is now at its maximum (100 per cent). So it is with a canoe, arrow, axe, dynamo, locomotive, or any other tool or machine.

We are now ready for some generalizations about cultural development. Let us return to our formula, but this time let us write it $E \times F = P$, in which E and P have the same values as before—E, the amount of energy expended; P the product produced—while F stands for the efficiency of the mechnical means with which the energy is expended. Since culture is a mechanism for serving human needs, cultural development may be measured by the extent to which, and the efficiency with which, need-serving goods or services are provided. P, in our formula, may thus stand for the total amount of goods or services produced in any given cultural situation. Hence P represents the status of culture, or, more accurately, the degree of cultural development. If, then, F, the efficiency with which human energy is expended, remains constant, the P, the degree of cultural development, will vary as E, the amount of energy expended per capita per year varies:

$$\frac{E_1 \times F}{E_2 \times F} = \frac{P_1}{P_2}$$

Thus we obtain the first important law of cultural development: *Other things being equal, the degree of cultural development varies directly as the amount of energy per capita per year harnessed and put to work.*

Secondly, if the amount of energy expended per capita per unit of time remains constant, then P varies as F:

$$\frac{E \times F_1}{E \times F_2} = \frac{P_1}{P_2}$$

and we get the second law of cultural development: *Other things being equal, the degree of cultural development varies directly as the efficiency of the technological means with which the harnessed energy is put to work.*

It is obvious, of course, that E and F may vary simultaneously, and in the same or in opposite directions. If E and F increase simultaneously P will increase faster, naturally, than if only one increased while the other remained unchanged. If E and F decrease simultaneously P will decrease more rapidly than if only one decreased while the other remained constant. If E increases while F decreases, or vice versa, then P will vary or remain unchanged, depending upon the magnitude of the changes of these two factors and upon the proportion of one magnitude to the other. If an increase in E is balanced by a decrease in F, or vice versa, then P will remain unchanged. But should E increase faster than F decreases, or vice versa, then P would increase; if E decreases faster than F increases, or vice versa, then P would decrease.

We have, in the above generalizations *the* law of cultural evolution: *culture develops when the amount of energy harnessed by man per capita per year is increased; or as the efficiency of the technological means of putting this energy to work is increased; or, as both factors are simultaneously increased.*

All living beings struggle to live, to perpetuate their respective kinds. In the human species the struggle for survival assumes the cultural form. The human struggle for existence expresses itself in a never-ending attempt to make of culture a more effective instrument with which to provide security of life and survival of the species. And one of the ways of making culture a more powerful instrument is to harness and to put to work within it more energy per capita per year. Thus, wind, and water, and fire are harnessed; animals are domesticated, plants cultivated; steam engines are built. The other way of improving culture as an instrument of adjustment and control is to invent new and better tools and to improve old ones. Thus energy for culture-living and culture-building is augmented in quantity, is expended more efficiently, and culture advances.

Thus we know, not only *how* culture evolves, but *why,* as well. The urge, inherent in all living species, to live, to make life more secure, more rich, more full, to insure the perpetuation of the species, seizes upon, when it does not produce, better (i.e., more effective) means of living and surviving. In the case of man, the biological urge to live, the power to invent and to discover, the ability to select and use the better of two tools or ways of doing something—these are the factors of cultural evolution. Darwin could tell us the consequences of variations, but he could not tell us how these variations were produced. We know the motive force as well as the means of cultural evolution. The culturologist knows more about cultural evolution than the biologist, even today, knows about biological evolution.

A word about man's motives with regard to cultural development. We do not say that man deliberately set about to improve his culture. It may well have been, as Morgan suggested, decades before Lowie emphasized the same point, that animals were first domesticated through whim or caprice rather than for practical, utilitarian reasons. Perhaps agriculture came about through accident. Hero's steam engine was a plaything. Gunpowder was first used to make pretty fireworks. The compass began as a toy. More than this, we know that peoples often resolutely oppose technological advances with a passionate devotion to the past and to the gods of their fathers. But all of this does not alter the fact that domesticated animals and cultivated plants have been used to make life more secure. Whatever may have been the intentions and motives (if any) of the inventors or discoverers of the bow and arrow, the wheel, the furnace and forge, the steam engine, the microscope, etc., the fact remains that these things have been seized upon by mankind and employed to make life more secure, comfortable, pleasant, and permanent. So we may disregard the psychological circumstances under which new cultural devices were brought into being. What is significant to the cultural evolutionist is that inventions and discoveries have been made, new tools invented, better ways of doings things found, and that these improved tools and techniques are kept and used until they are in turn replaced.

So much for the laws, or generalizations derived from our basic formula. Let us turn now to concrete facts and see how the history of culture is illuminated and made intelligible by these laws.

In the beginning of culture history, man had only the energy of his own body under his control and at his disposal for culture-living and culture-building. And for a very long period of time this was almost the only source of energy available to him. Wind, water, and fire were but rarely used as forms of energy. Thus we see that, in the first stage of cultural development, the only source of energy under man's control and at his disposal for culture-building was, except for the insignificant and limited use of wind, water and fire, his own body.

The amount of energy that could be derived from this source was very small. The amount of energy at the disposal of a community of 50, 100, or 300 persons would be 50, 100, or 300 times the energy of the average member of the community, which, when infants, the sick, the old and feeble are considered, would be considerably less than one "man-power" per capita. Since one "man-power" is about one-tenth of one horse-power, we see that the amount of energy per capita in the earliest stage of cultural development was very small indeed—perhaps 1/20th horsepower per person.

Since the amount of energy available for culture building in this stage was finite and limited, the extent to which culture could develop was limited. As we have seen, when the energy factor is a constant, cultural progress is made possible only by improvements in the means with which the energy is expended, namely, the technology. Thus, in the human-energy stage of cultural development progress is achieved only by inventing new tools—the bow and arrow, harpoon, needle, etc., or by improving old ones—new techniques of chipping flint implements, for example. But when man has achieved maximum efficiency in the expenditure of energy, and when he has reached the limits of his finite bodily energy resources, then his culture can develop no further. Unless he can harness additional quantities of energy—by tapping new sources—cultural development will come to an end. Man would have remained on the level of savagery indefinitely if he had not learned to augment the amount of energy under his control and at his disposal for culture-building by harnessing new sources of energy. This was first accomplished by the domestication of animals and by the cultivation of plants.

Man added greatly to the amount of energy under his control and at his disposal for culture-building when he domesticated animals and brought plants under cultivation. To be sure, man nourished himself with meat and grain and clothed himself with hides and fibers long before animal husbandry and agriculture came into being. But there is a vast difference between merely exploiting the resources of nature and of harnessing the forces of nature. In a wild food economy, a person, under given environmental conditions, expends a certain amount of energy (we will assume it is an average person so that the question of skill may be ignored) and in return he will secure, on the average, so much meat, fish, or plant food. But the food which he secures is itself a form and a magnitude of energy. Thus the hunter or wild plant-food gatherer exchanges one magnitude of energy for another: m units of labor for n calories of food. The ratio between the magnitude of energy obtained in the form of food and the magnitude expended in hunting and gathering may vary. The amount obtained may be greater than, less than (in which case the hunter-gatherer would eventually perish), or equal to, the amount expended. But although the ratio may vary from one situation to another, it is in any particular instance fixed: that is, the magnitude of energy-value of the game taken or plant-food gathered remains constant between the time that it is obtained and the time of its consumption. (At least it does not increase, it may in some instances decrease through natural deterioration.)

In a wild food economy, an animal or a plant is of value to man only after it has ceased to be an animal or a plant, i.e., a living organism. The hunter kills his game, the gatherer digs his roots and bulbs, plucks the fruit and seeds. It is different with the herdsman and the farmer. These persons make plants and animals work for them.

Living plants and animals are biochemical mechanisms which, of themselves, accumulate and store up energy derived originally from the sun. Under agriculture and animal husbandry these accumulations can be appropriated and utilized by man periodically in the form of milk, wool, eggs, fruits, nuts, seeds, sap, and so on. In the case of animals, energy generated by them may be utilized by man in the form of work, more or less continuously throughout their lifetime. Thus, when man domesticated animals and brought plants under cultivation, he harnessed powerful forces of nature, brought them under his control, and made them work for him just as he has harnessed rivers and made them run mills and dynamos, just as he has harnessed the tremendous reservoirs of solar energy that are coal and oil. Thus the difference between a wild plant and animal economy and a domestic economy is that in the former the return for an expenditure of human energy, no matter how large, is fixed, limited, whereas in agriculture and animal husbandry the initial return for the expenditure of human labor, augments itself indefinitely. And so it has come about that with the development and perfection of the arts of animal husbandry and agriculture—selective breeding, protection from their competitors in the Darwinian struggle for survival, feeding, fertilizer, irrigation, drainage, etc.—a given quantity of human labor produces much more than it could before these forces were harnessed. It is true, of course, that a given amount of human labor will produce more food in a wild economy under exceptionally favorable circumstances,—such, e.g., as in the Northwest Coast of America where salmon could be taken in vast numbers with little labor, or in the Great Plains of North America where, after the introduction of the horse and in favorable circumstances, a large quantity of bison meat could be procured with but little labor,—than could be produced by a feeble development of agriculture in unfavorable circumstances. But history and archeology prove that, by and large, the ability of man to procure the first necessity of life, food, was tremendously increased by the domestication of animals and by the cultivation of plants. Cultural progress was extremely rapid after the origin of agriculture. The great civilizations of China, India, Mesopotamia, Egypt, Mexico, and Peru sprang up quickly after the agricultural arts had attained to some degree of development and maturity. This was due, as we have already observed, to the fact that, by means of agriculture man was able to harness, control, and put to work for himself powerful forces of nature. With greatly augmented energy resources man was able to expand and develop his way of life, i.e., his culture.

In the development of culture agriculture is a much more important and powerful factor than animal husbandry. This is because man's control over the forces of nature is more immediate and more complete in agriculture than in animal husbandry. In a pastoral economy man exerts control over the animals only, he merely harnesses solar energy in animal form. But the animals themselves are dependent upon wild plants. Thus pastoral man is still dependent to a great extent upon the forces and caprices of nature. But in agriculture, his control is more intimate, direct, and, above all, greater. Plants receive and store up energy directly from the sun. Man's control over plants is direct and immediate. Further independence of nature is achieved by means of irrigation, drainage, and fertilizer. To be sure, man is always dependent upon nature to a greater or less extent; his control is never complete. But his dependence is less, his control greater, in agriculture than in animal husbandry. The extent to which man may harness natural forces in animal husbandry is limited. No matter how much animals are improved by selective breeding, no matter how carefully they are tended—defended from beasts of prey, protected from the elements—so long as they are dependent upon wild plant food, there is a limit, imposed by nature, to the extent to which man can receive profitable returns from his efforts expended on his herds. When this limit has been reached no further progress can be made. It is not until man controls also the growth of the plants upon which his animals feed that progress in animal husbandry can advance to higher levels. In agriculture, on the other hand, while there may be a limit to the increase of yield per unit of human labor, this limit has not yet been reached, and, indeed it is not yet even in sight. Thus there appears to be a limit to the return from the expenditure of a given amount of human labor in animal husbandry. But in agriculture this technological limit, if one be assumed to exist, lies so far ahead of us that we cannot see it or imagine where it might lie.

Added to all of the above, is the familiar fact that a nomadic life, which is customary in a pastoral economy, is not conducive to the development of advanced cultures. The sedentary life that goes with agriculture is much more conducive to the development of the arts and crafts, to the accumulation of wealth and surpluses, to urban life.

Agriculture increased tremendously the amount of energy per capita available for culture-building, and, as a consequence of the maturation of the agricultural arts, a tremendous growth of culture was experienced. Cultural progress was very slow during Eolithic and Paleolithic times. But after a relatively brief period in the Neolithic age, during which the agricultural arts were being developed, there was a tremendous acceleration of culture growth, and the great cultures of China, India, Mesopotamia, Egypt, Mexico, and Peru, came rapidly into being.

The sequence of events was somewhat as follows: agriculture transformed a roaming population into a sedentary one. It greatly increased the food supply, which in turn increased the population. As human labor became more productive in agriculture, an increasing portion of society became divorced from the task of food-getting, and was devoted to other occupations. Thus society becomes organized into occupational groups: masons, metal workers, jade carvers, weavers, scribes, priests. This has the effect of accelerating progress in the arts, crafts, and sciences (astronomy, mathematics, etc.), since they are now in the hands of specialists, rather than jacks-of-all-trades. With an increase in manufacturing, added to division of society into occupational groups, comes production for exchange and sale (instead of primarily for use as in tribal society), mediums of exchange, money, merchants, banks, mortgages, debtors, slaves. An accumulation of wealth and competition for favored regions provoke wars of conquest, and produce professional military and ruling classes, slavery and serfdom. Thus agriculture wrought a profound change in the life-and-culture of man as it had existed in the human-energy stage of development.

But the advance of culture was not continuous and without limit. Civilization had, in the main, reached the limit of its development on the basis of a merely agricultural and animal husbandry technology long before the next great cultural advance was initiated by the industrial revolution. As a matter of fact, marked cultural recessions took place in Mesopotamia, Egypt, Greece, Rome, perhaps in India, possibly in China. This is not to say that no cultural progress whatsoever was made; we are well aware of many steps forward from time to time in various places. But so far as general type of culture is concerned, there is no fundamental difference between the culture of Greece during the time of Archimedes and that of Western Europe at the beginning of the eighteenth century.

After the agricultural arts had become relatively mature, some six, eight or ten thousand years before the beginning of the Christian era, there was little cultural advance until the nineteenth century A.D. Agricultural methods in Europe and the United States in 1850 differed very little from those of Egypt of 2000 B.C. The Egyptians did not have an iron plow, but otherwise there was little difference in mode of production. Even today in many places in the United States and in Europe we can find agricultural practices which, the use of iron excepted, are essentially like those of dynastic Egypt. Production in other fields was essentially the same in western Europe at the beginning of the eighteenth (we might almost say nineteenth) century as in ancient Rome, Greece, or Egypt. Man, as freeman, serf, or slave, and beasts of burden and draft animals, supplemented to a meager extent by wind and water power, were the sources of energy. The Europeans had gunpowder whereas the ancients did not. But gunpowder cannot be said to be a culture-builder. There was no essential difference in type of social—political and economic—institutions. Banks, merchants, the political state, great land-owners, guilds of workmen, and so on were found in ancient Mesopotamia, Greece, and Rome.

Thus we may conclude that culture had developed about as far as it could upon the basis of an agricultural-animal husbandry economy, and that there were recessions from peaks attained in Mesopotamia, Egypt, Greece and Rome long before the beginning of the eighteenth century A.D. We may conclude further, that civilization would never have advanced substantially beyond the levels already reached in the great cultures of antiquity if a way had not been found to harness a greater magnitude of energy per capita per unit of time, by tapping a new source of energy: fuel.

The invention of the steam engine, and of all subsequent engines which derive power from fuels, inaugurated a new era in culture history. When man learned to harness energy in the form of fuel he opened the door of a vast treasure house of energy. Fuels and engines tremendously increased the amount of energy under man's control and at his disposal for culture-building. The extent to which energy has been thus harnessed in the modern world is indicated by the eminent physicist, Robert A. Millikan (1939:211)* as follows:

> In this country [the U.S.A.] there is now expended about 13.5 horsepower hours per day per capita—the equivalent of 100 human slaves for each of us; in England the figure is 6.7, in Germany 6.0, in France 4.5; in Japan 1.8, in Russia 0.9, in China, 0.5.

Let us return now, for a moment, to our basic principle—culture develops as (1) the amount of energy harnessed and put to work per capita per unit of time increases, and (2) as the efficiency of the means with which this energy is expended increases—and consider the evolution of culture from a slightly different angle. In the course of human history various sources of energy are tapped and harnessed by man and put to work at culture-living and culture-building. The original source of energy was, as we have seen, the human organism. Subsequently, energy has been harnessed in other forms—agriculture, animal husbandry, fire, wind, water, fuel. Energy is energy, and from the point of view of technology it makes no difference whether the energy with which a bushel of wheat is ground comes from a free man, a slave, an ox, the flowing stream or a pile of coal. But it makes a big difference to human beings where the energy comes from, and an important index of cultural development is derived from this fact.

To refer once more to our basic equation: On the one hand we have energy expended; on the other, human need-serving goods and services are produced. Culture advances as these two factors increase, hand in hand. But the energy component is resolvable into two factors: the human energy, and the non-human energy, factors. Of these, the human energy factor is a constant; the non-human energy factor, a variable. The increase in quantity of need-serving goods goes hand in hand with an increase in the amount of non-human energy expended. But, since the human energy factor remains constant, an increase in amount of goods and services produced means more goods and services per unit of human labor. Hence, we obtain the law: *Other things being equal, culture evolves as the productivity of human labor increases.*

In Savagery (wild food economy) the productivity of human labor is low; only a small amount of human need-serving goods and services are produced per unit of human energy. In Barbarism (agriculture, animal husbandry), this productivity is greatly increased. And in Civilization (fuels, engines) it is still further increased.

We must now consider another factor in the process of cultural development, and an important one it is, viz., the *social system within which energy is harnessed and put to work*.

We may distinguish two kinds of determinants in social organization, two kinds of social groupings. On the one hand we have social groupings which serve those needs of man which can be fed by drawing upon resources within man's own

*See p. 344 for references.

organism: clubs for companionship, classes or castes in so far as they feed the desire for distinction, will serve as examples. On the other hand, social organization is concerned with man's adjustment to the external world; social organization *is* the way in which human beings organize themselves for the three great processes of adjustment and survival—food getting, defense from enemies, protection from the elements. Thus, we may distinguish two factors in any social system, those elements which are *ends in themselves,* which we may call E; and elements which are *means to ends* (food, defense, etc.) which we may term M.

In any social system M is more important than E, because E is dependent upon M. There can be no men's clubs or classes of distinction unless food is provided and enemies guarded against. In the development of culture, moreover, we may regard E as a constant: a men's club is a men's club whether among savage or civilized peoples. Being a constant, we may ignore factor E in our consideration of cultural evolution and deal only with the factor M.

M is a variable factor in the process of cultural evolution. It is, moreover, a dependent variable, dependent upon the technological way in which energy is harnessed and put to work. It is obvious, of course, that it is the technological activities of hunting people that determine, in general, their form of social organization (in so far as that social organization is correlated with hunting rather than with defense against enemies). We of the United States have a certain type of social system (in part) because we have factories, railroads, automobiles, etc.; we do not possess these things *as a consequence* of a certain kind of social system. Technological systems engender social systems rather than the reverse. Disregarding the factor E, social organization is to be regarded as the way in which human beings organize themselves to wield their respective technologies. Thus we obtain another important law of culture: *The social organization (E excluded) of a people is dependent upon and determined by the mechanical means with which food is secured, shelter provided, and defense maintained.* In the process of cultural development, *social evolution is a consequence of technological evolution.*

But this is not the whole story. While it is true that social systems are engendered by, and dependent upon, their respective underlying technologies, it is also true that social systems condition the operation of the technological systems upon which they rest; the relationship is one of mutual, though not necessarily equal, interaction and influence. A social system may foster the effective operation of its underlying technology or it may tend to restrain and thwart it. In short, in any given situation the social system may play a progressive role or it may play a reactionary role.

We have noted that after the agricultural arts had attained a certain degree of development, the great civilizations of China, India, Egypt, the Near East, Central America and Peru came rapidly into being as a consequence of the greatly augmented energy resources of the peoples of these regions. But these great civilizations did not continue to advance indefinitely. On the contrary they even receded from maximum levels in a number of instances. Why did they not continue progressively to advance? According to our law culture will advance, other things being equal, as long as the amount of energy harnessed and put to work per capita per unit of time increases. The answer to our question, Why did not these great cultures continue to advance? is, therefore, that the amount of energy per capita per unit of time, *ceased to increase,* and, furthermore, the efficiency of the means with which this energy was expended *was not advanced beyond a certain limit.* In short, there was no fundamental improvement in the agricultural arts from say 2000 B.C. to 1800 A.D.

The next question is, Why did not the agricultural arts advance and improve during this time? We know that the agricultural arts are still capable of tremendous improvement, and the urge of man for plenty, security and efficiency was as great then as now. Why, then, did agriculture fail to progress beyond a certain point in the great civilizations of antiquity? The answer is, The social system, within which these arts functioned, curbed further expansion, thwarted progress.

All great civilizations resting upon intensive agriculture are divided into classes: a ruling class and the masses who are ruled. The masses produced the means of life. But the distribution of these goods is in accordance with rules which are administered by the ruling class. By one method of control or another—by levies, taxes, rents, or some other means—the ruling class takes a portion of the wealth produced by the masses from them, and consumes it according to their liking or as the exigencies of the time dictate.

In this sort of situation cultural advancement may cease at a certain point for lack of incentive. No incentive to progress came from the ruling class in the ancient civilizations of which we are speaking. What they appropriated from their subjects they consumed or wasted. To obtain more wealth the ruling class merely increased taxes, rents, or other levies upon the producers of wealth. This was easier, quicker, and surer than increasing the efficiency of production and thereby augmenting the total product. On the other hand, there was no incentive to progress among the masses—if they produced more by increasing efficiency it would only mean more for the tax-gatherers of the ruling class. The culture history of China during the past few centuries, or indeed, since the Han dynasty, well illustrates situations of this sort.

We come then to the following conclusion: *A social system may so condition the operation of a technological system as to impose a limit upon the extent to which it can expand and develop. When this occurs, cultural evolution ceases.* Neither evolution nor progress in culture is inevitable (neither Morgan nor Tylor ever said, or even intimated, that they are). When cultural advance has thus been arrested, it can be renewed only by tapping some new source of energy and by harnessing it in sufficient magnitude to burst asunder the social system which binds it. Thus freed, the new technology will form a new social system, one congenial to its growth, and culture will again advance until, perhaps, the social system once more checks it.

It seems quite clear that mankind would never have advanced materially beyond the maximum levels attained by culture between 2000 B.C. and 1700 A.D. had it not tapped a new source of energy (fuel) and harnessed it in substantial magnitudes. The speed with which man could travel, the range of his projectiles, and many other things, could not have advanced beyond a certain point had he not learned to harness more energy in new forms. And so it was with culture as a whole.

The steam engine ushered in a new era. With it, and various kinds of internal combustion engines, the energy resources of vast deposits of coal and oil were tapped and harnessed in progressively increasing magnitudes. Hydroelectric plants contributed a substantial amount from rivers. Populations grew, production expanded, wealth increased. The limits of growth of the new technology have not yet been reached; indeed, it is probably not an exaggeration to say that they have not yet even been foreseen, so vast are the possibilities and so close are we still to the beginning of this new era. But already the new technology has come into conflict with the old social system. The new technology is being curbed and thwarted. The progressive tendencies of the new technology are being held back by a social system that was adapted to the pre-fuel technology. This fact has become commonplace today.

In our present society, goods are produced for sale at a profit. To sell one must have a market. Our market is a world market, but it is, nevertheless, finite in magnitude. When the limit of the market has been reached production ceases to expand: no market, no sale; no sale, no profit; no profit, no production. Drastic curtailment of production, wholesale destruction of surpluses follow. Factories, mills, and mines close; millions of men are divorced from industrial production and thrown upon relief. Population growth recedes. National incomes cease to expand. Stagnation sets in.

When, in the course of cultural development, the expanding technology comes into conflict with the social system, one of two things will happen: either the social system will give way, or technological advance will be arrested. If the latter occurs, cultural evolution will, of course, cease. The outcome of situations such as this is not preordained. The triumph of technology and the continued evolution and progress of culture are not assured merely because we wish it or because it would be better thus. In culture as in mechanics, the greater force prevails. A force is applied to a boulder. If the force be great enough, the rock is moved. If the rock be large enough to withstand the force it will remain stationary. So in the case of technology-institutions conflicts: if the force of the growing technology be great enough the restraining institutions will give way; if this force is not strong enough to overcome institutional opposition, it must submit to it.

There was undoubtedly much institutional resistance to the expanding agricultural technology in late neolithic times. Such staunch institutions as the tribe and clan which had served man well for thousands of years did not give way to the political state without a fight; the "liberty, equality and fraternity" of primitive society were not surrendered for the class-divided, serf and lord, slave and master, society of feudalism without a struggle. But the ancient and time-honored institutions of tribal society could not accommodate the greatly augmented forces of the agricultural technology. Neither could they successfully oppose these new forces. Consequently, tribal institutions gave way and a new social system came into being.

Similarly in our day, our institutions have shown themselves incapable of accommodating the vast technological forces of the Power Age. What the outcome of the present conflict between modern fuel technology and the social system of an earlier era will be, time alone will tell. It seems likely, however, that the old social system is now in the process of destruction. The tremendous forces of the Power Age are not to be denied. The great wars of the twentieth century derive their chief significance from this fact: they are the means by which an old social order is to be scrapped, and a new one to be brought into being. The first World War wiped out the old ruling families of the Hapsburgs, Romanoffs, and Hohenzollerns, hulking relics of Feudalism, and brought Communist and Fascist systems into being. We do not venture to predict the social changes which the present war will bring about. But we may confidently expect them to be as profound and as far-reaching as those effected by World War I.

Thus, in the history of cultural evolution, we have witnessed one complete cultural revolution, and the first stage of a second. The technological transition from a wild food economy to a relatively mature agricultural and animal husbandry economy was followed by an equally profound institutional change: from tribal society to civil society. Thus the first fundamental and all-inclusive cultural change, or revolution, took place. At the present time we are entering upon the second stage of the second great cultural revolution of human history. The Industrial Revolution was but the first stage, the technological stage, of this great cultural revolution. The Industrial Revolution has run its course, and we are now entering upon the second stage, one of profound institutional change, of social revolution. Barring collapse and chaos, which is of course possible, a new social order will emerge. It appears likely that the human race will occupy the earth for some million years to come. It seems probable, also, that man, after having won his way up through savagery and barbarism, is not likely to stop, when at last he finds himself upon the very threshold of civilization.

The key to the future, in any event, lies in the energy situation. If we can continue to harness as much energy per capita per year in the future as we are doing now, there is little doubt but that our old social system will give way to a new one, a new era of civilization. Should, however, the amount of energy that we are able to harness diminish materially, then culture would cease to advance or even recede. A return to a cultural level comparable to that of China during the Ming dynasty is neither inconceivable nor impossible. It all depends upon how man harnesses the forces of nature and the extent to which this is done.

At the present time "the petroleum in sight is only a twelve year supply, . . . and new discoveries [of oil] are not keeping pace with use" (Furnas 1941:425). Coal is more abundant. Even so, many of the best deposits in the United States—which has over half of the world's known coal reserves—will some day be depleted. "Eventually, no matter how much we conserve, this sponging off past ages for fossil energy must cease . . . What then?" (Furnas 1941:426). The answer is, of course, that culture will decline unless man is able to maintain the amount of energy harnessed per capita per year by tapping new sources.

Wind, water, waves, tides, solar boilers, photochemical reactions, atomic energy, etc., are sources which might be tapped or further exploited. One of the most intriguing possibilities is that of harnessing atomic energy. When the nucleus of an atom of uranium (U 235) is split it "releases 200,000,000 electron volts, the largest conversion of mass into energy that has yet been produced by terrestrial means." Weight for weight, uranium (as a source of energy produced by nuclear fission) is 5,000,000 times as effective as coal. If harnessing sub-atomic energy could be made a practical success, our energy resources would be multiplied a thousand fold. As Dr. R. M. Langer (1940), research associate in physics at California Institute of Technology, has put it;

> The face of the earth will be changed. . . . Privilege and class distinctions . . . will become relics because things that make up the good life will be so abundant and inexpensive. War will become obsolete because of the disappearance of those economic stresses that immemorially have caused it. . . . The kind of civilization we might expect . . . is so different in kind from anything we know that even guesses about it are futile.

To be able to harness sub-atomic energy would, without doubt, create a civilization surpassing sober imagination of today. But not everyone is as confident as Dr. Langer that this advance is imminent. Some experts have their doubts, some think it a possibility. Time alone will tell.

But there is always the sun, from which man has derived all of his energy, directly or indirectly, in the past. And it may be that it will become, directly, our chief source of power in the future. Energy in enormous amounts reaches the earth daily from the sun. "The average intensity of solar energy in this latitude amounts to about 0.1 of a horse power per square foot" (Furnas 1941:426). "Enough energy falls on about 200 square miles of an arid region like the Mojave Desert to supply the [present needs of the] United States" (Furnas 1941:427). But the problem is, of course, to harness it effectively and efficiently. The difficulties do not seem insuperable. It will doubtless be done, and probably before a serious diminution of power from dwindling resources of oil and coal overtakes us. From a power standpoint the outlook for the future is not too dark for optimism.

We turn now to an interesting and important fact, one highly significant to the history of anthropology: The thesis set forth in the preceding pages is substantially the same as that advanced by Lewis H. Morgan and E. B. Tylor many decades ago. We have expounded it in somewhat different form and words; our presentation is, perhaps, more systematic and explicit. At one point we have made a significant change in their theoretical scheme: we begin the third great stage of cultural evolution with engines rather than with writing. But essentially our thesis is that of the Evolutionist school as typified by Morgan and Tylor. . . .

In the foregoing we have, we believe, a sound and illuminating theory of cultural evolution. We have hold of principles, fundamental principles, which are operative in all cultures at all times and places. The motive force of cultural evolution is laid bare, the mechanisms of development made clear. The nature of the relationship between social institutions on the one hand and technological instruments on the other is indicated. Understanding that the function of culture is to serve the needs of man, we find that we have an objective criterion for evaluating culture in terms of the extent to which, and the efficiency with which, human needs are satisfied by cultural means. We can measure the amounts of energy expended;

we can calculate the efficiency of the expenditure of energy in terms of measurable quantities of goods and services produced. And, finally, as we see, these measurements can be expressed in mathematical terms.

The theory set forth in the preceding pages was, as we have made clear, held by the foremost thinkers of the Evolutionist school of the nineteenth century, both in England and in America. Today they seem to us as sound as they did to Tylor and Morgan, and, if anything, more obvious. It seems almost incredible that anthropologists of the twentieth century could have turned their backs upon and repudiated such a simple, sound, and illuminating generalization, one that makes the vast range of tens of thousands of years of culture history intelligible. But they have done just this. The anti-evolutionists, led in America by Franz Boas, have rejected the theory of evolution in cultural anthropology—and have given us instead a philosophy of "planless hodge-podge-ism."

It is not surprising, therefore, to find at the present time the most impressive recognition of the significance of technological progress in cultural evolution in the writings of a distinguished physicist, the Nobel prize winner, Robert A. Millikan (1939:211):

> The changes that have occurred within the past hundred years not only in the external conditions under which the average man, at least in this western world, passes life on earth, but in his superstitions . . . his fundamental beliefs, in his philosophy, in his conception of religion, in his whole world outlook, are probably greater than those that occurred during the preceding four thousand years all put together. Life seems to remain static for thousands of years and then to shoot forward with amazing speed. The last century has been one of those periods of extraordinary change, the most amazing in human history. If, then, you ask me to put into one sentence the cause of that recent rapid and enormous change I should reply: "It is found in the discovery and utilization of the means by which heat energy can be made to do man's work for him."

Tucked away in the pages of Volume II of a manual on European archeology, too, we find a similar expression from a distinguished American scholar, George G. MacCurdy (1933:134–135):

> The *degree of civilization* of any epoch, people, or group of peoples *is measured by ability to utilize energy for human advancement or needs.* Energy is of two kinds, internal and external or free. Internal energy is that of the human body or machine, and its basis is food. External energy is that outside the human body and its basis is fuel. Man has been able to tap the great storehouse of external energy. Through his internal energy and that acquired from external sources, he has been able to overcome the opposing energy of his natural environment. *The difference between these two opposing forces is the gauge of civilization* (emphasis ours).

Thus, this view is not wholly absent in anthropological theory in America today although extremely rare and lightly regarded. The time will come, we may confidently expect, when the theory of evolution will again prevail in the science of culture as it has in the biological and the physical sciences. It is a significant fact that in cultural anthropology alone among the sciences is a philosophy of anti-evolutionism respectable—a fact we would do well to ponder.

34 EVOLUTION: SPECIFIC AND GENERAL
MARSHALL D. SAHLINS

Specific and General Cultural Evolution

Culture continues the evolutionary process [applying to living forms] by new means. Since these cultural means are unique, cultural evolution takes on distinctive characteristics. But still culture diversifies by adaptive specialization and still it successively produces over-all higher forms. Culture, like life, undergoes specific and general evolution.

The cultural anthropologist surveying the ethnographic and archaeological achievements of his discipline is confronted by variety if nothing else. There are myriads of culture types, that is, of the culture characteristic of an ethnic group or a region, and an even greater variety of cultures proper, of the cultural organization of given cohesive societies. How has this come about? In a word, through adaptive modification: culture has diversified as it has filled in the variety of opportunities for human existence afforded by the earth. Such is the specific aspect of cultural evolution. One of the best statements it has received belongs to Herbert Spencer, who, ironically, is commonly and pejoratively categorized today as a "unilinear" evolutionist.

Like other kinds of progress, social progress is not linear but divergent and re-divergent. Each differentiated product gives origin to a new set of differentiated products. While spreading over the earth mankind have found environments of various characters, and in each case the social life fallen into, partly determined by the social life previously led, has been partly determined by the influences of the new environment; so that multiplying groups have tended ever to acquire differences, now major and now minor: there have arisen genera and species of societies. (1897:3, 331.*)

That culture is man's means of adaptation is a common-place. Culture provides the technology for appropriating nature's energy and putting it to service, as well as the social and ideological means of implementing the process. Economically, politically, and in other ways, a culture also adjusts to the other cultures of its milieu, to the superorganic part of its environment. Cultures are organizations for doing something, for perpetuating human life and themselves. Logically as well as empirically, it follows that as the problems of survival vary, cultures accordingly change, that culture undergoes phylogenetic, adaptive development.

The raw materials of a culture's phylogenetic development are the available culture traits, both those within the culture itself and those that can be borrowed or appropriated from its superorganic environment. The orienting process of development is adaptation of these traits to the expropriation of nature's resources and to coping with outside cultural influence. In this orienting, adaptive process ele-

Reprinted from M. D. Sahlins and E. R. Service, *Evolution and Culture*, copyright © 1960 by The University of Michigan Press.
*See pp. 344–345 for references.

ments within a culture are synthesized to form new traits, an event we call "invention," and items made available from the outside are incorporated, a process we call "diffusion," or sometimes, "acculturation."

It is time we took stock of the specific evolutionary sophistication of our discipline. The culturological study of the mechanics of invention, diffusion, and cultural adaptation in general—including cultural ecology—is fairly well advanced. We need not bow before Huxley's invidious comparison of our understanding of cultural evolution and the "triumphant synthesis" of (specific) evolutionary biology. The synthesis exists in anthropology; it remains only to make it intellectually triumphant.

New cultural traits arising through adaptation can be considered adaptive advances. In this they are similar to structural and functional advances in species, although they are quite different in content. A cultural advance may appear as an innovation in kin reckoning, a "Dionysian" war complex, the elaboration of head-hunting, the development or the redefinition of the concept of mana, or any of a host of other things. . . . To cite further examples is unnecessary: recent years have witnessed an abundance of studies demonstrating that special cultural features arise in the process of adaptation. This is the kind of work in which Julian Steward has pioneered.

We are, unfortunately, still accustomed to speak of cultural adaptive modifications such as Easter Island stone images—or Australian section systems, Eskimo technical ingenuity, Northwest Coast potlatching, or Paleolithic cave art—as "cultural bents," manifestations of "cultural interest" or "cultural outlook." But to what purpose? Our understanding has not been enhanced (as usual) by restatement in anthropomorphic terms. In the evolutionary perspective these "bents" are adaptive specializations. So considered they can be interpreted in relation to selective pressures and the available means of maintaining a cultural organization given such pressures.

Adaptive advance is relative to the adaptive problem. In this context a Grecian urn is not a thing of beauty and a joy forever: it is not higher, or better, than a Chinese vase or a Hopi pot; among languages, suffixing tendencies are not more advanced than prefixing; Eskimo kin terminology is no higher than Crow; neither Eskimo nor Crow culture is more developed than the other. *Viewed specifically*, the adaptive modifications occurring in different historical circumstances are incomparable; each is adequate in its own way, given the adaptive problems confronted and the available means of meeting them. No one culture has a monopoly on or even necessarily more kinds of adaptive improvements, and what is selectively advantageous for one may be simply ruinous for another. Nor are those cultures that we might consider higher in general evolutionary standing necessarily more perfectly adapted to their environments than lower. Many great civilizations have fallen in the last 2,000 years, even in the midst of material plenty, while the Eskimos tenaciously maintained themselves in an incomparably more difficult habitat. The race is not to the swift, nor the battle to the strong.

When we look at the specific aspect of culture's evolution we are cultural relativists. But this is not justification for the extension or the distortion of the relativist injunction that says "progress" is only a moral judgment, and all "progress," like all morality, is therefore only relative. Adaptive advances considered as such are relative. Like morals they are to be judged as more or less effective specializations. But general progress also occurs in culture, and it can be absolutely, objectively, and nonmoralistically ascertained.

So far specific cultural evolution has been treated much like specific biological evolution, often in identical terms; but there are also important differences. The fundamental differences stem from the fact that cultural variation, unlike biological, can be transmitted between different lines by diffusion. Separate cultural traditions, unlike separate biological lineages, may converge by coalescence. Moreover, partial phylogenetic continuity sometimes occurs between successive general stages of cultural evolution as backward cultures, borrowing wholesale the achievements of higher forms, push on the new evolutionary heights without recapitulating all intermediate stages of development. By contrast, each new adaptive step is a point of no return for biological populations; they can only (at best) move forward to that full specialization which is ultimately the (dead) end of further progress. In the same connection, replacement of a less highly developed by a more progressive cultural form can be accomplished by diffusion or acculturation, which has the advantage for people that a higher culture may dominate without total destruction of the population, or even loss of ethnic or social integrity, of the lower. In the chapters to follow these unique qualities of cultural evolution are examined in detail.

While convergence by diffusion is common in specific cultural evolution, so is parallel independent development, as anthropology has learned well after years of controversy over "diffusion versus independent invention." Perhaps parallel, independent development—the consequence of similar adaptation to similar environment—is more common in culture than comparable phenomena seem to be in life because of the limitation on variation imposed by the generic similarity and unity of humanity, the "psychic unity of mankind." In any case, a professional anthropologist can immediately bring to mind a host of parallelisms or "regularities," as Steward calls them, in cultural evolution. Steward, incidentally, virtually equates parallelism with his term, "multilinear evolution," and, furthermore, asserts that multilinear evolution is anthropology's only road to profitable, albeit limited, evolutionary generalization (Steward 1953; 1955). We have something to say about this in the concluding section of the chapter.

Specific evolution is not the whole of cultural evolution. Culture not only produces adaptive sequences of forms, but sequences of higher forms; it has not only undergone phylogenetic development, but over-all progress. In brief, culture has evolved in a general respect as well as a specific one.

General cultural evolution is the successive emergence of new levels of all-round development. This emergent process, however, is not necessarily a historically continuous, phylogenetic one, for new levels of general standing are often achieved in unconnected (or only partially connected) cultural traditions. The relation between general and specific cultural evolution can thus be depicted as we have done before for comparable aspects of biological evolution. . . .

The general perspective on cultural evolution has been labelled, by its critics, "universal evolution." Readers other than anthropologists may find this difficult to believe, but the very term "universal" has a negative connotation in this field because it suggests the search for broad generalization that has been virtually declared unscientific (!) by twentieth-century, academic, particularistic American anthropology. Correlatively, "universal evolution" is criticized on the grounds that it *is* universal, i.e., so general as to be vague, obvious, or simply truistic. We hope the reader, then, will pardon us for a rather long digression concerning the scientific value of the study of general evolution.

The objectives of general evolutionary research are the determination and explanation of the successive transformations of culture through its several stages of overall progress. What progressive trends have emerged in warfare, for example, or in economy, in political institutions, or in the role of kinship in society? As the questions we ask are not posed in terms of adaptive modification, neither will our explanations be. In other words, studies of specific and general evolution lead in different directions, as has evolution itself.

Let us take for an example the evolutionary analysis of war. Considered phylogenetically or specifically, variations in warfare are related to the selective circumstances operating on the cultures involved. In this way we examine and explain the development of warfare among Plains Indians in the nineteenth century, or why it differs from war among California Indians or the Iroquois. Each type of warfare thus considered is a unique, historic type, to be interpreted with reference to its particular historical-ecological circumstances. Using a general perspective, however, we classify types of warfare as representatives of stages in the overall development of that aspect of culture, and then trace the progressive trends in war as they unfold through these successive stages. (Incidentally, anyone can see from the example we have chosen that "progress" is not here equated with "good.") The progressive trends discovered might include such things as increase in the scale of war, in the size of armies and the numbers of casualties, in the duration of campaigns, and the significance of outcome for the survival of the societies involved. These trends find their explanation not in adaptation but by reference to other developments accompanying them in the general progress of culture, such as increasing economic productivity or the emergence of special political institutions. Our conclusions now are of the form: war changes in certain ways, such as increases in scale, duration, etc., in proportion to certain economic or political (or whatever) trends, such as increasing productivity. It is obvious that the evolution of war has involved both diversification and progressive development, and only the employment of both specific and general perspectives can confront the evolutionary whole.

Distinguishing diversification from progress, however, not only distinguishes kinds of evolutionary research and conclusions, it dissipates long-standing misconceptions. Here is a question typical of a whole range of such difficulties: is feudalism a general *stage* in the evolution of economic and political forms, the one antecedent to modern national economy? The affirmative has virtually been taken for granted in economic and political history, and not only of the Marxist variety, where the sequence slave-feudal-capitalist modes of production originated. If assumed to be true, then the unilineal implications of the evolutionary scheme are only logical. That is, if feudalism is the antecedent stage of the modern state, then it, along with "Middle Ages" and "natural economy," lies somewhere in the background of every modern civilization. So it is that in the discipline of history, the Near East, China, Japan, Africa, and a number of other places have been generously granted "Middle Ages."

But it is obvious nonsense to consider feudalism, Middle Ages, and natural economy as the *general stage* of evolution antecedent to high (modern) civilization. Many civilizations of antiquity that antedate feudalism in its classic European form, as well as some coeval and some later than it in other parts of the world, are more highly developed. Placing feudalism between these civilizations and modern nations in a hierarchy of over-all progress patently and unnecessarily invalidates the hierarchy; it obscures rather than illustrates the progressive trends in economy, society, and polity in the evolution of culture. Conversely, identifying the specific antecedents of modern civilizations throughout the world as "feudalism" is also obviously fallacious and obscures the historic course of development of these civilizations, however much it may illuminate the historic course of Western culture.

Is not Marx [in the *Communist Manifesto*] in reality beginning with an analysis of the social development of Western Europe and the countries brought from time to time within its orbit from the Dark Ages to the growth of an advanced system of Capitalism, and then trying to apply the results achieved by this analysis to human history as a whole? May not the first of these steps be valid, and the second invalid . . . Were the Dark Ages really an advance over the Roman Empire? Civilisation for civilisation, can anyone possibly believe that they were? (Cole 1934:38-39.)

Feudalism is a "stage" only in a *specific* sense, a step in the development of one line of civilization. The stage of general evolution achieved prior to the modern nation is best represented by such classical civilizations as the Roman, or by such oriental states as China, Sumer, and the Inca Empire. In the general perspective, feudalism is only a specific, backward form of this order of civilization, an underdeveloped form that happened to have greater evolutionary potential than the others and historically gave rise to a new level of achievement. There is nothing unusual in evolutionary "leapfrogging" of this sort. The failure to differentiate these general and specific facets of the development of civilization can only be a plague on both houses of evolutionary research and a disgrace to the whole evolutionary perspective.

The reader may well feel disturbed, if not deceived, by the preceding discussion. How can an exposition of the course of evolution arbitrarily rip cultures out of the context of time and history and place them, just as arbitrarily, in categories of lower and higher development, categories that are presumed to represent *successive* states? We are confronting the taxonomic innovation that is required for the study of general evolution.

Perhaps it will help to point out that in biological evolution new forms of low degree are arising all the time, such as new forms of bacteria; in other words, the specific evolution of lower forms does not stop when they are by-passed by higher forms. It follows that the later form is not necessarily higher than the earlier; the *stages* or *levels* of general development are successive, but the particular representatives of successive stages need not be. To return to feudalism, it represents a lower level of general development than the civilizations of China, ancient Egypt, or Mesopotamia, although it arose later than these civilizations and happened to lead to a form still higher than any of them.

The fundamental difference between specific and general evolution appears in this: the former is a connected, historic sequence of forms, the latter a sequence of stages exemplified by forms of a given order of development. In general evolutionary classification, any representative of a given cultural stage is inherently as good as any other, whether the representative be contemporaneous and ethnographic or only archaeological. The assertion is strengthened very much by the knowledge that there is a generic relation between the technical subsystem of a culture and the social and philosophical subsystems, so that a contemporaneous primitive culture with a given technology is equivalent, for general purposes, to certain extinct ones known only by the remains of a similar technology.

The *unit* of general evolutionary taxonomy, it should be noted, is a cultural system proper, that is, the cultural organization of a sociopolitical entity. A *level* of general development is a class of cultures of a given order. But what are the criteria for placing particular cultures in such classes, for deciding which is higher and which lower?

In culture, as in life, thermodynamic accomplishment is fundamental to progress, and therefore would appear useful as a criterion of emergent development. It is well known that revolutionary all-round advance occurs when and where new sources of energy are tapped, or major technological improvements are applied to already available sources. But here we enter a caveat similar to that brought up in connection with the thermodynamic development of life: general progress is not to be equated with thermodynamic *efficiency*.

Technological innovation can raise efficiency, i.e., increase the amount of energy captured per unit of human energy expended, yet still not stimulate the progressive development of a culture. Whether or not, or to what extent, a gain in productive efficiency is actually employed in the build-up and maintenance of higher organization depends on local selective circumstances. An increase in efficiency may not be directed toward any advance whatsoever if the existing adaptation cannot accommodate it or the selective pressures remain insufficient to induce it. A people may adopt a technological innovation that theoretically might double output, but instead, they only work half as long (twice as efficiently) as they used to. Such, indeed, is a common outcome of the imposition, however "well-meaning," of Western technology the world over. Or, as Harris (1959) has pointed out, a gain in efficiency can as well be put into increasing population as into more goods and services, means of communication, new political systems, or the promulgation of transcendental philosophies, and so forth. A continuation on this course will eventually lead to an expansion of population beyond available social means of organizing it. In an open environment the society will fission into two or more societies, each at a relatively low level of cultural organization, rather than producing one cultural system of a high order of development. Progress is not the inevitable outcome of efficiency.

It seems to us that progress is the total transformation of energy involved in the creation and perpetuation of a cultural organization. A culture harnesses and delivers energy; it extracts energy from nature and transforms it into people, material goods, and work, into political systems and the generation of ideas, into social customs and into adherence to them. The total energy so transformed from the free to the cultural state, in combination perhaps with the degree to which it is raised in the transformation (the loss in entropy), may represent a culture's general standing, a measure of its achievement.

The reader will surmise from the qualified phraseology that we are once more on uncertain ground. It is hardly consolation that we share this unenviable position with our colleagues; it does not appear that any satisfactory and usable method of quantifying the thermodynamic achievements of different cultures has been developed—or even that, with a few exceptions, anyone is very much concerned. Perhaps a start can be made by estimating the total mechanical energy delivered per year by a society. Among primitives, where human beings are usually the sole form of mechanical energy, the calculation would be relatively simple: population size multiplied by average manpower (in energy units) over the year. In societies using nonhuman mechanical energy as well as human, the two are added together—statistics of the amount of nonhuman mechanical energy of many modern societies are available.

Although there is a lack, for the moment, of ready estimations of cultural progress in energy terms, the attempt to measure general standing need by no means be abandoned. There are good structural criteria. As in life, thermodynamic achievement has its organizational counterpart, higher levels of integration. Cultures that transform more energy have more parts and subsystems, more specialization of parts, and more effective means of integration of the whole. Organizational symptoms of general progress include the proliferation of material elements, geometric increase in the division of labor, multiplication of social groups and subgroups, and the emergence of special means of integration: political, such as chieftainship and the state, and philosophical, such as universal ethical religions and science. Long ago, Spencer described all this in painstaking, if not always accurate, detail. Although many social scientists deny that the idea of "progress" is applicable to culture, how can it be denied in the terms we have just stated it? As Greenberg remarks—despite the fact that he rejects the term "progress," after having defined it morally—a theory

> . . . which regarded all species as interconnected but which posited some mammalian form as the primeval ancestral type, whence descended in one line all the other vertebrates, in another the ancestor of all non-vertebrate phyla, with Protozoa first appearing in a very recent period, would not be adjudged a representative evolutionary theory. (1957:58–59.)

Similarly, culture has not fallen from evolutionary heights; it has risen to them.

The social subsystem of cultures is especially illustrative of progress in organization, and it is often used to ascertain general evolutionary standing. The traditional and fundamental division of culture into two great stages, primitive and civilized, is usually recognized as a social distinction: the emergence of a special means of integration, the state, separates civilization from primitive society organized by kinship. Within the levels *societas* and *civitas*, moreover, further stages can be discriminated on criteria of social segmentation and integration. On the primitive level, the unsegmented (except for families) and chiefless *bands* are least advanced—and characteristically, preagricultural. More highly developed are agricultural and pastoral tribes segmented into clans, lineages, and the like, although lacking strong chiefs. Higher than such egalitarian *tribes*, and based on greater productivity, are *chiefdoms* with internal status differentiation and developed chieftainship. Similarly, within the level of civilization we can distinguish the *archaic* form—characteristically ethnically diverse and lacking firm integration of the rural, peasant sector—from the more highly developed, more territorially and culturally integrated *nation state*, with its industrial technology.

General progress can also be viewed as improvement in "all-round adaptability." Higher cultural forms tend to dominate and replace lower, and the range of dominance is proportionate to the degree of progress. So modern national culture tends to spread around the globe, before our eyes replacing, transforming, and extinguishing representatives of millennia-old stages of evolution, while archaic civilization, now also falling before this advance, even in its day was confined to certain sectors of certain of the continents. The dominance power of higher cultural forms is a consequence of their ability to exploit greater ranges of energy resources more effectively than lower forms. Higher forms are again relatively "free from environmental control," i.e., they adapt to greater environmental variety than lower forms. . . .

General cultural evolution, to summarize, is passage from less to greater energy transformation, lower to higher levels of integration, and less to greater all-round adaptability. Specific evolution is the phylogenetic, ramifying, historic passage of culture along its many lines, the adaptive modification of particular cultures.

Some Implications

We should now like to relate the distinction drawn between specific and general evolution to current scholarly views of evolution, particularly to anthropological views.

But first a word about terms: "specific evolution" and "general evolution" are probably not the best possible labels for the adaptive and over-all progressive aspects of the evolutionary process. Friends and colleagues have suggested others: "lineal," "adaptive," "special," "particular," and "divergent" have been offered for "specific"; "emergent," "progressive," or "universal" for "general."

All the alternatives we judge to be somewhat inadequate, for one reason or another, although some were occasionally used in the preceding discussion. In a recent publication Greenberg (1959) distinguishes "transformism" from "advance" in evolution, which seems to correspond to our "specific" and "general." The reader is free to adopt any of the alternatives. The terms are not the issue; the issue is empirical realities. . . .

The traditional evolutionary concerns of anthropology have been precisely the reverse of those in biology, for until recently general evolution rather than specific has occupied first place in evolutionary anthropology. The way the great nineteenth-century cultural evolutionists, Tylor, Spencer, and Morgan, classified and considered cultures indicates that they were principally interested in general progress. Their procedure was to determine *stages* of development and to exemplify them with contemporaneous cultures.

For this reason alone it would be difficult to support the charge that evolutionary theory was grafted wholesale from biology onto culture, or that it was only "biological analogy." It also seems grossly inaccurate, however frequently it is done, to characterize the perspective of the anthropological pioneers as "unilinear," which is the idea that every culture in particular goes through the same general stages. The locus of unilinear evolutionism is not in anthropology, but, as we have seen with respect to the problem of feudalism, in "crude Marxism" (this phrase is a kind of current redundancy) and Bourgeois History . . . strange bedfellows. Considering only their procedures and obvious objectives—and not what they or others have said *ad hoc* about these—the nineteenth-century anthropological evolutionists should be acquitted of the unilinear charge, once and for all. Because the specific aspect of evolution was not given much attention does not warrant a criticism which says, in effect, that it was lumped with the general, thus yielding unilinear evolution. The error, if any, was omission not commission. And even so, we recall Spencer's words, "Like other kinds of progress, social progress is *not linear* but divergent and re-divergent" (our emphasis).

But they are dead, and it probably doesn't matter too much if exonerated or not. What progress has evolutionary anthropology made since the nineteenth century? The current revival of evolutionism in anthropology is, with the exception of White, decisively specifically oriented. By and large, it is particularistic and historically oriented, as anthropology in general has been throughout our century. Steward's "multilinear evolution" is now widely accepted and respectable. This is a gain, for as a platform, multilinear evolution conceivably embraces all of the specific trends in cultural evolution. But at what cost shall we secure this gain? In practice, Steward confines his attention to "regularities," which is to say, parallel developments in unrelated cultural lines, and at the same time belabors any more general evolutionary concerns. If anthropology continues on this theoretical course, then it can only fail to cope with the larger problem of the origin of diversity, not to mention the whole field of general evolution. Thus the total effect of widespread approval of Steward's position will mean undue limitation, a continuation of the reaction against the nineteenth century.

The historical orientation of twentieth-century American anthropology and of much of its current evolutionism has occasioned a rich controversy in recent years about the relation between "history" and "evolution." A set of interconnected issues are involved: (1) Is evolution to be concerned with historical developments in particular cultures or not? (2) Is environment a relevant, variable factor in the explanation of evolution or an irrelevant, constant factor? (3) Is evolution "history," or are these different real processes? The chief antagonists in the controversy are Kroeber (1946), Steward (1953; 1955), and White (1945; 1949; 1959a).

White distinguishes history as unique sequences of events located in time and space, whereas evolution is the progression of forms not considered in reference to specific times and places:

In the evolutionist process we are not concerned with unique events, fixed in time and place, but with a class of events without reference to specific times and places . . . The historian—devotes himself to a specific sequence of particular events; the evolutionist, to a sequence of events as a general process of transformation. (1945:238.)

Since evolution does not deal with specifics, since it is concerned with classes of cultural forms, culture is considered as a whole and particular environments are not relevant, in White's view:

The functioning of any particular culture will of course be conditioned by local environmental conditions. But in a consideration of culture as a whole, we may average all environments together to form a constant factor which may be excluded from our formula of cultural development. (1949:368.)

Not many accept White's attempt to distinguish history from evolution; many profess not to understand it. Perhaps that is why White is labelled a "neoevolutionary," although, as he says, all he states is the general evolutionary perspective of the nineteenth century.

Kroeber, in an exchange with White, insists that evolution is primarily the historic process, and that historians "do" evolution (1946). Murdock goes Kroeber one better: "The only cultural processes are historical," he writes (1949:116n). And ten years later, ". . . evolution consists of real events, not of abstractions from events, so that evolutionary development is historical in the strictest and most literal sense" (1959:129). Likewise, for Steward (multilinear) evolution is concerned with, "significant parallels in culture *history* . . . inevitably concerned with historical reconstruction" (1955:28, 18; emphasis ours). In turn, parallel development is parallel adaptation to environment; environmental considerations are indispensable (Steward 1955).

The distinction between general and specific evolution is relevant to—and we think, resolves—the debate. The historic development of particular cultural forms is specific evolution, phylogenetic transformation through adaptation. Environment, both natural and superorganic, is obviously essential to the understanding of such processes. The progression of classes of forms, or in other words, the succession of culture through stages of overall progress, is general evolution. This process is neither phylogenetic nor as such adaptive; consequently, environment is "constant," or better, irrelevant. That process which Kroeber labels "history," Steward, "multilinear evolution," and Murdock, "evolution," is the specific aspect of the grand evolutionary movement; that which White names "evolution" is the general aspect. Adopting the grand-movement perspective suggested here, evolution is in one respect "history," but in another not; in one aspect it involves particular events, but in another classes thereof; in one respect environment is relevant, but in another it is to be excluded from consideration. Each of the participants in the controversy is in one respect "right" but in another "wrong"—from our standpoint.

And, if we may be permitted to press home the implications, it seems to us then that evolutionism is the central, inclusive, organizing outlook of anthropology, comparable in its theoretical power to evolutionism in biology. ". . . the great principle that every scholar must lay firm hold of . . ."

SECTION INTRODUCTION REFERENCES* AND SUGGESTIONS FOR FURTHER STUDY

Adams, Robert M., 1966, *The Evolution of Urban Society: Early Mesopotamia and Prehispanic Mexico.* Chicago: Aldine.
Bee, Robert L., 1974, *Patterns and Processes: An Introduction to Anthropological Strategies for the Study of Sociocultural Change.* New York: Free Press.
Carneiro, Robert L., 1968, "Ascertaining, Testing, and Interpreting Sequences of Cultural Development. *Southwestern Journal of Anthropology* 24:354–374.
———, 1973, "The Four Faces of Evolution: Unilinear, Universal, Multilinear, and Differential." In J. J. Honigmann, ed., *Handbook of Social and Cultural Anthropology.* Chicago: Rand McNally, pp. 89–110.
Childe, V. Gordon, 1951, *Man Makes Himself.* New York: The New American Library of World Literature, Inc. (First published in 1936).
———, 1951, *Social Evolution.* London: Watts & Co.
———, 1954, *What Happened in History.* Baltimore: Penguin (First published in 1946).
Cottrell, William Frederick, 1955, *Energy and Society: The Relation between Energy, Social Change, and Economic Development.* New York: McGraw-Hill.
Durkheim, Emile, 1964, *Division of Labor in Society* (Trans. by G. Simpson.) New York: Free Press (First published in 1893).
Eisenstadt, S. N., 1968, "Social Evolution." *International Encyclopedia of the Social Sciences* 5:228–234.
Engels, Friedrich, 1972, *The Origin of the Family, Private Property, and the State, in the Light of the Researches of Lewis H. Morgan.* New York: International Publishers (First published in 1884).
Erasmus, C. J., 1969, "Explanation and Reconstruction in Cultural Evolutionism." *Sociologus* 19:20–38.
Fried, Morton H., 1967, *The Evolution of Political Society.* New York: Random House.
Goldschmidt, Walter, 1959, *Man's Way: A Preface to the Understanding of Human Society.* New York: Holt, Rinehart and Winston.
Hallowell, A. Irving, 1963, "Personality, Culture and Society in Behavioral Evolution." In

S. Koch, ed., *Psychology: A Study of Science*, Vol. 6. New York: McGraw-Hill, pp. 429–509.
Hockett, Charles F., and Robert Ascher, 1964, "The Human Revolution." *Current Anthropology* 5:135–168.
*Hoebel, E. Adamson, 1960, "William Robertson: An 18th Century Anthropologist-Historian." *American Anthropologist* 62:648–655.
Keller, Albert G., 1931, *Societal Evolution*, rev. ed. New York: Macmillan.
Huxley, Julian, 1942, "Evolutionary Progress." In *Evolution: The Modern Synthesis*. New York: Harper & Row, pp. 556–578.
Kluckhohn, Clyde, 1959, "The Role of Evolutionary Thought in Anthropology." In *Evolution and Anthropology*. Washington, D.C.: The Anthropological Society of Washington, pp. 147–157.
Lenski, Gerhard, 1970, *Human Societies: A Macrolevel Introduction to Sociology*. New York: McGraw-Hill.
Lewontin, R. C., 1968, "The Concept of Evolution." *International Encyclopedia of the Social Sciences* 5:202–210.
Lomax, Alan, and Norman Berkowitz, 1972, "The Evolutionary Taxonomy of Culture." *Science* 177:228–239.
Lowie, Robert, 1946, "Professor White and 'Anti-Evolutionist' Schools." *Southwestern Journal of Anthropology* 2:240–241.
*Malthus, Thomas R., 1817, *An Essay on the Principle of Population*. London: Murray.
Morgan, Lewis H., 1877, *Ancient Society*. New York: World.
Murdock, George P., 1949, *Social Structure*. New York: Macmillan.
———, 1959, "Evolution in Social Organization." In *Evolution and Anthropology*. Washington, D.C.: The Anthropological Society of Washington, pp. 126–143.
*Ostwald, Wilhelm, 1907, "The Modern Theory of Energetics." *The Monist* 17:481–515.
*———, 1915, "The System of the Sciences." *Rice Institute Pamphlet* 2(3):101–190.
Parsons, Talcott, 1964, "Evolutionary Universals in Society." *American Sociological Review* 29:339–357.
———, 1971, *The System of Modern Societies*. Englewood Cliffs, N.J.: Prentice-Hall.
Peel, J. D. Y., 1969, "Spencer and the Neo-Evolutionists." *Sociology* 3:173–191.
Sahlins, Marshall D., and Elman R. Service, eds., 1960, *Evolution and Culture*. Ann Arbor, Mich.: University of Michigan Press.
Sanders, William T., and Barbara J. Price, 1968, *Mesoamerica: The Evolution of a Civilization*. New York: Random House.
Segraves, B. Abbott, 1974, "Ecological Generalization and Structural Transformation of Sociocultural Systems." *American Anthropologist* 76:530–552.
Service, Elman R., 1962, *Primitive Social Organization: An Evolutionary Perspective*. New York Random House.
———, 1968, "Cultural Evolution." *International Encyclopedia of the Social Sciences* 5:221–228.
———, 1971, *Cultural Evolutionism: Theory in Practice*. New York: Holt, Rinehart and Winston.
*Steward, Julian H., 1955, *Theory of Culture Change: The Methodology of Multilinear Evolution*. Urbana, Ill.: University of Illinois Press.
———, 1956, "Cultural Evolution." *Scientific American* 194:69–80.
Tax, Sol, ed., 1960, *The Evolution of Man: Mind, Culture, and Society*. Vol. 2 of *Evolution After Darwin*. Chicago: University of Chicago Press.

Tönnies, Ferdinand, 1940, *Gemeinschaft und Gesellschaft* (Trans. and ed. by C. P. Loomis as *Fundamental Concepts of Sociology*). New York: American Book Co. (First published in 1887).

Tylor, Edward B., 1865, *Researches into the Early History of Mankind and the Development of Civilization*. London: Murray.

———, 1958, *Primitive Culture*. New York: Harper Torchbooks (First published in 1871).

White, Leslie A., 1947, "Evolutionism in American Anthropology: A Rejoinder." *American Anthropologist* 49:400–411.

———, 1959, *The Evolution of Culture: The Development of Civilization to the Fall of Rome*. New York: McGraw-Hill.

———, 1959, "The Concept of Evolution in Cultural Anthropology." In *Evolution and Anthropology*. Washington, D.C.: The Anthropological Society of Washington, pp. 106–125.

———, 1969, *The Science of Culture: A Study of Man and Civilization*, rev. ed. New York: Farrar, Straus and Giroux.

section XI

Function in Culture

Assignment of the topic of function in culture to the end of our compilation of readings does not represent an evaluation of the subject as less worthy than subjects which precede it. If the meaning of the term "function" is understood to be relationships, it is probably the single idea about culture that has had the greatest importance and seen the most frequent use in the history of anthropology. Considering "function" in a narrower sense to mean functionalist studies in anthropology, we may say that during the past several decades "holistic" studies of this kind have probably been by far the most abundant.

In an unabridged dictionary, the link among the meanings of function is relationship. Functional relationships are often expressed or implied in anthropology, and elsewhere, by a group of other words that includes the terms correlations, congruences, co-variations, and physiology, and, in a negative sense, such terms as disorder, dysfunction, malfunction, incongruence, incompatibility, and, referring to the social order, Durkheim's term "anomie." Function is important to both evolutionists and functionalists, who share the view of culture as a system. The primary distinction between the two lines of scholarship is that evolutionists treat functional relations diachronically, seeking to formulate statements of sequential development, whereas the concern of functionalists is either synchronic, at a fixed point in time, or timeless, since the traditional goal has been to understand how the system under study operates.

Most of the writings in this book may be regarded as functionalist since they concern relationships within culture, between culture and the human organism, and between culture and the physical environment.

What anthropologists call *functionalism* and *structural-functionalism*, however, generally has a narrower meaning, referring to a large group of studies centering principally upon the entire social order or certain features of the social order and their relationships to other aspects or elements of culture.

Like all other points of view and avenues of study which this book discusses, functionalism has a substantial history. Its outstanding early leaders in the twentieth century were the sociologist Emile Durkheim, and the anthropologists A. R. Radcliffe-Brown and Bronislaw Malinowski, representative writings of all of whom are included among our selections. In the history of ethnological theory, these scholars stand out as leaders of a trend of development which, after a long period of heavy emphasis on descriptive and historic studies, once again brought interpretive theory back to respectability. Although the stated primary concern of Radcliffe-Brown and Malinowski was society rather than culture and, for Malinowski, also psychological aspects of human life, from the viewpoint of cultural anthropology both were students of culture. Our selections throughout this book include no additional anthropologists primarily identified as functionalists, although all may be said to concern themselves with functional aspects of culture. But note that our selections on functionalism proper are amplified beyond this section by the selections in Section IV and that the sociologist Talcott Parsons is preeminently a "functionalist."

The readings by Radcliffe-Brown and Malinowski may be considered "traditional functionalism," now regarded as somewhat old-fashioned but nevertheless relatively little changed by later functionalists. The excerpt by Norbeck following these readings, although centered upon the subject of religion, presents a general review and critique of functionalist assumptions and procedures. Some additional comments may be useful in amplification of this review.

The categories of British social anthropology, social anthropology, and functionalism are generally synonymous; all are described as functionalist. Functionalism has a strong grounding in sociology, which is reflected in a number of ways in its studies: As we have noted, study and interpretation characteristically focus on the social order; the system under study has most frequently been called a social system, and the term "culture" is little used. We think it useful to emphasize that the strong tendency in functionalist interpretations has been upon socially supportive rather than disruptive functions or relationships which are implicit or not obvious to the human actors involved. This emphasis is consistent with the initial assumption that the cultural or social system is functionally congruent, that each element contributes to the integration of the whole. From this viewpoint, the ideas of functionalism seem tautologous, as does the functionalist concept, discussed in the critique by Edward

Norbeck, that a system cannot exist without the necessary conditions for existence. Yet it seems wholly justifiable, as functionalists have done, to attempt to understand the operation of a system not previously understood. It is amply clear that functionalist study toward this goal has often been illuminating. Certain subjects of functionalist study—for example, interpretations of the functional significance of various rites of passage—have indeed been strangely troubled by excellence. They appear to be so well done that they may serve as blueprints for the interpretation of similar rites in other societies. As a result, studies of these subjects are seldom made today.

With reference to the future of anthropological studies, we shall state the opinion that function will doubtless continue to be the keynote. As our introductory comments to Section IV express, the views and procedures of both functionalism and evolutionism have long been held jointly without antagonism and this appears to be the progressive trend for the future. The final article by Leslie A. White, points out the ways in which functionalist, evolutionist, and historic studies complement each other in the study of man and culture.

35 ON THE CONCEPT OF FUNCTION IN SOCIAL SCIENCE

A. R. RADCLIFFE/BROWN

The concept of function applied to human societies is based on an analogy between social life and organic life. The recognition of the analogy and of some of its important implications is at least as old as Protagoras and Plato. In the nineteenth century the analogy, the concept of function, and the word itself appear frequently in social philosophy and sociology. So far as I know the first systematic formulation of the concept as applying to the strictly scientific study of society was that of Emile Durkheim in 1895.

Durkheim's definition is that the "function" of a social institution is the correspondence between it and the needs of the social organism. This definition requires some elaboration. In the first place, to avoid possible ambiguity and in particular the possibility of a teleological interpretation, I would like to substitute for the term "needs" the term "necessary conditions of existence," or, if the term "need" is used, it is to be understood only in this sense. It may here be noted, as a point to be returned to, that any attempt to apply this concept of function in social science involves the assumption that there *are* necessary conditions of existence for

Reproduced by permission of the American Anthropological Association from the *American Anthropologist*, vol. 37, no. 3, 1935.

human societies just as there are for animal organisms, and that they can be discovered by the proper kind of scientific enquiry.

For the further elucidation of the concept it is convenient to use the analogy between social life and organic life. Like all analogies it has to be used with care. An animal organism is an agglomeration of cells and interstitial fluids arranged in relation to one another not as an aggregate but as an integrated whole. For the bio-chemist, it is a complexly integrated system of complex molecules. The system of relations by which these units are related is the organic structure. As the terms are here used the organism *is not* itself the structure; it is a collection of units (cells or molecules) arranged in a structure, i.e., in a set of relations; the organism *has* a structure. Two mature animals of the same species and sex consist of similar units combined in a similar structure. The structure is thus to be defined as a set of relations between the entities. (The structure of a cell is in the same way a set of relations between complex molecules, and the structure of an atom is a set of relations between electrons and protons.) As long as it lives the organism preserves a certain continuity of structure although it does not preserve the complete identity of its constituent parts. It loses some of its constituent molecules by respiration or excretion; it takes in others by respiration and alimentary absorption. Over a period its constituent cells do not remain the same. But the structural arrangement of the constituent units does remain similar. The process by which this structural continuity of the organism is maintained is called life. The life-process consists of the activities and interactions of the constituent units of the organism, the cells, and the organs into which the cells are united.

As the word function is here being used the life of an organism is conceived as the *functioning* of its structure. It is through and by the continuity of the functioning that the continuity of the structure is preserved. If we consider any recurrent part of the life-process, such as respiration, digestion, etc., its *function* is the part it plays in, the contribution it makes to, the life of the organism as a whole. As the terms are here being used a cell or an organ has an *activity* and that activity has a *function*. It is true that we commonly speak of the secretion of gastric fluid as a "function" of the stomach. As the words are here used we should say that this is an "activity" of the stomach, the "function" of which is to change the proteins of food into a form in which these are absorbed and distributed by the blood to the tissues. We may note that the function of a recurrent physiological process is thus a correspondence between it and the needs (i.e., necessary conditions of existence) of the organism.

If we set out upon a systematic investigation of the nature of organisms and organic life there are three sets of problems presented to us. (There are, in addition, certain other sets of problems concerning aspects or characteristics of organ life with which we are not here concerned.) One is that of morphology—what kinds of organic structures are there, what similarities and variations do they show, and how can they be classified? Second are the problems of physiology—how, in general, do organic structures function, what, therefore, is the nature of the life-process? Third are the problems of development—how do new types of organisms come into existence?

To turn from organic life to social life, if we examine such a community as an African or Australian tribe we can recognize the existence of a social structure. Individual human beings, the essential units in this instance, are connected by a definite set of social relations into an integrated whole. The continuity of the social structure, like that of an organic structure, is not destroyed by changes in the units. Individuals may leave the society, by death or otherwise; others may enter it. The continuity of structure is maintained by the process of social life, which consists of the activities and interactions of the individual human beings and of the organized groups into which they are united. The social life of the community is here defined as the *functioning* of the social structure. The *function* of any recurrent activity, such as the punishment of a crime, or a funeral ceremony, is the part it plays in the social life as a whole and therefore the contribution it makes to the maintenance of the structural continuity.

The concept of function as here defined thus involves the notion of a *structure* consisting of a *set of relations* amongst *unit entities*, the *continuity* of the structure being maintained by a *life-process* made up of the *activities* of the constituent units.

If, with these concepts in mind, we set out on a systematic investigation of the nature of human society and of social life, we find presented to us three sets of problems. First, the problems of social morphology—what kinds of social structures are there, what are their similarities and differences, how are they to be classified? Second, the problems of social physiology—how do social structures function? Third, the problems of development—how do new types of social structure come into existence?

Two important points where the analogy between organism and society breaks down must be noted. In an animal organism it is possible to observe the organic structure to a large extent independently of its functioning. It is therefore possible to make a morphology which is independent of physiology. But in human society the social structure as a whole can only be *observed* in its functioning. Some of the features of social structure, such as the geographical distribution of individuals and groups can be directly observed, but most of the social relations which in their totality constitute the structure, such as relations of father and son, buyer and seller, ruler and subject, cannot be observed except in the social activities in which the relations are functioning. It follows that a social morphology cannot be established independently of a social physiology.

The second point is that an animal organism does not, in the course of its life, change its structural type. A pig does not become a hippopotamus. (The development of the animal from germination to maturity is not a change of type since the process in all its stages is typical for the species.) On the other hand a society in the course of its history can and does change its structural type without any breach of continuity.

By the definition here offered "function" is the contribution which a partial activity makes to the total activity of which it is a part. The function of a particular social usage is the contribution it makes to the total social life as the functioning of the total social system. Such a view implies that a social system (the total social structure of a society together with the totality of social usages, in which that structure appears and on which it depends for its continued existence) has a certain kind of unity, which we may speak of as a functional unity. We may define it as a condition in which all parts of the social system work together with a sufficient degree of harmony or internal consistency, i.e., without producing persistent conflicts which can neither be resolved nor regulated.

This idea of the functional unity of a social system is, of course, a hypothesis. But it is one which, to the functionalist, it seems worth while to test by systematic examination of the facts.

There is another aspect of functional theory that should be briefly mentioned. To return to the analogy of social life and organic life, we recognize that an organism may function more or less efficiently and so we set up a special science of pathology to deal with all phenomena of disfunction. We distinguish in an organism what we call health and disease. The Greeks of the fifth century B.C. thought that one might apply the same notion to society, to the city-state, distinguishing conditions of *eunomia*, good order, social health, from *dysnomia*, disorder, social ill-health. In the nineteenth century Durkheim, in his application of the notion of function, sought to lay the basis for a scientific social pathology, based on a morphology and a physiology. In his works, particularly those on suicide and on the division of labor, he attempted to find objective criteria by which to judge whether a given society at a given time is normal or pathological, eunomic or dysnomic. For example, he tried to show that the increase of the rate of suicide in many countries during part of the nineteenth century is symptomatic of a dysnomic or, in his terminology, anomic, social condition. Probably there is no sociologist who would hold that Durkheim really succeeded in establishing an objective basis for a science of social pathology.

In relation to organic structures we can find strictly objective criteria by which to distinguish disease from health, pathological from normal, for disease is that which either threatens the organism with death (the dissolution of its structure) or interferes with the activities which are characteristic of the organic type. Societies do not die in the same sense that animals die and therefore we cannot define dysnomia as that which leads, if unchecked, to the death of a society. Further a society differs from an organism in that it can change its structural type, or can be absorbed as an integral part of a larger society. Therefore we cannot define dysnomia as a disturbance of the usual activities of a social type (as Durkheim tried to do).

Let us return for a moment to the Greeks. They conceived the health of an organism and the eunomia of a society as being in each instance a condition of the harmonious working together of its parts. Now this, where society is concerned, is the same thing as what was considered above as the functional unity or inner consistency of a social system, and it is suggested that for the degree of functional unity of a particular society it may be possible to establish a purely objective criterion. Admittedly this cannot be done at present; but the science of human society is as yet in its extreme infancy. So that it may be that we should say that while an organism that is attacked by a virulent disease will react thereto, and, if its reaction fails, will die, a society that is thrown into a condition of functional disunity or inconsistency (for this we now provisionally identify with dysnomia) will not die, except in such comparatively rare instances as an Australian tribe overwhelmed by the white man's destructive force, but will continue to struggle toward some sort of eunomia, some kind of social health, and may, in the course of this, change its structural type. This process, it seems, the "functionalist" has ample opportunities of observing at the present day, in native peoples subjected to the domination of the civilized nations, and in those nations themselves.

Space will not allow a discussion here of another aspect of functional theory, viz., the question whether change of social type is or is not dependent on function i.e., on the laws of social physiology. My own view is that there is such a dependence and that its nature can be studied in the development of the legal and political institutions, the economic systems and the religions of Europe through the last twenty-five centuries. For the preliterate societies with which anthropology is concerned it is not possible to study the details of long processes of change of type. The one kind of change which the anthropologist can observe is the disintegration of social structures. Yet even here we can observe and compare spontaneous movements towards reintegration. We have, for instance, in Africa, in Oceania, and in America the appearance of new religions which can be interpreted on a functional hypothesis as attempts to relieve a condition of social dysnomia produced by the rapid modifications of the social life through contact with white civilization.

The concept of function as defined above constitutes a "working hypothesis" by which a number of problems are formulated for investigation. No scientific enquiry is possible without some such formulation of working hypotheses. Two remarks are necessary here. One is that the hypothesis does not require the dogmatic assertion that everything in the life of every community has a function. It only requires the assumption that it may have one, and that we are justified in seeking to discover it. The second is that what appears to be the same social usage in two societies may have different functions in the two. Thus the practice of celibacy in the Roman Catholic Church of to-day has very different functions from those of celibacy in the early Christian church. In other words, in order to define a social usage, and therefore in order to make valid comparisons between the usages of different peoples or periods it is necessary to consider not merely the form of the usage but also its function. On this basis, for example, belief in a Supreme Being in a simple society is something different from such a belief in a modern civilized community.

The acceptance of the functional hypothesis or point of view outlined above results in the recognition of a vast number of problems for the solution of which there are required wide comparative studies of societies of many diverse types and also intensive studies of as many single societies as possible. In field studies of the simpler peoples it leads, first of all, to a direct study of the social life of the community as the functioning of a social structure, and of this there are several examples in recent literature. Since the function of a social activity is to be found by examining its effects upon individuals, these are studied, either in the average individual or in both average and exceptional individuals. Further the hypothesis leads to attempts to investigate directly the functional consistency or unity of a social system and to determine as far as possible in each instance the nature of that unity. Such field studies will obviously be different in many ways from studies carried out from other points of view, e.g., the ethnological point of view that lays emphasis on diffusion. We do not have to say that one point of view is better than another, but only that they are different, and any particular piece of work should be judged in reference to what it aims to do. . . .

There is not, and cannot be, any conflict between the functional hypothesis and the view that any culture, any social system, is the end-result of a unique series of historical accidents. The process of development of the race-horse from its five-toed ancestor was a unique series of historical accidents. This does not conflict with the view of the physiologist that the horse of to-day and all the antecedent forms conform or conformed to physiological laws, i.e., to the necessary conditions of organic existence. Palaeontology and physiology are not in conflict. One "explanation" of the race-horse is to be found in its history—how it came to be just what it is and where it is. Another and entirely independent "explanation" is to show how the horse is a special exemplification of physiological laws. Similarly one "explanation" of a social system will be its history, where we know it—the detailed account of how it came to be what it is and where it is. Another "explanation" of the same system is obtained by showing (as the functionalist attempts to do) that it is a special exemplification of laws of social physiology or social functioning. The two kinds of explanation do not conflict, but supplement one another.

36 THE GROUP AND THE INDIVIDUAL IN FUNCTIONAL ANALYSIS
BRONISLAW MALINOWSKI

Functionalism differs from other sociological theories more definitely, perhaps, in its conception and definition of the individual than in any other respect.[1] The functionalist includes in his analysis not merely the emotional as well as the intellectual side of mental processes, but also insists that man in his full biological reality has to be drawn into our analysis of culture. The bodily needs and environmental influences, and the cultural reactions to them, have thus to be studied side by side. . . .

In this brief preamble we have already insisted that the individual must be studied as a biological reality. We have indicated that the physical world must be part of our analysis, both as the natural milieu and as the body of tools and commodities produced by man. We have pointed out that individuals never cope with, or move within, their environment in isolation, but in organized groups, and that organization is expressed in traditional charters, which are symbolic in essence.

The Individual Organism under Conditions of Culture

Taking man as a biological entity it is clear that certain minima of conditions can be laid down which are indispensable to the personal welfare of the individual and to the continuation of the group. All human beings have to be nourished, they have to reproduce, and they require the maintenance of certain physical conditions: ventilation, temperature within a definite range, a sheltered and dry place to rest, and safety from the hostile forces of nature, of animals, and of man. The physiological working of each individual organism implies the intake of food and of oxygen, occasional movement, and relaxation in sleep and recreation. The process of growth in man necessitates protection and guidance in its early stages and, later on, specific training.

Reprinted by permission of the University of Chicago Press from Bronislaw Malinowski, "The Group and the Individual in Functional Analysis," *American Journal of Sociology* 44 (1939): 938–947.

[1] When I speak of "functionalism" here I mean the brand which I have produced and am cultivating myself. My friend, Professor R. H. Lowie of Berkeley, has in his last book, *The History of Ethnological Theory* (1937), introduced the distinction between "pure" and "tempered" functionalism—my brand being the pure one. Usually Professor Radcliffe-Brown's name is linked with mine as a representative of the functional school. Here the distinction between "plain" and "hyphenated" functionalism might be introduced. Professor Lowie has, in my opinion, completely misunderstood the essence of "pure" functionalism. The substance of this article may serve as a corrective. Professor Radcliffe-Brown is, as far as I can see, still developing and deepening the views of the French sociological school. He thus has to neglect the individual and disregard biology. In this article functionalism "plain and pure" will be briefly outlined with special reference to the problem of the group and the individual.

We have listed here some of the essential conditions to which cultural activity, whether individual or collective, has instrumentally to conform. It is well to recall that these are only minimum conditions—the very manner in which they are satisfied in culture imposes certain additional requirements. These constitute new needs, which in turn have to be satisfied. The primary—that is, the biological—wants of the human organism are not satisfied naturally by direct contact of the individual organism with the physical environment. Not only does the individual depend on the group in whatever he achieves and whatever he obtains, but the group and all its individual members depend on the development of a material outfit, which in its essence is an addition to the human anatomy, and which entails corresponding modifications of human physiology.

In order to present our argument in a synoptic manner, let us concisely list in Column A of Table 36–1 the basic needs of the individual. Thus "Nutrition (metabolism)" indicates not only the need for a supply of food and of oxygen, but also the conditions under which food can be prepared, eaten, digested, and the sanitary arrangements which this implies. "Reproduction" obviously means that the sexual urges of man and woman have to be satisfied, and the continuity of the group maintained. The entry "Bodily comforts" indicates that the human organism can be active and effective only within certain ranges of temperature; that it must be sheltered from dampness and drafts; that it must be given opportunities for rest and sleep. "Safety" again refers to all the dangers lurking in the natural environment, both for civilized and primitive: earthquakes and tidal waves, snowstorms and excessive insolation; it also indicates the need of protection from dangerous animals and human foes. "Relaxation" implies the need of the human organism for a rhythm of work by day and sleep at night, of intensive bodily exercise and rest, of seasons of recreation alternating with periods of practical activity. The entry "Movement" declares that human beings must have regular exercise of muscles and nervous system. "Growth" indicates the fact that the development of the human organism is culturally directed and redefined from infancy into ripe age.

It is clear that the understanding of any one of these entries of Column A brings us down immediately to the analysis of the individual organism. We see that any lack of satisfaction in any one of the basic needs must necessarily imply at least temporary maladjustment. In more pronounced forms, nonsatisfaction entails ill-health and decay through malnutrition, exposure to heat or cold, to sun or moisture; or destruction by natural forces, animals, or man. Psychologically the basic needs are expressed in drives, desires, or emotions, which move the organism to the satisfaction of each need through systems or linked reflexes.

The science of culture, however, is concerned not with the raw material of anatomical and physiological endowment in the individual, but with the manner in which this endowment is modified by social influences. When we inquire how the bodily needs are satisfied under conditions of culture, we find the systems of direct response to bodily needs which are listed in Column B. And here we can see at once the complete dependence of the individual upon the group: each of these cultural responses is dependent upon organized collective activities, which are carried on

Table 36–1 SYNOPTIC SURVEY OF BIOLOGICAL AND DERIVED NEEDS AND THEIR SATISFACTION IN CULTURE

A	B	C	D	E	F
Basic Needs (Individual)	Direct Responses (Organized, i.e., Collective)	Instrumental Needs	Responses to Instrumental Needs	Symbolic and Integrative Needs	Systems of Thought and Faith
Nutrition (metabolism)	Commissariat	Renewal of cultural apparatus	Economics	Transmission of experience by means of precise, consistent principles	Knowledge
Reproduction	Marriage and family				
Bodily comforts	Domicile and dress	Charters of behavior and their sanctions	Social control		
Safety	Protection and defense			Means of intellectual, emotional, and pragmatic control of destiny and chance	Magic Religion
Relaxation	Systems of play and repose	Renewal of personnel	Education		
Movement	Set activities and systems of communication				
Growth	Training and apprenticeship	Organization of force and compulsion	Political organization	Communal rhythm of recreation, exercise, and rest	Art Sports Games Ceremonial

according to a traditional scheme, and in which human beings not merely co-operate with one another but continue the achievements, inventions, devices, and theories inherited from previous generations. . . .

The Instrumental Imperatives of Culture

In glancing at our chart and comparing Columns A and B, we recognize that the first represents the biological needs of the individual organism which must be satisfied in every culture. Column B describes briefly the cultural responses to each of these needs. Culture thus appears first and foremost as a vast instrumental reality—the body of implements and commodities, charters of social organization, ideas and customs, beliefs and values—all of which allow man to satisfy his biological requirements through co-operation and within an environment refashioned and readjusted. The human organism, however, itself becomes modified in the process and readjusted to the type of situation provided by culture. In this sense culture is also a vast conditioning apparatus, which through training, the imparting of skills, the teaching of morals, and the development of tastes amalgamates the raw material of human physiology and anatomy with external elements, and through this supplements the bodily equipment and conditions the physiological processes. Culture thus produces individuals whose behavior cannot be understood by the study of anatomy and physiology alone, but has to be studied through the analysis of cultural determinism—that is, the processes of conditioning and molding. At the same time we see that from the very outset the existence of groups—that is, of individuals organized for co-operation and cultural give and take—is made indispensable by culture.

37 THE ROLE OF RELIGION: INTRODUCTION
EDWARD NORBECK

Out of a diverse background in which W. Robertson Smith, Durkheim, Malinowski, and Radcliffe-Brown stand out prominently has emerged a body of scholarly studies called "functionalist," which center upon the role of religion with reference to society and the individual, and the interrelationships between religion and other parts of culture. Functionalism has been the dominant theoretical orientation in modern analytical studies of religion among both anthropologists and sociologists. (Sociology has, as a matter of fact, made by far the greater contribution to the development of functionalist theory, and there is little beyond some attention to psychological aspects to distinguish the functionalism of anthropologists from sociological analysis.) As a preface to the chapters which follow, it is useful to know something of the basic assumptions and terminology of the studies based on these theoretical foundations.

Fundamental is the view of culture (or society, if one leans toward sociology) as a whole composed of interacting components. This system has a structure or

Reprinted by permission of the author from Edward Norbeck, *Religion in Primitive Society*, 1961, Harper & Row.

formal arrangement of its parts, and a set of relationships or interactions among these parts. As is customary in theories which involve the idea of systems, a tendency toward equilibrium or integration of the parts is generally assumed. Each part is held to operate toward the maintenance of the whole or to be functionally compatible with other parts. Change in any important aspect implies change in others, to bring the system back into equilibrium or integration. Perhaps in part because no whole societies have been found which lacked religion, theorizing along these lines has often included the implicit or explicit assumption that religion is an indispensable part of culture.

Within this general framework, scholars have had a variety of differing theoretical orientations and lines of emphasis, and their interpretations have followed several paths. Interests have generally been weighted toward the group rather than the individual and have relied heavily upon sociological theory. Especially as followed by Malinowski and his students, functionalism has also made use of psychological concepts in relating religion to the individual. The functions of religion may then be expressed as the contributions it makes toward the integration or maintenance of either the society or the individual. Malinowski and other scholars have hypothesized certain "basic needs" of the individual and society; and the function of religion or any other item of culture is then the part they play in filling these needs.

A few scholars have held that every element of culture is indispensable and serves a positive role in meeting individual and societal "needs." Some have observed that religion as well as other traits of culture may serve as disruptive or disintegrative forces. Very commonly the view has been that although religion may contribute toward societal or individual breakdown, its positive aspects outweigh these negative or disruptive effects, for, in order to survive, every society must have functional consistency or compatible enmeshing of its institutions, and the needs of individuals must also be met. When serious incompatibility arises, change leading to consistency must follow to prevent social disintegration or psychological breakdown of the individual.

Most studies have stressed the function of ritual and belief in supporting social structure and institutionalized customs—the family and other social units, the scheme of social stratification, moral or ethical codes, institutions such as marriage, and political and economic systems. By symbolically expressing customs and social relationships and placing upon them a stamp of sacred approval, ritual and belief are held to fortify the individual element expressed and also the whole. Interpretations have also commonly emphasized the role of group ceremonies in promoting social cohesion by jointly expressing and thereby reinforcing or teaching the values of the society. Group participation in any kind of activity presumably intensifies social cohesion, but religious rites are held to be particularly effective because of the formal seal of sanctification which they give to the cultural norms they express. As Radcliffe-Brown has stated this view, society depends for its existence upon common social sentiments, and ritual acts are symbolic expressions of these sentiments which reaffirm them and maintain their intensity.

A four-fold scheme of classification of types of functions has emerged in these analyses of the role of religion with reference to society and the individual. A distinction is made between positive functions, the contributions toward maintenance and support of society or the individual, and negative functions, the contributions toward disruption or disintegration. As we have implied, a distinction is also made between manifest functions, the purposes of religious acts as they exist in the thoughts of the actors, and implicit functions, the effects or consequences of the acts that are generally unclear or unknown to the members of society. The distinction between manifest and implicit functions may be made clear by a brief illustration. The expressed purpose of a rite may be to bring rain. The participants and observers may be well aware that participation in ceremonial serves such secondary purposes as providing entertainment and, perhaps, an opportunity to gain prestige by displaying wealth or standing out in some other way. They are much less likely to be aware that performance of the ritual gives them psychological assurance and promotes societal unity through joint action and common aims, effects which, following the four-fold terminology, are called positive implicit functions.

Many criticisms and doubts may be expressed about interpretations resting on the theoretical foundations as outlined above. Little agreement has been reached on hypothesized societal or individual needs, and it is tautologous to state that unless basic requirements for group or individual survival are met no society or individual can survive. Verification of the idea that religion is necessary for society to continue can hardly be made in any conclusive way. It would depend upon observation of societies entirely lacking religion, and no such society has been known. Moreover, existence of a trait that is seen to have functional significance does not mean that the trait is indispensable. An epidemic which carries off a large part of a society or a plague of locusts that causes crop failure and famine may be seen as serving the positive roles of uniting the people by mobilizing them to joint effort against a common enemy and of contributing to their economy through such things as providing employment for undertakers and stimulating the sale of mourning clothes. Crime may be looked upon as supporting society by providing a livelihood for law enforcement officers and the numerous specialists required to feed, house, clothe, and attempt to rehabilitate criminals. Disease, locusts, and crime are, however, indispensable to society only in the sense that cultural and social conditions would not be precisely the same if they did not exist. An additional critical comment is implied here, that functionalism of this persuasion refers to static conditions and ignores change. At its worst, this theorizing seems to say only that in order for society or culture to remain precisely as they are, they must not change.

All anthropologists do not, of course, think that religion is indispensable, and functionalist theory has been accommodated to embrace cultural change. Some scholars express the view that a "functional substitute," generally unidentified, may serve in the place of religion, and the idea of societal needs is not prominent today.

Many studies have avoided the question of societal or individual needs, but they still present us with the problems of determining the validity of the evaluations they make of the functions of religion. This is perhaps inevitable since the idea of positive and negative functions brings us within or dangerously close to the boundaries of value judgment. Using the same logic in analysis, different scholars may evaluate the effects they deduce so that they differ or even oppose each other. Any established belief or custom, for example, is negative in the sense that it inhibits acceptance of other beliefs or customs which might better foster societal unity or individual well-being. Final judgment of its positive or negative value is then difficult to make. Merton has pointed out that Marxists have labeled religion (i.e., Christianity) an opiate for the masses, making them content with their lot, whereas others see only its positive aspects in supporting the social *status quo*. The societally supportive and unifying effects of religion are, of course, most easily and satisfactorily deduced for small societies holding ritual in which all members participate. In large and socially segmented tribes, ceremonies which "rehearse the social order" may be seen as divisive of the whole because clan and other group social distinctions are preserved in them, or, dependent upon the interpreter's evaluation, they may be regarded as integrative of the whole for quite the same reason.

A trend of interpretation less prominent than those we have discussed but growing in recent years, has been to explain some forms of religious behavior as symbolic expressions of tensions arising from social or cultural sources. Making use of psychological concepts, these studies see religious acts as compensating for frustrations and dissatisfactions and providing channels for venting hostility which must otherwise be repressed. Ceremonial acts which seem to depart sharply from the norms of the society and have therefore resisted explanation along other avenues have often been approached in this way. Analysis of this kind has been used particularly in interpreting antisocial acts such as witchcraft, trying to account for its existence and for the variations of form it takes in different societies, and seeking in social structure for conflicts which give rise to tensions released either by acts or accusations of witchcraft.

Interpretations relating religion to tensions are difficult or impossible to verify and they often seem conjectural, but we shall reserve discussion of them for separate treatment.

It is difficult to escape the impression that the premises have shaped the conclusions of many functionalist studies. Dedication to the idea that all elements of culture are vital to support society in smooth articulation makes it imperative to see integrative functions, and it is no surprise that scholars have tended to see chiefly the positive roles of religion. Some scholars, following Durkheim, have carried the argument of the integrative effect of ritual into a full circle: joint participation in ceremonies promotes social unity, and the ceremonies come into existence because social life emotionally compels man to conduct them.

The accusation of tautology might also be made of the much-used hypothesis holding that communal rites which rehearse the social hierarchy by giving precedence to the actors in accordance with the established system of rank thereby reaffirm the social order. Since social relations in religious acts are unquestionably a part of social life, one might well ask if the observation of ritual is not simply one of the means by which the social order is deduced. He might also question whether this reasoning states anything more than that repetition reinforces habit. In response, the argument might be repeated that the religious cloak gives a special endorsement of sanctification to the social hierarchy and any other norm it expresses.

Another criticism that may be made of functionalism of the kind we have described is that much of it seems teleological. Explanations couched in terms of purpose have long been outlawed in the physical sciences. It strikes no modern, educated person as satisfactory to "explain" the existence of the sun by means of its roles in manufacturing chlorophyll, warming the earth, melting winter snows, and so on. Anthropological studies of religion relating it to society or the individual have indeed often seemed teleological although the word "purpose" has usually been expressed in terms of human or societal needs served by religion and disguised by such substitutes as "contribution," "significance," and "meaning." One reader will see teleology in these writings and another will not. It is probable that many scholars have unwittingly been trapped into seeming teleology by the nature of our language, which often conveys the idea of purpose when the speaker or writer has no such intent. Even when intentionally teleological, studies of this kind have value. Anthropocentric consideration of purpose in the physical sciences, such as the purpose of the planets or of the revolution of the earth, is both unprofitable and distracting and it has led to the formulation of no valid scientific theories. In human affairs, however, purpose is worthy of consideration. It is when we take teleological interpretations as explanations of causes and as unquestioned reasons for the existence of cultural phenomena that they are truly dangerous.

Despite the doubts and criticisms expressed here, it may fairly be said that functionalist studies have often presented reasonable interpretations of the role of religion in supporting the social scheme and other cultural norms. No study has been able to demonstrate a precise correspondence between the norms of a society and its religion, and there is probably never a point for point correspondence unless one follows the growing trend of defining religion as the "values" or "commitments" of a society. Religion and social norms often touch or coincide, but important values may find no religious expression. Systematic research comparing religion and value systems, it must be added, has hardly begun, and it is seriously inhibited by lack of effective techniques of defining and classifying "values." Scholarly formulations of important cultural norms seem, as a matter of fact, often to have proceeded by observation of what has been expressed or sanctioned by religious beliefs and acts. This course of action naturally follows from the view, advanced by Durkheim and held by many modern scholars, that the principal significance of religion derives from its role as a social device for expressing and reinforcing the values *most vital* to societal integration.

We must add that some of our criticisms at least partially dissolve when the results of functionalist studies are examined. In actuality, interpretations have not balanced positive and negative functions against each other or related them to the maintenance of society or the individual in any systematic, thoroughgoing way.

They have instead pointed out certain plausible effects of religious beliefs and practices, and they have often traced relationships between religion and other elements of culture in a useful and illuminating way.

Many recent analytic studies of somewhat different persuasion escape the charges of teleology and tautology. These are studies explicitly directed toward tracing interrelationships among elements of culture with no dedication to the idea that they are indispensable or to deducing societal or individual needs which they might serve. The usage of the term function in these studies is familiar to all fields of scientific research. As applied in the social sciences, it has sometimes been called the mathematically derived or quasimathematical usage of this word. In the sense used here, "function" means any quality, trait or fact so related to another that it is dependent upon and varies with the other. Functional relations or covariations of this kind have been sought between and among religion, economics, social and political organization, art, and other aspects of culture which scholars have chosen for attention.

38 HISTORY, EVOLUTIONISM, AND FUNCTIONALISM: THREE TYPES OF INTERPRETATION OF CULTURE

LESLIE A. WHITE

Summary

Contemporary anthropological theory has tended to recognize but two kinds of process in cultural phenomena, and, correspondingly, but two types of interpretation: a temporal process, the interpretation of which is called "history," and a non-temporal process, whose interpretation is termed "science." This view is a misleading and unfortunate one. First, it opposes "history" and "science," implying that a concern with chronological sequences of unique events is not science, whereas sciences such as astronomy, geology, and biology are interested in historic sequences as well as in other types of interpretation. History is one way of "sciencing." Secondly, the "history or science" view confuses the process which is history with the evolutionary process, or else conceals the evolutionary process entirely. Failure to distinguish and to recognize these two fundamentally different temporal processes is a major error. The elimination of the evolutionist point of view from anthropological theory is an expression of a reactionary anti-evolutionist philosophy which has flourished in certain schools of cultural anthropology in recent decades. The repudiation of evolutionism is an error of logical analysis, a blind spot in philosophy, and worst of all a great injury to anthropology as a science. It has

Reprinted from the *Southwestern Journal of Anthropology,* 1945, 1:221–248.

done much to emasculate cultural anthropology and to deprive it of its most valuable function: that of pointing out the course of cultural development in the past and its probable course in the future.

Logical analysis discloses three kinds of processes—temporal, temporal-formal, and formal-functional—on all levels of reality: physical, biological, and cultural. For each kind of process there is a corresponding type of interpretation: history, evolutionism, and functionalism. The *history* of science demonstrates that all sciences have cast their interpretations into these three forms. Prior to the reaction against the theory of evolution, cultural anthropology, too, employed all three types of interpretation. But in recent decades cultural anthropology, along with fundamentalist theology, has become a refuge for the anti-evolutionist point of view. The concept of evolution has proved itself to be one of the most important and fruitful theories in the whole field of science. Cultural anthropology cannot continue to oppose or ignore this concept and point of view indefinitely. The study of culture will again embrace evolutionary theory and be reanimated and invigorated by it. But this does not mean that we should ignore history or belittle functionalism. We need, and we must have, all three types of interpretation if we are to develop our science to the fullest extent.

SECTION INTRODUCTION REFERENCES* AND SUGGESTIONS FOR FURTHER STUDY

Barber, Bernard, 1956, "Structural-functional Analysis: Some Problems and Misunderstandings." *American Sociological Review* 21:129–135.

Bredemeier, Harry C., 1955, "The Methodology of Functionalism." *American Sociological Review* 20:173–180.

Cancian, Francesca M., 1960, 1961, "Functional Analysis of Change." *American Sociological Review* 25:818–827, 26:930–931.

Davis, Kingsley, 1959, "The Myth of Functional Analysis as a Special Method in Sociology and Anthropology." *American Sociological Review* 24:757–772.

Demerath, N.J., III, and R. A. Peterson, eds., 1967, *System, Change, and Conflict: A Reader on Contemporary Sociological Theory and the Debate Over Functionalism.* New York: Free Press.

Dore, Ronald P., 1961, "Function and Cause." *American Sociological Review* 26:843–853.

Driver, H. E., 1965, *An Integration of Functional, Evolutionary, and Historical Theory by Means of Correlations.* Indiana University Publications in Anthropology and Linguistics, Memoir 12.

Eggan, Fred, 1954, "Social Anthropology and the Method of Controlled Comparison." *American Anthropologist* 56:743–763.

Fallding, Harold, 1963, "Functional Analysis in Sociology." *American Sociological Review* 28:5–13.

Fortes, M., 1936 "Culture Contact as a Dynamic Process." *Africa* 9:24–55.

Gluckman, Max, 1968, "The Utility of the Equilibrium Model in the Study of Social Change." *American Anthropologist* 70:219–237.

Goldschmidt, Walter R., 1966, *Comparative Functionalism: An Essay in Anthropological Theory.* Berkeley: University of California Press.

Gregg, Dorothy, and Elgin Williams, 1948, "The Dismal Science of Functionalism." *American Anthropologist* 50:594–611.

Hemple, Carl G., 1959, "The Logic of Functional Analysis." In L. Gross, ed., *Symposium on Sociological Theory*. New York: Harper & Row, pp.271–307.

Homans, George, C., 1941, "Anxiety and Ritual: The Theories of Malinowski and Radcliffe-Brown." *American Anthropologist* 43:164–172.

Jarvie, I. E., 1973, *Functionalism*. Minneapolis: Burgess.

Levy, Marion, 1951, *The Structure of Society*. Princeton,N.J.: Princeton University Press.

Merton, Robert K., 1957, "Manifest and Latent Functions." In *Social Theory and Social Structure*, rev. ed. New York: Free Press.

Martindale, Don, ed., 1965, *Functionalism in the Social Sciences: The Strength and Limits of Functionalism in Anthropology, Economics, Political Science, and Sociology*. Philadelphia: American Academy of Political and Social Science.

Nagel, Ernest, 1956, "A Formalization of Functionalism." In *Logic Without Metaphysics*. New York: Free Press, pp. 247–283.

———, 1961, *The Structure of Science: Problems in the Logic of Scientific Explanation*. New York: Harcourt, Brace Jovanovich.

Parsons, Talcott, 1951, *The Social System*. New York: Free Press.

Spiro, Melford E., 1964, "Causes, Functions, and Cross-Cousin Marriage: An Essay in Anthropological Explanation." *Journal of the Royal Anthropological Institute* 94:30–42.

Thurnwald, Richard C., 1936, "Civilization and Culture: A Contribution Toward Analysis of the Mechanism of Culture." *American Sociological Review* 1:387–395.

Tumin, Melvin, 1965, "The Functionalist Approach to Social Problems." *Social Problems* 12:379–388.

Van Den Berghe, Pierre L., 1963, "Dialectic and Functionalism: Toward a Theoretical Synthesis." *American Sociological Review* 28:695–705.

Worseley, P. M., 1961, "The Analysis of Rebellion and Revolution in British Social Anthropology." *Science and Society* 21:26–37.

For further reference, see Section IV on the social order as culture.

reading references and notes

9 The Concept of Culture—LESLIE A. WHITE

Beals, Ralph L., and Harry Hoijer, 1953, *An Introduction to Anthropology*. New York: Macmillan.
Benedict, Ruth, 1934, *Patterns of Culture*. Boston and New York: Houghton Mifflin.
Bidney, David, 1946, "The Concept of Cultural Crisis." *American Anthropologist* 48:534–552.
———, 1954, *Review of* Culture, a Critical Review . . ." by Kroeber and Kluckhohn. *American Journal of Sociology* 59:488–489.
Boas, Franz, 1928, *Anthropology and Modern Life*. New York: Norton.
———, 1938, *The Mind of Primitive Man*, rev. ed. New York: Macmillan.
Cassirer, Ernst, 1944, *An Essay on Man*. New Haven, Conn.: Yale University Press.
Cohen, Morris R., 1931, "Fictions." *Encyclopedia of the Social Sciences* 7:225–228. New York: Macmillan.
Durkheim, Emile, 1938, *The Rules of Sociological Method*, George E. G. Catlin, ed. Chicago: The University of Chicago Press.
———, 1951, *Suicide, a Study in Sociology*, George Simpson, ed. Glencoe, Ill.: Free Press.
Einstein, Albert, 1934, *The World as I See It*. New York: Covici, Friede.
———, 1936, "Physics and Reality." *Journal of the Franklin Institute* 221:313–347, in German; 349–382 in English.
Hallowell, A. Irving, 1945, "Sociopsychological Aspects of Acculturation." In Ralph Linton, ed., *The Science of Man in the World Crisis*. New York: Columbia University Press.
Herrick, C. Judson, 1956, *The Evolution of Human Nature*. Austin: University of Texas Press.
Herskovits, Melville J., 1945, "The Processes of Cultural Change." In Ralph Linton, ed., *The Science of Man in the World Crisis*. New York: Columbia University Press.
———, 1948, *Man and His Works*. New York: Knopf.
Hoebel, E. Adamson, 1956, "The Nature of Culture." In Harry L. Shapiro, ed., *Man, Culture and Society*. New York: Oxford University Press.
Hooton, Earnest A., 1939, *Crime and the Man*. Cambridge, Mass.: Harvard University Press.
Huxley, Julian S., 1955, "Evolution, Cultural and Biological." In Wm. L. Thomas, Jr., ed., *Yearbook of Anthropology*.
Keesing, Felix M., 1958, *Cultural Anthropology*. New York: Holt, Rinehart and Winston.
Kluckhohn, Clyde, and Wm. H. Kelly, 1945, "The Concept of Culture." In Ralph Linton, ed., *The Science of Man in the World Crisis*. New York: Columbia University Press.
Kroeber, A. L., 1917, "The superorganic." *American Anthropologist* 19:163–213; reprinted in *The Nature of Culture*. Chicago: University of Chicago Press.
Kroeber, A. L., 1917, "The Superorganic." *American Anthropologist* 19:163–213; reprinted in *The Papers of the Peabody Museum of American Archaeology and Ethnology*, Harvard University, 47(1):1–223. Cambridge, Mass.
Linton, Ralph, 1936, *The Study of Man*. New York: Appleton.
———, 1945, *The Cultural Background of Personality*. New York: Appleton.
Lowie, Robert H., 1917, *Culture and Ethnology*. New York: Boni and Liveright.
Lynd, Robert S., 1939, *Knowledge for What?* Princeton, N. J.: Princeton University Press.
Malinowski, Bronislaw, 1941, "Man's Culture and Man's Behavior." *Sigma Xi Quarterly* 29:170–196.
Murdock, George P., 1937, Editorial Preface to *Studies in the Science of Society*. Presented to Albert Galloway Keller. New Haven, Conn.: Yale University Press.
———, 1951, "British social anthropology." *American Anthropologist* 53:465–473.
Osgood, Cornelius, 1940, *Ingalik Material Culture*. Yale University Publications in Anthropology No. 22.
———, 1951, "British Social Anthropology." *American Anthropologist* 53:465–473.
thropology 7:202–214.
Radcliffe-Brown, A. R., 1924, "The Mother's Brother in South Africa." *South African Journal of Science*, 21:542–555. Reprinted in *Structure and Function in Primitive Society*. Glencoe, Ill.: Free Press.
———, 1930–1931, "The Social Organization of Australian Tribes." *Oceania* 1:34–63; 206–246; 322–341; 426–456.

———, 1940, "On "Social Structure." *Journal of the Royal Anthropological Institute* 70:1–12; reprinted in *Structure and Function in Primitive Society*. Glencoe, Ill.: Free Press.
———, 1952, *Structure and Function in Primitive Society*. Glencoe, Ill.: Free Press.
Redfield, Robert, 1941. The Folk Culture of Yucatan. Chicago: The University of Chicago Press.
Sapir, Edward, 1916, *Time Perspective in Aboriginal American Culture*. Canada Department of Mines, Geological Survey Memoir 90. Ottawa.
———, 1917, Do We Need a Superorganic? *American Anthropologist* 19:441–447.
———, 1930, *Southern Paiute, a Shoshonean Language*. Proceedings of the American Academy of Arts and Sciences 65:1–296.
———, 1932, "Cultural Anthropology and Psychiatry." *Journal of Abnormal and Social Psychology* 27:229–242.
Spiro, Melford E., 1951, "Culture and Personality." *Psychiatry* 14:19–46.
Steward, Julian H., 1955, *Theory of Culture Change*. Urbana, Ill.: University of Illinois Press.
Strong, Wm. Duncan, 1953, "Historical Approach in Anthropology." In A. L. Kroeber, ed., *Anthropology Today*. Chicago: The University of Chicago Press, pp. 386–397.
Taylor, Walter W., 1948, *A Study of Archeology*. American Anthropological Association Memoir No. 69.
Tylor, Edward B., 1881, *Anthropology*. London.
———, 1913. *Primitive Culture*. 5th ed., London.
White, Leslie A., 1949, *The Science of Culture*. New York: Farrar, Straus and Cudahy; paperbound, 1958, New York: The Grove Press.
———, 1954, Review of *Culture, a Critical Review*, by Kroeber and Kluckhohn. *American Anthropologist* 56: 461–468.
Wissler, Clark, 1929, *Introduction to Social Anthropology*. New York: Henry Holt and Company.

11 The Superorganic: Science or Metaphysics—DAVID KAPLAN

Barnett, H. G., 1953, *Innovation: The Basis of Cultural Change*. New York: McGraw-Hill.
Bergmann, Gustav, 1954, "Reduction." In *Current Trends in Psychology and the Behavioral Sciences*. Pittsburgh: University of Pittsburgh Press.
Bidney, David, 1953, *Theoretical Anthropology*. New York: Columbia University Press.
Bradley, R. D., 1962, "Determinism or Indeterminism in Microphysics." *The British Journal for the Philosophy of Science* 13:193–215.
Brodbeck, May, 1955, "Methodological Individualisms: Definitions and Reduction." *Philosophy of Science* 25:1–22.
Copeland, John W., 1963, "Culture and Man: Leslie A. White's Thesis Reexamined." *Southwestern Journal of Anthropology* 19:109–120.
Durkheim, Emile, 1938, *The Rules of Sociological Method*. George E. G. Catlin, ed. Chicago: University of Chicago Press.
Fried, Morton H., ed., 1959, *Readings in Anthropology*. Vol. 1. New York: Crowell.
Goldenweiser, A., 1917, "The Autonomy of the Social." *American Anthropologist* 19:447–449.
Goldstein, Leon J., 1955, "Bidney's Humanistic Anthropology." *Review of Metaphysics* 8:493–509.
———, 1957, "On Defining Culture." *American Anthropologist* 59:1075–1081.
———, 1959, "Ontological Social Science." *American Anthropologist* 61:290–298.
Hempel, Carl G., 1951, "General Systems Theory and the Unity of Science." *Human Biology* 23:313–322.
Hempel, Carl G., and Paul Oppenheim, 1948, "Studies in the Logic of Explanation." *Philosophy of Science* 15:135–175.
Hospers, John, 1946, "On Explanation." *Journal of Philosophy* 43:337–356.
Jessor, Richard, 1958, "The Problem of Reductionism in Psychology." *Psychological Review* 65:170–178.
Kaplan, Bert, 1957, "Personality and Social Structure." In Joseph B. Gittler, ed., *Review of Sociology*. New York: Wiley.
Kroeber, A. L., 1917, "The Superorganic." *American Anthropologist* 19:163–213.
———, 1944, *Configurations of Culture Growth*. Berkeley: University of California Press.

Kroeber, A. L., and Clyde Kluckhohn, 1952, *Culture, a Critical Review of Concepts and Definitions.* Papers of the Peabody Museum of American Archaeology and Ethnology, Harvard University, 47 (1):1–223. Cambridge, Mass.
Lowie, R. H., 1936, "Cultural Anthropology: a Science." *American Journal of Sociology* 42:301–320.
Mandelbaum, Maurice, 1952, "Some Neglected Problems Regarding History." *Journal of Philosophy* 49:317–329.
——, 1955, "Societal Facts." *British Journal of Sociology* 6:305–317.
Mettler, Fred H., 1962, "Culture and the Structural Evolution of the Neural System." In M. F. Ashley Montagu, ed., *Culture and the Evolution of Man.* New York: Oxford University Press.
Murdock, George P., 1932, "The Science of Culture." *American Anthropologist* 34:200–215.
Nagel, Ernest, 1951, "Reflections on the Causal Character of Modern Physical Theory." In Salo W. Baron, Ernest Nagel and Koppel S. Pinson, eds., *Freedom and Reason.* Glencoe, Ill.: Free Press.
——, 1960, "Determinism in History." *Philosophy and Phenomenological Research* 20:291–317.
——, 1961, *The Structure of Science.* New York: Harcourt.
Opler, Morris E., 1963, "Cultural Anthropology: an Addendum to a 'Working Paper.'" *American Anthropologist* 65:897–903.
Sahlins, Marshall D., 1961, "The Segmentary Lineage: an Organization of Predatory Expansion." *American Anthropologist* 63:322–345.
Sapir, Edward, 1917, "Do We Need a Superorganic?" *American Anthropologist* 19:441–447.
Smart, J. J. C., 1956, "The Reality of Theoretical Entities." *The Australasian Journal of Philosophy* 34:1–12.
Spiro, Melford E., 1951, "Culture and Personality: The Natural History of a False Dichotomy." *Psychiatry* 14:19–46.
——, 1961a, "An Overview and a Suggested Reorientation." In Francis L. K. Hsu, ed., *Psychological Anthropology: Approaches to Culture and Personality.* Homewood, Ill.: Dorsey Press.
——, 1961b, "Social Systems, Personality and Functional Analysis." In Bert Kaplan, ed., *Studying Personality Cross-culturally.* Evanston, Ill.: Row, Peterson and Co.
Toulmin, Stephen, 1960, *The Philosophy of Science.* New York: Harper Torchbook Edition.
Tylor, E. B., 1871, *Primitive Culture: Researches into the Development of Mythology, Philosophy, Religion, Art and Custom.* London: J. Murray.
Waddington, C. H., 1960, *The Ethical Animal.* London: G. Allen.
Wallace, Anthony F. C., 1961, *Culture and Personality.* New York: Random House.
——, 1962, "The New Culture-and-Personality. In *Anthropology and Human Behavior.* Washington, D.C.: Anthropological Society of Washington.
White, Leslie A., 1949, *The Science of Culture.* New York: Farrar, Strauss.
——, 1959, "The Concept of Culture." *American Anthropologist* 61:227–251.
Wissler, Clark, 1923, *Man and Culture.* New York: Crowell.
Worsley, P. M., 1956, "The Kinship System of the Tallensi: A Revaluation." *Journal of the Royal Anthropological Institute* 86:37–75.

19 Psychological Anthropology—JOHN J. HONIGMANN

[1] David M. Schneider, *American Kinship: A Cultural Account* (New York: Prentice-Hall, 1968), pp. 2–3, 114–117.
[2] Ely Devons and Max Gluckman, "Conclusion: Modes and Consequences of Limiting a Field of Study," in Max Gluckman, ed., *Closed Systems and Open Minds* (Chicago: Aldine, 1964).
[3] Robert O. Lagacé, "Psychocultural Analysis, Cultural Theory, and Ethnographic Research," *Behavioral Science Notes*, vol. 1, no. 3, 1965, pp. 165–199.
[4] F. Kenneth Berrien, "Methodological and Related Problems in Cross-Cultural Research," *International Journal of Psychology*, vol. 2, no. 1, 1967, pp. 33–43.
[5] For brief historical treatments, see Marvin Harris, *The Rise of Anthropological Theory* (New York: Thomas Y. Crowell, 1968), ch. 15–17; John J. Honigmann, "The Study of Personality in Primitive Societies," in Edward Norbeck *et al.*, eds., *The Study of Personality* (New York: Holt, Rinehart and Winston, 1968); David G. Mandelbaum, "Edward Sapir: Contributions to Cultural Anthropology," *International Encyclopedia of the Social Sciences* (New York: The Macmillan Company & The Free Press, 1968).

⁶George A. DeVos and Arthur E. Hippler, "Cultural Psychology: Comparative Studies of Human Behavior," in Gardner Lindzey and Elliot Aronson, eds., *Handbook of Social Psychology,* 2nd ed. (Reading, Mass.: Addison-Wesley, 1968); John L. Fischer, "Psychology and Anthropology," in Bernard J. Siegel, ed., *Biennial Review of Anthropology, 1965* (Stanford, Calif.: Stanford University Press, 1965); Pertti J. Pelto, "Psychological Anthropology," in Bernard J. Siegel, ed., *Biennial Review of Anthropology, 1967* (Stanford, Calif.: Stanford University Press, 1967).

⁷Harris, *The Rise of Anthropological Theory;* I. S. Korolev, "Some Questions of Ethno-Psychological Studies Abroad," *Soviet Anthropology and Archaeology,* vol. 5, no. 2 (Fall 1966), pp. 3–10. See, however, V. V. Mshvenieradze and G. V. Osipov, "Sociology in the U.S.S.R.," *Information,* n.s., vol. 1, no. 3 (October 1962), pp. 49–73.

⁸The question has been asked whether a psychological viewpoint denotes any reference to emotions, ideas, or mental processes (in which case, even Durkheim explained social facts psychologically) or whether it indicates only the application of explanatory theories from the science of psychology. See Max Gluckman, "Psychological, Sociological and Anthropological Explanations of Witchcraft and Gossip: A Clarification," *Man,* n.s., vol. 3, no. 1 (June 1967), pp. 20–34; John G. Kennedy, "On Psychology and Social Anthropology," *Man,* n.s., vol. 3, no. 2 (June 1968), pp. 301–304. See also Percy S. Cohen's letter under the same title, *ibid.,* pp. 304–305.

⁹Robert Endleman, *Personality and Social Life* (New York: Random House, 1967); Robert Hunt, *Personalities and Cultures* (Garden City, N.Y.: Natural History Press, 1967).

¹⁰John J. Honigmann, *Personality in Culture* (New York: Harper and Row, 1967).

¹¹Lowell D. Holmes, *Anthropology* (New York: Ronald Press, 1965), ch. 15, Melville Jacobs, *Patterns in Cultural Anthropology* (Homewood, Ill.: Dorsey Press, 1964), ch. 4; Douglass R. Price-Williams, "Ethnopsychology I: Comparative Psychological Processes" and "Ethnopsychology II: Comparative Personality Processes," in James A. Clifton, ed., *Introduction to Cultural Anthropology* (Boston: Houghton Mifflin, 1968); Harry Holbert Turney-High, *Man and System* (New York: Appleton-Century-Crofts, 1968), ch. 8.

¹²Bert Kaplan, "The Methodology of the Study of Persons," in Norbeck *et al.,* eds., *The Study of Personality.*

¹³Melford Spiro, "Culture and Personality," in *International Encyclopedia of the Social Sciences.*

¹⁴Dorothea C. Leighton and John Adair, *People of the Middle Place* (New Haven, Conn.: Human Relations Area Files, 1966).

¹⁵Joel Aronoff, *Psychological Needs and Cultural Systems* (Princeton, N.J.: D. Van Nostrand, 1967).

¹⁶Joseph M. Lubart, "A Study of Basic Personality Traits of the Caribou Eskimos: A Preliminary Report," in George S. Goldman and Daniel Shapiro, eds., *Developments in Psychoanalysis at Columbia University* (New York: Hafner, 1966).

¹⁷L. Bryce Boyer, "Psychological Problems of a Group of Apaches: Alcoholic Hallucinosis and Latent Homosexuality among Typical Men," W. Muensterberger and S. Axelrad, eds., *The Psychoanalytic Study of Society,* vol. 3 (1964), pp. 203–277.

¹⁸John J. and Irma Honigmann, *Eskimo Townsmen* (Ottawa: Canadian Research Centre for Anthropology, 1965), ch. 6. The Rorschach test, the Thematic Apperception Test, and other tests, allowed Caroline E. Preston to make the important contribution to knowledge about West and North Alaskan Eskimo personality that she reports in "Psychological Testing with Northwest Coast Alaskan Eskimos," *Genetic Psychology Monographs,* vol. 69, no. 2 (May 1964), pp. 323–419.

¹⁹See papers by Henry Zentner and Cecil L. French in Arthur K. Davis, *A Northern Dilemma: Reference Papers,* 2 vols. (Bellingham, Wash.: Western Washington State College, 1967). Richard Slobodin, *Metis of the Mackenzie District* (Ottawa: Canadian Research Centre for Anthropology, 1966), examines "Metis Identity" in ch. 9.

²⁰Seymour Parker, "The Kwakiutl Indians: 'Amiable' and 'Atrocious,' " *Anthropologica,* n.s., vol. 6, no. 2 (1964), pp. 131–158. See also Helen Codere, "The Amiable Side of Kwakiutl Life: The Potlatch and Play Potlatch," *American Anthropologist,* vol. 58, no. 2 (April 1956), pp. 334–351.

²¹Benjamin N. Colby, "Psychological Orientations," in Manning Nash, ed., *Social Anthropology* (Austin: University of Texas Press, 1967). See also John Gillin, "Ethos and Cultural Aspects of Personality," in Sol Tax, ed., *Heritage of Conquest: The Ethnology of Middle America* (Glencoe, Ill.: Free Press, 1952).

²²Herbert P. Phillips, *Thai Peasant Personality* (Berkeley and Los Angeles: University of California Press, 1966).

²³John Gulick, *Tripoli: A Modern Arab City* (Cambridge: Harvard University Press, 1967), pp. 133–134; Herbert H. and Judith R. Williams, "The Definition of the Rorschach Test Situation: A

Cross-Cultural Illustration," in Melford E. Spiro, ed., *Context and Meaning in Cultural Anthropology* (New York: Free Press, 1965).

[24]Murray A. Straus, "Westernization, Insecurity, and Sinhalese Social Structure," *The International Journal of Social Psychiatry*, vol. 12, no. 2 (Spring 1966), pp. 130–138.

[25]Rita Mohr Weinberg, "Personality Characteristics of African Children: A Projective Analysis," *The Journal of Genetic Psychology*, vol. 113, no. 1 (September 1968), pp. 65–77.

[26]George A. De Vos and Hiroshi Wagatsuma, *Japan's Invisible Race* (Berkeley and Los Angeles: University of California Press, 1966).

[27]George A. De Vos, "Achievement Orientation, Social Self-Identity, and Japanese Economic Growth," *Asian Survey*, vol. 5, no. 12 (December 1965), pp. 575–589; "Social Values and Personal Attitudes in Primary Human Relations in Njiike," *Occasional Papers of the Centre for Japanese Studies, University of Michigan*, 1965, pp. 53–91.

[28]One need not seriously consider Z. A. Grabowski, *The English Psycho-Analysed* (London: Sidgwick and Jackson, 1967).

[29]Daniel Bell, "National Character Revisited: A Proposal for Renegotiating the Concept," in Edward Norbeck *et al.*, eds., *The Study of Personality;* Daniel J. Levinson, "Idea Systems in the Individual and in Society," in George K. Zollschan and Walter Hirsch, eds., *Explorations in Social Change* (Boston: Houghton Mifflin, 1964); Murray G. Murphey, "An Approach to the Historical Study of National Character," in Spiro, ed., *Context and Meaning in Cultural Anthropology;* Margaret Mead, "The Idea of National Character," in Robert L. Shinn, ed., *The Search for Identity* (New York: Harper and Row, 1964).

[30]De Vos, "Achievement Orientation, Social Self-Identity . . ."; George A. De Vos, "Achievement and Innovation in Culture and Personality," in Norbeck *et al.*, eds., *The Study of Personality*.

[31]Alan Howard, "Plasticity, Achievement, and Adaptation in Developing Economies," *Human Organization*, vol. 25, no. 4 (Winter 1966), pp. 265–272.

[32]Robert A. LeVine, *Dreams and Deeds* (Chicago: University of Chicago Press, 1966); James N. Morgan, "The Achievement Motive and Economic Behavior," in J. W. Atkinson, ed., *A Theory of Achievement-Motivation* (New York: John Wiley and Sons, 1966); Dennison Nash and Louis C. Schaw, "Achievement and Acculturation: A Japanese Example," in Spiro, ed., *Context and Meaning in Cultural Anthropology;* Stanley R. Barrett, "The Achievement Factor in Igbo Receptivity to Industrialization," *The Canadian Review of Sociology and Anthropology*, vol. 5, no. 2 (May 1968), pp. 68–83.

[33]Margaret Peil, "Aspiration and Social Structure: A West African Example," *Africa*, vol. 38, no. 1 (January 1968), pp. 71–78.

[34]Elizabeth Colson, "Competence and Incompetence in Context of Independence," *Current Anthropology*, vol. 8, nos. 1 and 2 (February-April 1967), pp. 92–111.

[35]Robert B. Edgerton, *The Cloak of Competence* (Chicago: University of Chicago Press, 1967).

[36]For a mainly sociological treatment, see Kenneth Little, "Voluntary Associations in Urban Life: A Case Study of Differential Adaptation," in Maurice Freedman, ed., *Social Organization: Essays Presented to Raymond Firth* (London: Frank Cass, 1967).

[37]For a comprehensive theory applying the concept mainly to social change, see George D. Spindler, "Psychocultural Adaptation," in Norbeck *et al.*, eds., *The Study of Personality*.

[38]George and Louise Spindler, "The Instrumental Activities Inventory: A Technique for the Study of the Psychology of Acculturation," *Southwestern Journal of Anthropology*, vol. 21, no. 1 (Spring 1965), pp. 1–23; George and Louise Spindler, "Researching the Perception of Cultural Alternatives: The Instrumental Activities Inventory," in Spiro, ed., *Context and Meaning in Cultural Anthropology*.

[39]David Gutman, "Aging Among the Highland Maya," *Journal of Personality and Social Psychology*, vol. 7, no. 1 (September 1967), pp. 28–35; David Gutman, "Mayan Aging—A Comparative TAT Study," *Psychiatry*, vol. 29, no. 3 (August 1966), pp. 246–259.

[40]L. Bryce Boyer, *et al.*, "Apache 'Learners' and 'Nonlearners,' " *Journal of Projective Techniques and Personality Assessment*, vol. 31, no. 6 (December 1967), pp. 22–29; *ibid.*, vol. 32, no. 2 (April 1968), pp. 146–159.

[41]A. Kimball Romney and Roy Goodwin D'Andrade, eds., "Transcultural Studies in Cognition, Part II," *American Anthropologist*, vol. 66, no. 3 (June 1964).

[42]John W. Berry, "Temne and Eskimo Perceptual Skills," *International Journal of Psychology*, vol. 1, no. 3 (1966), pp. 207–229; E. C. Theiner and M. Giffin, "A Comparison of Thought Processes in Three Cultures," *Comprehensive Psychiatry*, vol. 5, no. 1 (February 1964), pp. 54–63.

[43]Murray A. Straus, "Communication, Creativity, and Problem-Solving Ability of Middle- and

Working-Class Families in Three Societies," *American Journal of Sociology,* vol. 73, no. 4 (January 1968), pp. 417–430; Jacqueline H. Straus and Murray A. Straus, "Family Roles and Sex Differences in Creativity of Children in Bombay and Minneapolis," *Journal of Marriage and the Family,* vol. 30, no. 1 (February 1968), pp. 46–53.

[44] B. Berthold Wolff and Sarah Langley, "Cultural Factors and the Response to Pain: A Review," *American Anthropologist,* vol. 70, no. 3 (June 1968), pp. 494–501.

[45] Barbara B. Lloyd, "Choice Behavior and Social Structure: A Comparison of Two African Societies," *The Journal of Social Psychology,* vol. 74, no. 1 (February 1968), pp. 3–12.

[46] J. W. Berry, "Independence and Conformity in Subsistence-Level Societies, Part I," *Journal of Personality and Social Psychology,* vol. 7, no. 4 (December 1967), pp. 415–418.

[47] For a comprehensive account of large-scale methods, see John W. M. Whiting, "Methods and Problems in Cross-Cultural Research," in Lindzey and Aronson, eds., *Handbook of Social Psychology.*

[48] Gerald D. Berreman, "Aleut Reference Group Alienation, Mobility, and Acculturation," *American Anthropologist,* vol. 66, no. 2 (April 1964), pp. 231–250; Seymour Parker, "Ethnic Identity and Acculturation in Two Eskimo Villages," *American Anthropologist,* vol. 66, no. 2 (April 1964), pp. 325–340; Anthony F. C. Wallace, "Identity Processes in Personality and in Culture," in Richard Jessor and Seymour Feshbach, eds., *Cognition, Personality, and Clinical Psychology* (San Francisco: Jossey-Bass, 1967).

[49] John J. Honigmann, "Interpersonal Relations in Atomistic Communities," *Human Organization,* vol. 27, no. 3 (Fall 1968), pp. 220–229.

[50] George M. Foster, "Peasant Society and the Image of Limited Good," *American Anthropologist,* vol. 67, no. 2 (April 1965), pp. 293–315.

[51] Evon Z. Vogt and Ethel M. Albert, eds., *People of Rimrock: A Study of Values in Five Cultures* (Cambridge: Harvard University Press, 1966).

[52] See the discussion in Charles A. Valentine, *Culture and Poverty* (Chicago: University of Chicago Press, 1968), ch. 5, esp. p. 130.

[53] For recent examples, see Warner Muensterberger and Sidney Axelrad, eds., *The Psychoanalytic Study of Society,* vols. 3, 4, and 5 (New York: International Universities Press, 1964, 1966, 1967); and John Frosch and Nathaniel Ross, eds., *The Annual Survey of Psychoanalysis,* vols. 8 and 9 (New York: International Universities Press, 1964, 1968).

[54] John H. Kunkel, "Values and Behavior in Economic Development," *Economic Development and Cultural Change,* vol. 13, no. 3 (April 1965), pp. 257–277. See also Myron Weiner's "Introduction" to his *Modernization: The Dynamics of Growth* (New York: Basic Books, 1966), esp. pp. 9–10.

[55] For recent thoughts on the controversy and bibliography, see Melford E. Spiro, "Causes, Functions, and Cross-Cousin Marriage: An Essay in Anthropological Explanation," *Journal of the Royal Anthropological Institute,* vol. 94, no. 1, 1965, pp. 30–43; Harris, *The Rise of Anthropological Theory,* pp. 501–512. Morris Opler reviews the same issue with respect to evolutionary theory in "Cultural Dynamics and Evolutionary Theory," in Herbert R. Barringer *et al.*, eds., *Social Change in Developing Areas* (Cambridge, Mass.: Schenkman, 1965); and see John G. Kennedy, "Psychological and Social Explanations of Witchcraft," *Man,* vol. 2, no. 2 (June 1967).

[56] L. Bryce Boyer and Ruth M. Boyer, "A Combined Anthropological and Psychological Contribution to Folklore" (in press) reviews the controversies and contributions made by psychoanalytic theory. See also L. Bryce Boyer, "Stone as a Symbol of Apache Mythology," *American Imago,* Vol. 22, Nos. 1 and 2 (Spring-Summer 1965), pp. 14–39.

[57] William A. Lessa and Evon Z. Vogt, eds., *Reader in Comparative Religion,* 2nd ed. (New York: Harper and Row, 1965).

[58] Anthony F. C. Wallace, *Religion: An Anthropological View* (New York: Random House, 1966); Annemarie de Waal Malefijt, *Religion and Culture* (New York: The Macmillan Company, 1968).

[59] Melford E. Spiro, "Religious Systems as Culturally Constituted Defense Mechanisms," in Spiro, ed., *Context and Meaning in Cultural Anthropology.*

[60] John G. Kennedy, "Mushahara: A Nubian Concept of Supernatural Danger and the Theory of Taboo," *American Anthropologist,* vol. 69, no. 6 (December 1967), pp. 685–702.

[61] Erika Bourguignon, "The Self, the Behavioral Environment, and the Theory of Spirit Possession," in Spiro, ed., *Context and Meaning in Cultural Anthropology.*

[62] Raymond D. Fogelson, "Psychological Theories of Windigo 'Psychosis' and a Preliminary Application of a Models Approach," in Spiro, ed., *Context and Meaning in Cultural Anthropology.* See also Honigmann, *Personality in Culture,* pp. 399–403.

[63] Ari Kiev, ed., *Magic, Faith, and Healing* (New York: Free Press of Glencoe, 1964); G. M. Carstairs,

"Healing Ceremonies in Primitive Societies," *The Listener,* vol. 72, no. 1845 (August 1964), pp. 195–197; John G. Kennedy, "Nubian Zar Ceremonies as Psychotherapy," *Human Organization,* vol. 26, no. 4 (Winter 1967), pp. 185–194.

[64]David G. Mandelbaum, "Alcohol and Culture," *Current Anthropology,* vol. 6, no. 3 (June 1965), pp. 281–293. Specific papers include Margaret K. Bacon, et al., "A Cross-Cultural Study of Drinking," *Quarterly Journal of Studies on Alcohol,* supp. no. 3 (April 1965), pp. 1–114; Richard T. Curley, "Drinking Patterns of the Mescalero Apache," *Quarterly Journal of Studies on Alcohol,* vol. 28, no. 1 (March 1967), pp. 116–131; Edward P. Dozier, "Problem Drinking among American Indians," *Quarterly Journal of Studies on Alcohol,* vol. 27, no. 1 (March 1966), pp. 72–87; Frances Northend Ferguson, "Navaho Drinking: Some Tentative Hypotheses," *Human Organization,* vol. 27, no. 2 (Summer 1968), pp. 159–167; John H. Hamer, "Guardian Spirits, Alcohol, and Cultural Defense Mechanisms" (in press); Edward J. Jay, "Religious and Convivial Uses of Alcohol in a Gond Village of Middle India," *Quarterly Journal of Studies on Alcohol,* vol. 27, no. 1 (March 1966), pp. 88–96; Robert E. Kuttner and Albert B. Lorinez, "Alcoholism and Addiction in Urbanized Sioux Indians," *Mental Hygiene,* vol. 51, no. 4 (October 1967), pp. 530–542.

[65]John M. Roberts et al., "Pattern and Competence: A Consideration of Ticktacktoe," *El Palacio,* vol. 72, no. 2 (Autumn 1965), pp. 17–30; John M. Roberts and Brian Sutton-Smith, "Cross Cultural Correlates of Games of Chance," *Behavioral Science Notes,* vol. 1, no. 3, 1965, pp. 131–144; Brian Sutton-Smith and John M. Roberts, "Studies of an Elementary Game of Strategy," *Genetic Psychology Monographs,* vol. 75, no. 1 (February 1967), pp. 3–42; Brian Sutton-Smith and John M. Roberts, "Rubrics of Competitive Behavior," *The Journal of Genetic Psychology,* vol. 105, no. 1 (September 1964), pp. 13–37.

[66]Anthony F. C. Wallace, "Psychological Preparations for War," in Marvin Harris et al., eds., *War: The Anthropology of Armed Conflict and Aggression* (Garden City, N.Y.: Natural History Press, 1968); (Margaret Mead, "Alternatives to War," *ibid.;*) Margaret Mead and Rhoda Métraux, "The Anthropology of Human Conflict," in Elton B. McNeil, ed., *The Nature of Human Conflict* (Englewood Cliffs, N.J.: Prentice Hall, 1965).

[67]Jerome David Frank, *Sanity and Survival* (New York: Random House, 1967).

[68]Herbert Hendin, *Suicide and Scandinavia* (New York: Grune and Stratton, 1964); Jerrold Levy, "Navajo Suicide," *Human Organization,* vol. 24, no. 4 (Winter 1965), pp. 308–318; David Lester, "Suicide, Homicide, and the Effects of Socialization," *Journal of Personality and Social Psychology,* vol. 5, no. 4 (April 1967), pp. 466–468; Thomas W. Maretzki, "Suicide in Okinawa: Preliminary Exploration," *International Journal of Social Psychiatry,* vol. 11, no. 4 (Autumn 1965), pp. 256–263; Russell Noyes, Jr., "The Taboo of Suicide," *Psychiatry,* vol. 31, no. 3 (May 1968), pp. 173–183.

[69]T. Adeoye Lambo, "Socioeconomic Changes in Africa and their Implications for Mental Health," in G. E. W. Wolstenholme and M. O'Connor, eds., *Man and Africa* (Boston: Little, Brown, 1966).

[70]Stephen Kellert, et al., "Culture Change and Stress in Rural Peru," *Millbank Memorial Fund Quarterly,* vol. 45, no. 4 (October 1967), pp. 391–415.

[71]L. Bryce Boyer and Ruth M. Boyer, "Some Influences of Acculturation on the Personality Traits of the Old People of the Mescalero and Chiricahua Apaches," in W. Muensterberger and S. Axelrad, eds., *The Psychoanalytic Study of Society,* vol. 3; L. Bryce Boyer et al., "Effects of Acculturation on the Personality Traits of the Old People of the Mescalero and Chiricahua Apaches," *International Journal of Social Psychiatry,* vol. 11, no. 4 (Autumn 1965), pp. 264–271. L. Bryce Boyer et al., "Apache Age Groups," *Journal of Projective Techniques and Personality Assessment,* vol. 28, no. 4 (December 1964), pp. 397–402.

[72]Seymour Parker, "Ethnic Identity and Acculturation in Two Eskimo Villages," *American Anthropologist,* vol. 66, no. 2 (April 1964), pp. 325–340.

[73]Erik H. Erikson, *Identity, Youth, and Crisis* (New York, W. W. Norton, 1968).

[74]Robert Lifton, "Individual Patterns in Historical Change: Imagery of Japanese Youth," *Journal of Social Issues,* vol. 20, no. 4 (October 1964), pp. 96–111.

[75]William Madsen, "Value Conflicts in Cultural Transfer," in Philip Worchel and Donn Byrne, eds., *Personality Change* (New York: John Wiley & Sons, 1964).

[76]Homer G. Barnett, "Psycho-Social Models of Change," in Zollschan and Hirsch, eds., *Explorations in Social Change.* See also Donald T. Campbell, "Variation and Selective Retention in Socio-Cultural Evolution," in Barringer, et al., eds., *Social Change in Developing Areas.*

[77]L. L. Langness, *The Life History in Anthropological Science* (New York: Holt, Rinehart and Winston, 1965).

[78] Charles C. Hughes, "The Life History in Cross-Cultural Psychiatric Research," in Jane M. Murphy and Alexander H. Leighton, eds., *Approaches to Cross-Cultural Psychiatry* (Ithaca, N.Y.: Cornell University Press, 1965).

[79] J. Van Velsen, "The Extended-Case Method and Situational Analysis," in A. L. Epstein, ed., *The Craft of Social Anthropology* (London: Tavistock Publications, 1967).

[80] Oscar Lewis, *Pedro Martínez* (New York: Random House, 1964); "Seventh Day Adventism in a Mexican Village: A Study in Motivation and Culture Change," in Robert A. Manners, ed., *Process and Pattern in Culture* (Chicago: Aldine, 1964); *La Vida: A Puerto Rican Family in the Culture of Poverty* (New York: Random House, 1966).

[81] Dilim Okafor-Omali. *A Nigerian Villager in Two Worlds* (London: Faber and Faber, 1965).

[82] Paul Friedrich, "An Agrarian 'Fighter,' " in Spiro, ed., *Context and Meaning in Cultural Anthropology*.

[83] Emerson Blackhorse Mitchell and T. D. Allen, *Miracle Hill: The Story of a Navaho Boy* (Norman; University of Oklahoma Press, 1967); and Peter Nabokov, *Two Leggings: The Making of a Crow Warrior* (New York: Thomas Y. Crowell, 1967).

[84] [Robert Cockney] *I, Nuligak,* translated by Maurice Meyayer (Toronto: Peter Martin Associates, 1966); Don Handelman, "The Development of a Washo Shaman," *Ethnology,* vol. 6, no. 4 (October 1967), pp. 444–464.

[85] Albert Maori Kiki, *Kiki* (New York: Frederick A. Praeger, 1968).

[86] Walter H. Slote, "Case Analysis of a Revolutionary," in Frank Bonilla and Jose A. Silva Michelena, eds., *The Politics of Change in Venezuela,* Vol. I: *A Strategy for Research on Social Policy* (Cambridge: Massachusetts Institute of Technology Press, 1967).

[87] For example Eleanor E. Maccoby, "Effects of the Mass Media," in Martin L. Hoffman and Lois W. Hoffman, eds., *Review of Child Development Research, I* (New York: Russell Sage Foundation, 1964); and Bettye M. Caldwell, "The Effects of Infant Care," *ibid.* Other important recent publications that any social scientist who is interested in socialization should know, but that only incidentally incorporate a comparative cultural perspective, include John A. Clausen, ed., *Socialization and Society* (New York: Little, Brown, 1968); and Orville G. Brim, *Socialization after Childhood* (New York: John Wiley & Sons, 1966).

[88] Aronoff, *Psychological Needs and Cultural Systems;* Lubart, *Study of Basic Personality Traits of the Caribou Eskimo;* Honigmann and Honigmann, *Eskimo Townsmen;* De Vos and Wagatsuma, *Japan's Invisible Race;* Vogt and Albert, *People of Rimrock;* Hendin, *Suicide and Scandinavia.*

[89] Mary Ellen Goodman, "Influences of Childhood and Adolescence," in Edward Norbeck *et al.*, eds., *The Study of Personality.*

[90] George M. Guthrie and Pepita Jiminez Jacobs, *Child-Rearing and Personality Development in the Philippines* (University Park: Pennsylvania State Press, 1966).

[91] A. I. Rabin, *Growing Up in the Kibbutz* (New York: Springer, 1965).

[92] Herschel Alt and Edith Alt, *The New Soviet Man* (New York: Bookman Associates, 1964).

[93] Murray A. Straus, "Society as a Variable in Comparative Study of the Family by Replication and Secondary Analysis," *Journal of Marriage and the Family,* vol. 30, no. 4 (November 1968), pp. 565–570.

[94] Leigh Minturn and William W. Lambert, *Mothers of Six Cultures* (New York: John Wiley & Sons, 1964).

[95] Alex Inkeles, "Society, Social Structure, and Child Socialization," in John A. Clausen, ed., *Socialization and Society;* Margaret Mead, "Adult Roles," in A. V. S. de Reuck and Ruth Porter, eds., *Ciba Foundation Symposium on Transcultural Psychiatry* (London: J. and A. Churchill, 1965).

[96] Yehudi A. Cohen, *The Transition from Childhood to Adolescence* (Chicago: Aldine, 1964). See also Norman Kiell, *The Universal Experience of Adolescence* (New York: International Universities Press, 1964), who argues that the internal turmoil and external disorders accompanying adolescence are only moderately affected by culture.

[97] John W. M. Whiting *et al., Field Guide for a Study of Socialization* (New York: John Wiley & Sons, 1966).

[98] Murray L. Wax and Rosalie H. Wax, "Formal Education in an Indian Community," Supplement to *Social Problems,* vol. 11, no. 4 (Spring 1964).

[99] G. Alexander Moore, Jr., *Realities of the Urban Classroom* (Garden City, N.Y.: Doubleday, 1967).

[100] Harry F. Wolcott, *A Kwakiutl Village and School* (New York: Holt, Rinehart and Winston, 1967).

[101] Richard L. Warren, *Education in Rebhausen* (New York: Holt, Rinehart and Winston, 1967).

[102] John Singleton, *Nichū, A Japanese School* (New York: Holt, Rinehart and Winston, 1967).
[103] John Gay and Michael Cole, *The New Mathematics and an Old Culture* (New York: Holt, Rinehart and Winston, 1967).
[104] Frederica de Laguna, "Childhood among the Yakutat Tlingit," in Spiro, ed., *Context and Meaning in Cultural Anthropology*.
[105] For example: Laurence Wylie, ed., *Chanzeaux, A Village in Anjou* (Cambridge: Harvard University Press, 1966); and John A. Hostetler and Gertrude Enders Huntington, *The Hutterites in North America* (New York: Holt, Rinehart and Winston, 1967). For the Hutterites, see also Joseph W. Eaton, "Adolescence in a Communal Society," *Mental Hygiene*, vol. 48, no. 1 (January 1964), pp. 66–73.
[106] Edith Iglauer, *The New People* (Garden City, N.Y.: Doubleday, 1966).
[107] Marvin K. Opler, "Cultural Induction of Stress," in Mortimer H. Appley and Richard Trumbull, eds., *Psychological Stress* (New York: Meredith, 1967); Richard S. Lazarus, *Psychological Stress and the Coping Process* (New York: McGraw-Hill, 1966).
[108] Richard Jessor, *et al.*, *Society, Personality, and Deviant Behavior* (New York: Holt, Rinehart and Winston, 1968).
[109] See also Dozier, "Problem Drinking among American Indians"; Theodore D. Graves, "Acculturation, Access, and Alcohol in a Tri-Ethnic Community," *American Anthropologist*, vol. 69, nos. 3 and 4 (June-August 1967), pp. 306–321.
[110] Charles Savage, Alexander H. Leighton, and Dorothea C. Leighton, "The Problem of Cross-Cultural Identification of Psychiatric Disorders," in Murphy and Leighton, eds., *Approaches to Cross-Cultural Psychiatry*.
[111] Honigmann, *Personality in Culture*, ch. 13.
[112] Keiichi Mizushima and George De Vos, "An Application of the California Psychological Inventory in a Study of Japanese Delinquency," *Journal of Social Psychology*, vol. 71, no. 1 (February 1967), pp. 45–51.
[113] Harry H. L. Kitano, "Japanese-American Crime and Delinquency," *Journal of Psychology*, vol. 66, no. 2 (July 1967), pp. 253–263.
[114] Richard T. Sollenberger, "Chinese-American Child-Rearing Practices and Juvenile Delinquency," *The Journal of Social Psychology*, vol. 74, no. 1 (February 1968), pp. 13–23.
[115] S. Kirson Weinberg, "Juvenile Delinquency in Ghana. A Comparative Analysis of Delinquents and Nondelinquents," *Journal of Criminal Law, Criminology, and Police Science*, vol. 55, no. 4 (December 1964), pp. 471–481.
[116] Alexander H. Leighton and Jane M. Murphy, "Cross-Cultural Psychiatry," in Jane M. Murphy and Alexander H. Leighton, eds., *Approach to Cross-Cultural Psychiatry;* Marvin K. Opler, *Culture and Social Psychiatry* (New York: Atherton Press, 1967); Marvin K. Opler, "The Social and Cultural Nature of Mental Illness and Its Treatment," in Stanley Lesse, ed., *An Evaluation of the Results of the Psychotherapies* (Springfield, Ill.: Charles C Thomas, 1968); E. D. Wittkower, "Cultural Factors in Mental Illness," in Norbeck *et al.*, eds., *The Study of Personality*.
[117] Seymour Parker and Robert J. Kleiner, *Mental Illness in the Urban Negro Community* (New York: Free Press, 1966); Kent S. Miller, ed., *Mental Health and the Lower Social Classes* (Tallahassee: Florida State University, 1966).
[118] Carmi Schooler and William W. Caudill, "Symptomatology in Japanese and American Schizophrenics," *Ethnology*, vol. 3, no. 2 (April 1964), pp. 172–178. A mimeographed paper by Caudill and Schooler, "Symptom Patterns and Background Characteristics of Japanese Psychiatric Patients," is abridged in *Transcultural Psychiatric Research*, vol. 5 (October 1968), pp. 133–136.
[119] Y. Kumasaka, "A Culturally-Determined Mental Reaction Among the Ainu," *Psychiatric Quarterly*, vol. 38, no. 4 (October 1964), pp. 733–739; Philip L. Newman, " 'Wild Man' Behavior in a New Guinea Highlands Community," *American Anthropologist*, vol. 66, no. 1 (February 1964), pp. 1–19; L. L. Langness, "Hysterical Psychosis in a New Guinea Highlands: A Bena Bena Example," *Psychiatry*, vol. 28, no. 3 (August 1965), pp. 258–277. In connection with Langness, see also Richard Salisbury, "Possession Among the Siane (New Guinea)" and "Possession on the New Guinea Highlands: Review of the Literature," both mimeographed papers being abridged in *Transcultural Psychiatric Research*, vol. 3 (October 1966), pp. 103–116.
[120] Ari Kiev, *Curanderismo: Mexican-American Folk Psychiatry* (New York: Free Press, 1968); William Madsen, *The Mexican-Americans of South Texas* (New York: Holt, Rinehart and Winston, 1964); Arthur J. Rubel, "The Epidemiology of a Folk Illness: *Susto* in Hispanic America," *Ethnology*,

vol. 3, no. 3 (July 1964), pp. 268–283; Thomas S. Langner, "Psychophysiological Symptoms and the Status of Women in Two Mexican Communities," in Murphy and Leighton, eds., *Approaches to Cross-Cultural Psychiatry.*

[121] Jane M. Murphy and Alexander H. Leighton, "Native Conceptions of Psychiatric Disorder," in Murphy and Leighton, eds., *Approaches to Cross-Cultural Psychiatry;* Frank G. Vallee, "Eskimo Theories of Mental Illness in the Hudson Bay Region," *Anthropologica,* n.s. vol. 8, no. 1 (1966), pp. 53–83.

[122] Seymour Parker and Tom T. Sasaki, "Society and Sentiments in Two Contrasting Socially Disturbed Areas," in Murphy and Leighton, eds., *Approaches to Cross-Cultural Psychiatry.*

[123] John J. Honigmann, "Social Disintegration in Five Northern Canadian Communities," *The Canadian Review of Sociology and Anthropology,* vol. 2, no. 4 (November 1965), pp. 199–214.

[124] Norman Chance, Hsien Rin, and Hung-Ming Chu, "Modernization, Value Identification, and Mental Health: A Cross-Cultural Study," *Anthropologica,* vol. 8, no. 2, 1966, pp. 197–216.

[125] L. Bryce Boyer *et al.,* "Comparisons of the Shamans and Pseudoshamans of the Apaches of the Mescalero Indian Reservation: A Rorschach Study," *Journal of Projective Techniques and Personality Assessment,* vol. 28, no. 2 (June 1964), pp. 173–180; Don Handelman; H. S. Morris, "Shamanism Among the Oya Melanau," in Maurice Freedman, ed., *Social Organization;* Yuji Sasaki, "Psychiatric Study of the Shaman in Japan," abridged in *Transcultural Psychiatric Research,* vol. 4 (April 1967), pp. 15–17; Julian Silverman, "Shamans and Acute Schizophrenia," *American Anthropologist,* vol. 69, no. 1 (February 1967), pp. 21–31.

20 Biosocial Influences on Culture—A Neglected Category—EDWARD NORBECK

[1] Gabriel de Tarde, *Le Lois de l'Imitation, 1890.*
[2] Hiroshi Wagatsuma, "The Social Perception of Skin Color in Japan," *Daedalus, Proceedings of the American Academy of Arts and Sciences,* Vol. 96, No. 2, Spring, 1967, pp. 407–443.
[3] Eiichirō Ishida, "Japan Rediscovered," *Japan Quarterly,* Vol. XI, 276–282.

23 American Kinship Terms Once More—ROBBINS BURLING

Bock, Phiip K., 1968, "Some Generative Rules for American Kinship Terminology." *Anthropological Linguistics* 10:6:1–6.
D'Andrade, Roy G., MS, "Semantics and Syntax in the Componential Analysis of Kinship Terminologies" (in press).
Goodenough, Ward, 1965, "Yankee Kinship Terminology: a Problem in Componential Analysis." In E. A. Hammel, ed., *Formal Semantic Analysis,* pp. 259–287. *American Anthropologist,* Special Publication, vol. 67, no. 5, part 2.
Romney, A. Kimball, and Roy G. D'Andrade, 1964, "Cognitive Aspects of English Kin Terms." In A. K. Romney and R. G. D'Andrade, eds., *Transcultural Studies in Cognition,* pp. 146–170. *American Anthropologist,* Special Publication, vol. 66, no. 3, part 2.
Sanday, Peggy R., 1968, "The 'Psychological Reality' of American-English Kinship Terms: an Information-Processing Approach." *American Anthropologist* 70:508–523.
Schneider, David M., 1965, "American Kin Terms and Terms for Kinsmen: a Critique of Goodenough's Componential Analysis of Yankee Kinship Terminology." In E. A. Hammel, ed., *Formal Semantic Analysis,* pp. 288–308. *American Anthropologist,* Special Publication, vol. 67, no. 5, part 2.
―――, 1968, *American Kinship: a Cultural Account.* Englewood Cliffs, N.J.: Prentice-Hall.
―――, MS, "Componential Analysis: a State-of-the-Art Review" (in press).
Wallace, Anthony F. C., MS, "Relational Analysis of American Kinship Terminology" (in press).
Wallace, Anthony F. C., and John Atkins, 1960, "The Meaning of Kinship Terms." *American Anthropologist* 62:58–80.
Weinreich, Uriel, 1966, "Explorations in Semantic Theory." In T. A. Sebeok and others, eds., *Current Trends in Linguistics, Volume III: Theoretical Foundations,* pp. 395–497. The Hague: Mouton.

26 Biological Adaptation to Culture—FREDERICK S. HULSE

Bonné, B., 1969, "Polymorphic Systems in the Habbanite Isolate." *Abstracts of the XII International Congress of Genetics,* I, Tokyo.
Dorjahn, V. R., 1958, "Fertility, Polygyny and Their Interrelations in Temne Society." *American Anthropologist* 60:838–860.
Washburn, S. L., and I. DeVore, 1961, "Social Behavior of Baboons and Early Man." *Social Life of Early Man.* Viking Fund Publications in Anthropology, 31, New York.

27 How Culture Affects Genetics—FREDERICK S. HULSE

Boas, F., 1894, The Half Blood Indian. *Popular Science Monthly* 14:761.
Bonné, B., 1969, "Polymorphic Systems in the Habbanite Isolate." *Abstracts of the XII International Congress of Genetics* 1, Tokyo.
De Vos, G., and H. Wagatsuma, 1966, *Japan's Invisible Race.* Berkeley: University of California Press.
Dunn, L. C., 1959, *Heredity and Evolution in Human Populations.* Cambridge, Mass.: Harvard University Press.
Harrison, G. A. and J. J. T. Owen, 1964, "Studies on the Inheritance of Human Skin Colour." *Annals of Human Genetics* 28:27.
Henriques, F. N., 1953, *Family and Color in Jamaica.* London: G. Allen.
Manuila, A., 1956, "Distribution of ABO Genes in Eastern Europe." *American Journal of Physical Anthropology,* n.s. 14:577–588.
Mendel, G., 1866, Experiments in Plant Hybridization. *Proceedings of the Natural History Society of Brünn.* English Translation, Harvard University Press, Cambridge, 1948.
Penrose, L. S., 1955, "Evidence of Heterosis in Man." *Proceedings of the Royal Society B* 140:203.
Rodenwaldt, E., 1927, *Die Mestizen auf Kisar.* Jena: Fischer.
Sanghvi, L. D., and V. R. Khanolkar, 1949, "Data Relating to Seven Genetical Characters in Six Endogamous Groups in Bombay." *Annals of Eugenics* 15:52–64.
Shapiro, H. L., 1929, *Descendants of the Mutineers of the Bounty.* Memoirs of the Bernice P. Bishop Museum, vol. 9.
Trevor, J. C., 1953, "Race Crossing in Man." *Eugenics Laboratory Memoirs,* vol. 36.
Williams, G. D., 1931, "Maya-Spanish Crosses in Yucatan." *Papers of the Peabody Museum,* vol. 113.
Workman, P. L., B. S. Blumberg, and A. J. Cooper, 1963, "Selection, Gene Migration, and Polymorphic Stability in U.S. White and Negro Populations." *American Journal of Human Genetics* 15:429–437.

29 The Ecological Approach in Anthropology—JUNE HELM

[1] This is a slightly expanded version of a paper read at the annual meeting of the American Sociological Association, 1961, as part of a multidisciplinary symposium on human ecology with Otis Dudley Duncan as chairman. I am indebted to Robert Braidwood, Fred Eggan, and Stanley Lieberson for critical readings of the draft of this paper. They are not, of course, responsible for the deficiencies of the final version.

[2] O. D. Duncan, "Human Ecology and Population Studies," in P. Hauser and O. Duncan (eds.), *The Study of Population* (Chicago: University of Chicago Press, 1959), pp. 678–715.

[3] E. Tylor, *Primitive Culture* (3d ed., revised; London: John Murray, 1871), chap. ii, and L. Morgan, *Ancient Society* (New York: Henry Holt & Co., 1877).

[4] F. Ratzel, *The History of Mankind* (London: Macmillan Co., 1896–98).

[5] "Influence of Environment upon Human Industries or Arts" (*Smithsonian Institution Annual Report, 1895*), pp. 639–65, and his "Environment," in F. W. Hodge (ed.), *Handbook of American Indians* (Bureau of American Ethnology, Bull. 30 [Washington, D.C.: Bureau of American Ethnology, Smithsonian Institution, 1905]).

[6] C. Wissler, *Man and Culture* (New York: Thomas Y. Crowell Co., 1923), and his *The Relation of Nature to Man in Aboriginal North America* (New York: Oxford University Press, 1926).

[7] See, e.g., K. Birket Smith, *The Caribou Eskimos, Material and Social Life and Their Cultural Position* (Report of the 5th Thule Expedition, 1921–24, Vol. V, 2 parts [Copenhagen, 1929]), and his "Eskimo Cultures and Their Bearing upon the Prehistoric Cultures of North America and Eurasia," in G. G. MacCurdy (ed.), *International Symposium on Early Man* (New York, 1937), pp. 293–302; W. Bogoras, "Elements of the Culture of the Circumpolar Zone," *American Anthropologist*, XXXI (1929), 576–601; G. Hatt, *Moccasins and Their Relation to Arctic Footwear* ("Memoirs of the American Anthropological Association," No. 3, 1916), pp. 151–250; and H. Steensby, *An Anthropogeographical Study of the Origin of Eskimo Culture* (Copenhagen: Meddelelser om Grønland, 1917), Vol. LIII.

[8] *Habitat, Economy and Society* (London: Methuen & Co., 1934).

[9] A. Kroeber, *Cultural and Natural Areas of Native North America* (Berkeley: University of California Press, 1939).

[10] J. Steward, "The Economic and Social Basis of Primitive Bands," *Essays in Honor of A. L. Kroeber* (Berkeley: University of California Press, 1936), pp. 331–50; "Ecological Aspects of Southwestern Society," *Anthropos*, XXXII (1937), 87–104; and *Basin-Plateau Aboriginal Sociopolitical Groups* (Bureau of American Ethnology, Bull. 120 [Washington, D.C.: Bureau of American Ethnology, Smithsonian Institution, 1938]).

[11] G. Childe, *Man Makes Himself* (London: Watts & Co., 1936), and J. D. G. Clark, *Archaeology and Society* (London: Methuen & Co., 1939). My ignorance of British technical publications in archeology at this and prior periods does not allow me to point to possible academic antecedents.

[12] *A Study of Archeology* ("Memoirs of the American Anthropological Association," No. 69, 1948), p. 89.

[13] See, e.g., C. Meighan et al., "Ecological Interpretation in Archaeology: Part I," *American Antiquity*, XXIV (1958), 1–23, and "Part II," *American Antiquity*, XXIV (1958), 131–50.

[14] For summations and assessments, see R. Firth, "Function," in W. L. Thomas (ed.), *Yearbook of Anthropology, 1955* (Baltimore: Lord Baltimore Press, 1955), pp. 237–58, and G. Willey, "Archeological Theories and Interpretation: New World," in Kroeber et al., *Anthropology Today* (Chicago: University of Chicago Press, 1953), pp. 361–85. Kingsley Davis' point is well taken that functionalism is "synonymous with sociological analysis" which, in anthropology had to struggle for admission as "one among a plurality of distinct anthropological interests" ("The Myth of Functional Analysis as a Special Method in Sociology and Anthropology," *American Sociological Review*, XXIV [1959], 757–72).

[15] J. G. D. Clark, *Prehistoric Europe: The Economic Basis* (New York: Philosophical Library, 1952); H. Movius, "Old World Prehistory: Paleolithic," in Kroeber et al., op. cit., pp. 163–92; W. Wedel, "Some Aspects of Human Ecology in the Central Plains," *American Anthropologist*, LV 1953), 499–514.

[16] E. Haury et al., "An Archaeological Approach to the Study of Cultural Stability," in *Seminars in Archaeology, 1955* ("Memoirs of the Society for American Archaeology," Vol. XI [1956]).

[17] R. and L. Braidwood, "The Earliest Village Communities of Southwestern Asia," *Journal of World History* (Paris), I (1953), 278–310; R. Braidwood, "Means toward an Understanding of Human Behavior before the Present," and his "The Old-World: Post-Paleolithic," in *The Identification of Non-artifactual Archaeological Materials* (National Research Council, Publication 565 [Washington, D.C.: National Academy of Sciences, National Research Council, 1957]), pp. 14–16, 26–27; R. Braidwood, B. Howe, and E. Negahban, "Near Eastern Prehistory," *Science*, CXXX, No. 3402 (1960), 1536–41.

[18] B. Meggers, "Environmental Limitations on the Development of Culture," *American Anthropologist*, LVI (1954), 801–24.

[19] An excellent summation of the advances in British archeology in these respects is provided by W. Haag ("Recent Work by British Archaeologists," *Annals of the Association of American Geographers*, XLIII [1957], 298–303).

[20] G. Willey (ed.), *Prehistoric Settlement Patterns in the New World* ("Viking Fund Publications in Anthropology," XXIII [New York: Wenner-Gren Foundation, 1956]).

[21] Classic Maya civilization is one case in point (see G. Willey, "The Structure of Ancient Maya Society: Evidence from the Southern Lowlands," *American Anthropologist*, LVIII [1956], 777–82).

[22] See, e.g., S. Miles, "An Urban Type: Extended Boundary Towns," *Southwestern Journal of Anthropology*, XIV (1958), 339–51.

[23] K. Chang, "Study of the Neolithic Social Grouping: Examples from the New World," *American Anthropologist,* LX (1958), 298–334.

[24] R. Beardsley et al., "Functional and Evolutionary Implications of Community Patterning" in *Seminars in Archaeology, 1955* ("Memoirs of the Society for American Archaeology," Vol. XI [1956]), pp. 131–51.

[25] In this regard A. I. Hallowell some years ago explicated for anthropologists the reformulation of standard ethnological aim and method that an "ecological hypothesis" requires: non-cultural (e.g., demographic and biotal) data must be taken into account, and it is inadequate to operate exclusively with "generically descriptive traits that purport to characterize the normative aspects of an institution considered as a whole"—precise information about variabilities and consistencies is required ("The Size of Algonkian Hunting Territories: A Function of Ecological Adjustment," *American Anthropologist,* LI [1949], 35–45.)

[26] R. Spencer, *The North Alaskan Eskimo. A Study in Ecology and Society* (Bureau of American Ethnology, Bull. 171 [Washington, D.C.: Bureau of American Ethnology, Smithsonian Institution, 1959]); R. Dunning, "Rules of Residence and Ecology among the Northern Ojibwa," *American Anthropologist,* LXI (1959), 806–16; E. Leacock, *The Montagnais 'Hunting Territory' and the Fur Trade* ("Memoirs of the American Anthropological Association." No. 78, 1954); see also Hallowell, *op cit*. The fruitfulness of an ecological stance in viewing environmentally marginal societies is demonstrated in M. Lantis' review, at the request of the Arctic Institute, of research on the human ecology of the Eskimo ("Research on Human Ecology of the American Arctic" [Washington, D.C.: Arctic Institute, 1953]) (mimeographed). The bibliography of 160 items includes studies in archeology, ethnography, geography, biology, and psychology that are cross-cut by an ecological outlook.

[27] F. Barth, "Ecologic Relationships of Ethnic Groups in Swat, Northern Pakistan," *American Anthropologist,* LVIII (1956), 1079–89.

[28] *Ibid.,* p. 1079.

[29] J. Steward, *Theory of Culture Change* (Urbana: University of Illinois Press, 1955), p. 121.

[30] Birket-Smith's writings on the "oecumene" of the Caribou Eskimo (*op. cit.*) is the immediate source from which I adopted this term, here emphasizing its implications of the "known world" of any particular people.

[31] For recent Northern Amerind studies along these lines, see J. Helm and O. Lurie, *The Subsistence Economy of the Dogrib Indians of Lac La Martre in the Mackenzie District of the Northwest Territories* (Ottawa: Northern Research and Co-ordination Centre, Department of Northern Affairs and National Resources, 1961), and R. W. Dunning, *Social and Economic Change among the Northern Ojibwa* (Toronto: University of Toronto Press, 1959). A. Lesser has recently published a theoretical treatment of "the social-field" concept that accords with the concept of oecumene as I have presented it ("Social Fields and the Evolution of Society," *Southwestern Journal of Anthropology,* XVII [1961], 40–48). Also, on the segmentary lineage system as developing "specifically in a tribal society which is moving against other tribes in a *tribal intercultural environment,*" see M. Sahlins, "The Segmentary Lineage: An Organization of Predatory Expansion," *American Anthropologist,* LXIII (April, 1961), 322–45.

[32] Kroeber, *op. cit.*

[33] Childe, *op. cit.,* and Steward, *Theory of Culture Change, op. cit.*

[34] "The Effects of Depopulation upon Social Organization as Illustrated by the Tapirape Indians," *Transactions of the New York Academy of Sciences,* Series 2, III, No. 1 (1940), 12–16.

[35] C. Wagley, "Cultural Influences on Population: A Comparison of Two Tupi Tribes," *Revista do Museu Paulista,* V (N.S., 1951), 95–104.

[36] B. Malinowski, *A Scientific Theory of Culture and Other Essays* (Chapel Hill: University of North Carolina Press, 1944), chap. vii.

[37] R. Redfield, *The Primitive World and Its Transformations* (Ithaca, N.Y.: Cornell University Press, 1953); A. Spoehr, "Cultural Differences in the Interpretation of Natural Resources," in W. L. Thomas, Jr. (ed.), *Man's Role in Changing the Face of the Earth* (Chicago: University of Chicago Press, 1956), pp. 93–102.

[38] A. Gayton, "Culture-Environment Integration: External References in Yokuts Life," *Southwestern Journal of Anthropology,* II (1946), 252–68; E. Evans-Pritchard, *The Nuer* (Oxford: Clarendon Press, 1940).

[39] A. Kardiner with R. Linton, *The Individual and His Society* (New York: Columbia University Press, 1939); H. Barry, I. Child, and M. Bacon, "Relation of Child Training to Subsistence Economy," *American Anthropologist,* LI (1959), 51–63.

⁴⁰For examples in archeology, see Clark, *op. cit.,* and G. Quimby. "Habitat, Culture, and Archaeology," in G. Dole and R. Carneiro (eds.), *Essays in the Science of Culture in Honor of Leslie A. White* (New York: Thomas Y. Crowell Co., 1960), pp. 380–89; in physical anthropology, G. Bartholomew and J. B. Birdsell, "Ecology and the Proto Hominids," *American Anthropologist,* LV (1953), 481–98; in social anthropology, E. Evans-Pritchard, *op. cit.,* and L. Thompson, "The Relations of Men, Animals, and Plants in an Island Community (Fiji)," *American Anthropologist,* LV (1949), 253–76.

⁴¹L. Hobhouse, G. Wheeler, and M. Ginsberg, *The Material Culture and Social Institutions of the Simpler Peoples* (London: Chapman & Hall, Ltd., 1915).

⁴²F. Eggan, "Social Anthropology and the Method of Controlled Comparison," *American Anthropologist,* LVI (1954), 743–63.

⁴³W. Goldschmidt, "Social Organization in Native California and the Origin of Clans," *American Anthropologist,* L (1948), 444–56; F. Eggan, *The Social Organization of the Western Pueblos* (Chicago: University of Chicago Press, 1950).

⁴⁴J. Steward, "Ecological Aspects of Southwestern Society," *op. cit.*

⁴⁵C. D. Forde, "The Anthropological Approach in Social Science," in M. Fried (ed.), *Readings in Anthropology* (New York: Thomas Y. Crowell Co., 1959), II, 59–78 (reprinted from *Advancement of Science,* IV [1947], 213–24). Forde's sensitivity to physiographic, technological-exploitative, and demographic factors and their interplay exemplifies ecological perspectives in contemporary social anthropology: witness the view, e.g., that various African tribes "differ significantly in the scale of their clan organization and in the political relations based thereon, in close relation to the extent to which the physical conditions enforce frequent and large-scale dispersal" (p. 75); that the basic lineage "appears to represent a recurrent adjustment to the scale of co-operation and mutual aid elicited under stable conditions" (p. 73); and that clan fission in certain societies is a consequence of a population pressure too great to permit continued territorial unity (p. 74).

⁴⁶M. Sahlins, *Social Stratification in Polynesia* (Seattle: University of Washington Press, 1958).

⁴⁷M. Nimkoff and R. Middleton, "Types of Family and Types of Economy," *American Journal of Sociology,* LXVI (1960), 215–25. The establishment of the Human Relations Area Files has contributed greatly to the development of such studies.

⁴⁸H. Driver and W. Massey, *Comparative Studies of North American Indians* ("Transactions of the American Philosophical Society," Vol. XLVII, 1957). Also relevant is G. Murdock, *Social Structure* (New York: Macmillan Co., 1949), and his "Evolution in Social Organization," in B. Meggers (ed.), *Evolution and Anthropology: A Centennial Appraisal* (Washington, D.C.: Anthropological Society of Washington, 1959), pp. 126–43.

⁴⁹R. Naroll, "A Preliminary Index of Social Development," *American Anthropologist,* LVIII (1956), 687–715.

⁵⁰M. Edmonson, *Status Terminology and the Social Structure of North American Indians* (Seattle: University of Washington Press, 1958).

⁵¹B. Aginsky, "The Evolution of American Indian Culture: A Method and Theory," *Thirty-second International Congress of Americanists* (1956), pp. 79–87.

⁵²Steward, *Theory of Culture Change.*

⁵³Statement in Sol Tax *et al., An Appraisal of Anthropology Today* (Chicago: University of Chicago Press, 1953), p. 243.

⁵⁴Steward, *Theory of Culture Change,* p. 37.

⁵⁵*Ibid.,* p. 5.

⁵⁶An example of studies in an allied field consonant with Steward's efforts to establish a typology based on cultural core features that represent similar integration levels is the historian K. Wittfogel's delineation of the hydraulic or irrigation society as a culture type deriving from sociopolitical responses in agriculture societies to environmental conditions that stimulate the establishment of systems of water control ("The Theory of Oriental Society," in M. Fried [ed.], *op. cit.,* II, 94–113; from a translation and revision of K. Wittfogel, "Die Theorie der orientalischen Gesellschaft," *Zeitschrift fur Sozialforschung,* VII [1938], 90–122). Wittfogel has joined Steward and other anthropologists in a comparative study of irrigation civilizations (J. Steward *et al., Irrigation Civilization: A Comparative Study* ["Social Science Monographs,"] I (Washington, D.C.: Pan American Union, 1955)]).

⁵⁷J. Weiner, "Physical Anthropology: An Appraisal," in B. Meggers (ed.), *op. cit.,* p. 27.

⁵⁸F. C. Howell, "Pleistocene Glacial Ecology and the Evolution of 'Classic Neandertal Man,'" *Southwestern Journal of Anthropology,* VIII (1952), 337–410.

⁵⁹B. Kraus and C. White, "Micro-evolution in a Human Population: A Study of Social Endogamy and

Blood Type Distribution among the Western Apache," *American Anthropologist,* LVIII (1956), 1017–43.

[60]M. Slater, "Ecological Factors in the Origin of Incest," *American Anthropologist,* LXI (1959), 1042–59.

[61]"The Superorganic," in A. Kroeber, *The Nature of Culture* (Chicago: University of Chicago Press, 1952), pp. 22–51.

[62]R. Redfield, *The Folk Culture of Yucatan* (Chicago: University of Chicago Press, 1941), p. 133.

[63]See, e.g., M. Titiev, *The Science of Man* (New York: Henry Holt & Co., 1954), chaps. xxi–xxiii; K. Davis, *Human Society* (New York: Macmillan Co., 1949), pp. 321 ff.

[64]Steward, *Theory of Culture Change,* p. 142.

[65]R. Redfield, *The Little Community* (Chicago: University of Chicago Press, 1960).

[66]See discussion by A. Spoehr in S. Tax *et al., op. cit.,* p. 142.

[67]C. Hawkes, "Archeological Theory and Method: Some Suggestions from the Old World," *American Anthropologist,* LVI (1954), 155–68.

[68]Wagley, *op. cit.* (1940–41); C. Levi-Strauss, "Social Structure," in A. Kroeber (ed.), *op. cit.,* pp. 524–53; L. Krader, "Ecology of Central Asian Pastoralism, *Southwestern Journal of Anthropology,* XI (1955), 301–26; E. Service, "Sociocentric Relationship Terms and the Australian Class System," in G. Dole and R. Carneiro (eds.), *op. cit.,* pp. 416–36; and Naroll, *op. cit.*

[69]See R. Firth, "Function," in W. Thomas (ed.), *op. cit.,* pp. 237–58.

[70]The evolutionism of Leslie White (e.g., *The Evolution of Culture* [New York: McGraw-Hill Book Co., 1959]) has, in its technological determinism, a tangential relevance here. I have eschewed consideration of the Whitean school, however, because it is antipathetic, in its sweeping universalism, to the empirical tradition that has fostered the ecological approach in anthropology.

[71]Levi-Strauss suggests that the "urban ecology" school of Chicago, in its stress on spatial configurations, would perhaps have been better served if the approach had been first "through small and relatively isolated communities with which the anthropologist usually deals." He goes on to point out, however, anthropology has in this respect been remiss in that "there have been practically no attempts to correlate the spatial configurations with the formal properties of other aspects of social life" (*op. cit.,* p. 533).

33   Energy and the Evolution of Culture—LESLIE A. WHITE

Furnas, C. C., "Future Sources of Power" (*Science,* Nov. 7, 1941).
Langer, R. M., "Fast New World" (*Collier's,* July 6, 1940).
MacCurdy, George C., "Human Origins" (*New York,* 1933), vol. II).

34   Evolution: Specific and General—MARSHALL D. SAHLINS

Greenberg, Joseph, 1957, *Essays in Linguistics.* Viking Fund Publications in Anthropology 24. New York.
———, 1959, Language and Evolution." In *Evolution and Anthropology: A Centennial Appraisal,* pp. 61–75. Washington, D.C.: The Anthropological Society of Washington.
Harris, Marvin, 1959, "The Economy Has No Surplus?" *American Anthropologist* 61:185–99.
Kroeber, A. L., 1946, "History and Evolution." *Southwestern Journal of Anthropology* 2:14.
———, 1952, *The Nature of Culture.* Chicago: University of Chicago Press.
Murdock, George Peter, 1949, *Social structure.* New York: Macmillan.
———, 1959, Evolution in Social Organization." In *Evolution and Anthropology: A Centennial Appraisal,* pp. 126–43. Washington, D.C.: The Anthropological Society of Washington.
Spencer, Herbert, 1897, *The Principles of Sociology.* Vol. 3. New York: Appleton.
Steward, Julian H., 1953, Evolution and Process. In A. L. Kroeber, ed., *Anthropology Today,* pp. 313–26. Chicago: University of Chicago Press.
———, 1955, *Theory of Culture Change: The Methodology of Multilinear Evolution.* Urbana: University of Illinois Press.

White, Leslie A., 1949, *The Science of Culture*. New York: Farrar Straus (Paperbound ed. 1958, Grove Press).
———, 1959, *The Evolution of Culture*. New York: McGraw-Hill.
———, 1959a, The Concept of Evolution in Cultural Anthropology. In *Evolution and Anthropology: A Centennial Appraisal,* pp. 106–25. Washington, D.C.: The Anthropological Society of Washington.

name index

Adelung, J. C., 33
Aginsky, B., 261–262
Allport, G., 73

Bain, R., 19
Barnett, H., 164
Barth, F., 260, 264
Bastian, A., 174
Bates, M., 267
Beals, R. L., 56, 64
Benedict, R., 119, 136, 144
Bidney, D., 35, 63, 71–80, 82–84, 92
Boas, F., 65, 66, 116, 175, 297
Bock, K., 199
Bonné, B., 232
Bruner, E. M., 154–160
Buettner-Janusch, J., 220–231
Burling, R., 198–207

Cassirer, E., 19, 20–26
Chomsky, N., 176–177, 188–198
Cohen, M., 67
Cole, G. D. H., 302
Collingwood, R. G., 186
Copeland, J. W., 89

D'Andrade, R. G., 199
d'Aquili, E. G., 6
Darwin, C., 278, 286, 288
de Tarde, G., 168
Dewey, J., 73

Dixon, R. B., 74
Dorjahn, V. R., 233
Douglas, M., 176
Duncan, O. T., 257, 263
Dunn, L. C., 238
Durkheim, E., 19, 32, 44–47, 64, 68, 97, 312, 313, 316, 325

Edmonson, M., 261
Erikson, E., 164

Fodor, J., 195
Forde, C. D., 248, 258, 261
Frake, C. O., 270–275
Frank, J., 164
Freud, S., 79, 150, 154
Fromm, E., 158

Geertz, C., 155
Gillin, J., 161
Ginsberg, M., 261
Goodall, J., 223, 230
Goodenough, W., 199, 203, 271
Greenberg, J., 306

Halle, M., 195
Hallowell, A. I., 66, 67
Harrison, G. A., 244
Hawley, A., 268–269
Helm, J., 257–265
Henriques, F. N., 237

347

Name Index

Herskovitz, M. J., 56
Hobhouse, L., 261
Hoebel, E. A., 64
Hoijer, H., 56, 64
Hollingshead, A. B., 267
Honigmann, J. J., 152, 160–167
Howell, C., 155
Hulse, F., 231–245
Huxley, J., 299
Hymes, D., 271

Jerison, H. J., 223–224
Jung, C., 150

Kaplan, B., 85
Kaplan, D., 5, 81–92
Kardiner, A., 163
Klemm, G., 32–33, 34
Kluckhohn, C., 5, 29, 56, 63, 67–68, 128–146, 159
Köhler, W., 68
Kroeber, A. L., 5, 6, 9, 10, 29, 34, 48–55, 63, 67–68, 73, 79–80, 89, 115–117, 121–128, 175, 221, 248, 250–258, 263, 307

Langer, S., 19
Laughlin, C. D., Jr., 6
Lévi-Strauss, C., 176
Lévy-Bruhl, L., 174
Lewis, O., 165
Linton, R., 56, 68, 78, 107–111, 136, 141
Lowie, R. H., 12, 34, 56, 65
Lynd, R., 65–66

MacCurdy, G. C., 297
Madsen, W., 164
Maine, H. S., 280, 282–283
Malinowski, B., 68, 73, 76, 97, 175, 312, 319–322, 323
Mandelbaum, D., 164
Marx, K., 32, 80, 302
Mason, O. T., 258
Meggers, B. J., 259
Merton, R. K., 325
Miller, G., 196
Millikan, R., 297
Moore, J. H., 6
Morgan, L. H., 10, 257, 279–280
Murray, H. A., 159

Naroll, R., 261
Norbeck, E., 7–14, 168–171, 322–327

Opler, M. E., 90
Osgood, C., 63–64, 68
Ostwald, W., 281
Owen, J. J. T., 244

Parker, S., 161
Parsons, T., 111–117, 312
Penrose, L. S., 242
Perchonock, E., 196

Quine, W., 188

Radcliffe-Brown, A. R., 56, 66, 67, 86, 95, 97, 99–107, 154, 312, 313–318, 323
Ratzel, F., 247, 258
Roberts, J., 164
Robertson, W., 278
Romney, K., 199
Rouse, I., 227

Sahlins, M., 220, 261, 280, 298–308
Sapir, E., 67, 70, 73, 74, 129, 130–131, 132, 136, 140, 175
Savin, H. B., 196–197
Service, E. R., 216–220
Simmel, G., 97
Slater, M., 262
Sorokin, P., 80
Spencer, H., 32, 72, 263, 278, 298
Spiro, M. E., 56–57, 64, 89
Steward, J., 248, 258, 262, 263, 265–270, 300, 306
Straus, M., 166

Taylor, W. W., 64, 258
Trevor, J. C., 241–242
Turner, V., 176
Tyler, S. A., 177–188
Tylor, E. B., 10, 13, 18, 33, 34, 36–43, 56, 64, 257, 278, 279–280

von Humboldt, W., 189, 197

Wagatsuma, H., 171
Wagley, C., 260, 264
Wallace, A. F. C., 86, 89–90, 158–159, 199
Washburn, S. L., 219
Wheeler, G., 261
White, L. A., 19, 26–30, 34, 55–71, 89, 154, 249, 280, 283–297, 307, 327–328
Willey, M., 34
Winckelmann, J. J., 33
Wissler, C., 68, 121, 247–248

Zuckerman, S., 229

subject index

Achievement theory, 162
Acculturation, 124, 300
Adaptive neurons, 223–224
Agriculture and cultural evolution, 289–293
Allele frequencies, 237–238
Animal husbandry, 289
Anthropological linguistics, 175
　See also Cognitive anthropology; Language; Semantic features
Anthropology, as a science, 12–14
　early trends of, 257–258
　evolutionary school of, 79
　origins of, 8–9
Apache Indians, 164
Archeology, 7
　and ecology, 259
Associations, 98
Athapaskan linguistic stock, 239

Basques, 239
Binary opposition, 176
Biotic community, 271
Bipedalism, 230

Caste, and blood type, 237
　defined, 240
　and gene flow, 236–237
Ceylon, 166
Chimpanzees, meat-eating of, 230
Civilization, 36, 49–55
　definition of, 36

grades of, 36
and the individual, 49–55
scientific study of, 38–39
uniformity of, 36
Cognitive anthropology, 174–188
　definitions of, 174–177
Cognitive order and chaos, 179–186
Cognitive unity, 176
Cognitive processes, 162
"Collective thought", 44
Comparative sociology, 99
Componential analysis, 199
Configurations, cultural, 133, 141–145
　See also Patterns, cultural
Controlled eliciting, 185–186
Copulation, of primates, 228–229
Cranial volume and toolmaking, 223–224
Cultural adaptation, 299
Cultural anthropology, goals and procedures of, 3–15
　history of, 7–14
　methods of, 13–14
　as a science, 187
Cultural core, 269
Cultural determinism, 79–80, 82, 90–91, 322
Cultural diffusion, 39, 40, 270, 300
Cultural equilibrium, 13
Cultural lag, 77
Cultural norms, 78, 157
Cultural recessions, 290

Subject Index

Cultural relativism, 33, 299–300
Cultural revolution, 295
Cultural universals, 4, 5, 11
Culture, and biology, 213–246
 biosocial influences on, 168–171
 and climate, 253–254
 as a cognitive system, 174–210
 definitions of, 3–14, 18–30, 32–36, 55–80, 85–86, 115–117, 174–207
  as an abstraction, 5–7, 56–57, 62–63, 67–68, 85–86, 143
  as characteristic traits, 69
  as a cognitive system, 174–207
  as communicated knowledge, 72
  functional definition of, 6
  idealistic definitions of, 5
  as ideas, 62–72
  as learned behavior, 5
  realistic definitions of, 5
  as *sui generis*, 65
  superorganic concept of, 10, 32–93, 116
  as symbols, 18–30, 69
  as a system, 12–14
 evolution of (*see* Evolution, cultural)
 and genetics, 231–234
 and geographic environment, 247–277
 and human needs, 156–157
 and the individual, 11, 165, 319–321
 innovations in, 89
 integrating principle of, 145
 and intelligence, 10
 and language, 75
 locus of, 61–62
 man's capacity for, 220–231
 material, 64, 74, 76
 and natural vegetation, 253
 non-material, 74
 patterning of, 119–147
 See also Patterns, cultural
 as personality, 149–173
 See also Personality
 and race, 10
 reification of, 64
 and society, 5, 94–118
 as a superorganic phenomenon, 32–93
 as symbols, 18–31
 as a system, 6
 theories of, 179, 186–187
 science of, 36–43
 See also Culturology
 stages of, 38

Culture change, 158–159, 164
 See also Cultural evolution
Culture contact, 106
Culture history, 32
Culture and personality, 11–12, 13, 85, 154–160
 See also Personality; Psychological anthropology
Culture traits, 63, 75, 133–135
 and psychological dynamics, 163
Culture wholes, 250
Culturology, 29, 30, 34, 57–58, 251

Diet, and biological traits, 244–245
Diffusion (*see* Cultural diffusion)
Dominance, 219–220
Dunkers, 238
Dysnomia, 316

Ecocultural structure, 260–261
Ecological niche, 260
Ecological zones, North American, 250–257
Ecology, animal, 263
 cultural, 8, 247–275, 299
  concepts and methods of, 265–270
  objectives of, 265–269
 human, 263
Economic institutions, study of, 104
Egypt, 290
Enculturation, 148, 165–166
Endogamy, 232–233
Energy, and cultural evolution, 283–297
 human, 291
 resources of, 295–296
Environment, and archaeology, 259
 and exploitive patterns, 259
Environmental determinism, 250, 269
Eskimo, 258
Estrus, of mammals, 227
Eta of Japan, 240
Ethnography, 8
Ethnology, 8
Ethnic group, defined, 240
Eugenics, 215
Eunomia, 316–317
Evolution, cultural, 8, 9, 13, 38, 73, 220, 222, 262, 278–310
 biological, 35, 54, 106, 155, 213–245, 220–221, 265–266, 300, 302–303
 definitions of, 106–107
 and energy, 283–297
 and functionalism, history, 327–328

inorganic, 54
multilineal, 262, 306
neurological, 225
social, 106–107
unilineal, 268, 280, 298
universal, 301
Evolutionist school, 296–297
Exogamy, 232–233

Family, human, 4, 10, 229, 282
Food sharing, 217, 218
Formal analysis, linguistic, 185–186, 199
Free will, 37
French structuralism, 176
Fuels, and cultural evolution, 290–291
Function in culture, 311–329
Functionalism, 13, 28, 76, 264, 311–328
    analysis in, 319–322
    and evolution, history, 327–328
    and organic analogy, 314
    in social sciences, 313–318
Functional substitute, 324
Functional unity, 316
Functions, manifest and implicit, 324
    negative and positive, 324
    types of, 324

Gene flow, barriers to, 236–239
Genetic drift, 238
Genetics, 231–234

Hanunóo, 271–272
Hardy-Weinberg Law, 231
Heterosis, 241
History, evolutionism, and functionalism, 327–328
Holism, 33
Homo sapiens, traits of, 221–222
    and brain size, 224–225
    See also Man; Racial differences
Hunting groups, 230

Ifugao, 122
Incest taboo, 231–232
Industrial Revolution, 295
Intelligence, and culture, 235–236
Inventions, simultaneous, 11

Japanese concept of beauty, 169–171
Japanese personality, 168–171
Jews in Rome, 238

Kinship terminology, American, 198–207
    principles of, 200–207

Koyas, 178–179

Labor, division of, 103
Language, acquisition of, 193–194
    anthropological concepts of, 130–131
    and culture, 18
    and deep structures, 195
    emotional, 22–23
    empiricist theories of, 198
    labeled bracketing in, 195–196
    and the mind, 188–198
    origin of, 21
    and the percept, 191–193
    propositional, 22–23
    and surface structures, 194
    study of, 41
    and symbols, 21–26
Learning models, 190
Linguistic universals, 198
Linguistics (*see* Cognitive anthropology; Language)

Maize farming and environment, 252
Man, and animals compared, 48
    definition of, 20–21
    as an organism, 3–4, 9, 11
    as a political animal, 48
    as a social organism, 48
Mankind, unity of, 6, 9–10, 18
Marriage, customs of, 233–234
Memory and cognition, 196–197
Mental codes, 179
Mental processes, rationalist and empiricist theories of, 188–189
Mentifacts, 75
Mesopotamia, 290
Microcebus, 228
Miscegenation, effects of, 240–245
Mother-in-law taboo, 62
Mythology, 41

Navaho culture, 128–146
Needs, human, 320–322
    societal, 323–325
Neurological adaptations in human evolution, 223–225
Nuclear family, 156

Oecumene, 260

Pair formation, in sexual evolution, 229–230
PAM (population, area, and mobility), 262

Paradigms, in linguistic analysis, 183
Patterns, cultural, 119–146, 163–164, 266
  assemblage of, 140
  awareness of, 137–138
  concepts of, summarized, 146
  and configurations, 133
  covert, 141–145
  defined, 132–133
  of idea and action, 136–137
  ideal and behavioral, 135–136
  major and minor, behavioral, 140
  in Navaho culture, 128–146
  nuclear conception of, 131–133
  overt, 133–141
  in personality studies, 163–164
  role of, 128
  and structural regularity, 134–135
  of style, 125, 127–128
  and sub-patterns, 138–140
  systemic, 122–124
  total-culture, 124–125
  universal, 121–122
  verbal, 143
  in verbal responses, 129–130
Pecking order, 219
Perception, active and passive views of, 189–190
Perceptual models, 190–192
Personality, cross-cultural research on, 152
  as culture, 5, 148–171
  definitions of, 151–153
  early studies of, 152–153
  social, 102, 161–162
Personality formation, biological factors in, 149
  biosocial factors in, 150
  in childhood, 165–166
  cultural factors in, 149–153
  geographical-environmental factors in, 149
  situational factors in, 150
  and sociocultural change, 164–165
  See also Psychological anthropology
Physical anthropology, 7, 26?
Pitcairn Islanders, 241
Pleistocene Man, 225–226
Polyandry, and genetics, 233
Polygyny, and genetics, 233
Population patterns, 260
Primates, lower, and human societies, 216–220
  social organization of, 234
Progress in cultural evolution, 304–305
Psychic unity, 174, 187, 300

Psychological anthropology, 155–167
  See also Personality; Personality formation
Psychology, distinguished from anthropology, 57–58, 87–88, 154–160

Racial differences, 10, 48–49
Ramopithecus, 230
Reductionism, 83–84, 86–87
Religion, functionalist study of, 322–327
  role of, 322–327
  and social norms, 326
  as symbolic expression, 325
  and tension, 325
Revivals in culture, 41
Ritual and belief, 323

Semantic domains, 181–184
Semantic features, and paradigms, 183
  and taxonomies, 181–183
  techniques and methods of study, 185
  and trees, 183–184
Settlement patterns, 273
Sexual behavior, of primates, 217–218
Sexual dimorphism, 228
Signs, and symbols, 19, 23, 27–30, 45
Slavery, 236–237
Social anthropology, 8, 96–98, 102–107, 115
  definition of, 99
  methods of, 102–107
Social change, 164
Social character, 159
Social constraints, 46
Social ecology, 266
Social groups, 291–292
Social institutions, 95–96
  functions of, 105
Social morphology and physiology, 102–103
Social order, as culture, 94–117
Social organization, comparative studies of, 261–262
  and population size, 264
Social personality, 102, 161–162
Social phenomena, definition of, 99
Social psychiatry, 166–167
Social relations, 100–101
  definition of, 104
Social structure, 99–101
  and economics, 103–104
  and rituals, 323
Social system, concept of, 111–113, 115–117
  elements of, 292

Socialization, 78, 155–156, 158, 165–166
Society, composition of, 94
  and culture, 70
  See also Social order as culture
  definitions of, 94–98, 113
  primitive, 282–283
  and sex, 227–231
  sub-categories of, 121
  as systems of human action, 111–114
Sociofacts, 75
Speech (*see* Language)
Speech groups, and drainage zones, 256
Status
  ascribed and achieved, 96, 109–111
  vs. contract, 282–283
  and role, 96, 107–111
Structural systems, classification of, 102
Structure, and function, 312, 315
  See also Functionalism
Style, patterns of, 125, 127–128
Subanun, 272–273
Survivals in culture, 40–41
Swidden farmers, 273–274
Symbolates, 29–30
Symbolic faculty of man, 6, 12, 19–26
Symboling, definition of, 58, 231, 222–223
Symbols, and culture, 18–31, 58–61, 71, 221–223, 231
  definition of, 18, 26–27

and language, 21–26
religious, 325
Syntactic structures, 194–195
Systems theory, 13–14

Taboos, 218
Tapirapé Indians, 260
Technology, and cultural evolution, 284–285, 293–296, 303
Teleology, in functionalism, 326
Telugu, 178
Territoriality, 217–219
Thermodynamics, 303–304
Tools, and culture, 222–227
  and energy, 284–285
  flakes and bifaces, 227
  pebble, 226
  Pleistocene, 225–226
Transformational grammar, 196
Tri-Ethnic Project, 166–167

Values, 168

War, evolutionary analysis of, 301
World view, and ecology, 260–261

Yankees, definitions of, 240–241
Yurok Indians, 122

Zuni Indians, 161